E. W. KENYON AND HIS MESSAGE OF FAITH: THE TRUE STORY

CREATION HOUSE
Orlando, FL

Joe McIntyre

E. W. KENYON AND HIS MESSAGE OF FAITH: THE TRUE STORY by Joe McIntyre
Published by Creation House
Strang Communications Company
600 Rinehart Road
Lake Mary, Florida 32746
Web site: http://www.creationhouse.com

Unless otherwise noted, all Scripture quotations are from the King James Version of the Bible.

Scripture quotations marked NKJV are from the New King James Version of the Bible. Copyright © 1979, 1980, 1982 by Thomas Nelson Inc., publishers. Used by permission.

Scripture quotations marked TLB are from The Living Bible. Copyright © 1971. Used by permission of Tyndale House Publishers Inc., Wheaton, IL 60189. All rights reserved.

To my wonderful and supportive wife Pam,

and my "great kid" Tory

Acknowledgments

Many people have greatly helped in the writing of this book—too many to name them all.

I would like to thank my church family at Word of His Grace Fellowship for their support and intercession for me as I wrote this book. They also gave me lots of grace (and space) to work on this book. May the Lord repay you abundantly!

Thanks to Denny Daniels for his many suggestions, and to William DeArteaga for his helpful critique.

Bonnie Dofelmier and Barbara Jaap of Kenyon's Gospel Publishing Society have been a great help and very supportive. Gretchen Scott at Northwest College Library endured hundreds of interlibrary loan requests. Thank you, Gretchen.

Thanks to Geir Lie and Dr. Dale Simmons who shared the benefits of much of their research with me. Thanks to Al Houghton for his much encouragement and for critiquing the earlier manuscript.

Thanks to Deborah Poulalion and Christina Williams for their hours of editing work on the manuscript, and to the editorial staff at Creation House for their help with getting this book ready for publication.

Contents

INTRODUCTION

Any story sounds true until someone tells the other side and sets the record straight.

—Proverbs 18:17, TLB

I N THE EARLY 1970s I wandered into a Christian bookstore and purchased two books that were destined to change my life.

The books were *In His Presence* and *Jesus the Healer* by E. W. Kenyon (1867–1948). I discovered that God was, first and primarily, a Father God. I also discovered that Jesus loved me enough to bear my sicknesses and pains as well as my sins. I received my healing from asthma that had plagued me since I was a child. I am no longer bothered by asthma. Praise the Lord!

In 1980 the Lord led me to begin a Bible study that eventually became the church I now pastor, Word of His Grace Fellowship in Kirkland, Washington. I would tell people who wanted to know what the church believed to read *In His Presence*. That book was foundational to our church.

In the mid-eighties some books were released that viciously attacked Kenyon and the Faith movement. These books misrepresented both Kenyon and the modern Faith movement, and one book suggested that Kenyon mixed metaphysics—specifically Christian Science and New Thought ideas—into Christianity, resulting in heresy.[1] The supposition of Kenyon's heresy is the key piece in a larger argument which asserts that the modern Faith movement is heretical because it has drawn heavily from Kenyon's ideas.

Is there truth in these criticisms? If there is, then Kenyon's writings *deserve* to come under close scrutiny and people *should* be warned of their delusive content. But if these accusations are false, the truth should be made known so the body of Christ can make an unbiased evaluation of Kenyon's teachings.

When a book that included criticisms of Kenyon became a best-seller, I began to write a response, primarily for my congregation. In my writing, I used the information about Kenyon that was openly available—books in print and publically available magazine articles. I concluded that Kenyon did not mix metaphysics and Christianity. In fact, he was an outspoken opponent of the cults and was deeply influenced by the orthodox Christian leaders of his day.

Having completed a rough draft, I sought to communicate with Ruth Kenyon Housworth, who at that time ran Kenyon's Gospel Publishing Society with her husband Norm. I had spoken to her a number of times over the years, and I thought she might be blessed to know someone was responding to her father's critics. Sadly, Ruth was in the hospital and went to be with the Lord about a month later. The staff at Kenyon's Gospel Publishing Society asked me to perform the memorial service for Ruth, which I was honored to do.

Around this time I asked the staff if they knew about the "rumored" boxes of unpublished materials that both Ruth and her husband had mentioned to me on separate occasions years earlier. The staff was unaware of these materials.

Three weeks later I received a phone call from Kenyon's Gospel Publishing Society. They had found about five boxes full of old materials—unpublished articles, sermons, previously unknown periodicals from Kenyon's early days, some manuscripts, an old Bible, and some hymn books, a brief journal, many, many, sermon notebooks, lots of poems, and other odds and ends. It was a gold mine of material for someone trying find out more about Kenyon's theological development!

This find, of course, was a tremendous blessing. New statements about Kenyon's mentors were found. A clear picture of his early years emerged. Much more documentation for my previous conclusions was found. Many historical gaps were filled in. But the conclusions themselves were much the same.

The fact that my conclusions were not significantly altered indicates that Kenyon's critics have not presented an honest case. By not exploring documentable influences—influences that were clear from the previously available materials—they built a believable case against him. But when we look at the writings of those whom Kenyon said were his mentors, Kenyon's theology and its developments prove to be in harmony with the orthodox Christian leaders of his day. His critics' accusation of cultic influence no longer makes sense.

I wrote this book to provide factual information about the true influences on Kenyon's theology, the influences Kenyon openly acknowledged. This book is not intended to be a complete biography of the man. Although there is much biographical information, the book is more a focused view of the forces that shaped Kenyon's message— his message of faith.

Section one describes his conversion, the two to three years when he was out of fellowship with the Father, the truth about his time at Emerson College of Oratory, and his restoration to faith.

Section two focuses on the three key years of Kenyon's theological development—1894–1897. It was during these years that he was ordained with the Free Will Baptists and pastored a church in New York.

Section three looks at Kenyon's fruitful years of ministry. It shows the many relationships that he had with the orthodox Christian leaders of his day and concludes with his death and the various stories surrounding it. The Faith-Cure movement, a Christian healing movement which predates the Metaphysical movement, is introduced.

Section four takes a topical look at issues where Kenyon's teaching has been attacked. In this section, I am not so much defending Kenyon's theology as pointing out that his views were very similar to those whom he said were his mentors. The reader is free to disagree with Kenyon's perspective, but I believe this section establishes beyond doubt that Kenyon's influences were completely orthodox. His teachings reflect the ideas that were common among the evangelical community of his formative years. The writings of many of his stated mentors are examined and compared with Kenyon's writings.

My research for this book has led me to believe that a little information went a long way in accusing Kenyon of heresy. It brings to mind the story told about Mark Twain when there were widespread rumors that he had died. He responded by sending a cablegram which read, "The reports of my death are greatly exaggerated."

Like the reports of Twain's death, the reports of Kenyon's heretical teachings are "greatly exaggerated." It is time to tell the true story to this generation.

—Joe McIntyre
Kirkland, Washington

CHAPTER 1

EARLY DAYS

*I can remember the night that I received eternal life. It seemed
as though I hardly touched the sidewalk on my way home. It was a
cold winter night in January, but, oh, how beautiful the snow and
frost. Yes, the trees stripped of their foliage assumed a beauty I
had never noted before.*

—E. W. Kenyon

I CAN REMEMBER the night that I received eternal life. It seemed as
though I hardly touched the sidewalk on my way home. It was a
cold winter night in January, but, oh, how beautiful the snow and frost.
Yes, the trees stripped of their foliage assumed a beauty I had never
noted before.

E. W. Kenyon was reared in circumstances that were not likely to
produce the remarkably fruitful author and teacher that he would
become. The son of William A. Kenyon and Ann Eliza Knox, he was
born on April 24, 1867, at a lumber camp, the fourth son in a family of
ten. The family remained there in Hadley Hills, New York, for a few
years and then moved to the nearby village of Amsterdam.

Due to his family's poverty, he left school at the age of ten at which
time he could only write his name in capital letters. At twelve he went
to work at one of the local carpet mills, where he typically worked
from 6 A.M. to 6 P.M. six days a week. His frustration with life at this
time led "Will" Kenyon to become "familiar with all forms of wicked-
ness." He dreamed of becoming an actor, which was a disreputable

profession at the time, and described himself as an agnostic.[2]

KENYON'S CONVERSION

PROBABLY MOTIVATED BY the mindless nature of mill work and the sinful lifestyle he was living, Will Kenyon began to hunger spiritually in his teen years. His family did not attend church, so Will had only been to church three times in his life. When his friend Wesley Craig invited him to the week of prayer at the local Methodist church which was meeting at an old schoolhouse, he consented. The first night Will raised his hand at the giving of the invitation. The second night when an altar call was given he went forward. He described his walk home on that cold night in the quote above. The next morning Will fell on the ice. But something had changed in him. "I knew," he said, "I had religion."[3]

E. W. Kenyon was dramatically and soundly converted at seventeen years of age. He began to devour the New Testament that an older man in the church had given him. His conversion stirred within him a longing to get an education and to preach.

> Just as soon as a man receives eternal life he wants an education. At the time I was born again, I was working in a factory. I had no education whatever. The third night when I came home from the service my mother asked me where I had been, and I told her.
>
> My brother, older than I, a witty fellow, said, "Mother, that fool will be preaching next."
>
> I ran upstairs to get away from him, for I dreaded his wit, but I said as I went, "Eddie, you are right; I am going to have an education, and I am going to preach."[4]

According to Ruth Kenyon Housworth, E. W. Kenyon's daughter, he "had a thirst for knowledge, and what he learned he wanted to pass on to others. That desire for study was the driving force of his life." And although he worked long hours as a carpet weaver, her father devoted "every spare minute . . . to study."[5] A newspaper article said of the young Kenyon:

> As he plied the shuttle in his loom there raged more and more fiercely within the longing for an education. There were no night

schools, so he studied as best he might; often registering a vow that he would obtain the coveted treasure.[6]

Kenyon wrote:

> I vowed I would do it, and I have done it. I stood by the loom as a boy and vowed that I would become an educator. I did not know what it meant, but I knew that within me was a teaching gift, an undeveloped thing. I vowed I would do it. I did it. I was handicapped as few men have been handicapped, but I did it. I am passing it on to you to show that they cannot conquer you if you will to do it.[7]

After Will Kenyon gave his life to the Lord, he delighted in the joy of sins forgiven. Filled with zeal and the wonder of the new life, he was an enthusiastic soul winner. His witnessing at the factory had a far-reaching influence on the workers.[8]

After three months he began to conduct cottage prayer meetings and street meetings where he led many to Christ. He was eventually given an exhorter's license by the Methodist Episcopal Church in Amsterdam, New York, and was pastoring by the age of nineteen.[9] He also led his mother and father to faith in Christ.[10]

Kenyon also pursued his dream of education. He received permission to leave the factory to attend a three-month term at the academy in his home town and later had another term at Kent's Hill, a local school.

PROBLEMS ARISE

EVEN THOUGH KENYON enthusiastically pursued converts, he was never solidly established in the basic doctrines of the faith himself. "Do you know," he wrote, "when I accepted Jesus Christ, not one word was said to me about justification, the new birth, or the great doctrines of redemption?"[11] With such a shaky foundation, problems soon arose. After a few years of faithfully attempting to serve the Lord, E. W. Kenyon gave way to discouragement. The distracted and disillusioned young preacher "left the Lord's vineyard and turned to the affairs of this world."[12]

What were the factors that contributed to Kenyon's falling away from the faith? This is an important question to answer, because he would revisit these points in his teaching for the rest of his life.

LACK OF TRAINING

THE FOREMOST REASON Kenyon attributed to his falling away was a lack of training in scriptural truths. He explained, "I got a wonderful experience [his conversion], but I did not know what that experience was."[13]

> I went to the altar and didn't know what I had. I only knew I had my sins forgiven. No one ever told me I had been born again or had received eternal life. I had been in the ministry for years before I knew I had eternal life. Before that time I had never heard anyone teaching about eternal life.[14]

Because of his personal experience, Kenyon determined to establish new converts in the scriptures and give them the tools to live the Christian life. He described from his own experience what happens when this foundation is missing.

> I remember when I was born again. I said to myself that nothing could happen to me. I was so happy. Joy seemed to run out my fingers. How I labored with the boys to bring them to meeting. One day I went to a picnic with a company of young people. I was amusing the crowd that day; I amused them to such an extent that I got out of fellowship with the Father, and I did not know what ailed me. I had grieved the Spirit.
>
> That night we were going down to The Salvation Army. None of the boys were Christians. I always testified, and God gave me great liberty in testimony in those days, but I waited until toward the end. But I had to speak; it seemed as though I should burst. I got on my feet and told them how miserable I was and how unhappy. I told them that I did not believe that I was a Christian any longer, that I had sinned and I was lost. I had no one to help me. As I went down the stairs with the boys, they told me that I ought to go to the altar and be justified again. . . . Days and days went past before I got my fellowship back again.[15]

A few years later while pastoring he met the same struggle.

Although one of his key teachings eventually would be the difference between *relationship* and *fellowship,* this event was the beginning of a downhill slide for Kenyon.

> Years went by before I knew the difference between fellowship and relationship. I could not help my people. I would see young people accept Christ and come into the church and their testimony would ring out with great joy for weeks, then it was gone. I would do my best, but could not get them back. I did not know how to help them. Many a choice man and woman did I lose out of my church. I knew they were born again.[16]

Although Kenyon experienced some troubled years due to his lack of grounding in the Word, God would use it for good. His desire to firmly establish new converts in the Word emerged from this negative event and marked Kenyon forever—in a good way.

Near the end of his life (1943) Kenyon wrote about someone who had lost their fellowship with the Father after a glorious conversion. Kenyon explained to this inquirer that he hadn't lost his salvation, he had broken fellowship with the Father. "I can understand that. I think every believer goes through that experience unless he has been correctly instructed at the beginning. . . . I passed through that myself."[17]

E. W. instructed him to take his correspondence course and read his books. Kenyon's books and courses were designed to help believers avoid falling into the same pit Kenyon did. "Great enthusiasm and joy come at the new birth," Kenyon wrote, "but unless that is cared for and fed by the mind being renewed through feeding on the Word and practicing it, that joy will die out."[18]

SKEPTICISM

BECAUSE OF HIS LACK of scriptural understanding, E. W. Kenyon wrote that he became dominated by his skeptical nature.[19]

Skepticism is ignorance in the saddle; one is skeptical about a thing he does not know or understand. When he knows or understands it, he is no longer skeptical.[20]

Young Will was quite sensitive of nature and was beset by doubts. Not having a basis in the fundamental truths of Christianity from Scripture his mind was besieged by questions. Although he experienced great joy when his fellowship with the Lord was rich, if it was marred in any way he became helpless and vulnerable. This increased his susceptibility to wonder if Christianity was "a bag of holes." Ignorance was creeping into the saddle and skepticism was grasping the reins.

LIBERAL INFLUENCES

LIKE MANY YOUNG MINISTERS, Will looked to the elder ministers around him for help and instruction. Unfortunately for Kenyon, those he looked to were not a good influence on him. He shared that his "first view of Jesus the Nazarene was through the eyes of others. Almost all my early experience was through the mental eyes of my elders. I learned my theology from men rather than from God Himself.[21]

Being young and naive, Kenyon allowed his desire for an education to be fed by ministers with a liberal bent. One minister gave E. W. a book that he had authored on annihilationism, which Kenyon eagerly read. "There was a time when I denied the sufferings of the wicked. I believed in the annihilation of the wicked. I believed it because I was led into it by a man who gave me his book."[22] Kenyon later reflected that the book didn't contain much Scripture at all, but many quotes from well-known clergy.

Kenyon also noted the devastating effects of one sermon he heard as a young minister. The preacher argued that "God knew Adam was going to fall, and that knowing that, He was not just in creating him." This message totally disarmed the zealous young soul-winner. Kenyon wrote, "The man that preached it didn't know what seed he was sowing in my young heart. I was trying to be true to God. When I got into the work and met this argument, I lost faith. I lost everything. For three years I was in darkness."[23]

The justice of God in creating man would later become an important theological theme in Kenyon's writings. He made this theme the subject of a chapter in his first book *The Father and His Family*.

Kenyon swallowed some poor and damaging teaching. He assumed the integrity of these older ministers and accepted their ideas without examining the Scriptures. After he was restored to the Lord, he would not make *that* mistake again.

LACK OF RESULTS

ANOTHER WIND OF DISCOURAGEMENT assaulted the tender faith of the zealous young minister: the lack of results he was seeing in those he was attempting to nurture in the Lord. We see a glimpse of this emerging discouragement in the above quotes. It began to really get to him as he attempted to lead others. Kenyon wrote about these early days that he "wondered why the largest percentage of church members and those whom I had led to Christ myself were spiritual failures. I wondered if after all, Christianity was a bag full of holes." Compared to his zeal, those around him seemed pathetically uncommitted. As he said of himself at the time "I was very zealous. I had consecration services every week," to fire them up. But, he reported, "I preached hard and worked hard, but my people failed to attend prayer meetings despite all that I could do."[24]

NOT RECEIVING THE HOLY SPIRIT

KENYON ALSO POINTED OUT that due to lack of teaching, he had not received the Holy Spirit in the first years after his conversion. ("I had never received the Holy Spirit; if I had, I should never have got in that condition [fallen away].[25]") Kenyon's teaching on the Holy Spirit has come under discussion, and we will examine his beliefs thoroughly in a later chapter. For here, let it suffice to say that he did believe Christians needed to receive the Holy Spirit *after* their conversion.

THREE DARK YEARS

KENYON'S FIRST WIFE, Evva (who died in 1914), said that her husband was disillusioned by "disgust arising from the many inconsistencies in the motives and lives of Christian leaders," and some failings in his own life, namely, "the pride of life, desire for fame and money in his own nature."

Kenyon spent between two and three years in darkness.

> Years went by and I lost it and went back into sin; I dropped back deeper and deeper until I went into agnosticism. Yet all through those dark days of my doubts, I had a consciousness that I was a child of God. I never left my Bible behind me during those two or

three years in which I was in darkness, but I never breathed a prayer to God Almighty. I was a son, but I was a prodigal. When I came back, I came into fellowship with my Father.[26]

We will examine what Kenyon did during these days of darkness in the next chapter. This crucial chapter will answer the question, "Was Kenyon influenced by the metaphysical cults?"

CHAPTER 2

DAYS OF DARKNESS

When faith dies, philosophy flourishes. A living Christ and a living Father God perfectly satisfies, and we have no need of philosophy, we have no need of metaphysics. It is when we lose Christ out of our daily life that we turn to metaphysics and philosophical theories that have no place in the life of faith.

—E. W. Kenyon[1]

E. W. KENYON had fallen away from the Lord. Always energetic and zealous, where can he direct his energy? He had to pursue some means of livelihood, so, at the age of twenty-one, Kenyon began to sell pianos. He recalled, "I didn't know anything about the sales game when I went into it as a boy of twenty-one."[2] His older brother George was already successful in the piano business, so E. W. went to work for the same piano and organ company. He became quite successful as a piano salesman, throwing himself into it with the zeal that marked his nature.

His evangelistic gift appeared to find an outlet in the sales business, and his success in it likely began to feed his desire for money. He testified to a genuine desire to help and bless people while in the business world and referred to this as a major factor in his success.[3] His experience in sales would eventually lead to Kenyon teaching on success in his periodicals and later in his little book *Sign Posts on the Road to Success*. Yet he clearly was drifting away from his calling and with each dollar earned his spiritual emptiness grew.

9

REASON DARKNESS

HAVING BEGUN TO DOUBT the gospel as revealed in the Scriptures, his inquisitive mind sought other sources of light. He described the reason for this spiritual hunger in his book *The Two Kinds of Righteousness*. "Man has no approach to God. The sense of condemnation has given to him an inferiority complex that makes him a coward. It robs him of faith in himself, in man, in God and in His Word. This sin consciousness holds him in bondage."[4] Kenyon felt that the only type of prayer a man in this condition could pray would be a prayer of desperation.

Having lost his fellowship with the Lord, his own sense of sin plagued him. He referred to this struggle in a sermon he preached years later in the church where he rededicated his life to the Lord: A. J. Gordon's Clarendon Street Baptist Church in Boston. He recalled that he "once heard Dr. [A. T.] Pierson, in a discourse, say that there were seven steps in the Resurrection life of Jesus, and that they illustrate our own life." This struck Kenyon as incredible. He said to himself, "No, it cannot be, for Jesus was a perfect man; I am a failure, and hence what is true of Him cannot be true of me." This sense of unworthiness dominated his early days because, he said," I then believed that sin still ruled over me, and not the Lord."[5]

Dr. Pierson, a close friend of A. J. Gordon and a respected fellow preacher and author, had a great influence on Kenyon. Kenyon heard Pierson teach on our identification with Christ. Our identification with Christ would become a major theme in all of Kenyon's writings. Pierson's influence will be shown in more detail later.

Continuing his thoughts on where sin consciousness and unworthiness leads an individual Kenyon wrote:

> This [sin consciousness] has led him into philosophy. He could no more keep away from the subject of God and religion than a hungry man can keep away from food.
>
> The sense of guilt, inferiority, failure, and weakness makes him reason, and that reasoning we call philosophy.[6]

Kenyon spoke from his own experience here. Out of fellowship with the Lord, his spiritual hunger motivated him to investigate philosophy and metaphysics to satisfy *on a mental level* what he later would understand to be his own deep spiritual hunger for reality in Christ.

10

Kenyon referred to his battle with fear and unworthiness:

> The solution of the fear problem is found in the fact that Jesus did conquer Satan, He did put sin away, He did restore lost righteousness to the heart of man. This lost righteousness is the cause of the inferiority complex, or the sense of unworthiness. The sense of unworthiness is a dark corner in the heart where fear propagates, where doubts come into full strength and vigor, where unbelief sinks its roots. If God can destroy this age-old sense of inferiority that came to us through the fall of Adam, then fear has lost its torments.
>
> I sought for a cure for fear. It is not in philosophy, it is not in metaphysics, it is not in human religion, scientific or otherwise. Fear can only be destroyed by the truth coming to us of our emancipation from the power of Satan, of our being right with God. That will destroy fear.[7]

DENOUNCING PHILOSOPHY

KENYON ACKNOWLEDGED his search for freedom from fear while he was away from the Lord. He investigated some philosophical and metaphysical literature. Some modern researchers have argued that Kenyon used metaphysical ideas to construct pseudo-Christian doctrine. It should be noted that he was not seeking to enhance his pastoral or teaching ministry when he read this literature—he was not a minister at this time. Nor was he seeking to learn about metaphysical healing. Healing would not become a part of his ministry until a few years after his restoration to the Lord. Kenyon was seeking to overcome his guilt and fear while he was out of fellowship with the Lord.

Kenyon believed philosophy was a quest for reality—man's attempt to know God and spiritual things without the help of the Holy Spirit. But, he stated, "the man who really knows Jesus Christ, who has received eternal life, never turns to philosophy. If he has been a philosopher, he gives it up because he has arrived at reality in Christ."[8] Throughout his ministry he would refer to philosophy as the "swan song of human failure."[9]

Kenyon found what he was looking for when he came back into fellowship with God and had a realization of his justification. Righteousness by faith, or justification, was to become one of the

11

foundational planks of his developing theology. His book *The Two Kinds of Righteousness* is the expression of this truth and its importance to the believer's life. He believed that the right-standing which God offered in the gospel was what those in the metaphysical cults were really hungering for.

E. W. Kenyon would reflect back on his time of deception in many places in his writings. On this period of darkness he commented:

> For years I was living in the light of reason. I was reading books on philosophy, metaphysics, and psychology, *thinking I was getting light from them.* All the time I felt a struggle in my own inner being, a conflict was going on. It was God in my spirit trying to make me see that the light I thought I had was *reason darkness,* and that it was shutting me away from the deeper unveilings of the grace of God in His Word.
>
> There came a time when I had to make a choice between *the works of reason* and the Word of God, and you know the choice I made.
>
> And I want to say to my good friends who are living *in the realm of reason,* who feel the teaching about the blood of Christ, and the new birth, and the sacrifice of Christ on the cross and His Resurrection, are relics of heathen darkness and must be interpreted in the light of reason—I want to tell you, friends, that *that light of reason is darkness,* it is shutting you away from redemption and from the big things of God.
>
> Our philosophical friends have created a new god, a philosophical god. He does not look a bit like Jesus or the Father or the Holy Spirit. He is a man-made god.
>
> I want you to come back—yes, come back to the God of the Bible, the God and Father of our Lord Jesus Christ. Come back to Him. You will find rest for your soul, and joy for your spirit, and healing for your body.[10]

Who was Kenyon calling back to the God of the Bible? He told us:

> Vast numbers of men and women are today exchanging the living grace of Jesus Christ for Christian Science, Unity, and the other philosophical and psychological cults.[11]
>
> Modern philosophical religions claim to have light and they claim that it is *the* light, but this is light that they have originated

in their own intellects, it is the product of their own spiritual light and understanding of God, for all these writers declare that God is not a person but a principle.[12]

THE TRUE THEOLOGICAL IMPACT OF THE CULTS

IT IS TRUE THAT KENYON'S exposure to metaphysical and philosophical writings did affect his teaching—but not in the way his critics have implied. He used his knowledge of the cults to point out their weaknesses and call those ensnared in them to the satisfaction provided by the *true* gospel.

The understanding he gained after recovering from this investigation into philosophy and metaphysics undergirded all his later teaching about sense knowledge and revelation knowledge. Philosophy and metaphysics, Kenyon came to see at this early period of his life, were the fruit of reason without the assistance of the Holy Spirit. Kenyon always referred to the cults as "sense knowledge" religions.

Challenging those deceived by the metaphysical cults to return to the simple truths of the Bible would be a life-long burden for him. Many of his contemporaries in the evangelical church were likewise lamenting how many genuine Christians were being lured into these false cults.

It is important to note that Kenyon's brief flirtation with metaphysical and philosophical teachings took place in the two to three year period he was out of fellowship with the Lord. He was not a minister at this time. Nor is there any evidence that he associated with any metaphysical groups. He acknowledged that he did read books on these subjects.

This understanding Kenyon gained explains why his writings contain many references to the cults. Not because he was secretly sympathetic to these cults as some have suggested. If he was sympathetic to them, he was a master of disguise! His writings contain many references to the cults because he wanted to warn people that there was no light in them.

God used this period of struggle in Kenyon's life. Though he "had a skeptical, atheistic trend for a number of years," God's call on his life still smoldered within him. Even in his darkness he still "thought of going into the ministry." But the effects of his "reason darkness" plagued him and "when it came to the Lord Jesus I couldn't accept the literal Resurrection."[13]

But a merciful God was about to change this. For Kenyon, the

Resurrection and deity of Christ would soon become two truths that he would feel particularly called to defend. He would understand the struggles of those who had skeptical minds and would make it his aim to convince them of the essential and absolute necessity of these two truths. They would be foundational to all of his future teachings. But at this season of his life he was floundering in doubt and reasoning himself into unbelief.

During this period he apparently attended services held by a Unitarian minister by the name of Minot J. Savage.[14] Kenyon did not attempt to hide this fact. (Unitarianism, which is a form of liberal Christianity that denies the Trinity and deity of Christ, should not be confused with Unity, which is a metaphysical cult that developed out of New Thought). In his early publications—after he was restored to the Lord—he often refers to his time of darkness. It is obvious, however, to anyone reading these articles that he thoroughly repudiated and denounced all of the teaching he was exposed to at this period of his life.[15]

An Acting Career?

During his two or three years of broken fellowship with the Lord, Kenyon was making lots of money and living an ungodly lifestyle. His desire for the stage reemerged somewhere during this period of his life, and he thought it would be helpful to get some training. He decided to attend *Emerson College of Oratory* in Boston, not to study metaphysics, or for the ministry, but to prepare himself for the stage.

Some say that he became sympathetic to the cults at Emerson. In the next chapter, we'll see whether this is true.

CHAPTER 3

EMERSON COLLEGE
OF ORATORY

Prof. C. W. Emerson . . . is one of the few elocutionists fit to be trusted to teach people how to speak in the name of the Lord.
—Charles Cullis[1]

E. W. Kenyon entered the student body of Emerson College of Oratory in the autumn of 1892 at the age of twenty-five. He had decided to hone his acting skills to "get ready for the stage," a dream he had entertained as a young man and had resurrected in recent years.

His choice of school ultimately became a center for the philosophy that developed into the metaphysical movement known as New Thought. Ralph Waldo Trine, who became one of the most articulate spokesmen for the New Thought movement, was also one of Kenyon's classmates. These facts have provided fuel for attempts to "roast" Kenyon theologically.[2]

Kenyon attend Emerson from September of 1892 to May of 1893, after which he was restored to the Lord. Let's look at the college during this period. Was it really overwhelmed with New Thought ideas? Also, how open was Kenyon to religious influences at this period of his life? We'll look at Trine and see what he was doing during the one year Kenyon was on campus. Then we'll examine some of Kenyon's teaching for evidence of New Thought influence.

STRANGE CONTRADICTIONS

Both Emerson College of Oratory and its founder, Charles Wesley Emerson (1837–1908), embodied striking contradictions. Originally known as the *Boston Conservatory of Elocution, Oratory, and Dramatic Art,* Emerson was one of the most prominent schools in America for training in vocal expression from 1890 to 1920.[3] It would later become known as a center for New Thought philosophy, but at the time Kenyon attended, it trained men for *Christian* ministry, as well as oratory and drama. Kenyon wrote "[I] fought the men [at Emerson College] that were getting ready for the ministry. I wrecked one young man who was one of the cleanest boys studying for the ministry. I was so mad, but God got hold of me and brought me back into fellowship with Him. I got this man back."[4]

There wasn't any other kind of ministry to prepare for other than traditional Christian ministry, so it seems safe to assume this is what Kenyon referred to in his statement. The fact that some Emerson students were preparing for Christian ministry is quite significant in the light of arguments that Kenyon was influenced by New Thought just because he attended Emerson.

Notice also that Kenyon got this young man "back." "Back" would surely refer to bringing him back to orthodoxy. Kenyon's comment also suggests that Kenyon was more influential on the students than the faculty was on him!

Charles Wesley Emerson, founder of the college, was an interesting mixture of the orthodox and the unorthodox.[5] He began his career as a licensed minister in a Congregationalist church. He later assumed the pastorate at two Unitarian churches. After a short stint of studying law, he pursued studies in oratory. He was naturally gifted and soon opened his own school of oratory.

What is not generally known is that he first taught oratory at Faith Training College in Boston, an institution raised up to further the ends of the Holiness movement.[6] Its founder was the homeopathic doctor and Holiness advocate Charles Cullis, who would become internationally known as the central figure of a movement of orthodox divine healing known as the Faith-Cure.

Emerson taught oratory classes at this Holiness college for eleven years (1876–1887) on a totally volunteer basis! No salaries were paid to any of the teachers. Emerson was in the company of other very well known Holiness ministers, including Daniel Steele, William McDonald, and A. B. Earle. The stated purpose of the college was to "bring the earnest, honest souls of our students as quickly as possible face-to-face with their duty and privilege of receiving the Holy Ghost, the 'Promise of the Father.'"[7]

This experience of *receiving the Holy Ghost,* described a post-conversion crisis of consecration which was also referred to as the *second work of grace* or *entire sanctification.* Having received this experience, one was then said to able to walk in complete victory over sin.

The Holiness movement and its teachings hold a significant place in the unfolding of Kenyon's story. C. W. Emerson's involvement with this institution identified him with this group. As historian Dale Simmons noted, "Because of the tremendous amount of press attention Cullis's work had attracted over the years, Emerson was well aware of the costs involved in associating with the faith work."[8] Emerson was comfortable with this association.

One of the speakers at Emerson's funeral (in 1908), a Rev. Benjamin F. Kidder, stated, " . . . I personally know that he was in deepest and truest sympathy with the highest and holiest ideals of truth and life as held by the Methodists."[9] The Methodist church at this time was the fountain of most of the Holiness teaching. Cullis himself reported that "Prof. C. W. Emerson . . . is one of the few elocutionists fit to be trusted to teach people how to speak in the name of the Lord."[10]

In one of his annual reports, Cullis noted Emerson's colorful past and then quoted Emerson as saying that he was becoming more and more convinced of "the wisdom and power in the name of Jesus" and for him the *text of texts* seemed to be, "If I be lifted up, I will draw all men unto Me." Emerson concluded, "What we need for power is to lift up the Lord Jesus Christ."[11]

Dale Simmons observed, "The fact that neither Cullis nor any of the other leading Holiness figures who served on Faith Training College's faculty were sufficiently alarmed by Emerson's teachings is telling." He added, "The evidence then strongly favors the conclusion that, at least during that period, [Charles Wesley] Emerson embraced the 'full gospel message of Jesus as Savior, Sanctifier, Healer, and Coming King,' which Cullis and his associates advocated."[12]

Nevertheless, Emerson also embraced evolution and clearly taught what we *now* know as New Thought metaphysics. His documentable influences are highly unorthodox and his Christianity certainly questionable. These strange contradictions regarding Emerson illustrate how the language of Christianity was used in numerous contexts with varied meanings. Emerson felt he was doing a work for God. It quite possible Emerson embraced the gospel as expressed by the Holiness movement while teaching at Cullis's school but gradually drifted away from it as he developed his own school.

How did Kenyon react to Emerson? Simmons speculated, "Given the fact that Kenyon was going through a period in which he was openly antagonistic toward the Christian faith and those who professed it, it is just as reasonable to assume that Kenyon might have found Emerson to be too 'orthodox' for his liking."[13]

THE TRINE CONNECTION

While Kenyon attended Emerson College (September 1892–May 1893), Ralph Waldo Trine was both a freshman student and professor. Trine taught rhetoric at Emerson from 1892–1894, and all students would have attended his class.

Some say that Trine influenced Kenyon toward New Thought. In order for Trine to do this, he had to know about New Thought himself at the time, correct? One critic incorrectly speaks of Trine as "a chief expositor of New Thought at Emerson College of Oratory."[14] Trine could not have been a "chief expositor" of New Thought while he was at Emerson for one simple reason: he was just being exposed to New Thought ideas himself.

Emerson College historians tell us "Trine apparently did not become known as an exponent of the faith [New Thought] until *after* his leaving Dr. Emerson's college [in 1894]. "

Historians do not agree on exactly how Trine was imbued with New Thought. Emerson College historians say it is possible Trine first learned of its doctrines from Charles Wesley Emerson."[15] Trine moved to Boston for his first year at Emerson, so if C. W. Emerson was his source for New Thought concepts it would have been during 1892. A different biographical sketch states "In Boston he became heavily influenced by the thought of his namesake Ralph Waldo Emerson [not Charles Wesley] . . . whose work would become a major source for New Thought philosophy at the end of the century."[16]

Whether he learned New Thought concepts from the writings of transcendentalist Ralph Waldo Emerson or professor Charles Wesley Emerson, the evidence is clear that Trine's exposure to New Thought ideas was during his first year in Boston while teaching at Emerson. This hardly allows for Trine to have passed on much New Thought influence to Kenyon!

According to the historians of the New Thought movement, Trine's influence began with the publication of his first book, *What All the World's A-Seeking,* in 1896.[17] This date is very significant because by 1893 Kenyon was restored to the Lord and by early 1894 he was ordained with the Free Will Baptists, a very conservative denomination. New Thought was not a recognized movement until years after Kenyon was restored to the Lord. (New Thought should not be confused with Christian Science, which *was* a developing movement in Boston when Kenyon was there. We'll discuss his opinion of Christian Science in chapter nineteen).

To say that Trine influenced Kenyon is only speculation based on two people being in the same place at the same time. There is no other evidence to suggest that Trine influenced Kenyon. Some statements of Trine's that are quoted by Kenyon's critics sound similar to Kenyon, but the similarity is only superficial.[18] Kenyon was opposed to just about everything Trine stood for, spiritually speaking.

DISCERNING DRUMMOND

There is a theologian and author from Scotland who can help us see something about the character of both Kenyon and Emerson. His name is Henry Drummond (1851–1897). Drummond was an influential man in the Christian community in the late 1800s. He worked closely with D. L. Moody, sharing his burden for evangelism, and wrote an influential book *Natural Law in the Spiritual World* (1883), which was popular among evangelicals. A book he wrote about 1 Corinthians 13, *The Greatest Thing in the World,* is still sold in Christian bookstores.

However, Drummond became quite controversial as time went on, and his orthodoxy was brought into question. He acknowledged that he read the writings of many who were considered heretics. He believed and taught evolution.

One of Drummond's greatest admirers was none other than Charles Wesley Emerson. When Drummond came to Boston in May 1893 to deliver a series of lectures, he also visited Emerson College. (This was the last month of Kenyon's year of attendance at the college.) Emerson introduced him as a man who was "in hearty sympathy with the spirit of this college." After Drummond spoke, Emerson concluded:

> Of all the living men whom I had not seen but whom I came to know for their writings, the one man whom I desired to see in the flesh and have visit this institution was Professor Drummond . . . We thank Professor Drummond for his visit with us and . . . wish him great success and happiness in the noble Christian work in which he is engaged.[19]

A large part of the "noble Christian work" in which Drummond was engaged was evangelism! It was "the master passion of his life" and the reason for his association with Moody.[20] To have Emerson say that Drummond was in sympathy with the spirit of his college shows how comfortable Emerson was with evangelicals. It also illustrates the ambivalence in the spiritual environment of Boston. Attendance at Emerson College would not necessarily have brought its students into any metaphysical philosophy, at least in these early years.

Kenyon may well have attended Drummond's lecture, and we do know Kenyon read a number of Drummond's books and at one time published a series of excerpts from *The Greatest Thing In the World* in one of his periodicals. Yet Kenyon drew the line at accepting Drummond's teaching on evolution. Kenyon was convinced that evolution undermined the believer's confidence in his being created for a divine destiny as a son of God. Kenyon also believed that if the first three chapters of Genesis could be challenged, the whole Bible would be threatened.

During the last quarter of the nineteenth century, the language of Christianity was used in numerous contexts with varied meaning. Kenyon warned against the false teachings of the metaphysical cults early in his ministry, exhibiting no sympathy with them at all. Having briefly fallen victim to these things, he was qualified to warn others.

In a recommendation for Kenyon's evangelistic ministry, one pastor commends him as being "familiar with all the 'isms' of the day."[21] Obviously, this pastor did not mean *sympathetically* familiar!

A Test of Influence

The case of those who suggest that Kenyon's exposure to Emerson and Trine strongly influenced his doctrine is, at best, weak. An examination of their teaching on the nature of man may illustrate the fact.

Emerson taught that man is "soul ruling the mind, and mind ruling the body."[22] Ralph Waldo Trine wrote in a similar vein, "It is through the instrumentality of the mind that we are able to connect the real soul life with the physical life, and so enable the soul life to manifest and work through the physical."[23] Both men described man in three aspects with the soul as the deepest part which finds expression though the mind.

If Kenyon's thinking had been stimulated much by these men regarding man's nature, we would expect evidence of it in his writings closest to his time at Emerson. Yet Kenyon's published writings, which began in 1898, show him to consider man to be two-fold—soul and body. It wasn't until twelve years after leaving Emerson that he described man in three aspects. Kenyon then wrote:

> Man is a trinity in his nature: body, soul, and spirit. There is the outer realm of the senses; the realm of the soul; and the inner realm of the spirit, the holy of holies of our being. . . .[24]

Like most conservative evangelicals who believed man to consist of three distinct elements, Kenyon taught that the spirit was the deepest part of man and the soul was synonymous with the mind. (Actually, the soul was said to be the mind, emotions, and will.) Kenyon's teaching in this statement is far more likely reflective of the influence of Jessie Penn-Lewis, whose teaching Kenyon said he was "entranced with" for many years.[25] Among Kenyon's personal library remaining after he died were some books by Jessie Penn-Lewis. One of the books articulated man's nature this way.

> If your spirit is strong your body must become strengthened. Your body is not to carry your spirit, but your spirit should control your body:
>
> When your spirit is strong, it assimilates the Spirit-food in the Bible, and you feed your spirit. You need a strong spirit more than a strong body, and even a "strong" mind. Your mind will be

stronger, if you have a strong spirit to quicken it, for in that spirit dwells the Holy Spirit. It is the shrine of God. It is the place where God dwells, and the strength of the might of God is to get into your spirit until your spirit is "strong in the Lord, and in the strength of His might."[26]

This quote sounds very similar to many of Kenyon's statements on the necessity of feeding the spirit man by meditating in the Scriptures. In his understanding of the nature of man, Kenyon followed Penn-Lewis, A. T. Pierson and the other Keswick-influenced teachers (more about them later). The evidence does not support the idea that Emerson and Trine had much influence on Kenyon at all.[27]

AN OBSERVATION

Kenyon did feel he benefited from his time at Emerson. He would later include oratory in his Bible school curriculum as an important part of training the students for public ministry. The need of training for effective public speaking was appreciated by Kenyon in these days when there were no public address systems to enhance the voice.

Kenyon's critics have built their case by majoring on one of *many* spiritual streams (the metaphysical cults) that were flowing in the world and around the church at this time. The so-called "Kenyon Connection" gains much of its fire power from the premise that Kenyon imbibed a philosophy at Emerson that colored the rest of his ministry. This argument boils down to guilt by association for the most part. It might be described as speculation based upon presupposition. I think it's safe to say that Kenyon's time at Emerson College can tell nothing all that significant about his future ministry. Kenyon's next few years, however, will tell us everything.

Kenyon would have finished his only year at Emerson in May of 1893. Two important events took place very close to one another in his life at this time. He married his first wife, Evva, and he was restored to the Lord. We will look at these events in the next chapter.

CHAPTER 4

RESTORED

We have believed a lie in the past, and discovered it to be a lie.
We believed we had light and that it was God's light, when it was
only human light and it was dangerous . . . Jesus is the only light,
and if you turn down Jesus and His substitutional sacrifice, His
literal Resurrection, and try to get a Jesus that is but a metaphys-
ical concept, you will have another Jesus, and not my Lord.

—E. W. Kenyon[1]

Having been successful as a salesman, Kenyon had no reason to
think he wouldn't be successful as an actor. Kenyon was ready
to start a new life, with a special companion at his side who was a
member of a prominent New England family. Evva Spurling and
Kenyon were married at the Tremont Street Methodist Church in
Boston on May 8, 1893, by Reverend W. W. Ramsay, D. D. At this
time neither of them were professing Christians and, according to
Evva, they "had no intention of making His [Christ's] work the business of our lives."[2]

Evva admitted to being very bitter toward God due to sufferings and
hardship she endured during her earlier days. She didn't go into
details, but these experiences hardened her heart against believing in
God. For reasons described earlier, Kenyon was just as hardened
toward God. Yet for some unknown reason, one month after they
were married the young couple paid a visit to the Clarendon Street
Baptist Church in Boston. This church was quite well known due to

the reputation of its pastor, A. J. Gordon.

At this service, Evva Kenyon reported that "Mr. Kenyon heard the voice of the Lord. Upon our return home he unreservedly and forever gave himself back to the Lord for service. The Spirit came upon him in marvelous power."[3]

According to Evva, her husband's rededication to the Lord left her "astonished and bewildered. What was I to do? I did not know that there was a God. I did not want to serve Him if there was a God," she said. But she was quite concerned that she and her new husband walk together. So, she said, "I got upon my knees beside him, and the best I knew how I gave myself to that hard, indefinite God of my imagination," but to her surprise, " the gentle, compassionate Jesus met me and bound me to Himself forever. We were called together to the blessed service of the Lord."[4]

Roughly ten months after Kenyon's move to Boston and entrance to Emerson College, in June 1893, he and his bride entered together into the service of the Lord. In a journal entry dated July 17, 1896, Kenyon poured out his joy at his walk with the Lord. Notice what he says about the "hours of darkness."

> The strong, tender, ever-watchful friend with me, His very presence upholds, encourages, strengthens me. I can as He draws near feel the fruits of the Spirit grow in my soul. Love, new and holy, thrills me. I love Him, His people for whom He died, love that makes me jealous for Him, that makes me forget my own desires and long to be all and in all my life in the sacred shadow of a love so deep and pure. Joy fills my heart and I am glad for the hours of darkness now, His presence, my Lord's real presence, He of Galilee, of Calvary, praise His dear name, my soul is filled with a joy unknown . . . Mary Magdalene on Easter Morning must have felt this joy. Oh, praise His dear name. Peace creeps in and such peace, heavenly peace filled with love and joy set to music.[5]

As he rejoiced in the joy of his restored fellowship with the Lord, Kenyon was even glad for the years that he struggled in darkness. The deep, rich communion he experienced after he was restored gave some value to the painful years of wandering.

Evangelistic Work

Kenyon soon began evangelistic work. The Lord opened doors and paid him with souls. Before long he felt the Lord wanted him to pastor a church.[6] This brought the Kenyons face to face with a difficult question: with what denomination should they unite?

Evva commented:

> Mr. Kenyon was, by conversion, in the Methodist church. I had been brought up in the Congregational church. We both believed in baptism by immersion, and were both (even then) inclined to take the Bible literally. Many points with which we could not heartily agree seemed to debar us from truthfully assenting to the creed of any denomination with which we were acquainted.[7]

This quote documents the dramatic change in Kenyon from his Emerson days. This was just a few months after leaving Emerson. Any sympathy Kenyon had with philosophy and metaphysics while away from the Lord was left behind. He was now concerned about joining any group that failed to uphold a literal interpretation of Scripture. He would still need to deal with his skeptical mind and divest himself of some doubt and false doctrines he had embraced. But he would do this based on the Bible as the Word of God.[8]

Kenyon's Ordination

While conducting services in Amesbury, Massachusetts, the Kenyons met the pastor of a Free Baptist church. They considered this man to be a "dear brother" and became "interested in him and the creed he represented."[9] Evva wrote that they decided to unite with the Free Baptists after "much deliberation."[10]

The common practice for ordination was to bring the candidate to the quarterly meeting and in that setting ask the candidate a series of simple questions.[11] The questions had to do with the candidate's belief in the infallibility of Scripture, agreeing that the Free Will Baptists were consonant with the Scriptures, a personal confidence in a divine call, full fellowship with the brethren, and a commitment to earnestly contend for the faith as expressed in the Free Will Baptist denomination.

Kenyon went to pastor a Free Will Baptist congregation in Elmira, New York, in November 1893. On January 17 of the next year he was "ordained to the Christian ministry by Dr. G. H. Ball of Keuka College and others of that quarterly meeting."[12]

We can assume, then, that the Kenyons were aware of what the Free Will Baptists taught, and endorsed it. For that reason, let us explore their creed. It reveals to us Kenyon's thinking at this point in his life. It also shows us the foundation for Kenyon's teaching and ministry for the rest of his life.

THE FREE WILL BAPTISTS

Sacred and non-negotiable doctrines among the Free Baptists were a general atonement, the believer's baptism, the authority of the Word, the deity of Christ, and the unity of the Trinity.[13] The Free Will Baptists formed as a reaction against the strong Calvinism in other parts of the Baptist church. They were also distinguished from other Baptists by their intense conservatism.[14] They believed in free will and general atonement as opposed to predestination and limited atonement. They embraced the idea of entire sanctification and the premillenial return of Christ.[15]

Most of the traditional denominations at this time were postmillenial, believing Jesus would not return until after a prolonged season of peace and prosperity on the earth through the spread of the gospel. The rise of the popularity of premillenialism is one of the phenomena of nineteenth century theological development. The Free Will Baptists were premillenial before that view assumed the popularity it did at the turn of the century.

The group practiced two unusual doctrines—footwashing and anointing with oil for healing.[16] We will establish later that Kenyon first learned about divine healing while among the Free Will Baptists.

This denomination had a strong vision for foreign and home missions and encouraged their ministers to travel and plant many churches and to support overseas mission work as well. "Freewill Baptist leaders took advantage of every opportunity to overcome objections to missions, to raise support for mission endeavors, and to recruit personnel for foreign service."[17] Interestingly, this missions emphasis was centered in New England.

When Kenyon founded a training school a few years later, he guided his students toward home and foreign missions. Planting new churches was a constant activity in Kenyon's ministry while he remained in New England.

ESTABLISHING STUDY HABITS

Kenyon's approach to Bible study seems to have been particularly affected by the Free Will Baptists' attitude toward education. Part of an 1840 conference on education resolved the following:

- The Scriptures accompanied by the aids of the Holy Spirit are the only source which the servant of God can derive or desire that instruction which is requisite to qualify him for teaching the great truths of religion.
- As all uninspired writings are liable to contain error, through the productions of pious men they should be consulted with great caution, lest errors be imbibed with truth.
- In case any one wishes to consult any of these helps on any significant point, he should first examine the Scripture thereon, carefully comparing Scripture with Scripture, and thus get as good understanding upon it himself, unaided by any book other than the Bible. He will then be prepared to read to advantage men's views; and will know far better to receive his truth and reject his error.[18]

Having at one time lost out with God by being too open to men's opinions, this attitude toward the Scriptures and philosophy toward uninspired writings led Kenyon to examine all ideas in the light of his own study of the Word. He wrote:

Perhaps in all the years of my Bible study, I was never so shocked as I was in my early days to find that the word "atonement" did not occur in the New Testament.

I had had a period of darkness and doubt, and there had been many questions as to whether the Bible was the Word of God or not, and when I saw this, for a little while it seemed to me as though I must give up everything . . .

I remember how I walked the floor, debating whether I had

better stay in the ministry or go into business. [This was not long after his restoration.]

I remember how I finally said to myself, "I am going to look this thing up; I have depended upon books and other men's opinions long enough, I am going to know the Bible for myself now . . .

This marked the beginning of my real study of the Scriptures. I gathered all the critical writings I could find on the Old Testament Hebrew, and began a careful study of the words used in the great sacrifices of Israel.[19]

Kenyon's determination to study the Word for himself brought him into fellowship with like-minded brethren. The Free Will Baptists provided him with a creed that he could agree with and a philosophy of learning that stayed with Kenyon throughout his ministry.

THE EFFECT OF THE HOLINESS REVIVAL

Some say Kenyon never preached the distinctives of the Holiness tradition. That is why it should be noted that during the 1890s the Free Will Baptists embraced the Holiness revival then in progress. Historian Robert M. Anderson writes, "Numbers of Free Will Baptists had been swept into the Second Work Holiness revivals of the 1890s."[20] They already had a history of believing in entire sanctification—the belief that man could live in complete victory over sin—so the movement easily accommodated the second work of grace concept of a post-conversion crisis experience followed by a victorious life.

The Free Will Baptists, who, according to researcher Vinson Synan, "from the beginning accepted the basic premises of Methodism," moved closer to the Holiness movement's teachings on sanctification during this time. "It was not until the height of the holiness crusade of the 1880s that this group adopted a strictly Wesleyan perfectionist creed . . . sanctification was presented [in the North Carolina *Discipline* of 1889] as "an instantaneous work of God's grace in a believer's heart whereby the heart is cleansed from all sin and made pure by the blood of Christ."[21]

Kenyon's early days among the Methodists and the fact that the Free Will Baptists embraced second work of grace Holiness teaching had a profound effect on his life, both positively and negatively. We will look at this in the following chapters.

FRUITFUL MINISTRY

The question of a denomination answered, the Kenyons settled in to some fruitful and exciting months of ministry. Evva reported that the Lord wonderfully blessed her husband's labors in Elmira. Many souls were brought into the kingdom. Nearly every service for months was a revival service.[22]

Kenyon next assumed the pastorate of a larger church in Springville, New York, from July 1, 1894, until June 1897. Evva wrote, "Here three happy, profitable years were passed, years in which the Lord taught him many of the precious truths that moulded his life for today. It was here that he sought and found the Holy Spirit as a person."[23]

These three years in Springville were the most crucial in the development of Kenyon's theology. Kenyon came under the influence of some ministries that profoundly affected him and, most significantly, he received the Holy Spirit. The next chapter explores these developments in detail.

CHAPTER 5

FORMATIVE YEARS

Here [in Springville, New York] three happy, profitable years [1894–1897] were passed, years in which the Lord taught [Kenyon] many of the precious truths that moulded his life for today. It was here that he sought and found the Holy Spirit as a person."

—Evva Kenyon[1]

One book about Kenyon states that the "crucial period of his religious and educational development appears to have taken place during his stay in the city of Boston during the early 1890s." This author then suggests that Kenyon was being influenced by a man who was a significant figure in Unitarian circles in Boston "from 1895 to 1899, about the time Kenyon was in Boston."[2] The biggest problem with these statements is that Kenyon did not spend "the early 1890s" or from 1895 to 1899 in Boston. He was there for only one year, autumn 1892 to summer 1893.[3] The years 1894–1897 were, in fact, crucial times of development for Kenyon, but not in Boston or under metaphysical influences.

What was Kenyon doing and what were his influences during these crucial years? What ministries was he exposed to? What books did he read? In this chapter we will provide some answers.

For these three years Kenyon was pastor of the Free Will Baptist church of Springville, New York. While providing leadership for others, Kenyon also focused on his own spiritual growth. He wanted to avoid a repeat performance of the "years of darkness." In New York he discovered a method of Bible study for himself that was so insightful it found its way into the Scofield Bible. He also spent a considerable effort in learning more about the Holy Spirit, which is documented by handwritten notes from lectures that he attended. As a result of this teaching and in quest of sanctification, Kenyon received the Holy Spirit.

This chapter will describe Kenyon's system of Bible study and then take a look at how Kenyon learned about the Holy Spirit and from whom.

THE SEVENFOLD TEST

Having been led astray at one time, Kenyon had a concern about avoiding deception. As he turned to study Scripture himself, he asked the Lord to help him. "This danger of being led into false teaching stood at the threshold of every new truth in the early days of my Bible study, and I prayed much that the Lord would give me a real testing tube, scales, weight, and measure, whereby every step could be satisfactorily proved."[4]

He wrote, "I asked the Lord one day if He wouldn't give me something by which I might measure and try every doctrine that came to me. As I waited before Him, this came. It was no mental process, for I did not know enough to work it out—He gave it to me." The year after Kenyon left Springville, he described this process in a magazine he founded called *The Tabernacle Trumpet*. Notice how he insisted that any doctrine must be in harmony with the whole Word. (Some have claimed Kenyon taught that only the New Testament, particularly the Pauline epistles, were legitimate sources of revelation knowledge.)[5]

> All New Testament teaching conforms to Old Testament types, and if all doctrine were built of the units of testimony of the whole Word, much false teaching would be done away with.
>
> Take this sevenfold test. All New Testament doctrines must be found: 1) In Genesis, in germ form; 2) In the Law, in type; 3) In Psalms, in sacred song; 4) In the Prophets, as prophecy; 5) In the Gospels, taught by Christ; 6) In Acts, practiced by the Apostles; 7) In the Epistles, as doctrine.
>
> . . . Every truth, or doctrine taught in the New Testament can

be found by the Spirit-taught student in these sevenfold steps. It gives the Christian an entire Bible. Then let us see, if the whole Word sends forth clear tones in perfect harmony with each other as we ascend the scale from Genesis to Revelation.[6]

Kenyon would certainly, in the years ahead, receive from many other respected ministries, but the Word would always be his final court of appeal.

Interestingly, Kenyon told an audience in 1928 that this "seven-fold, God-given test" had been borrowed by a well-known scholar. "You will find it in Scofield's Bible. He changed the name of it, but he got it from a tract of mine. That was over thirty years ago.

Kenyon recommended that his readers imitate his method for any subject under discussion. This appears in his magazine *Reality,* March-April 1906:

> We must know how to "divide the Word." So try this plan. Take a good concordance, Young's is the best, and look up different subjects and find out what God says about them in the Book.
>
> Whenever you hear anyone discuss a subject, go through the Book from Genesis to Revelation, and see what you can learn. I did this for years, until it would be hard to ask a question of everyday life that I have not found out what He said about it.
>
> You will not have men's theories then, but God's Word.[7]

Kenyon taught his students to study through the primary verses of a subject being studied, noting the shades of meaning for both the Greek and Hebrew words in their context. I interviewed a man who in his youth had been with Kenyon when he pastored in Seattle (1934–1948 roughly) and Kenyon had given him his Young's concordance and taught him this very method of study. Kenyon's method was also very much in line with the suggestions of the Free Will Baptists discussed in the previous chapter. His reverence for and reliance on Scripture was established early and lasted a lifetime.

Even though Kenyon relied exclusively on the Word, some say Kenyon practiced a metaphysical style of Scripture interpretation.[8] All the metaphysical cults, particularly Christian Science and New Thought, handle the Scriptures quite loosely, employing much fanciful interpretation, probably to avoid the implications of the text taken literally. In contrast, unless he was interpreting the types, Kenyon consistently took the text in its most obvious, literal sense. In this he reflected the influence of J. N. Darby and the other Brethren authors whom he greatly respected. A little closer to home, we see the influence of A. J. Gordon, A. T. Pierson, R. A. Torrey, and A. B. Simpson, all of whom Kenyon greatly admired.

One respected charismatic Bible teacher (who passed away a few years ago), is quoted as saying "he [Kenyon] probably wasn't formulating his faith positions entirely *sola scriptura.*" *With all due respect, this opinion isn't consistent with the evidence.*[9] During Kenyon's Seattle years, the latter part of his life, he stated, "I cannot accept a man's word when there is no God-word to back it up."[10]Anyone reading Kenyon's writings in much depth would be struck by his high regard for the Scriptures. All the metaphysical cults use the Bible, but consistently disregard what they don't like or what doesn't fit their systems. Kenyon's respect for the Word places an impassable gulf between him and the cults.

KENYON LEARNS ABOUT THE HOLY SPIRIT

In addition to establishing the preeminence of the Word, Kenyon received the Holy Spirit during this three year period (1894–1897). Keep in mind that "receiving the Holy Ghost" or "baptism in the Holy Ghost" was the terminology used to describe the experience of sanctification in the Methodist and Holiness movements. *Sanctification* was a crisis of consecration that occurred after conversion, often referred to as a *second work of grace* or *entire sanctification.* Kenyon was actually seeking a sanctification experience when he received the Holy Spirit. We will go into more detail on his quest for sanctification later.

There was a tremendous amount of interest in the ministry of the Holy Spirit in the late 1800s. Kenneth Mackenzie, an associate of A. B. Simpson for many years as well as a featured speaker for one of Kenyon's conferences, wrote in 1900 of increased interest in the ministry of the Holy Spirit. "A recent announcement of one of the leading publishing houses gives the titles of twenty-one books on the Holy Spirit, all of which have been written within the past twenty-five years."[11]

A modern historian noted the roots of this increased interest.

There was a marked intensification of interest in the doctrine of
the Holy Spirit shortly before the Civil War ... The quest for
"vitality" flourished in the context of the revivalism and social
reform optimism of the 1840s and 1850s. Interest was further
fueled by the publishing in 1856 of *The Tongue of Fire* by British
Methodist William Arthur, a work that quickly gained widespread
readership in America ... [12]

Shortly after this book was published, the 1857–58 revival
occurred. Revival at that time served to further spread the belief
that God was about to pour out His Spirit for the renewal of His
church in a way similar to the day of Pentecost.[13]

A POWERFUL BOOK

I mention Arthur's book because of its key place in revival history. So,
did Kenyon read it? Yes, he wrote, "I remember reading Arthur's
book ... It is a marvelous book! Arthur describes this scene with the
prayers of the one hundred and twenty awaiting for the power of God
to fall upon them."[14]

Kenyon's theology later reflected a significant emphasis from
Arthur's book: the premise that the Holy Spirit spread His "fire" by
using the human tongue. True to his Methodist background with its
emphasis on testimony Arthur wrote:

> The symbol is a tongue, the only instrument of the grandest war
> ever waged: a *tongue*—man's speech to his fellow man ... a
> tongue of *fire*—a man's voice, God's truth; man's speech, the
> Holy Spirit's inspiration; a human organ, a superhuman power."[15]

Kenyon also went on to emphasize the importance of the tongue in
maintaining a victorious Christian life.

KENYON'S PENTECOSTAL BELIEFS

It is claimed that Kenyon rejected two distinctives of Pentecostalism:
subsequence and initial evidence. "He [Kenyon] believed that subsequence—the Pentecostal doctrine of Spirit baptism as a second definite
work of grace—was "erroneous teaching concerning the Baptism of
the Holy Spirit."[16]

This is one of many examples of misunderstanding and misrepresentation of Kenyon's teachings. Kenyon believed in subsequence. He taught that immediately after one was born again one should ask the Holy Spirit to come and live in his body. Statements of this idea are in almost every book he wrote. What Kenyon did not believe was that this experience of receiving the Holy Spirit was the *baptism* of the Holy Spirit. He believed that the phrase *baptism of the Holy Spirit* referred to conversion. After conversion the believer was to ask the *Person* of the Holy Spirit to enter his body. Kenyon's detractors have tripped over this semantic stumbling block and fallen into misrepresentation.

Kenyon did not accept the *initial evidence* doctrine. (Initial evidence is the idea that speaking in tongues is the only valid evidence that one is filled with the Holy Spirit.) This is the distinctive doctrine of most of the Pentecostal denominations. Kenyon received the Holy Spirit as an experience subsequent to salvation in 1897. The Pentecostal experience of speaking in tongues as the initial evidence of receiving the Holy Spirit was not taught until after the Azusa revival around 1906. It wasn't formulated into a formal doctrinal position until around 1914.

When Kenyon made application to the Assemblies of God in 1924, he stated that he did speak with tongues and was in agreement with the doctrinal position of the Assemblies.[17] The evidence suggests that for a while he embraced tongues as initial evidence (during the 1920s) but later backed away from that position and said tongues were not necessary to *prove* one had received the Spirit.

Kenyon believed that speaking in tongues was a valid experience, but for him the evidence for being filled, or receiving the Holy Spirit, was the promise of Scripture itself. Faith in the Word *was* the evidence. Kenyon wanted people to look to the Word of God *alone* as evidence that they had received the Holy Spirit.

Kenyon was not alone in this perspective. He was inspired by four orthodox Christian leaders under whose teaching he sat. All four believed that receiving the Holy Spirit was subsequent to conversion, and none insisted on tongues as evidence. (Their receiving of the Holy Spirit, as I pointed out, predates the Pentecostal movement.) We can specifically document what teaching Kenyon heard from these men and how he reacted to it. These details should lay to rest the argument that because Kenyon was not a Pentecostal he had to draw from the cults for inspiration.

HOLY SPIRIT MENTORS

A. J. Gordon

As you may recall, Kenyon rededicated his life to the Lord in A. J. Gordon's church, which was a prominent evangelical establishment. Gordon bitterly opposed Mary Baker Eddy and Christian Science, opposing her teachings in word and in print in Boston. He was also a leader in divine healing and the premillenial prophetic movement.

Gordon's most popular books included *The Ministry of Healing* (1882) and *In Christ* (1872). But it is Gordon's book Ministry of the Spirit that is quoted in Kenyon's writings more than any other author's work.[18] This work was finished in December 1894, shortly before Gordon's death.[19] In it Gordon taught that the church began on the Day of Pentecost.[20] Kenyon echoed that thought in all his later writings. Kenyon taught receiving the Holy Spirit in almost identical language to Gordon. Many ideas in this book influenced Kenyon other than the idea of subsequence.

One quote from Kenyon's Basic Bible Course indicates Gordon's obvious influence.

> A. J. Gordon, in his book entitled, *The Ministry of the Holy Spirit,* asks, "Why not employ the same method in writing about the Third person of the Trinity as is employed in considering the Second person."
>
> In his book he follows that method and we wish to use this method here in our study of the Holy Spirit.[21]

Later in his life when Kenyon revised his first book *The Father and His Family* (1936), it was Gordon's book *Ministry of the Spirit* that Kenyon reached for when he wanted to add some relevant quotations. In his new introductions to the chapters, he quotes from that book at least twice.

A. T. Pierson

Among the materials Kenyon kept until the end of his life is an old-fashioned notebook. On the front in Kenyon's distinctive handwriting is written, "E. W. Kenyon, Springville, N.Y." This book contains notes

Kenyon took during lectures by several different Bible teachers.

One set of notes bears this inscription over the top: "Collected from lectures of Dr. A. T. Pierson at Bible Institute Nov. 1–8, 1895." (This is most likely Chicago Bible Institute, later Moody Bible Institute.)[22] Then follows ten pages of notes consisting of Scripture references under various headings which described the ministry of the Holy Spirit. Kenyon obviously sat under Pierson's ministry for a week of teaching on the ministry of the Spirit.[23]

At the turn of the century, Arthur T. Pierson was one of the strongest voices for evangelism and world missions. From 1891–1893, Pierson served as interim pastor at the famous Metropolitan Tabernacle founded by Charles Haddon Spurgeon. After the Metropolitan Tabernacle found a permanent pastor, Pierson returned to the States and assumed, among many other responsibilities, the oversight of A. J. Gordon's Missionary Training School in Boston.

In October 1895 he finished writing a book about the ministry of the Holy Spirit called *The Acts of the Holy Spirit*. Notice his use of the word *incarnates* in this excerpt.

> In them [the recipients of the Holy Spirit] He so incarnates Himself that through them He works upon others, so that by the indwelling Holy Spirit they become, like Him, teachers of truth, guiding into all truth; anointed witnesses, testifying to Christ, and glorifying Christ; inspired witnesses, not speaking from themselves, but receiving of the things of Christ and showing them to men; effective witnesses, convincing the world of sin, of righteousness, and of judgment; and even prophetic witnesses, showing things to come.

For many, the thought that God the Holy Spirit, would actually dwell in man was becoming increasingly awe-inspiring and important. The concept of the Holy Spirit "incarnating" Himself in the believer was popular in the writings of many at this time (more documentation later). Kenyon used similar language, which points to the influence of Pierson and others. Yet Kenyon has been severely criticized for his choice of words. This may indeed have been a poor choice of words, the idea of the Holy Spirit *incarnating* Himself in men, but it was a common theme among orthodox evangelicals of the day.

R. A. Torrey

In Kenyon's same notebook mentioned earlier, there is also a set of notes from "Rev. R. A. Torrey." The heading of the first page reads, "Holy Spirit, April 1, '96." The notes continue through April 4. The notes and Scripture references parallel almost exactly the section on the Holy Spirit in Torrey's 1898 book, *What the Bible Teaches*.[24] The notes do not indicate where the teaching took place, quite possibly in Chicago, where Kenyon's ministry would take him frequently in the years ahead.

Torrey was a prolific writer, authoring or editing more than forty books. D. L. Moody frequently used Torrey in his conferences and crusades to teach on receiving the Holy Spirit for power in ministry. In 1889 Torrey became the superintendent of Chicago Training Institute (later known as Moody Bible Institute). From 1894–1906 he also pastored the Chicago Avenue Church.

Torrey and the other authors I discuss in this chapter (excepting Arthur) challenged Kenyon's ideas about the Holy Spirit. Because of his background with the Methodist church and the Holiness-influenced Free Will Baptists, Kenyon would have believed that the purpose of baptism in the Holy Spirit was to eradicate the sinful nature (resulting in sanctification). On the issue of the Holy Spirit, Torrey's teaching was a definite departure from Holiness thought. Torrey believed that baptism in the Holy Spirit is not for sanctification, but for power.

"There is a line of teaching," Torrey wrote, "put forward by a very earnest but mistaken body of people, that has brought the whole doctrine of the baptism with the Holy Spirit into disrepute." Then Torrey listed where he agreed and disagreed with the Holiness teachers. First, he said, they teach that it is a further experience, subsequent to conversion. Torrey agreed. Second, it can be instantaneously received. Torrey also agreed. Third, it is the eradication of the sinful nature. With this point Torrey took issue.

Kenyon would have been challenged to examine the Scriptures by Torrey's assertion. In Kenyon's notebook of Torrey's teachings, there is a concluding statement written and underlined as though it had really hit home. It says, *"Holy Spirit is a Person."*

Eventually Kenyon followed Torrey's lead and rejected Holiness teaching on sanctification. Kenyon also appeared to echo Torrey in his teaching about receiving the "baptism" by faith (though he used a different term for the experience, calling it "receiving the Holy Spirit" or "being filled with the Holy Spirit"). Torrey, like Kenyon, predated the Pentecostal movement and did not believe that tongues were necessary to demonstrate that the Spirit had come.

> God's most positive and unqualified promises must be appropriated by faith . . . There is a faith that goes beyond expectation, a faith that just puts out its hand and takes what it asks. This is brought out very clearly by Mark in 11:24: "What things soever ye desire, when ye pray, believe that ye receive them, and ye shall have them."
>
> When one who has a clear title to a piece of property deeds it to me, it is mine as soon as the deed is properly executed and recorded, though it may be some time before I enter into the experimental joy of it . . . In like manner, as soon as we, having met the conditions of prevailing prayer, put up to God a petition for anything according to His will, it is our privilege to know that the prayer is heard, and that thing which we have asked of Him is ours.
>
> Now apply that to the baptism with the Holy Spirit . . .
>
> If the conditions have been met, any reader may ask God to baptize him with the Holy Spirit. He can then say when the prayer has gone up, "That prayer was heard; I have what I have asked; I have the baptism with the Holy Spirit."
>
> I know of no better way of knowing than by God's Word. I would believe God's Word before my feelings any day.[25]

Torrey's teaching on receiving the Holy Spirit by faith illustrates perfectly the concept of faith Kenyon taught throughout his ministry: Determine the will of God by the Word of God, ask in faith, and believe that you receive without any other evidence but God's Word.[26]

It might be pointed out that Torrey encouraged the one desiring the Holy Spirit to believe he receives and *then to confess he has* (present tense) the Holy Spirit without any other evidence than the Word of God.

A. B. Simpson

A. B. Simpson, founder of the Christian and Missionary Alliance and pioneer in divine healing, was another voice that stressed the person of the Holy Spirit. Simpson's teaching further challenged Kenyon's view of sanctification and pointed him toward inviting the Holy Spirit to live in him as his "indwelling life."

Simpson wrote a two-volume study on the Holy Spirit entitled *The Holy Spirit, or, Power from on High* (1896). It is a Genesis-through-Revelation study of the Spirit's ministry. In volume 2 he wrote:

> What is the baptism imparted to us by Christ?
>
> Sometimes we hear this spoken of as if He baptized us with something different from Himself, some sort of influence, or feeling, or power. The truth is, the Spirit Himself is the baptism. Christ baptizes, and it is with or in the Spirit that He baptizes us . . . the Holy Ghost Himself is our indwelling life.[27]

Because Simpson influenced Kenyon in many areas of his theology, he will be examined in more detail in a later chapter.

KENYON'S UNIQUE PERSPECTIVE

Kenyon followed the philosophy of Bible study shown him by the Lord along with that recommended to him by the Free Will Baptists. He took in the teachings of respected and devout men, investigated the Scriptures for himself, and then settled on what he determined was the most biblical view. His notes from Pierson and Torrey consist mostly of the various headings and the Scripture references used to validate them.

His general teaching on the Holy Spirit's ministry is consistent with all of these respected teachers. Kenyon taught, as did all these men, that the Holy Spirit was received subsequent to salvation. Kenyon, like each of them, emphasized the receiving of the *Person* of the Holy Spirit, not primarily a blessing or sanctification or power, which were *the fruit* of receiving Him.

R. A. Torrey felt very strongly about this. "He considered that doctrine so vital that he charged that any who failed to stress the personhood of the Holy Spirit were essentially self-confident and self-centered."[28]

The lead article in the first publication Kenyon ever produced was *How To Receive The Holy Spirit* (1898). The quote used earlier to describe Kenyon's method of Bible study was from this article. He used the seven-fold method in his personal study of the Holy Spirit. He did a thorough Genesis to Revelation study on the Holy Spirit, examining all the relevant words and concepts. His conclusions, though influenced by his respected mentors, were the fruit of his own searching of the Scriptures.

Kenyon strongly emphasized that receiving the Holy Spirit wasn't receiving an experience or sanctification, but rather it was receiving a divine person. The article was quickly put into tract form and made available through his ministry. Kenyon rejected the terminology used by many, even the above respected mentors, in their referring to receiving the Holy Spirit subsequent to conversion as the *baptism* of the Holy Spirit. But he was in complete agreement with them in their essential teaching. In aligning himself with them he was distancing himself from his Holiness roots.

Now we want to take a closer look at the impact of the Holiness movement on Kenyon as a young pastor. We will do this in the next chapter.

CHAPTER 6

THE HOLINESS MOVEMENT

All we have been taught was that God forgave us our sins, and that by a second work of grace, sin was eradicated from us. But if we did wrong ignorantly or knowingly we had to be justified again.

—E. W. Kenyon[1]

The fact that Kenyon did not teach second-work-of-grace holiness in his published works has emboldened some of his critics to suggest that he was not a part of this movement and did not learn healing from those in the Holiness stream. In the absence of historical data they freely speculate as to Kenyon's influences.

Kenyon did reject some distinctive teachings of the Holiness movement. This has made him difficult to categorize among the Christian groups of his day. One researcher wrote:

> Admittedly, Kenyon could be historically grouped with the non-Pentecostal healers, such as John Alexander Dowie, Charles Cullis, and a whole host of other participants in the divine healing movement who came from the Wesleyan-Holiness tradition, many of whom became Pentecostals. Grouping Kenyon with these Wesleyan-Holiness healers would be inaccurate, however, for the same reason that Kenyon cannot be classified a Pentecostal. Kenyon never preached the doctrinal distinctives of the Wesleyan-Holiness movement: the second work of grace,

instantaneous sanctification, and sinless perfection.[2]

Because he rejected Holiness teaching, it is argued that Kenyon must have turned to the metaphysical cults for inspiration.[3] That is why this chapter is devoted to showing Kenyon's real experience with the Holiness movement.

Instead of saying Kenyon "never preached" Holiness distinctives, it would be more accurate to say his study of the Scriptures led him to reject much of this teaching. He did embrace Holiness second-work-of-grace teaching early in his Christian walk—resulting in much frustration and contributing to his temporary loss of faith. The real question is, Why did he reject these teachings? As you read this section, you will observe that Kenyon was, for a season, deeply invested in the Holiness movement and its teachings. He eventually jettisoned much of the teaching on sanctification but retained some important truths he gleaned while a part of this movement.

The rest of the chapter demonstrates how principles from Holiness teaching undergirded Kenyon's doctrine on faith, confession, and healing. This was the wellspring from which Kenyon drew ideas—not the metaphysical cults.

WELCOME TO HOLINESS

The Holiness movement in America was rooted in the Methodist church, which was the largest Protestant denomination during the nineteenth century. John Wesley had taught the doctrine of Christian perfection in earlier years, and many voices were calling the church, within and without Methodism, *back* to a "higher Christian life." In the 1890s fresh waves of revival swept the church, but these all found their roots, for the most part, in the earlier teachings within Methodism.[4]

The most distinctive doctrine of the Holiness movement was what was known as the second work of grace. At conversion the believer's sins were forgiven, and he was justified. Then the convert was to seek an experience known as entire sanctification. This was the "second work of grace." It consisted of an instantaneous crisis of consecration, or total abandonment to the Lord, believed to remove the sin nature which was not affected by conversion. After this crisis the believer was able to live without sinning. This experience was often referred to as the baptism of the Holy Spirit.

We can easily establish that Kenyon was exposed to these teachings. Kenyon was converted in a Methodist church. He spent his first years with the Lord attending a Methodist church and other Holiness meetings. He also attended services with The Salvation Army (who were among the second-work-of-grace Holiness advocates).

Kenyon described the negative effect of sanctification teaching on him. "All of this time there was an undercurrent in my life, a sense of unworthiness. The adversary seemed to delight in making me conscious of unworthiness." He sought relief by embracing the popular teaching. But he found no cure for this burden. He related, "I tried everything that man had taught. I sought the 'clean heart,' 'entire sanctification,' 'second work of grace,' everything that was preached. I was blessed for a while, but it would all fade away."[5]

The sanctified life for Kenyon was a mirage in the desert. In another place he confessed, "Some of us know what it means to have had a time somewhere in our lives where we spent a great deal of our time trying to consecrate ourselves to the Lord; what it means to have humbled ourselves and cried before God trying to surrender ourselves to Him."[6]

It is easy to hear the frustration of Kenyon's early attempts to walk with God following Holiness teaching. These early discouragements eventually resulted in him falling away from the Lord.

But after his restoration to the Lord, he still was quite sympathetic to his Methodist roots and his Holiness background. He may have assumed that the problem was not with the teaching, but rather with himself. The Free Will Baptists were in many ways similar to the Methodists in regard to sanctification, but they put more emphasis on doctrine than on seeking an experience.

A HOLINESS PREACHER

Kenyon was, for the most part, a Holiness preacher when he pastored the Free Will Baptist church in Springville, New York (1894–1897). As noted earlier, "Numbers of Free Will Baptists were swept into the Second Work Holiness revivals of the 1890s."[7] The doctrinal fruit from the Holiness root is evident in a statement made by Kenyon in 1899 about his beliefs.

1. We insist that the Bible is the word of God. 2. Absolute obedience

to the word of God. 3. That men live what they profess. 4. We insist that men are saved body, soul, and Spirit from sin but are not saved while in sin. 5. That God will and does fulfill every promise in His word, when we meet His requirements. 6. That the God of Israel is the God of today, and does the same mighty works today that He did then. 7. That Jesus is the same yesterday, today, and forever, and that the same signs that followed the apostles, today follow those who believe.[8]

Notice particularly point four: " . . . not saved while in sin." The Holiness movement, at least the more Methodist-influenced wing, taught that one could lose his salvation if he fell into sin.[9] After sinning, you had to be justified again and seek sanctification again. This teaching sounds like Holiness author Phoebe Palmer, who wrote, "for the Saviour came to save you *from* your sins, not *in* your sins."[10]

Personally, and as a pastor, Kenyon attempted to enter into an experience of entire sanctification. "In a church of which I was pastor we used to have consecration services from one to three times a week. I cannot tell you how many times I personally tried to do this," he mourned.[11]

This was no light thing for Kenyon. His desire to please God motivated him to seek the deepest possible commitment. But he ended up frustrated. He further shared, "If I did not groan and cry and sweat and sob and wait on God to get rid of the Adamic nature, then I am no preacher!"[12] Try as he might, he still had to battle with sin and the resulting sense of unworthiness and condemnation.

However, as Kenyon searched the Scriptures for himself he came to see things differently. Gordon, Torrey, Pierson, and Simpson had sown the seeds. Kenyon's own study watered them. He found fault with Holiness sanctification doctrine because he felt it undervalued the new birth and placed an overemphasis on the so-called second work of grace.[13]

His search for sanctification ended when he simply invited the Holy Spirit to dwell inside. He remembered, "I hunted for sanctification and second blessings . . . but one day when alone before the Lord, my eyes were opened, and I opened my heart and asked Him to come in." After Kenyon received the person of the Holy Spirit, he ended his quest for sanctification. Satisfied at last, he added, "From that hour to this He has been inside."[14] Kenyon believed that if he had received the Holy

Spirit earlier in his walk he never would have fallen away from the Lord.[15]

HOLINESS ROOTS

We've seen which Holiness doctrines Kenyon embraced and then rejected. Now we need to look at the teachings that Kenyon held to and used as a foundation in his ministry. It is important to see how the Holiness movement had significant teachings on these issues because this shows that Kenyon did not lack in orthodox Christian influence.

The widespread teaching on expressing faith by confession or testimony was clearly drawn from the Holiness movement. The evidence suggests that the metaphysical cults learned "affirmations"—the practice of declaring aloud one's beliefs in order to believe them more deeply—from the Holiness movement rather than the cults having much influence on the church.

In the next section I am going to quote quite a few Holiness advocates. Observe how similar they sound to Kenyon and the modern Faith movement. This is not to suggest that everyone in the Faith-Cure movement practiced faith and confession for divine healing exactly as taught by Kenyon. It *is* to suggest that the theological roots of the doctrine of faith and confession are documentably (and abundantly) present in the Holiness movement *and* that Kenyon *was* influenced by this movement.

PALMER AND PUBLIC CONFESSION

Phoebe Palmer (1807–1874) was one of a handful of people who shaped nineteenth century Christianity. A biographer wrote, "One could develop nearly an entire study around Palmer's direct impact upon the organizations and churches that began to form in the 1870s and after. . . . Her distinctive system of thought was that which had the greatest ongoing influence."[16] Many of the people who greatly impacted Kenyon's life were touched by Phoebe Palmer's ministry, including Charles Cullis, Carrie Judd Montgomery, and A. B. Simpson. It would be difficult for Kenyon *not* to have been influenced by her!

Phoebe Palmer . . . exercised continuous influence over Methodist

preachers and their wives and over the outstanding leaders in
America's largest Protestant denomination for twenty-five
years . . . She also became one of the nation's best-known religious writers and one of Methodism's most powerful public
speakers.[17]

The writings of Phoebe Palmer are what alerted the Christian community (and ultimately Kenyon) to scriptural teaching on confession
and testimony. The church did not need to borrow these concepts from
the cults. Here's how Palmer taught it.

Palmer advocated what she called the "shorter way" into the experience of holiness. She taught that holiness was available, like
justification, on the basis of faith alone. The necessary thing was to
meet the conditions set forth in the Scriptures and then to believe the
promises, accepting the Word of God alone as the evidence. Phoebe
came to a conclusion regarding the Scriptures: "Whatever my feelings
may be, I will believe God's immutable Word unwaveringly, irrespec-
tive of emotions."[18]

Taking Jesus' teaching that "the altar sanctifies the gift," she
believed Christ Himself was the New Testament altar (Matt. 23:19). If
the believer presented himself to Christ without reservation, the only
scriptural thing to do was to believe that God would do His part and
sanctify the offering.

In her own personal quest for total consecration to the Lord, she
found herself instructed to rely exclusively on the *"naked* word of
God." After she settled the issue with God entirely without emotional
evidence, she then experienced God's overwhelming grace.

Palmer felt God had led her to see the necessity of believing without
any other evidence than the Word of God. If God's conditions were
met, God was to be trusted to do His part, with or without any emotional witness. Holiness was to be accepted by faith *before* there was
any conscious change or witness of the Spirit.

The Free Will Baptists, with whom Kenyon was aligned at the time,
were one of the denominations that embraced this teaching on holiness
by faith. In the latter part of the nineteenth century—when Kenyon
would have been exposed to it—the Holiness movement drifted away
from her emphasis on "naked faith" in the Word of God, and began to
emphasize joy or other emotions as evidence of sanctification.[19]
Perhaps Kenyon's experience wouldn't have been so negative if the

Holiness movement had stayed closer to Palmer's emphasis.

Significantly, after holiness was accepted by faith, Palmer emphasized that it was to be testified to publicly.

> I was convinced that for years I had been hindered from rising in holiness by a neglect to comply with the order of God, implied in the passage, "With the heart man believeth unto righteousness, and with the mouth confession is made unto salvation."[20]

The significance of this idea of confessing publicly to a blessing received from God as a means of receiving and maintaining it should not be overlooked. A positive confession of receiving the grace of sanctification was widely taught and practiced in the Holiness movement. Historically, this precedes the use of affirmations by the metaphysical cults by many decades.

Palmer wrote in 1848, many years before Christian Science or New Thought developed:

> But do not forget that believing with the heart, and confessing with the mouth, stand closely connected, and "what God hath joined together, let not man put asunder." To the degree that you rely on the faithfulness of God, O hasten to make confession with the mouth of your confidence; and to the degree you honor God, by reposing on His faithfulness, will God honor you, by conferring on you the graces of His Holy Spirit in their rich plenitude.[21]

The majority of the voices in the Holiness movement emphasized the importance of testifying to the grace received, both as a means of receiving and of keeping the "Blessing." This is the same in principle as Kenyon's teachings on faith and confession. Notice his description of his discovery of being righteous by faith:

> Strange, I had never noticed it before. God Himself was to become my Righteousness the moment that I accepted Christ and confessed Him as my Lord. Then I remembered Romans 10:10, "For with the heart man believeth unto righteousness, and with the mouth confession is made unto salvation."
>
> Then 2 Corinthians 5:21, "For he hath made him to be sin for us, who knew no sin; that we might be made the righteousness of

God in him." I couldn't believe it at first. I struggled for days and days on this scripture. I knew that if I became the righteousness of God in Christ that I would never again depend on experiences. I had arrived. The thing that my heart had craved was here, but it would never become real to me until I confessed it before the world.

That Sunday morning, when I dared to say, "I am the right-eousness of God in Christ," was when I experienced what it meant. A strange quietness filled my whole being. A joy that I had never before experienced, filled my heart.[22]

In this telling testimony we see Kenyon's Holiness roots clearly. "It would never become real to me until I confessed it before the world," he wrote. But notice also that his discovery of righteousness in the Scriptures and his testimony to it was weaning him from the dependence on experiences so common in the Holiness movement.

PALMER ON FAITH

Palmer's teaching predated the metaphysical cults and their teachings about "spiritual laws," which did not become widespread until the 1880s and 1890s. Other influential teachers, including Kenyon, later reflected Palmer's ideas of faith as a law and an unchanging principle of the kingdom.

One historian summarized her teachings this way:

There are laws which govern God's "moral universe" just as there are laws governing the physical universe. This structure of moral or spiritual cause and effect is revealed primarily in the Bible . . . If one understands these laws and acts in accordance with them, it is certain that the designated means will achieve the desired ends . . . Faith's "effects must of necessity follow, because the principles by which the kingdom of grace is governed are unchangeable."[23]

The "law of faith" was not some rigid demand that caused God to bow to the believer's whim, but rather a principle by which the believer met the conditions of God's covenant promises and God performed His promise for them every time (Rom. 3:27).

49

SAMUEL LOGAN BRENGLE ON CONFESSION

Salvation Army Commissioner Samuel Logan Brengle (1860–1939) was another Holiness advocate. Brengle, like Palmer, emphasized the necessity of testimony to *keep* sanctification. In his book *Heart Talks on Holiness* (1897) he wrote:

> A lieutenant got the blessing of a clean heart in one of my meetings the other day, and then told us he had had the blessing once before but had lost it because he failed to testify to it . . . Paul says: 'For with the heart man believeth unto righteousness; and with the mouth confession is made unto salvation' (Rom. 10:10). The confession is as necessary as the believing. We insist upon this in the matter of justification, and it is equally important in the matter of sanctification. If we do not testify definitely, humbly, and constantly to the blessed experience, we put our light under a bushel, and it goes out.

The Holiness movement had seen that not only justification, but also sanctification, was to be believed in the heart and confessed with the mouth. Many from this background would soon embrace the idea that healing was also part of our salvation. The foundational principle of faith was already established. Not all among the Holiness people embraced divine healing, but a surprising number did. Many backed off in later years when healing became associated with Pentecostalism.

In another of Brengle's works, *Helps to Holiness,* he refers again to faith and confession. When a believer says, "I must have the blessing *now,*" he explained:

> This is where the devil really begins. Many people who say they are fighting the devil do not know what fighting the devil means. It is a fight of faith in which the soul takes hold of the promise of God, and holds on to it, and believes it, and *declares it to be true in spite of all the devil's lies, in spite of all circumstances and feelings to the contrary,* and in which it obeys God, whether God seems to be fulfilling the promise or not. When a soul gets to the point where he will do this, and will hold fast the profession of his faith without wavering, he will soon get out of the fogs and mists and twilight of doubt and uncertainty into the broad day of

perfect assurance (italics added).[24]

Standing on the Word when the promises of God are challenged by the devil was enjoined by Holiness teachers. The battle was against "all the devil's lies, circumstances, and feelings." Sounds a lot like today's Faith teachers, doesn't it?

These books were popular and in circulation when Kenyon was *forming* his theology. He had no books of his own in print until 1916. Many years later Kenyon wrote an article that reflected the Holiness understanding of the necessity of testimony or confession.

> Confession or testimony holds a larger place in the drama of redemption than the church has ever given it. When the Word tells us to "hold fast our confession," it means that we are to hold fast to our testimony of what God is to us, what He has done for us, what He has done in the past, and what He is doing in us now . . .
>
> If the Lord heals you, you must tell it; if the Lord heals your spirit, heals your mind, heals your body, you must tell it. Go home and tell what wondrous things the Lord has wrought. If you are afraid to tell it out you will lose the blessing that belongs to you. If men can frighten you so you will not give your testimony, in a little while you will have no testimony to give. Public confession, or giving your testimony, and faith are so closely related that, if you lose your testimony, you will know that your faith will die out immediately. You keep your testimony clear by continuously giving in wisely in the spirit, and your faith will grow by leaps and bounds.[25]

The similarity between this quote of Kenyon's and many of the other quotes in this chapter is striking. The idea of a "clear testimony" is a carry over from Holiness teaching. Yet Kenyon wrote the above in 1934, still reflecting his roots quite clearly.

DANIEL STEELE

Daniel Steele, a respected teacher in the Holiness movement, ex-president of Syracuse University, and considered by many a foremost authority on the Greek New Testament (at Boston University) in his day, wrote regarding confession in 1878, "Jesus, as a *complete*

Saviour, able to save to the uttermost from fear and doubt and indwelling sin, is to be confessed to his honor, to the praise of the Holy Ghost, the efficient Agent, and to the glory of the Father." Steele then quoted another author who stated, "The mouth is the chief and foremost of these channels which lead the soul out of its invisible sanctuary; it is by speech that man communicates the secret converse which is his real life." Affirming this statement, Steele added, "Let him, by his testimony, make known to an unbelieving church "the exceeding greatness of Christ's power to us-ward who believe."[26]

GEORGE D. WATSON

Holiness teacher George D. Watson was admired by Kenyon, and Kenyon published more than one article by Watson in his magazine the *Bethel Trumpet*.[27] Watson was a frequent speaker in Christian and Missionary Alliance conferences. Charles Cullis's Willard Tract Society published some of Watson's books, one of them on divine healing.

In his book *Love Abounding,* Watson wrote in the chapter titled "The Principles of Faith:"

> They do not know enough about the Bible to know that any faith that does not grow and that does not mature to the degree of confession is a lie and a cheat and a fraud. God never has, from the days of Abel until this hour, taken the trouble to pay any attention to faith that did not express itself. Dumb faith, say-nothing faith, cowardly faith, does not have the respect of God or angels, and the Bible never mentions that kind of faith . . . God mentions only that kind of faith that comes to the point of a grand, stalwart testimony. David says, "I believed, therefore have I spoken." And St. Paul quotes him and says, "We believe and therefore speak." Why, why that "therefore"? Because genuine faith and an expression of that faith are absolutely essential to the existence of each other.
>
> I have seen hundreds and hundreds who didn't have one bit of feeling or emotion stand and say, "Well, I will dare say it; the blood cleanses." And they kept on saying it, and it wasn't five minutes before their faith had brought consuming fire down from heaven.

Why? Because your faith is not perfect until that faith comes out of your mouth.[28]

Watson traced the truth of personal testimony back to the early Methodists. "It is thrilling to read the history of the various revivals ... and in the modern Holiness movement, and trace the same feature among them all: of reaction from formalism, and of personal testimony to the inward work of the Holy Spirit. Just as fire will die without ventilation, so the heat and power of divine love will die out of the heart without testimony."[29]

Kenyon wrote in this same vein: "The thing that made Methodism so mighty in its early days was a continual confession of the things for which Mr. Wesley stood." Echoing Watson's thoughts, he continued, "When they stopped affirming, faith stopped growing, and believing or acting upon the Word became more and more difficult."[30]

Here, again, Kenyon displayed his familiarity with Methodism and the place testimony held in the scheme of things. In this context, he was relating it to the need of affirming the Scriptures constantly. This practice he elsewhere refers to as *positive confession.*

In another of his books, *White Robes,* George Watson exhorted:

> The two acts of heart-faith and mouth-confession are so con-joined in the Bible, they are woven together in such multiplied forms of expression, that no ordinary Bible student can doubt that they sustain an inherent and essential relation to each other. An inner faith and an audible confession are the two wings of religious life. God has in infinite wisdom ordained them both as conditions of His blessing. Faith in the heart is the condition by which we obtain the fact of God's blessing, and confession with the mouth is the condition by which we obtain the experience or emotion of God's blessing ... Heart-faith and mouth-confession are twin-born of the Holy Ghost, and that which the Spirit has joined together, we dare not put asunder.[31]

Watson also believed in divine healing and saw it as part of our present redemption. In Kenyon's teachings we see the ideas about faith expressed by these individuals applied to divine healing and the other aspects of redemption.

HANNAH WHITHALL SMITH AND THE PRAYER OF CONSECRATION

In November 1896 Kenyon received a gift from the Sunday school teachers of the church he pastored in Springville, New York. It was a nice, leather-bound Revised Version Bible that Kenyon used for many years. It remained among his belongings after his death, stuffed full of notes and outlines. Among them is a page inserted into the spine with Hannah Whithall Smith's prayer of consecration. In the 1890s Kenyon used Smith's prayer to lead congregations into this consecration.

Smith (1832–1911) is a respected and well-known author still today. Her book *The Christian's Secret of a Happy Life* is still quite widely read. She included a prayer of dedication in her book, advocating a once-and-for-all committing of the believer to the Lord.

> Lord Jesus, I believe that Thou art able and willing to deliver me from all the care and unrest and bondage of my Christian life. I believe Thou didst die to set me free, not only in the future, but now and here. I believe Thou art stronger than sin, and that Thou canst keep me, even me, in my extreme weakness, from falling into its snares or yielding obedience to its commands. And, Lord, I am going to trust Thee to keep me. I have tried keeping myself, and have failed, and failed most grievously. I am absolutely helpless. So now I will trust Thee. I give myself to Thee. I keep back no reserves. Body, soul, and spirit, I present myself to Thee, as a piece of clay to be fashioned into anything Thy love and Thy wisdom shall choose. And now I *am* Thine. I believe Thou dost accept that which I present to Thee; I believe that this poor, weak, foolish heart has been taken possession of by Thee, and that Thou has even at this very moment begun to work in me to will and to do of Thy good pleasure. I trust Thee *utterly,* and I trust Thee *now* (italics hers).[32]

SMITH ON CONFESSION

Smith's book and its teachings on faith and consecration are a great representation of the teaching of the Higher Life movement, as it was often called. The idea of confession is not missing from her teaching either. She encouraged her readers:

To begin at once to reckon that you are His, that He has taken you, and that He is working in you to will and to do His good pleasure. And keep on reckoning this. You will find it a great help to put your reckoning into words, and say over and over to yourself and to your God, "Lord, I am Thine; I do yield myself up entirely to Thee, and I believe that Thou dost take me. I leave myself with Thee. Work in me all of the good pleasure of Thy will, and I will only lie still in Thy hands and trust Thee."

Make this a daily, definite act of your will, and many times a day recur to it as being your continual attitude before the Lord. Confess it to yourself. Confess it to your God. Confess it to your friends. Avouch the Lord to be your God, continually and unwaveringly and declare your purpose of walking in His ways and keeping His statutes; and sooner or later, you will find in practical experience that He has avouched you to be one of His peculiar people, and will enable you to keep all His commandments.[33]

In another of her books, *The God of All Comfort,* in the chapter titled "The Shout of Faith," she says:

The secret of all successful warfare lies in this shout of faith. It is a secret incomprehensible to those who know nothing of the unseen divine power that waits on the demands of faith; a secret that must seem, to those who do not understand it, the height of folly and imprudence.

It may sometimes seem so impossible that the Lord can or does save [in the sense of victory over sin] that the words will not say themselves inside, but have to be said aloud, forcing one's lips to utter them over and over, shutting one's eyes, and closing one's ears against every suggestion of doubt no matter how plausible it may seem. These declarations of faith often seem untrue at first, so apparently real are the seen reasons for doubt and discouragement. But the unseen facts are truer than the seen, and if the faith that lays hold of them is steadfastly persisted in, they never fail in the end to prove themselves to be the very truth of God.[34]

Hannah Whithall Smith advocated speaking the promises aloud as a means of overcoming doubt and coming to a place of faith. She encouraged a continual saying of these things until doubt is overcome and assurance filled the heart. If this sounds to you like confessing the word until faith comes as practiced by Kenyon and the modern Faith movement, it should.

In *Jesus the Healer* Kenyon wrote, "Make your lips do their duty. Fill them with His Word."[35] Kenyon frequently encouraged his readers to confess the Scriptures as a means of building faith. Elsewhere Kenyon stated, "They [the outstanding facts of our redemption] may not mean much the first time you repeat them, but you constantly re-affirm them. By and by the Spirit will illumine them and your soul will be flooded with joy and light."[36]

KENYON'S CRISIS OF CONSECRATION

Kenyon, like many other Christians of his day, had a crisis of consecration and wrote his own statement of consecration. He referred to this experience a number of times, mostly in his unpublished articles, so this event in his life is not widely known.

In 1897, while still pastoring in Springville, his health was failing and reaching a point of crisis. He described the illness as peritonitis, which is the inflammation of the membrane lining the abdominal cavity. In severe cases, this inflammation causes abdominal tenderness, high fever, and vomiting. Without surgery there can be abdominal distention, dehydration, and death. In rare cases it can also be a chronic condition.[37]

Kenyon related his own struggles in 1897 with the Lordship of Christ. In an article called *Why Trusting Is So Hard for Many,* he wrote "Before I knew Him, for more than a year I struggled and fought with the Lordship of Christ. I did not want to let Jesus Christ take me over and do as He wanted to with me. I was afraid that He would rob me of some of the joys I wanted, some of the pleasures that I craved." Kenyon was quite transparent about his struggles with his personal flaws and shortcomings.

A deeper revelation of the Lord melted away Kenyon's resistance. "I did not know that He loved me more than I loved myself. I did not know that He knew more than I knew in this sense of which we are speaking. I did not take it in. I did not know that He was more ambitious for me than I was." Before he saw this truth, he resisted absolute surrender to the Lordship of Christ. "But," he reported, "one day I saw it, in a measure at least, I yielded to His Lordship. I yielded to His dominion over me. As I did, this poor, sick, wrecked body was instantly made whole."

Kenyon was quite sick. He believed himself to be near death. He related, "I could not have lived much longer. I was breaking under the thing. The heart was in bad condition; stomach and bowels were in bad condition; my nerves were breaking under the pressure. I was suddenly, instantly emancipated, just the moment I recognized His blessed dominion."

Yielding to the Lordship of Christ would become a major theme in Kenyon's preaching. "You see," Kenyon explained, "the dominion of Christ is the dominion of love. The dominion of love is the divine dominion of self, and when self yields to love's dominion, then 'peace that passeth all understanding' fills the heart and life, and healing comes to the body."[38]

When Kenyon says "before I knew Him," in the above quote, he doesn't mean before he knew Him as Savior. He means before he knew Christ intimately enough to yield himself totally to His Lordship. This deeper knowledge of Christ—knowing Christ as more than Savior—was an important theme in Kenyon's later writings.

In an article dictated the same day as the above-quoted one, he told more about his healing.

> If the Spirit of him that raised up Jesus from the dead dwelleth in you, that Spirit can bring life to those dying members in your body, renew and heal and make you well and strong. He has done it again and again. He did that for me. I was dying; the nurse stood by and said, "He's dying." My fingers had turned purple, my feet had turned purple and cold and dead. I was dying of peritonitis.
>
> A man rushed into the room and stood by me; he offered just a few words of prayer, and the life of the Son of God came pouring through my body. My bowels, where mortification had set in, where death reigned—the life of God came pouring in and drove death out, and I was instantly healed at eleven o'clock at night. In the morning I was up and dressed and rode downtown.

Death had come for him, but God had other plans. "He took me right out of death's grip, absolutely delivering me from the hand of death. That is the Resurrection power of Jesus Christ."[39] Small wonder Kenyon believed in the healing power of God!

Kenyon, while struggling with the issue of Christ's Lordship or the necessity of total consecration of his life to God, faced, as mentioned in the above quotes, a number of what he described as "life-threatening" illnesses. He surrendered to the best of his ability to Jesus. He was dramatically healed as a result of this surrender and of the prayer of an unknown brother.

He had written out a prayer of consecration and signed it on the day of his healing—February 7, 1897. He later had it made into a large wall hanging that he hung on his ministry office wall. It now resides on the wall of the Kenyon's Gospel Publishing Society office. It reads:

I have tried to do Your will and failed.
Now, by Thy grace, I come to place in Thy care my all;
I will to be Thine, I will to do Thy will,
I will to believe Thee, I will to obey Thee,

I will to know Thy will as revealed in Thy Word,
I will to trust Thy Holy Spirit to indwell me, to implant, culture, and
    bring to perfection the graces with which thou wouldst adorn my
    life.
I will to be led into all Thy Truth.

I will to let Him control my temper, my passions, feelings, habits,
    emotions, conversation, and conduct, both in business and social
    life.
I acknowledge my own helplessness in making these conform to Thy
    will;
They have brought weakness into Thy service, sorrow and unrest into
    my life, and dishonor to Thee.

In weakness I come to Thee. I turn them over, yield them up,
Yea, gladly surrender them all to Thee,
and now, dear Lord, I have willed away myself, my all,
And now, I will my will, to Thee.
I can do no more, have no more to give;
All is Thine, and what is Thine thou canst use or lay aside.

All I ask is that this may be final.
I rest on John 6:37, "Him that cometh to me, I will in no wise cast out."
I have simply come, and come to stay, in the name and merits of my
    Redeemer, Thy Son, amen.

Now *"For me to live is Christ."*[40]

In the November 1936 *Living Bible Studies* lesson Kenyon sent out
to the radio audience, the above-quoted prayer is recorded on the back
page with this note amended to it:

> The above covenant was written and signed by our pastor, Dr. E.
> W. Kenyon, February 7, 1897. When Dr. Kenyon, on his knees,
> signed this covenant, he was instantly healed of several diseases
> which were threatening his life.[41]

In this episode of Kenyon's life we see both the influence of the
Holiness movement and a definite experience with divine healing. His
own study and other documentable and orthodox influences in his life
would alter his views on sanctification, but during this period he was
heavily influenced by the teachings on the second work of grace and
the crisis of consecration.

He had come to believe in healing through the Free Will Baptists,
but now his own experience had confirmed this doctrine dramatically.

In the next chapter we will examine one of the most fascinating
movements of the late nineteenth century, a movement known as the
Faith-Cure. This earlier Faith movement surely left its mark on E. W.
Kenyon. Our examination of this movement will also answer the question of who really influenced E. W. Kenyon in his teaching on divine
healing.

CHAPTER 7

THE FAITH-CURE

*The evidence that "diseases can be and are cured by prayer"
has become so palpable in this country and on the continent of
Europe as to convince most absolutely not a few of our most intelligent physicians, ministers of the gospel, and men and women of
all classes, and this conviction is constantly widening and deepening in all directions.*

—Asa Mahan, 1884[1]

One of my most exciting experiences while writing this book
was finding out about a nineteenth-century revival of divine
healing that was international in scope and took the center stage in the
church, among both its advocates and its foes. This revival of healing,
known as the Faith-Cure movement lasted from around 1873 until its
teachings were absorbed into the Pentecostal movement in the early
1900s. Its earliest advocates began teaching divine healing by faith as
early as 1846. Significantly, a historian noted, "the faith healing movement was stronger in America during the 1890s than at any previous
point."[2] These were the years Kenyon was learning about divine
healing.

It is only because so few today are aware of this revival that
Kenyon's critics have been as influential as they have been. A review

of its teachers and teaching reveals a great similarity between the Faith-Cure movement and the Faith movement. This refutes the assertion that the Faith movement must have metaphysical roots since no other roots can be found.

Kenyon helped to bridge the gap between the two movements. Others who bridged the gap included F. F. Bosworth, John G. Lake and Carrie Judd Montgomery. Bosworth's classic statement on divine healing, *Christ the Healer,* quotes many of the champions of the Faith-Cure. Bosworth himself was associated with John Alexander Dowie (in Dowie's orthodox years) and also with A. B. Simpson's Christian and Missionary Alliance for many years. Bosworth knew Kenyon (who met both him and Dowie in Chicago) and eventually added much material from Kenyon to his book on divine healing.

John G. Lake was also associated with John Alexander Dowie in Lake's early days and learned divine healing from him. He also greatly admired A. B.Simpson who was a part of the Faith-Cure movement.

Carrie Judd Montgomery was friends with and a ministerial associate of Cullis, A. J. Gordon, and A. B. Simpson, sharing the platform with them in conferences.

Bosworth, Lake, Montgomery, and Kenyon carried the torch of divine healing into the next generation and into the Pentecostal movement.

In the next few pages you will learn how Kenyon discovered divine healing, almost by accident. Then we'll show how Kenyon was influenced by the three most prominent leaders of the Faith-Cure movement—A. B. Simpson, Charles Cullis, and John Alexander Dowie.

KENYON'S DISCOVERY OF DIVINE HEALING

The Kenyons had become open to the idea of divine healing while among the Free Baptists, who believed in anointing the sick with oil. Evva Kenyon wrote, "The Lord now began to lead us into the knowledge of healing, which we had partially accepted before we left the denomination." Note that their partial acceptance of divine healing came from the Free Will Baptist denomination, not from Kenyon's time at Emerson or his exposure to metaphysical teachings.[3]

Both Kenyon and Evva had experienced God's healing power personally. Yet Kenyon had a dread of being considered a fanatic and had decided he would never preach healing or make it prominent in his work. If it might hinder evangelism, Kenyon didn't want it in his ministry. "Nevertheless," Evva explained, "God intended that he should preach the whole gospel."[4]

Just a couple months after the Kenyons entered their new life, the Lord told Evva to lay hands on an Irishman who was staying upstairs from them, suffering from consumption. (Consumption is the obsolete name for tuberculosis.) She didn't want to obey, but she finally submitted, and the man was made perfectly whole.[5]

Kenyon was similarly reluctant when he was asked to pray for the sick.

I saw the first miracles of healing in my ministry in [the Free Baptist church at] Springville, New York, where I was pastor.

Before this I had always been suspicious of anyone who claimed their prayers were answered along the line of healing. I felt we had doctors and surgeons and sanitariums for that purpose. Why did we need anything else? I then firmly believed that God had given us the physicians and the other methods of healing.

I knew nothing about the name of Jesus and that healing was part of the plan of Redemption, but my heart was very hungry and I was studying the Word diligently. I had just received the Holy Spirit. The Word had become a living thing. I had awakened faith in many hearts by my newfound love for the Word.

One day the clerk of our church came down and asked me if I would pray for his wife. She had been ill for many months. I will never forget how I shrank from it. I had to go. She lay in bed, and I prayed for her the best I knew how. I did not understand about the name of Jesus, but God in His great grace honored me and she was instantly healed. That night she came to church and gave her testimony. It created a great deal of sensation and some criticism. Some said it was her time to get well anyway. A few gave credit where it belonged.

A young women in a neighboring town was healed next. She was helpless, unable to walk. If I remember correctly, she had had an operation and it had left her in a fearful condition. I prayed for her. She was instantly healed and got up and went about her work. She is now on our correspondence list.

From that day on healings came—not many, for not many

people asked to be prayed for. While we were holding services in Massachusetts, healing became more frequent. One day I discovered the use of the name of Jesus. Then miracles became a daily occurrence.

In concluding his article Kenyon stated, "All these things mean God is cooperating with us as He cooperated with the Lord Jesus . . . Through all these years I have witnessed the power of that name and the grace of the Lord Jesus."[6]

After God began healing people through Kenyon, he "gave healing the place, in his ministry, designed by God." They prayed for people in need, and Evva reported, "Many healings, up to the present date [January, 1901], have taken place among us. Cases of consumption, abscesses, scaldings, heart disease, pneumonia, dysentery, compound rupture, diseases of the eyes, fevers, and so on indefinitely have been healed by simple faith in the word of our God."[7]

The Kenyons ultimately parted ways with the Free Will Baptists, but not over the issue of healing. Kenyon clashed with the denomination because he insisted that his FWB church get out of debt and stop using manipulative methods to raise his salary. After they resigned, the Kenyons, at the instruction of the Lord, started a new work. Kenyon cautiously introduced divine healing to their new nondenominational church, called the Tabernacle.

In our work at the Tabernacle, I did not teach healing except in a very guarded way. Yet as the people began to obey the Word and to test its promises, healings and other signs followed, and I could not suppress the truth. Had I any right to hold down the truth through fear of persecution or misrepresentation when I knew that God could heal, and was healing the sick?[8]

So the Kenyons committed to serving the body of Christ through praying for divine healing.

Kenyon was a zealous soul-winner, and if a few weeks went by without seeing anyone brought to the Lord, he was concerned. As time went on, he saw the value of divine healing as a tool for evangelism. He set out to train others in the healing ministry so that they could also win souls. This cause some of his contemporaries to complain that he was trying to "raise up an army of divine healers."[9] That may have been meant as an insult, but it sounds almost like a compliment in retrospect!

A. B. SIMPSON AND THE BELIEVER'S PRIVILEGES

A. B. Simpson was one of three men, according to Kenneth Mackenzie, Jr., who were in the forefront of the divine healing movement. Mackenzie, an Episcopal minister who was associated with A. B. Simpson throughout his ministry and authored two books on divine healing, believed that A. B. Simpson, Charles Cullis, and John Alexander Dowie were the three men who were the trailblazers in this doctrine. He wrote "Three great figures loom against the skyline of the last quarter of the nineteenth century . . . They were called 'faith-curists.'"

Simpson's influence, however, would overshadow the influence of the others. Simpson also taught much about the believer's privileges in Christ, which would eventually dominate Kenyon's teachings as much as divine healing. This will be examined in another chapter.

Kenyon's accolades for Simpson were effluent. In 1902 Kenyon wrote, "Dr. A. B. Simpson, who has done more than any other living man to spread the knowledge of the believer's privileges in Christ, has been an expositor of the Word. His songs and books are an unfolding of the mind of the Spirit in the Word."[10] Because of his Christlike spirit, Simpson was respected not only by Kenyon, but also by many who disliked his teaching about divine healing.

Simpson, the founder of the Christian and Missionary Alliance, was a man of character and dedication. After hearing a great number of testimonies (more than two hundred!) of healing at a Charles Cullis Faith Convention, he went apart with the Lord and settled the question between himself and God as to the truth of God's Word and divine healing. He became convinced that healing was a part of "Christ's glorious gospel for a sinful and suffering world, and the purchase of His blessed cross, for all who would believe and receive His Word."[11]

Simpson had struggled with his health for over twenty years. While preparing for college at fourteen he had "broke hopelessly down with nervous prostration" and came very near death.[12] At twenty-one he broke down again with heart trouble. A few months before he discovered Christ as his healer, a physician told him he did not have enough strength to last more than a few months.[13]

When he discovered Christ as his healer, he vowed before the Lord that he would accept this doctrine as true and would never question it again. He took Christ as his physical life for all the needs of his body, and further vowed that he would use this truth for the glory of God and speak of it and minister it any way which God would require of him.

Two days later, he was invited to preach in a Congregational church. He attempted to preach a sermon of his own choosing and was unable to do so. He knew the Lord wanted him to testify to his new unveiling of truth. He recalled, "God did not ask me to testify of my feelings or experiences, but of Jesus and His faithfulness. And I am sure He calls all who trust Him to testify before they experience His full blessing. I believe I should have lost my healing if I had waited until I felt it."

Simpson said testifying to Christ as his healer probably did him more good that any of his listeners, and, he added, "I believe if I had withheld it I should not now be writing the pages of the *Gospel of Healing*."[14] Notice again that Simpson believed he was healed, having taken Jesus as his healer, and testified to it before it was manifested in his body. He even implied that he would not have been alive and writing the book if he had not obeyed the Lord in public testimony to his healing.

The following day another test of faith came to Simpson. He was asked to join a party that was ascending a three-thousand-foot mountain. He still felt no better than when he had committed himself to the Lord as his healer. "So," he wrote, "I ascended that mountain. At first it seemed as if it would almost take my last breath. I felt all the old weakness and physical dread; I found I had in myself no more strength than ever." Initially surprised at his lack of strength after having trusted the Lord as his Healer, Simpson noted, "But over against my weakness and suffering I became conscious that there was another Presence. There was a Divine strength reached out to me if I would have it, take it, claim it, hold it, and persevere in it . . . I pressed closer, closer, closer, to His bosom, and every step seemed stronger until, when I reached that mountain top, I seemed to be at the gate of heaven . . . from that time I have had a new heart in this breast, literally as well as spiritually, and Christ has been its glorious life."[15]

Simpson, like so many of those involved in the Faith-Cure movement, advocated testimony and actions of faith before the healing was manifested. He had this to say about confession:

Faith drives the nail, but confession clinches it; and until we step out, committing ourselves and making our attitude irrevocable and public, we are liable to be moved and shaken . . . Christ required confession from those whom He healed, and He still requires it. If we would make any advance in spiritual blessing, we must commit ourselves irrevocably to what our faith claims, and go forward without doubt or calculation. It is a sublime spectacle to behold a human spirit that has committed itself to God's Word before all the universe, standing and waiting upon heaven to help and answer. For such a spirit all heaven must be concerned, and we can imagine God upon His throne, saying, "Something must be done for this heart that thus fully trusts me." Beloved, are you wholly committed to God, and have your lips sealed your covenant and claim?[16]

Although Simpson did not advocate second-work-of-grace sanctification in the same way as the Holiness movement, he obviously believed in the importance of testimony. He is very likely one of the voices that moved Kenyon away from the second-work-of-grace concept. We will examine Simpson's influence on Kenyon's teaching about sanctification later.

CHARLES CULLIS

Kenyon also cited Charles Cullis, the central figure of the Faith-Cure teachers, as a great inspiration to him in his walk of faith.[17] Dr. Cullis, a homeopathic physician from Boston, was so popular that his summer healing conventions were thronged with seekers for healing. A new location had to be sought to accommodate all the crowds. New buildings were erected by the owners of the resort where they were meeting to handle the multitudes.[18] Speakers there included Ethan O. Allen, A. J. Gordon, R. Kelso Carter, Daniel Steele, William Boardman, Carrie Judd Montgomery and Europeans Mrs. Michael Baxter and Otto Stockmeyer. It would be hard to imagine anyone ministering in New England and teaching divine healing, as Kenyon was, not knowing about the ministry (Cullis's) that brought the truth of divine healing to the forefront.

It is strange to note that one researcher, who denied Kenyon was influenced by Cullis as a teacher of divine healing, admitted Kenyon admired Cullis's life of faith and modeled his Bible school in part after Cullis![19]

Kenyon was greatly touched by reading Charles Cullis's story.

> Today, my mind goes back to the time, when in the southern part
> of Massachusetts, I saw in a bookcase the life story of Charles
> Cullis. I cannot describe to you the emotions that stirred my heart
> as I began to read it. I went into it chapter after chapter until I
> came to some of his great battles. I lived with him in his fights; I
> knew what it meant. It was like a soldier who, having just gone
> through a severe engagement, is reading the field notes of the
> other parts of the battle. I read of long hard struggles, sometimes
> month after month, with but just enough to meet the needs of the
> inmates of his great institution. At times darkness seemed to settle
> down over his life and work; his friends thought he had made a
> mistake, and that a life of faith could never be lived in Boston. I
> saw him on his knees, writing out the promises that the eternal
> God had made to encourage us to trust Him.[20]

Charles Cullis, who made quite an impact on Kenyon, garnered the
respect of his admirers and his critics alike. He had opened a number
of homes to take in the incurables given up to die by the medical profession. He helped them as much as possible as a homeopathic doctor
and led the majority of them to Christ before they died. He eventually
discovered divine healing and prayed (quite successfully) for the sick
as well. Cullis's sacrificial dedication to help the needy in Boston won
him an honored place in church history in his day.

Cullis shared his discovery of divine healing with many leaders in
the Holiness movement who also embraced the doctrine. He also rallied
many who had been teaching divine healing for years to teach at his
many faith conventions, and he published their books. His publishing
ministry was one way in which the Faith-Cure movement arose out of
the Holiness movement and reached many, many lives. E. W. Kenyon was
a great admirer of the man who did "more than any other man to bring
healing by faith to the attention of the church in the last century."[21]

JOHN ALEXANDER DOWIE

Arguably the most gifted—and the most tragic—character in the
Faith-Cure movement was John Alexander Dowie. Used mightily of
God for a season, Dowie came to believe in his latter years (from 1901

until his death in 1907) that he was Elijah the Restorer, the great end-time prophet.

In a previous chapter, I mentioned one writer's opinion that Kenyon could not be classed with Cullis and Dowie because he did not preach the distinctives of the Holiness tradition. I have to disagree. Kenyon was very familiar with their teachings and was inspired by some of them. Oddly, it was on a taped interview with Ruth Kenyon Housworth (taped by this researcher) that I heard her say that her father had met Dowie (and F. F. Bosworth) in Chicago.[22]

Dowie's boldness of faith inspired many, including Kenyon. While preaching in Chicago in 1908, Kenyon said "Here and there I find a man or woman who really has extraordinary faith . . . even as I believe God called John Alexander Dowie."

Elsewhere Kenyon said of Dowie:

> Why, when Dr. Dowie was in the fullness of grace in Chicago, again and again he spoke to cancers and they dropped off the body instantly. The power of that man's dominating faith thrilled the audiences.
>
> He spoke to a leg that was too short, infantile paralysis had paralyzed it, took hold of it, and said, "In the name of Jesus, come down," and that leg grew four inches right in front of the audience.
>
> For years you could go into the old Zion Tabernacle in Chicago and see hundreds of crutches and surgical appliances hanging on the walls; then you knew what dominating faith and creative faith meant.[23]

In one of his books, Kenyon referred again to the power of God in Dowie's ministry. He wrote, "You and God are linked together. You become invincible. We see a glimpse of this in Luther's ministry. We saw it in John Alexander Dowie's ministry. We have seen it in individuals here and there—God and man linked together, doing the impossible."[24]

Fully aware of Dowie's downfall to error and delusion, he acknowledged the powerful ministry of divine healing as a gift from God to Dowie. "I believe that since the days of the apostles no other man has had the gift of healing which he had. But he did as thousands of others have done with lesser gifts; he used this gift to further his own cause."[25] Kenyon saw Dowie as a man uniquely gifted by God who succumbed to the flesh and misused his gifts to build his own empire.

A WORD ABOUT MEDICINE

An aspect of healing ministry that is still debated today is the use of medical treatment. The abysmal state of medicine was probably one of the underlying reasons why some Faith-Cure healers rejected medical treatment. Bloodletting, the practice of letting out the blood of the patient to "cleanse" him of disease, was highly thought of in the medical profession of the late nineteenth century. Arsenic, opium, and morphine were popular tonics. The practice of medicine was primitive and barbarous. The cure might be worse than the disease![26] Faith healers were often called upon to pray for people who had had surgery or some other treatment and were suffering because of it.

John Alexander Dowie represented one extreme in his total renunciation of the medical profession. Charles Cullis, himself a homeopathic doctor, never advocated stopping medical treatment. Others took various positions between these two poles. It was common in both the Holiness movement and the early Pentecostal movement to trust God alone for physical health and healing.

The Kenyons gave up medicine while among the Free Will Baptists. It is not clear what the Free Will Baptist position was on the subject, but the Kenyons gave up medicine while among the Baptists.[27]

SUMMARY

Kenyon's healing ministry, as we've seen, was developed under completely orthodox influences. While he was in Springville, New York (about 1897), the Lord began to open his eyes to the promises of Scripture regarding healing. In his writings, Kenyon recorded his respect for three of the greatest leaders of the Faith-Cure movement—Simpson, Cullis and Dowie. But a multitude of other voices were singing the chorus of divine healing. In the next chapter we will examine some other strong voices from the choir.

CHAPTER 8

MORE FAITH-CURE INFLUENCES

*There is no belief rising more swiftly before the churches
everywhere than that of divine healing.*

—R. Kelso Carter, 1897[1]

As he entered into his healing ministry, Kenyon found much
encouragement and support, both in books and ministries, in
New England. Besides the Free Will Baptists, many other orthodox
believers were praying for healing. Many of those who believed in
healing had derived their faith doctrine from the Holiness movement,
especially the writings of Phoebe Palmer, who was immensely influential, as I noted earlier.

In this chapter I am going to examine the Holiness concept of faith as
exemplified in Palmer's writings. Then I will give examples from ministers of divine healing who applied this same concept of faith in their
teaching about divine healing. They are: Ethan O. Allen, Elizabeth Mix,
Carrie Judd Montgomery, and Andrew Murray. All four of these individuals knew Charles Cullis. Allen, Mix, and Montgomery spoke at Cullis's
faith conventions regularly. Murray, who was from South Africa, visited
Cullis and attended one of his conventions. With the exception of Mix,
all wrote books on healing as well. Finally, I will review some of the
popular written defenses of the healing movement by authors William
Boardman, A. J. Gordon, R. L. Stanton, and R. Kelso Carter.

Note: You may need to remind yourself that the material you are
reading is more than one hundred years old. That is because it sounds

so similar to the Faith teaching of today.

THE HOLINESS CONCEPT OF FAITH

Phoebe Palmer, one of the most influential Christian figures of the nineteenth century, sparked a revival of Holiness teachings and experience. Documentably the revival of divine healing sprang out of the roots of the Holiness revival. Faith and confession were foundational to this movement.

I want to emphasize again that Holiness teaching (Palmer's influence dates from about 1835) preceded the metaphysical cults with their affirmations by many years. The metaphysical cults didn't begin to blossom until the 1880s with Mary Baker Eddy's Christian Science. New Thought became a recognizable movement in the latter 1890s.

Palmer had great influence in regard to the concept of faith which permeated the Holiness movement. Eventually this concept of faith was extended to apply not only to sanctification, but also to healing. Palmer wrote in *Faith and Its Effects,*

> Had your faith been wholly founded on the faithfulness of God, and not dependent on your feelings, you would not in any way have lost anchorage, as a consequence of this destitution of emotion.
>
> If *feeling* were the principle commanding religious action, instead of calm, deliberate, steady faith, how often should we be led astray, even when in our most pious moods.[2]

Palmer further stated concerning receiving sanctification by faith, describing her own questions:

> Shall I venture upon these declarations [of Scripture] without previously realizing a change sufficient to warrant such conclusions? Venture now, merely because they stand recorded in the written word! She [Palmer, writing about herself] here perceived that the declarations of Scripture were as truly the *the Word of the Lord* to her soul, as though they were proclaimed from the holy mount in the voice of thunder, or blazoned across the vault of heaven in characters of flame. She now saw into the simplicity of faith in a manner that astonished and humbled her soul; she was astonished

71

she had not before perceived it, and humbled because she had been so slow of heart to believe God. The perceptions of faith and its effect that then took possession of her mind were these: Faith is taking God at His word—relying unwaveringly upon his truth.

Here she saw an error which, during the whole of her former pilgrimage in the heavenly way, had been detrimental to her progress. She now perceived that she had been much more solicitous about *feeling* than *faith*,—requiring *feeling,* the *fruit* of faith, previous to having exercised faith.[3]

In a previous chapter I showed how important confession or testimony was to *receiving* the sanctification experience. Palmer also taught that it was by continually confessing or testifying before men to the possession of sanctification, that the sanctification was maintained. She wrote, "Now, though I well know that this blessing is the gift of God through our Lord Jesus Christ; yet I fully believe, if I had not yielded to these convictions relative to confession, I could not have retained it."[4]

Ethan Allen and Elizabeth Mix applied what they had learned about sanctification by faith to healing by faith. They encouraged people to believe, act, and testify to what *they believed they had received* before any conscious change occurred in their souls (or bodies!). Let us see how they did this.

The Father of Divine Healing

Ethan O. Allen, known as the father of divine healing in the United States, was the first American known to have a full-time traveling ministry focused on healing. For fifty years he traveled throughout the Eastern United States praying for the sick and teaching divine healing. Allen was a frequent guest at A. B. Simpson's conferences. Kenyon may well have heard him there. Allen also spoke regularly at the faith conventions organized by Charles Cullis, who published Allen's book *Faith Healing.*

Kenyon's teaching is strikingly similar to Allen's. A good example is Allen's description of his own healing from tuberculosis in a Methodist class meeting in 1846.

I had been thinking that day how Christ used to heal the sick, and

I believed He could heal me if I could only exercise faith enough . . .

I then laid my case of infirmity before the Lord, grasping hold of the Saviour as confidently as if He had been personally present. I told Him about the sickness in my side, and believed He could help me then. I claimed the promise, and in a moment was blessed in a wonderful manner. I knew the Lord had heard my prayer; the evidence was very clear. I began to praise the Lord, exclaiming, "I am healed, I am healed!" But Satan was not far off, and soon attempted to defeat the work. As I started for home a sharp pain commenced in my side, even while I was declaring I was healed. I still held on in faith, declaring I was healed, pain or no pain. I walked on, the pain continuing, and the tempter saying: "You have more pain than ever." I exclaimed: "I have got the evidence, pain or no pain. Begone Satan! Begone pain! It is done! I believe it!" And here all pain and soreness left me, and I was as happy as I could be.[5]

It would be hard to find closer parallel to Kenyon's teaching about divine healing. Let's review the steps Allen took. He claimed the promise of God by faith and stated that the "evidence" of his healing "was very clear." The "evidence" was the witness of the Holy Spirit that his prayer was heard and that God had given the healing to him by faith. Note that he said, "I have got the evidence, pain or no pain." Even when pain struck his body, Allen *declared* he was healed and *commanded* Satan and the pain to leave his body.

Allen applied the Methodist understanding of faith for receiving sanctification to receiving healing. He spoke out of the witness of the Spirit rather than his physical condition. Some people today call this "sensory denial;" the Methodists and Faith-Cure people called it faith in God and His Word.

Allen, also in the Methodist tradition, stressed the need for confession that a healing is received.

The next Sabbath at meeting I had nearly forgotten to confess this work [his healing], when suddenly the pain in my side returned more death-like than ever, and a burden of mind at the same time, but as soon as I opened my mouth to give testimony of what I had experienced I was free again from all pain, and as clear as the noonday sun in regard to my acceptance with the Lord and His approval of me.[6]

Allen's understanding of this principle came, either directly or indirectly, from Phoebe Palmer, who had taught that holiness was obtained by consecration, faith, and confession. She, following the lead of older Methodists such as Hester Ann Rogers and John Fletcher, taught that sanctification was *kept* by continual public confession.[7] This idea was normative in Methodism as early as 1846.

A Mother in the Healing Ministry

Elizabeth Mix, a black woman from Wolcottville, Connecticut, was healed of tuberculosis under Ethan O. Allen's ministry.[8] She and her husband, Edward, were among the first traveling companions of Allen in the healing ministry. She was a well-educated, articulate and persuasive person. Eventually she and her husband devoted themselves full-time to their own independent faith healing ministry.[9]

Though as far as I am aware Mrs. Mix had no direct contact with Kenyon, she was an important voice in the Faith-Cure movement. I want to cite an anecdote from Mrs. Mix's ministry to show how her methodology resembled what Kenyon taught. This is the story of a young invalid named Carrie Judd. Miss Judd's sister Eva wrote to Mrs. Mix to request her prayers for her sister's recovery. Mrs. Mix responded:

> I can encourage you, by the Word of God, that "according to your faith" so be it unto you; and besides you have this promise, "The prayer of faith shall save the sick, and the Lord shall raise him up."
>
> Now the promise is to you, as if you were the only person living. Now if you can claim that promise, I have not the least doubt but what you will be healed . . .
>
> I want you to pray for yourself, and pray believing, and then *act faith*. It makes no difference how you feel, but get right out of bed and begin to walk by faith. Strength will come, disease will depart, and you will be made whole.[10]

Carrie Judd prayed at the appointed time suggested in the letter.

(Those at Mrs. Mix's prayer meeting were praying for Carrie at that arranged time.) After being unable to get out of bed for two years, she got out of bed and walked a few steps. She was walking around her room in about three weeks. This was February 1879, and by April she was out walking through the neighborhood rejoicing in the mercy of God. Her recovery was completed, and she entered into a ministry of divine healing herself.[11] Later she and her husband became close friends with Kenyon.

Notice the methodology. Mrs. Mix encouraged Miss Judd that the promise of God was for her. At an appointed time she was to believe that she received her healing and then begin to act healed, *even though she may feel no better.* She was encouraged that *as she acted* God's power would begin to work and *eventually* she would have the healing manifested in her body.

Paul Chappell, in his study of divine healing in America, wrote, "It is significant to note Mrs. Mix's articulation of an important and universal principle of the divine healing movement. She instructed patients to pray in faith and then to act upon their faith. She emphasized that it is not necessary to feel some particular emotion, but it is essential for patients to act as though they believe what they profess to believe."[12]

Mix learned to minister healing from Ethan O. Allen, so surely she also believed in the importance and necessity of testimony as well. Believe, profess, and act is the consistent recurring theme.

A BRIGHT STAR

Carrie Judd Montgomery (1858–1946), healed under the ministry of Mrs. Mix, was to become one of the bright stars of the nineteenth century revival of divine healing. Kenyon was close friends with Carrie and her husband George, at least in later years when Kenyon moved to the West Coast. We will discuss their relationship in a later chapter. At this point we'll review some of Montgomery's teaching to show its relationship to Holiness thought and today's Faith movement.

After her healing Montgomery wrote a book called *The Prayer of Faith,* which resulted in her becoming internationally known as an advocate of divine healing. It was translated into German, French, Swedish, and Dutch. In 1885 she received an invitation to be a featured speaker at the International Conference on Divine Healing and True Holiness held in London.

Carrie Judd Montgomery also had contacted Charles Cullis and read his annual reports of healings. She requested his prayers as she was recovering from her illness and maintained a relationship with Cullis until his death, speaking regularly at his faith conventions.

Montgomery's ministry began in the Faith-Cure movement and continued into the Christian and Missionary Alliance movement under A. B. Simpson (as the recording secretary, she was a founding member of the leadership of that organization), and later embraced the Pentecostal movement, aligning with the Assemblies of God until her death. She is another direct link with today's Faith movement. Her ministry has striking parallels with E. W. Kenyon's ministry, both in her teachings on faith and healing, and her spiritual evolution.[13]

Her publication, *Triumphs of Faith: A Monthly Journal Devoted to Faith-Healing and to the Promotion of Christian Holiness,* became one the most significant publications in the divine healing movement. She began publishing it in January 1881. The title emphasizes the link between healing and holiness by faith. For example, she taught that both healing and holiness (sanctification) required testimony.

> Let Jesus reign in your heart, and He, the Sinless One, will continually live out His holiness in and through you. This blessing of sanctification is a most precious and definite work of grace in the heart, *and it is necessary that we should testify definitely to this blessing if we want to abide in such a precious experience. With the heart we believe, and with the mouth we confess, as in every other blessing.* If you are not willing to confess that Jesus Christ has saved you, you have not salvation, or have so little that it will all leak away. When you get sanctified you must confess it as definitely as you confess salvation. People come to me in great sorrow, saying, "I used to have the blessing of sanctification, but I have lost it." And when we probe deep to find the reason, we find very often it is because of failure to testify.
>
> *.And it is the same with divine healing.* If people are not willing to testify to the healing power of the Great Physician, they are apt to lose their health again. Also, I would warn you *not to wait for certain feelings or emotions before you testify to the work which God has wrought in your heart or in your body.* "Faith is the evidence of things not seen," and if we really believe God's Word we shall not be afraid to stand upon it, and to tell all the world of its

truth. Are you not willing to believe absolutely God's Word, and to count it worth more than any flitting emotion? You must first stand upon God's truth, and God's Holy Spirit will then come and witness that truth. God will give you plenty of feeling sooner or later, but He first requires you to stand upon His naked Word (italics added).[14]

Notice the similarity of Montgomery's teaching to that of Phoebe Palmer. Only she extends the principle of faith that Palmer taught for sanctification to divine healing, much the same as Allen and Mix.

A WRITER FOR ALL TIMES

Another advocate of divine healing who documentably influenced Kenyon was South African evangelist and teacher Andrew Murray (1828–1917). Kenyon attended Moody's Northfield conference where Murray spoke. Kenyon also published excerpts from Murray's books in his periodical.

Having lost his voice and reportedly finished his career as a preacher, Murray sought out the truth of divine healing. Eventually he went to London to the divine healing home established by William Boardman called Bethshan. He was so completely healed he was never troubled again by any weakness of the throat or voice.[15]

Murray was influenced by William Boardman's book *The Lord Thy Healer* and by Charles Cullis's ministry, which he visited. In 1884 Murray wrote the Dutch version of his book on divine healing called *Jesus, The Physician of the Sick.* It was published in English in 1900. Concerning faith and healing Murray wrote:

> Prayer without faith is powerless . . . If you have already asked for healing from the Lord, or if others have asked it for you, you must, before you are conscious of any change, be able to say with faith, "On the authority of God's Word, I have the assurance that He hears me, and that I am healed."
>
> Faith receives healing as a spiritual grace which proceeds from the Lord, even while there is no conscious change in the body. Faith can glorify God and say, "Bless the Lord, O my soul . . . who healeth all thy diseases" (Ps. 103:1, 3). The Lord requires this faith that He may heal . . .

> It is necessary to testify to the faith one has . . . Praise the Lord
> without waiting to feel better, or to have more faith. Praise Him,
> and say with David, "O Lord my God, I cried unto thee, and thou
> hast healed me" (Ps. 30:2).
> Divine healing is a spiritual grace which can only be received
> spiritually and by faith, before its effect is felt on the body . . . If,
> therefore, your sickness does not yield at once, if Satan and your
> own unbelief attempt to get the upper hand, do not heed them.[16]

Here another respected leader whose devotional writings are still
popular today, expressed himself in terms that Kenyon could easily
have used. Healing is received by faith, testified to before it is manifested, and rejoiced in because God's Word is true. The reality of
sickness is not denied. The right of sickness to exist in the believer's
body—when Jesus provided healing in the atonement—is denied. The
satanic source of sickness is reiterated.

Kenyon wrote in his book on divine healing, *Jesus the Healer:*

> You have a right to freedom from pain or sickness. In that name
> you command it to leave. You are not demanding it of the Father,
> because the Father has given you authority over these demoniacal
> forces.[17]

Kenyon, like the others in the Faith-Cure movement, saw healing in
the context of spiritual warfare. It was widely taught that Satan was the
author of sickness and disease. It was also widely taught that because
of what Jesus did at the cross, Satan had no right to afflict the believer
with sickness. The reality of sickness wasn't denied, but rather its right
to afflict the redeemed.

It might be pointed out that the metaphysical cults do not believe in
demons or a personal devil. Only the orthodox divine healing movement saw sickness as a work of Satan and demon spirits. Christian
Science taught that sickness was an "error of the mortal mind," *a
wrong belief in the existence of physical matter!*

THEOLOGICAL DEFENSES OF DIVINE HEALING

As was mentioned earlier, Charles Cullis became the central figure in
the Divine Healing movement. His personal ministry, his influence on

leaders in the Holiness movement, and his faith conventions all contributed to this notoriety. But it was his publishing company, the *Willard Tract Repository,* that put the movement's ideas in print.[18] By the time of Cullis's death in 1892, due to the books that he published, "the faith healing doctrine was a firmly established feature in the expansive landscape of American Christianity."[19]

Cullis published three books of testimonies of healing that he authored himself: *Faith Cures; or Answers to Prayer in the Healing of the Sick* (1879), *More Faith Cures* (1881), and *Other Faith Cures* (1885). These books were the first of their kind in America, presenting dozens of testimonies of divine healing.

During the 1880s Cullis also began to publish the first doctrinal and theological treatises on divine healing. Carrie Judd Montgomery also published a journal and books. In the next few pages we'll examine several of these books and the theological contributions they made.

THE FULLNESS OF GOD

The first of these was written by Cullis's long-time friend and coworker in the Higher Life movement, William Boardman (1810–1886). It was called *The Great Physician (Jehovah Rophi).* Boardman's earlier work, *The Higher Christian Life* (1859), was tremendously influential in bringing the message of sanctification into non-Methodist circles. Notice how Boardman says that "spirit, soul, and body" are transformed by faith.

> By faith man accepts Christ as the fullness of God. It is already true in Christ, and is true also in us the moment we accept the reality as a reality of God, and let ourselves go into His hands as His own true, lawful, rightful habitation, to be possessed, filled, dwelt in, transformed, and controlled by Him. This is alike true of spirit, soul, and body . . .
>
> His fullness will be our fullness in so far as we accept it. It is already true in Him to the full, and will be true in us at once as far as our faith takes Him.[20]

Boardman expressed the idea that everything we need is already a reality in Christ, only awaiting the believer's faith to claim it. In the above quote he was referring to sanctification, yet note that he suggests its application to spirit, soul, *and* body. He later came to see healing as a part of our redemption and applied this same premise (that sanctification and everything we need is already true in Christ and awaiting our claiming it by faith) to healing. This is exactly what Kenyon taught. The Holiness movement had embraced the idea of sanctification as well as justification being provided for in Christ. Many, such as Boardman, began to understand healing to be included in Christ's finished work as well.

HEALING IN THE ATONEMENT

A. J. Gordon, who spoke regularly at Cullis's faith conventions and was on the board of Cullis's ministry, wrote a book titled, *The Ministry of Healing: Miracles of Cure in All Ages,* which Cullis published in 1882. It was a historical and doctrinal study of faith healing from the early church fathers, the post-Reformation period, and modern ministries of healing.

Kenyon certainly read this book since he quoted from Gordon's writings more frequently than any other author. In fact, the major theme in Kenyon's writings—the believer's identification with Christ—was probably sparked by Gordon's classic book, *In Christ.*

In his book on healing, Gordon traced the history of healing since the Reformation, referring to Dorothea Truedel as the modern pioneer of divine healing. In an advertisement for his book *Jesus the Healer,* Kenyon wrote, "Healing was first discovered by Dorothea Truedel in the Swiss Mountains. She was the first one to teach healing after the dark ages. Year by year the message has been growing clearer."[21] Kenyon saw himself and his writings in the unfolding drama of the restoration of God's truth. He felt he was carrying the torch handed on from these pioneers of healing.

Gordon believed that healing was included in the atonement of Christ. Even the critics of the doctrine acknowledged Gordon's skillful treatment of the subject.[22] Gordon wrote:

> The yoke of His cross by which He lifted our iniquities took hold also of our diseases; so that it is in some sense true that as God "made Him to be sin for us who knew no sin," so He made Him to be sick for us who knew no sickness. He who entered into mysterious sympathy with our pain which is the fruit of sin, also put

80

himself underneath our pain which is the penalty of sin . . .

If now it be true that our Redeemer and substitute bore our sicknesses, it would be natural to reason at once that He bore them that we might not bear them.[23]

But, it is asked, if the privilege and promise in this matter are so clear, how is it that the cases of recovery through the prayer of faith are so rare? Probably because the prayer of faith itself is so rare, and especially because when found it receives almost no support in the church as a whole.[24]

Healing in the atonement became widely regarded as the basis for claiming healing as the believer's covenant privilege. The necessity of a living faith was underscored by many of those teaching divine healing, Gordon obviously included.

DELIVERANCE FROM SIN AND DISEASE

In 1884 Carrie Judd Montgomery published *Gospel Parallelism: Illustrated in the Healing of Body and Soul.* Authored by R. L. Stanton, the book was originally published in her journal as a series of articles. Stanton, a former president of Miami University and a moderator of the General Assembly of the Presbyterian Church, insisted that it was absolutely necessary "to include both [healing of body and soul] in any true conception of what the gospel offered to mankind."

It is my aim . . . to endeavor to show that the atonement of Christ lays a foundation equally for deliverance from sin and for deliverance from disease; that complete provision has been made for both; that, *in the exercise of faith,* under the conditions prescribed, we have the same ground to believe that the body may be delivered from sickness that we have that the soul may be delivered from sin.

The removal of sin, with all its defilements and corruptions of the soul, is fully provided for, so also, the removal of disease, with all its infirmities and deformities of the body, is equally embraced in the Lord's gracious design.[25]

This quote indicates that Stanton was thinking of sanctification by faith as taught in Holiness circles. Stanton extended the idea of complete cleansing of the soul to reach complete healing of the body. He indicated that it is *received by faith in the one atoning sacrifice of Christ.* Kenyon would agree!

SALVATION FOR SOUL AND BODY

Another popular defense of divine healing was published by Charles Cullis. It was written by his good friend and associate, R. Kelso Carter, and was entitled *The Atonement for Sin and Sickness; or, A Full Salvation for Soul and Body* (1884). Carter was healed of a "stubborn heart disease" when prayed for by Cullis in 1879. Carter and George McCalla organized the first convention exclusively on the subject of divine healing in 1882. (Charles Cullis's conferences were focused on both holiness *and* divine healing.)

Carter's book reveals the Holiness roots of the healing doctrine as he taught it. Carter's first chapters establish a basis in the atonement for pardon from all past sins and cleansing from all inbred sin before developing a basis for physical healing being in the atonement as well.

> I began to believe that my Divine Master not only took upon himself my sins, but also bore my bodily sicknesses, and that I might, through simple faith, be free from the latter, just as well as from the former . . . I had come to see that my Jesus is able and willing to save me from my sins, and was trusting Him for it . . . I was trusting Him to keep me from sinning; then why not trust Him to keep me from being sick? . . .
>
> I trusted in Him, and strove hard not to lean to my own understanding. But in this way at least, I did not publicly acknowledge Him; that is I did not profess my faith on the subject. In the course of two years, however, I was led into a firm belief; and then the conviction grew upon me that I must make public confession.

About two years before writing the book he publicly announced his belief in divine healing. He was attacked with sickness a short time before this public confession, and he believed it to be from the devil. He told the devil that he was trusting Jesus to keep him. He said, "Jesus has the keeping part, I have the believing and confessing."[26] He continued:

This then is my confession. I believe that Jesus "bare my sins—all of them—in his own body on the tree;" and I believe that "he took my infirmities, and bore my sicknesses." Now if He bore them for me, I am not obliged to carry them myself; so I just believe it, and cry from my inmost being, Praise the Lord!

... I do boldly avow my belief that sin and sickness are from the devil; while holiness and health are from God. If I sin, it is because the devil gets the advantage in my soul, and I am sick, it is because he gets the advantage in my body. In neither case does any necessity exist.[27]

A Taste of Kenyon's Healing Theology

Kenyon would later state his belief about deliverance from sin and sickness being included in the finished work of Christ in his book, *Jesus the Healer.* Notice how similar his teaching sounds to the books we've previously quoted.

We have come to believe that it is just as wrong for a believer to bear his sickness when Jesus bore it, as it is for him to bear his sins when Christ bore them.

We have no right to live in sin and to bear those hateful habits that make life a curse, because Christ bore them.

It was wrong for Him to bear them if we are going to bear them too. It is wrong for us to have sickness and disease in our bodies when God laid those diseases on Jesus. He became sick with our diseases, that we might be healed.[28]

Kenyon, like most of the voices in the Faith-Cure movement, saw in the work of Christ at Calvary a basis for holy living *and* healing and health. Claiming the provisions of Christ's work by faith and confessing them before men was common practice among them. Acting on the promise without any apparent change was also regularly encouraged.

Kenyon emphasized confession in his later years much more than in his earlier ministry, probably to make up for the fact that the Holiness movement with its emphasis on confession was no longer very influential. Not as many voices were proclaiming the need to testify to what was received from God. Seeing Kenyon's roots, however, it is obvious why confession, or testimony, was of continuing importance to him.

During Kenyon's theologically formative years, he came under the influence of many respected Bible teachers who gathered under the headship of D. L. Moody. Although we have already mentioned a number of them, they play a significant enough role in the development of Kenyon's teachings that they require a closer look. In the next chapter we will examine some of the highly influential mentors in the life of E. W. Kenyon.

CHAPTER 9

MOODY'S WARRIORS

If we honor God's Word, he will honor us. Look at George Müller and D. L. Moody. They both honored God enough to believe his Word and shape their lives by it. Therefore God honored them, and gave them a place exalted among men. Look over the names of those now counted as mighty men of God. You will find they are all great Bible students and Bible preachers.

—E. W. Kenyon[1]

Kenyon wrote the above in his periodical the *Bethel Trumpet* in 1901. He elsewhere referred to Moody as the "spiritual genius of the nineteenth century."[2] It would be hard to imagine higher praise for a fellow minister. In this chapter I want to look at the influence of Moody and those who surrounded him on E. W. Kenyon.

Dwight L. Moody was a—if not *the*—central figure in late nineteenth-century evangelicalism. In addition to being a preeminent preacher whose crusades in various cities (and countries) were very successful, he also was a great organizer and founded a number of conferences and educational institutions. The summer Bible conferences that Moody began in his hometown of Northfield, Massachusetts, proved to be very important in the life of E. W. Kenyon.

The year that Kenyon was restored to the Lord in A. J. Gordon's church (1893) was the year that Gordon was overseeing the Northfield conference for Moody who was doing evangelistic work at the Chicago World's Fair. Through Gordon, Kenyon was brought into the circle of influences he would refer to as "Moody's warriors."

THE NORTHFIELD CONFERENCES

In 1880 Moody gathered together a number of Bible teachers for a conference emphasizing the need of the Holy Spirit's ministry in the believer's life. These developed into annual gatherings at Northfield for the deepening of the spiritual life until Moody's death in 1899, after which the conferences waned in influence.

Some time after World War I, Kenyon wrote a tribute to an author and Bible teacher he greatly admired (S. D. Gordon). In this tribute he lamented the loss of the spirituality since the war but praised Moody and his comrades.

> Hardly any of those deeply spiritual before the war maintained their spiritual life through the war. Something happened to them. We do not know what, whether compromise with the world or otherwise, but they lost out.
>
> Men with that rare spiritual genius of [F. B.] Myers, the [G. Campbell] Morgan we used to know, Andrew Murray, Webb Peploe, and A. J. Gordon, they all belong to the other generation.
>
> They belong to that era of spiritual grace that focalized under Mr. Moody's matchless ministry. We don't have Bible conferences anymore. We don't have conventions for the deepening of the spiritual life that attracts the nation's attention and brings men from all parts of the world.[3]

Here we have Kenyon's view of the Northfield conferences under Moody's leadership. All the above-mentioned men were speakers at Northfield during Kenyon's formative years (1894–1897).

The quote also indicates that Kenyon attended Northfield and heard Gordon there. That would have been in 1893 and 1894. Gordon was at Northfield in 1893 (as coordinator) and 1894 (as speaker). Those are the only years Kenyon could have heard Gordon at Northfield, because he died in early 1895. Kenyon was restored to the Lord in 1893 a few months before the conference.

Kenyon's respect for Moody and his peers was rooted in his gratitude for the tremendous help their teaching brought him. Kenyon was attracted to these people because of their respect for God's Word

Kenyon wrote in 1902, "These men love the Word. Luther, the Wesleys, Whitfield, Spurgeon, Müller, [A. B.] Simpson, [J. N.] Darby and Moody *with his army of warriors* all take us to the Book and leave us there, knowing that 'These are they that testify of Me'" (italics added).[4] Moody's warriors, as Kenyon called them, were spiritual leaders and Bible teachers who greatly influenced his ministry.

Let us look at three men who spoke at Northfield conferences the years Kenyon attended and about whom Kenyon wrote in his books or magazines.

A CHIEF WARRIOR

A. J. Gordon was one of Moody's chief warriors and quite influential on Kenyon. Kenyon said he read a number of Gordon's books and was quite familiar with his personal testimony and ministry. Kenyon eventually preached at Gordon's Clarendon Street Baptist Church some years after Gordon's death. The fact that he preached there is a clear indication of the circle in which Kenyon's ministry moved.

I mentioned previously that Gordon's book *In Christ* appears to have significantly impacted Kenyon's life. The believer's position in Christ became a central aspect of Kenyon's theology. Much of Gordon's language in that book resembles Kenyon's language and his teaching on these themes. I will show some of the remarkably similar ideas in a later chapter.

Gordon, who is not well known today, was one of the most respected scholars and Bible teachers of his day. His writings were also widely read among the early advocates of the Pentecostal movement which emerged after Gordon's death. His association with the Faith-Cure movement and with Kenyon makes him quite significant to our story.

A SECOND WARRIOR

Another warrior whom Kenyon acknowledged as inspiring him was A. T. Pierson. He spoke at Northfield every year from 1894 to 1898, years that Kenyon would have attended.[5] Kenyon also published other articles by Pierson in his periodicals.

Pierson was well-received in Christian circles in the United States and abroad. He served as interim pastor for Charles Haddon Spurgeon in London. In the states, he preached for A. B. Simpson and many Alliance conventions.[6]

Pierson's closest friend was A. J. Gordon. Both Gordon and Pierson's mother died in the same year (1895). At the Northfield conference that year, somewhat shattered by his loss, Pierson had a life-changing encounter with the Lord which changed his ministry emphasis from missions to the higher Christian life.

The encounter with the Lord that so touched Pierson's life, was poured through two "vessels" who had ministered earlier that year at the Keswick conference: Andrew Murray and H. W. Webb-Peploe. Pierson heard them both at Northfield. The teaching that year on faith by these two speakers forever changed the emphasis of Pierson's ministry. Pierson began writing on higher-life themes from this conference onward. Kenyon was there and wrote about hearing the same messages that touched Pierson so significantly. It was the higher-life themes in the later part of Pierson's ministry that were so influential on Kenyon.

During his life Pierson wrote some thirty-five books on missions and the Christian life. He edited an outstanding and influential missionary periodical known as *The Missionary Review of the World*. A number of his books on the deeper life showed the influence of the British Keswick movement. (The Keswick movement also played a role in Kenyon's life.)

In his book *In Christ Jesus* (1898) Pierson gives a somewhat systematic survey of Paul's epistles, examining them in the light of our identification with Christ. Pierson published *Shall We Continue in Sin?* (1897) which was a thorough exposition of the believer's union with Christ. Kenyon heard Pierson preach on union and identification and was challenged by it.

Kenyon recalled in 1904, "I once heard Dr. Pierson, in a discourse, say that there were seven steps in the resurrection life of Jesus, and that they illustrate our own life . . . I went home, and that statement kept coming up in my mind, and at last I said, 'Lord, let me have it out once and for all; show me the truth concerning it.'" A challenged Kenyon plunged into a deep study on the life of victory and realized "that I had come into an inheritance. At once I said, 'I will begin to draw on my bank,' and from that moment I have had victory. Victory was mine."[7] Pierson's teachings contributed to a spiritual turning point in Kenyon's life. Significantly, the themes Pierson expounded were our identification and union with Christ and who we are in Christ.

ANOTHER WARRIOR

R. A. Torrey was a close associate of D. L. Moody, and Moody frequently asked him to teach on the baptism of the Holy Spirit in his meetings. In 1889 Torrey became the superintendent of the Chicago Training Institute, which was later known as Moody Bible Institute.

We have already noted that Kenyon sat under Torrey's teaching ministry for a number of days, learning about the Holy Spirit. Kenyon also heard Torrey speak at Northfield from 1893 to 1897, as well as hearing him speak in Chicago at the institute.

Kenyon commented upon Torrey's evangelistic success in Australia in 1903. Notice that he characterized Torrey as preaching "the Finished Work of Christ," which was a great theme in Kenyon's ministry.

> The secret of Dr. Torrey's marvelous success in Australia lies in the fact that he is enabled from the Scriptures to prove that Jesus of Nazareth actually died for our sins. Nothing establishes a man as the knowledge of the finished work of Christ. When we *know* beyond any question that Jesus of Nazareth was the Son of God— not *a son*—but *the only begotten* of God, and that in Him only there is life and light; and when we know that His dying actually put away *sin,* that hideous wall which stood between God and humanity, and by that matchless sacrifice God is enabled, today, to remit the voluntary transgressions and sins of man and give him a standing with Himself without condemnation, this is peace, this is the foundation, this is the doctrine that saves men, this is the teaching that the Holy Spirit can use.[8]

In other places in his periodicals, Kenyon reported on the success of Torrey's ministry in England and in other locations. He invited his readers to pray for worldwide revival. In his written and spoken ministry Torrey pointed Kenyon away from the second-work-of-grace teaching and helped Kenyon see the finished work of Christ. Torrey's teaching on faith and prayer is also quite similar to that of Kenyon. Torrey held to a more conservative view of divine healing than Kenyon, but believed that healing was in the atonement and available to the believer.

OTHER WARRIORS

Gordon, Pierson, and Torrey were among the most prolific of the warriors on the American side, but there were others who documentably influenced Kenyon as well. Dr. Henry C. Mabie, a close friend of A. J. Gordon's, spoke every year at Northfield from 1894–1898. Mabie wrote three books on the atonement that will be referred to later. James M. Gray, C. I. Scofield and A. C. Dixon spoke during these years at Northfield as well. Each of these men touched the life of E. W. Kenyon. Kenyon taught the Scofield type of dispensationalism as opposed to Darby's style.

THE KESWICK CONNECTION

The evidence seems clear that coming under the influence of these men, many of whom were of the Reformed tradition rather than the second-work-of-grace Holiness tradition, caused Kenyon to examine the Scriptures on the subject of sanctification, a doctrine of major importance to Kenyon. The Reformed part of the church (Calvinist) emphasized doctrine and objective truth more than the subjective or experiential side of things which the Methodist/Holiness tradition focused on. Kenyon, as a fruit of receiving from these men, eventually moved away from the Methodistic view of sanctification toward the Keswick view.

The Keswick view maintained that growth in holiness was the appropriation of the finished work of Calvary, rather than a second-crisis experience of sanctification that removed indwelling sin. The Keswick teachers held that the believer continued to have a sin nature as well as the new nature received in regeneration. This sin nature was subdued rather than eradicated as the second work of grace advocates avowed.

Kenyon eventually parted ways with the Keswick teachers' view of sanctification as well. He came to believe that the scriptures taught man's sin nature was removed in the new birth. Unconditional surrender to the Lordship of Christ, and renewing of the mind were the missing ingredients for living a victorious life, Kenyon held. His respect for these Keswick-influenced men, however, would not be diminished by his disagreement with them over the finer points of sanctification.

In a sermon preached in 1928, Kenyon reviewed the various ideas about the new birth that found expression in the church.

> First there is the old Methodist view. It was perhaps the most common. It was propagated more than any other. The Methodists never stressed the new birth. They stressed justification. That is why they called you to the altar. *I never heard the new birth opened up or discussed in the Methodist church.* They say if you are justified, you are forgiven. They said that if you lived godly you would keep your justification. They did not believe you were a new creation. They told you you had to have a second work of grace. That second work would eradicate or take out the sin nature, and you would be wholly sanctified.
>
> But after that nature was out could you keep it out?
>
> You kept your sanctification until you did something wrong. Then you lost everything, your sanctification and justification, and you had to go back and be converted over again and sanctified again.
>
> We are taking this seriously—for it is not our province to ridicule anybody's religious convictions . . . I never heard a Methodist evangelist tell anyone that he was born again. I had been teaching several years before I knew anything about it myself.
>
> The old Keswick movement which began in England, had in it such men as Andrew Murray, F. B. Meyer, G. Campbell Morgan, and H. W. Webb-Peploe. These men went before great congregations. You perhaps can remember when the Keswick movement swept over this nation. They taught if one would make an entire surrender to Jesus Christ he would receive the Holy Spirit. They believed that when a man was born again he received a measure of the Holy Spirit, and then it was possible to be filled. *It was the most healthy movement that ever came.* It produced some of the finest men and women we have among Christians today . . . They held that the new birth was not a new creation but was the incoming of a new nature. When a man received eternal life, he received the nature of God but the other nature remained in him (italics added).[9]

This is a very important overview by Kenyon of the influences he imbibed in his earlier years. He moved away from the Methodist view and toward the Keswick view. Although greatly influenced by Moody's warriors—both American and British (Andrew Murray was, however, South African), by the time he wrote his first book he had rejected both the second-work-of-grace and the dual-nature theories in favor of his belief in the new creation.

Yet these men (along with A. B. Simpson and a few other notables) were the mentors with whom Kenyon identified himself in the body of Christ. From his statements about the Keswick movement, which focalized under Moody's ministry at Northfield in America, it is clear that it was "water in the desert" for Kenyon as he was seeking stability in his walk with the Lord. The emphasis on the "naked Word," which was lost for the most part in the experience-oriented Holiness movement (even though Phoebe Palmer had strongly emphasized the "naked Word") was strong among Moody's warriors and the Keswick teachers.

When someone believes in another's ministry he will likely encourage his friends to pray for that ministry. Kenyon encouraged readers of his magazine to pray for evangelists Dr. Torrey, Dr. A. C. Dixon, Dr. Simpson, Andrew Murray, F. B. Meyer, G. Campbell Morgan, and a few others. "Pray for a worldwide work of grace," he wrote.[10]

SUMMARY

It should be clear that the most significant influences in Kenyon's life while he was living in New England were those who rallied around D. L. Moody. The Northfield conferences, particularly from 1893 to 1898, were very influential upon Kenyon. Moody's death on December 22, 1899, shocked all those who admired him and looked to him for leadership. Kenyon, deeply grieved at the loss of the "spiritual genius of the nineteenth century," traveled to Chicago to attend Moody's memorial.

Kenyon, while attending Moody's memorial, wrote in his Bible (the one given to him by his church in Springville) what appears to be a commitment to evangelism that those attending the service all made in honor of the departed evangelist:

> By the enabling grace of God, I pledge myself to seek with untiring zeal, the salvation of men under all circumstances where men can be reached.

I will know the Almighty, and make Him known to the world. Will suffer, will live the life of Christ among men. Assist me by Thy grace. I ask Thee for the love of Christ, the love that makes the cross an object of desire. I ask Thee for the confidence of men, let Thy life live itself in me, my God, from now until Thy desire is wrought in and through me. In His name, amen.

—Moody's Memorial, February 2, 1900,
Moody Church, Chicago, Ill.

Kenyon deeply loved and respected Moody. I'm sure he identified with and considered himself—in his own way—among Moody's warriors.

In the next chapter, we will examine Kenyon's entrance into the life of faith, inspired by another of his heroes, George Müller.

CHAPTER 10

THE LIFE OF TRUST

What is trust? Trust is the living assurance, the quiet rest of
having believed . . . It is that quiet, restful consciousness that
"underneath are the everlasting arms," that the Word of God
cannot fail you; it is the rock on which you have built your house.
—E. W. Kenyon[1]

During the early years of Kenyon's ministry, churches raised money much differently than they do now. The pastor's salary came from pew rents and subscriptions (pledges) of giving. As a result, the wealthy and even the unsaved could have a prominent place in the service or undue influence over the church because of their giving. People also felt pressure to pledge beyond their means, and then experienced tremendous guilt if they were unable to pay.

This system troubled the Kenyons. In this state of mind Kenyon met a man named Tamil David at a Northfield conference. David was living by faith as George Müller taught, which meant that he did not ask people for money but rather trusted God to supply his needs. It is quite likely that David gave to Kenyon a copy of Müller's book, *The Life of Trust*.

Kenyon was impressed with David and invited him to preach at his church. By this time the Kenyons had accepted a call to pastor the Wellington Street Church, a Free Will Baptist church in Worcester, Massachusetts (in May 1897). David went there, and the seeds of the life of faith, or *trust* as Müller called it, were planted in the Kenyons' hearts and soon bore fruit. Evva concluded, "In many other ways God showed us His plan for us, that we were not to be hired by men to do God's work, but simply to work under His dictation and trust Him alone for support."[2]

The Kenyons felt that the Lord wanted them to stop using pew rents and pledges and trust Him entirely. George Müller, A. J. Gordon, and A. B. Simpson, to mention three, also felt the common ways of raising a salary for the pastor were unbiblical and should be discontinued. Essek and Evva believed that their commitment to the Scriptures required them to follow in the footsteps of their mentors.

In this chapter we'll examine the repercussions of the Kenyons' decision. First we'll look at George Müller and see why so many in Kenyon's day were inspired by him. Then we'll see how the life of trust caused the Kenyons to leave their church and their denomination and set out on their own. They started a church and a Bible school at this time. Kenyon was not afraid to challenge the status quo if the Word and the Spirit led him to do so.

MÜLLER'S LIFE OF TRUST

Kenyon followed the example of Müller to make one of the most impacting decisions of his life. However, Müller's influence didn't stop there. Kenyon continued to run his Bible school by Müller's principles, despite opposition.

Let's see who Müller was and how he became one of the most respected men in the church in the nineteenth century. Müller, who operated orphanages in Bristol, England, became known through his book, *The Life of Trust*, which was a record of how he trusted God to provide for his orphanages. The first American edition of *The Life Of Trust* was published in 1860 and a revised edition was produced in 1877.

The introduction to the American edition of his book gave an overview of the theological issues and practical accomplishments that Müller's life brought to light.

A single man, wholly destitute of funds, is supporting and educating seven hundred orphans, providing everything needful for their education, is in himself an extensive Bible and Tract and Missionary society, the work is daily increasing in magnitude, and the means for carrying it on are abundantly supplied, while he is connected with no particular denomination, is aided by no voluntary association, and he has asked the assistance of not a single individual. He has asked no one but God, and all his wants have been regularly supplied. In these labors of love he has, up to this present time, expended nearly a million dollars. It is thus that he has endeavored to show to an unbelieving world that God is a living God, and that he means what he has said in every one of his promises.[3]

Many of those Kenyon acknowledged as influences (Moody, Torrey, Pierson, Gordon, Simpson, Cullis) were touched by Müller's example and followed it to some degree, if not entirely.

Müller himself wrote concerning his purpose:

The chief and primary object of the work was not the temporal welfare of the children, nor even their spiritual welfare, blessed and glorious as it is, and much as, through grace, we seek after it and pray for it; but the first and primary object of the work was, to show before the world and the whole church of Christ, that even in these last evil days the living God is ready to prove Himself as the living God, by being ever willing to help, succor, comfort, and answer the prayers of those who trust in Him; so that we need not go away from Him to our fellow men, or to the ways of the world, seeing that He is both able and willing to supply us with all we can need in His service.[4]

Kenyon later made this observation about George Müller:

George Müller did more for the church than will ever be known this side of the judgment; thousands have been helped to trust the unseen Father God by his victories of faith, the writer received his first inspiration to trust by reading the life of Müller.[5]

AN EXPENSIVE DECISION

One of Kenyon's observable traits was that once he saw something to be biblical, that settled the question of whether or not to implement it. Kenyon felt the Scriptures backed up Müller and other witnesses that

God brought to the Kenyons, so they entered in to the "life of trust."

This decision was expensive for the young pastoral couple. They became convinced that not only should they stop receiving a salary, but also that the church should trust God for its expenses, including the money they needed to pay off the debt on the auditorium the church was building. The Kenyons said that collection baskets should be discontinued and a box by the door substituted. At this time they believed this was the only biblical way to receive offerings.

The Kenyons felt they had to make changes because, as Evva wrote, "God had, previous to this, led us to accept the Bible literally." The church in Worcester, unfortunately, did not think this was the best course. So, feeling he had no other choice, Essek turned in his resignation May 1, 1898. Apparently, the denomination supported the church and not the Kenyons, because Kenyon severed connection with the Free Will Baptists as well. The Kenyons stepped out in "naked faith" to follow the Lord.[6]

As in their acceptance of divine healing, the Kenyons were compelled by the Word of God and confirming witnesses God brought into their lives to "follow the cloud." Evva reported, "God pushed us into a life of faith. We had to do as we did or incur God's displeasure. It was God's way for us, and in walking His way we walked out of the denomination. We had no other reason at that time for coming out."[7]

Kenyon left the Free Will Baptists because of his desire to live by faith. He wanted his finances—both personal and church-related— placed in the hands of the Lord. The fact that Evva stated, "We had no other reason at that time for coming out," indicates that in 1901 they still agreed with at least the majority of the movement's doctrines.

Kenyon was apparently well thought of in the movement at the time of his departure. Only a few months before his departure he preached the conference sermon for the February 16, 1898, meeting of the Massachusetts Association of Free Baptists.[8]

THE NEW MINISTRY

At this point the Kenyons did not know where they were headed. All they knew was that God had called them to trust Him for their support. "One thing we were sure of, that God wished to prove to us, and the people, that He could support us financially without resorting to man's methods," Evva reported.[9]

The Kenyons desired to leave Worcester because they did not want to seem to be in opposition to the church from which they had resigned. After some successful meetings in the South, they asked the Lord to let them go south and work among the "colored" people, but the Lord "withheld His consent."[10] Another option the Kenyons considered was joining with Frank Sandford. Evva reported, "We had met and loved brother Sandford and thought perhaps we might go and help him, but God said our place was not Shiloh [a Christian community Sandford established]."[11]

Frank W. Sandford (1862–1948) was a celebrated healing evangelist who was ordained by the Free Will Baptists.[12] Kenyon shared his passion for souls and his belief that signs and wonders were needed to bring people to salvation. Though Sandford was orthodox and well-respected at this point in the Kenyons' lives, he later fell into delusion. He came to believe he was the Elijah that was to come (as did John Alexander Dowie. Two Elijahs in the same part of the country!).

Sandford was quite visible in New England and for a season was somewhat the "man of the hour." He preached for R. A. Torrey and A. B. Simpson and discovered divine healing listening to Simpson and Charles Cullis. A great admirer of D. L. Moody, Sandford attended Northfield conferences and fellowshiped among the same crowd as Kenyon. He had attended Emerson College of Oratory, embraced second-work-of-grace Holiness, had a Free Will Baptist background, and was a celebrated evangelist among them until he departed to found his own ministry.

One of the turning points in Sandford's life was reading Hannah Whithall Smith's *Christian's Secret of a Happy Life.* Sandford may have introduced Kenyon to Smith's writings, though this is not certain. Frank W. Sandford also embraced the life of faith and was likely a strong influence on the Kenyons for a season. Sandford was the main speaker for the Kenyon's first Bible conference after they left the denomination (in 1898).

Perhaps the Lord steered the Kenyons away from Sandford so that they would not be brought down with his error. Later Kenyon was probably disturbed when Sandford became critical of everyone who didn't share his vision, including Kenyon's heroes, Moody and Simpson. Kenyon never mentioned Sandford again after this time in 1901.

A CHURCH AND A SCHOOL

The Kenyons came to the conclusion that the Lord had closed every other door but one—that they must begin a new work in Worcester. In naked obedience, Kenyon hired a hall in the Worcester YMCA. Evva wrote:

> The services in the hall prospered. Souls were born and many covenanted to obey the Word. The YMCA hall was, in a month, over-crowded, and another place was rented for services. The money placed in the box [the Kenyons put a box in the back instead of receiving collections] paid the expenses of the meetings; that for our own needs came in various ways.[13]

It was shortly after this that the Kenyons began to incorporate divine healing into the ministry, again at the prompting of the Lord. (This was discussed in chapter 7).

As Kenyon preached in neighboring towns, young people became interested in his message and desired to study God's Word. Kenyon began a series of lectures for them in mid-August 1899. As more and more young people were drawn to the Kenyons, the question of whether to begin a Bible training school found a place in their prayers.

Kenyon felt that a farm where the students could work while they studied would be a godly way to learn responsibility and stay separate from the world. A farm was placed in their hands in the latter part of January 1900. Bethel Bible School became an established fact February 1, 1900.[14]

The Kenyons operated the school on faith, charging no tuition to the students. Their first year without salary and denomination—1899— proved to be successful. Evva reported:

> During that year, standing practically alone, amid false representation, slander and persecution, God sent to us, for our support and his work, more money than was raised by the church from which we came out. We were enabled, without salary, to support a large family of students and fellow workers, to publish tracts and a paper, to hold continuous service in Worcester, to travel almost constantly holding meetings elsewhere, and to give many dollars to missions and charitable work. In addition to that, many people

were healed from incurable diseases, and best of all, a *living God* had become a fact in our lives.[15]

Sharing her husband's burden for the lost, she said, "Even the Bible school is but a means toward one end, saving sinners. He desires it to be a place where young men will first learn to conquer themselves then go out to conquer Satan in others. A real West Point, training soldiers for Jesus."[16]

CHALLENGING THE STATUS QUO

The Kenyons openly taught divine healing and trusted God for finances. Apparently in challenging the status quo they made some enemies.

The headline of the Spencer (Mass.) *Leader* for January 13, 1900, stated:

> Followers Angry. Rev. Kenyon's Sympathizers Complain of Religious Intolerance. Efforts to Start an Assembly of Divine Healers Are Opposed.

Kenyon's teachings on the believers' privilege to receive healing and their responsibility to minister divine healing, his repudiation of salaries and fund-raising efforts, and his forsaking of denominational ties were perceived negatively by the other churches and pastors. Kenyon was in these years a fiery young preacher. He might not have been overly tactful in expressing his convictions. His sincerity is, however, unquestionable.

They experienced a major battle as they looked to God in the "life of trust" and sought Him for property for the Bible school. Kenyon wrote:

> I walked the streets an outcast in feelings; the daily papers had fought me for months; my old friends would cross the streets when they saw me coming, or dodge into a store or hallway. It seemed as though all men dreaded or hated me, they shunned me at least . . . Those were days of testing . . .
>
> I had a chance to build a church that would have given me a standing in my denomination and the Christian world. All

100

conceded me the ability to have done it, but God had another plan and *made* me follow Him; that plan meant humiliation. I say it modestly, that I question if any man and wife in New England have suffered more abuse from the public than my wife and I have for three years.[17]

Attempting to follow the Lord fully and not compromise on the Scriptures, the Kenyons found themselves persecuted and rejected by much of the church. Yet they felt strongly that the Lord's hand was in their decisions. They had seen the blessing of the Lord in the midst of the difficulties. He confirmed His Word both in healing and provision.

The foundation was laid for further developments in Kenyon's theology. Yet Kenyon cannot be understood unless due emphasis is given to the driving force in his life: evangelism. All he did was fueled by his passion to see people saved. In the next chapter we will look at the heart of E. W. Kenyon, the evangelist.

CHAPTER 11

EVANGELIST, PASTOR, AND TEACHER

What most forcibly impressed the writer about Brother Kenyon were the qualities of conviction *and* thoroughness. *He believed what he preached, and he preached what he believed.*
—Frank W. Sabean

A love for souls burned within Essek Kenyon. When he was pastoring, if a month went by without seeing someone saved he was deeply troubled and sought God to find out where the problem was. His books and periodicals, even though they contained much teaching for the believer, always appealed to the lost to receive Christ and come into the Father's family. Divine healing was also seen as a tool to win the lost. He referred to healing as God's "advertising method."

In this chapter I will try to characterize Kenyon in the roles he played as evangelist, pastor, and teacher. Many people who have read Kenyon's books have little knowledge of his personality, because Kenyon didn't write about himself very much. But by looking through old issues of his periodicals and speaking to some people who attended his church as teenagers, I was able to get a sense of the personality and presence of this talented man.

KENYON THE EVANGELIST

Kenyon's efforts as an evangelist were quite successful, and he printed reports about his crusades regularly in his periodical *Reality*. Many were saved, received the Spirit, and were healed as he circulated around New England and Canada. The local pastors where he preached often wrote their impressions of Kenyon's ministry, which were sometimes printed in *Reality*.

After Kenyon spoke at the Annual Convention for the Deepening of the Christian Life in Nova Scotia, Canada, in September of 1903, a Frank W. Sabean recorded his impressions. He wrote, "Mr. Kenyon is a young man, and we predict for him, if he walks humbly with God, a wonderful future of usefulness in the Master's vineyard. Nature has endowed him with extraordinary intelligence and strong physique to which have been added years of diligent study and training."

Commenting on Kenyon's attitude toward the Scriptures, Sabean added, "He has implicit faith in the inspiration of the Book as the immutable Word of God. The God of the Word and the Word of God are realities to him, and he has unbounded faith in both."

Kenyon was, even in his early days, a voice and not an echo. Those who heard him knew they were hearing someone who walked with God. Sabean continued, "What most forcibly impressed the writer about Brother Kenyon were the qualities of *conviction* and *thoroughness*. He believed what he preached, and he preached what he believed . . . He had evidently taken Paul's admonition to Timothy: 'Study to shew thyself approved unto God, a workman that needeth not to be ashamed, rightly dividing the word of truth' (2 Tim. 2:15)."

Sabean was convinced after his exposure to Kenyon's preaching that Kenyon was a man who "must know for himself what God taught in His Word, not what others said was truth. He evidently has the gift of teaching for, though profound, he is easily understood. His appeal was from the plain teaching of the Word of God to the intelligence of his hearers, and not a play upon the emotions." As a result of Kenyon's preaching, "men were made to clearly understand what God has to say about sin, judgment, and salvation through Christ, the results of their intelligent choice and their responsibility in making that choice."[1]

Sabean was so impressed with Kenyon that he later joined him in working at Bethel Bible School.

Years of diligent Bible study, prayer, and seeking God had put behind Kenyon the doubt and skepticism of his early days. He now preached with conviction what God had made real to him from the Scriptures. Reporting on the above convention himself, Kenyon noted, "One especially blessed feature of the work was the large number of men who accepted Christ as their Saviour."[2] Many pastors commented on the strong appeal Kenyon had to men, as well.

THE EVANGELIST'S GOALS

Kenyon had a two-fold emphasis in his evangelistic meetings—saving the lost and stirring the saints. This is illustrated by a report on the revival in Rockland, Massachusetts. After eight weeks under the "forceful, earnest preaching of Mr. Kenyon," the Rev. B. H. Lane related: "Sinners have been saved, and the whole town has been moved as it has not for years. Fifty or more have accepted Christ as their personal Savior . . . [and] Christians are taking hold of God mightily in prayer, and He is honoring their faith."[3]

Kenyon's stirring of the saints was noted in the revival in Kingston, Massachusetts, in June 1904.

> We feel that the meetings in Kingston were in many ways among the most successful of all our evangelistic efforts, not so much in the number of souls saved, as that the Lord permitted us to so witness to the town of the great doctrines of redemption that it was deeply stirred.

Throughout his life, Kenyon made it a priority to teach those in the church about the great truths of redemption. He realized that these doctrines held the key to successful Christian life. In Kingston the churches had become weak because of a lack of this teaching. The report noted:

> The spirit of Unitarianism had slowly crept into all the churches, and unconsciously the people seemed weakened in faith and apparently powerless to combat against the forces of unbelief which surrounded them.

Unitarianism is a system of doctrine that denies the Trinity and the deity of Christ. New England being a center for Unitarian influences,

Kenyon saw himself as one of the voices raised up to destroy the grip of this error over the people wherever he ministered. As a result of the Kenyon's visit to Kingston:

> A number of people accepted Christ, and many received the Holy Spirit. The chief success, however, lay in the fact that the town was moved over the evidence given proving that Jesus of Nazareth was the Christ, the very Son of God, and that no one can be saved except he be "born again."[4]

Kenyon seemed to have an ability to draw together many churches in a town and cause them to work together for the salvation of the lost. He would enter a town and begin meetings in one church, and because of the success of those meetings other pastors would want to join together with the original church. Kenyon and his team were able to move entire communities to repentance and awakening. He also called those at his school (Bethel) to the same kind of dedication and abandonment to the Lord that Kenyon himself demonstrated.

THE PERSONAL EVANGELISM COURSE

Kenyon was so focused on the need for evangelism that he prepared the Personal Evangelism Course to train others. His desire to call others to the work of evangelism and equip them is evident in the introduction to his own training material, where he wrote:

> Until soul winning becomes the business of our lives we will not lead many men from darkness to light. Soul winning is the art of arts. We should study carefully the lives and methods of the great soul winners. Get every book possible on the subject, but never neglect the Bible by being so occupied with other books . . . You want to realize that you have been engaged by the Master to do this kind of work, that your time is not your own, that every unsaved man is an opportunity.[5]

Although Kenyon wanted the Christian to enjoy the benefits of his redemption, this did not mean a complacent life of coveting blessings. "It is not enough for us to have the Word in our own lives and to be enjoying the realities of redemption," he wrote. This would be dishonoring to the Lord. Kenyon reminded the believer that "Jesus Christ would have us be channels through which He can send out a message of life and freedom already purchased and awaiting those in bondage."[6]

Kenyon insisted that the soul winner have a solid walk with the Father. "The personal worker must walk in the fullest fellowship with the Father. The person with whom he is dealing must have a consciousness of His love for him, of His desire to help him." This put responsibility on the one sharing the gospel to express the Father's love. "If a man sees you love him, are really interested in him," this will disarm him, Kenyon said, and "he opens up to you. He makes it easy for you to speak to him."[7]

E. W. Kenyon saw evangelism as the greatest drama in the world. It was essential that the child of God be moved with the same compassion as Christ. "Christ is the head of a mighty organization engaged in taking men out of the dominion of Satan and bringing them into the realm of love and life eternal. The love of Christ must dominate the actions of every person who takes part in this great work, regardless of whether they are a minister or a layman."[8] Training believers to win the lost was an important part of Kenyon's ministry from beginning to end.

A TEACHER OF THE WORD

From his earliest days of ministry, Kenyon expressed his teaching gift in the written word. In October 1898 he began *The Tabernacle Trumpet,* an eight-page monthly periodical published "in the interest of Bible study and faith in God." In February 1901 the name was changed to the *Bethel Trumpet.* Kenyon doubled the size of the publication in April 1903 and changed the name to *Reality. Reality* remained the voice of his ministry until some time in 1916.

The Father and His Family was Kenyon's first book. It was published in 1916 and gave expression to his understanding of the plan of redemption. After he moved to Southern California, Kenyon published *The Wonderful Name of Jesus* (1927). That same year he began a new periodical known as the *Kenyon Herald.* This was a four-page paper that carried teaching articles and news of Kenyon's church, which was known as the Church of the Living Word.

The *Kenyon Herald* was expanded to eight pages and renamed

Living Messages ("A magazine devoted to live issues of the day") in January 1928. The last known issue was published in 1931 after which Kenyon moved to the Seattle area. Kenyon's *Herald of Life* was born in 1935 and continued many years after Kenyon's death in 1948. It has recently been revived and is now available from Kenyon's Gospel Publishing Society.[9] Throughout his ministry Kenyon published many tracts, often containing teaching articles from his magazines that he considered useful.

Kenyon's teaching ministry through books flourished after 1935. He first revised and released his two previously published books. All his other titles were compiled and released from 1938–1945. Two books were published posthumously by the Society (edited by his daughter Ruth) in 1949 and 1955. Three correspondence courses became available in 1943. In 1943 a child evangelism course was also offered.

Because Kenyon is primarily known today through his many books, he is regarded more as a teacher than as an evangelist. Although evangelism was a primary focus with him, he also was strongly moved to teach so that believers would know their place in Christ and the truths of redemption. As we have shown previously, this motivation came out his own experience of falling away from the Lord because of a lack of instruction. Kenyon learned from his failures as well as his successes, and he wanted to spare others the pain he had endured.

RESPONSES TO HIS TEACHING

What would it have been like to sit under Kenyon's ministry? Let's look at him through the eyes of two people who attended his services—Dr. Lydia Berkey and Gordon Lindsay.

Lydia Berkey was a Pentecostal preacher who was healed of stammering as a young girl and later ordained by Aimee Semple-McPherson. She sat under the ministries of Smith Wigglesworth, Maria Woodworth-Etter, John G. Lake, and Aimee Semple-McPherson during her years in ministry. Regarding Kenyon she wrote:

> I've never been around a man as spiritual as he was, or a man who walked with God like he did . . . I learned so much from him. I never missed hearing him when he was in our area. And when he passed away, it seemed like we lost so much, because he had so

much to give. His ministry was a ministry of great compassion . . .

When he would preach, the glory of God would shine on his face until you would forget what he looked like, because you were conscious of the fact that it was Jesus manifesting himself through him. And even while he was teaching, people would be healed and set free without his even touching them. As far as I'm concerned, he's the top of my list."[10]

Gordon Lindsay was the founder of Christ for the Nations in Dallas, Texas. Lindsay made a comment about the time John G. Lake spoke at Kenyon's church. "Dr. Lake had a speaking engagement at the church pastored by Dr. E. W. Kenyon, the famous writer and author. I had the privilege of hearing this brilliant teacher." Lindsay felt that Kenyon's writings had great merit.[11] He referred to Kenyon as a "genius."

KENYON'S LOVE FOR THE WORD

After Kenyon was restored to the Lord, his brother invited him to join him in a business venture. "My brother George didn't want me to preach—he wanted me to go into business with him. But I went ahead, and one day he sat in my audience. After the service I was very anxious to know what he thought. He said, 'I guess you will make a preacher all right, but let me give you some advice—the one who helps the people is the one who knows and preaches the Word of God. You get so full of the Bible that they can punch a hole in you anywhere and you will run a stream.'" Kenyon embraced his brother's counsel.

Kenyon saturated himself in the Word. He related his dedication to preaching only the Word of God in one of his sermons. He said, "For seven years of my ministry I didn't give a single illustration outside of the Word of God because I wanted the Word to become all in all to me."[12] In 1928 Kenyon told his congregation that "a few years ago you couldn't quote a verse in the New Testament that I couldn't tell you chapter and verse."[13]

In his teaching, though he desired to be thorough in the scholarly sense of diligent study and research, Kenyon was focused on the practical application of the Word to life. Everything Kenyon taught expressed his desire to encourage believers in victorious and fruitful living. He was a thorough student of the Word and his Basic Bible

Study course gives an overview of the Old Testament that reveals a solid grasp of the whole Bible. One of his favorite teachers was the Brethren author C. H. Mackintosh, whose writings on the Pentateuch [first five books of the Bible] Kenyon read and recommended. Referring to Mackintosh's notes on Leviticus, Kenyon remarked, "Possibly the best thing that has been written on it [the Book of Leviticus] as a whole is the "Notes" by C. H. M."[14] Kenyon learned much from the Brethren—J. N. Darby and C. H. Mackintosh in particular.

Kenyon expressed his desire to teach and train others in a statement he made in 1928. He said, "If I were a young man I believe I would set myself to the establishing of a school here on the [West] coast. An academy, college, or university where men that believe in this Book which is the foundation of our civilization—the foundation of our government and the foundation of the laws of our land, would have first place." In the same message just quoted, he went on to say, "After twenty-five or thirty years of intensive Bible study I have reached this place in my mental processes where I absolutely know this is a divine Book."[15]

PASTOR KENYON

By the time Kenyon assumed the pastorate of his church in Los Angeles, he had pastored off and on for many years. Always a hard worker, he got up every morning between four and five and worked until late in the evening. Constantly writing, studying, and meditating on the Word, he prepared diligently for each service. Seeing people saved, healed, and receiving the Holy Spirit brought him continuous delight. He designed his services to accomplish these goals.

The churches he pastored were always training centers to equip the saints. He was most happy when his congregation took hold of his message and ran with it. He gushed with delight in his later years when he reported that he had no more to give to some of those he had trained, because he had already given them all that he had received from God.

Ministers who knew him personally had good things to say about him. One commented on his "loving, fatherly way" in which he dealt with people. This same minister also said Kenyon was "in many ways . . . a great man of God."[16] Another minister for whom Kenyon preached described him as "a very pleasant, fatherly person" who "stands out as a very gentle and kindly man."[17] In his later years in Seattle when his ministry was centered in a downtown bank building, he was known to all the merchants and people working on the streets. Kenyon addressed them all by name.

In his Northwest years the church he pastored reflected his maturing emphasis on love. His message of faith truly became a message of faith working by love (Gal. 5:6). The slogan for the church was "Where Love Reigns and God Is Real." Kenyon was remembered as a man who never spoke a critical word about anyone. He said there was too much work to do to waste time being critical of others. He was always encouraging and looking for the best in people.

I was able to contact a number of people who had been in the youth group at Kenyon's church in Seattle. They gave some fascinating insights into Kenyon's personality and ministry. In the Sunday morning service, Kenyon would have one of the youth get up and give a five-to-seven-minute message to the congregation. When the young person was finished Kenyon would get up and praise the message saying, "Wasn't that wonderful?" He would then, in a supportive and encouraging way, take up the theme that had been brought forth in the brief message and elaborate on it for about ten minutes. The result of this would affirm the revelation the young person had shared and also instruct them on how to further develop the subject. The young people were greatly encouraged to keep digging and study more.

Kenyon gave the entire Sunday evening service to the youth. They did everything from leading worship to teaching the Word. His desire to train and release ministry through others was clearly exhibited in his giving opportunity to the youth. If "The Doctor" (as they called him) saw any potential that could be developed in any of the young men or women, he would encourage them to study, take lessons, or in some way cultivate their gifts. This was especially true if he saw potential in the ministry of the Word.

Everyone in the congregation was encouraged to get the American Revised Version of the Bible, which Kenyon used, and follow along closely as he taught. "Now, remember that," or, "Now, don't forget that," he often exhorted. A charismatic, dynamic, and dramatic speaker, he captivated his audience with his clear, articulate prose. One who heard him many times noted that The Doctor gave his listeners the impression they were hearing a well-educated man.

His usual attire for preaching was a double-breasted suit, unbuttoned, with a vest underneath. As he preached, he would come out from behind the pulpit and, grasping his Bible in his left hand and pointing the index finger of his right hand at the people, grip his congregation with the intensity of his gaze. As he preached he often dramatically used the back of his hand to toss back the wave of unruly hair that would fall across his forehead. He held them spellbound.

Although Kenyon was intense there was such love in his countenance and message that his powerful preaching wasn't intimidating. People saw beyond the man into the heart of the Jesus Kenyon proclaimed. As he unveiled the great truths of redemption, they came alive in the hearts of his listeners. Many, many lives were transformed. People were set free from sin, sickness, and depression. Broken homes, families, and hearts all found healing and encouragement. The victory of the resurrection was translated into the circumstances of life for those who sat under E. W. Kenyon's inspiring ministry.

Many of those who looked back on their years at the church commented on the sense of community and fellowship that was among them. One commented, "The scripture, 'behold, how they love one another' was truly demonstrated in their midst." Another said the "hallmark" of the church was love. Divine healing was preached, and there were many testimonies given to miraculous recovery, yet, one commented, the teaching on healing was "not to the extreme that you couldn't go to the doctor." Yet healing was strongly emphasized. Kenyon and many of those he trained frequently went into the homes of sick people who contacted the ministry and prayed for them. Many came to the church as a result of being healed.

One of the men I contacted, who later worked with Billy Graham, remembered how his family came into contact with The Doctor. His mother had severe arthritis that kept her from doing work around the house. One day (he was 13 at the time) he heard his mother downstairs scream out. He went downstairs to find out what had happened only to discover that his mother, while listening to Kenyon on the radio, had been healed of her arthritis. The family eventually became great supporters of the church and The Doctor.

Kenyon was a very loving father to his daughter Ruth and son Essek. Some said he spoiled them a bit, but he was very generous and gave them all he could. He lived by faith all his life and was never a wealthy man. His grandchildren were very fond of him, and he was delighted with them. His daughter-in-law Jerry Kenyon said he was extremely kind and tender in all his dealings with the family. She considered him a very loving man. And of course, his daughter Ruth, who carried on the ministry after his death, was devoted to him. Dale Simmons, who interacted much with Ruth while studying her father, commented that her tender devotion to her father "is something any parent would covet."[18]

Although his writings are bold and outspoken, personally Kenyon was not desirous of constantly being center stage. One who walked with him for many years said that if you walked into a room of people with Kenyon among them, it would be unlikely that you would pick him out as a preacher or leader. When not ministering, he was quiet and retiring. E. W. Kenyon did, however, have a good sense of humor and liked a good story. His laugh was described as "delightful."

A BOLD DEFENDER OF ORTHODOXY

E. W. Kenyon could be quite bold and outspoken if he felt the occasion required it. He told a story from his early days when the controversy over Modernism raged in New England. The Modernists were liberals who wanted the church to get "back to Jesus." What this really meant was getting back to the moral teachings of Jesus without His deity or the supernatural and away from the teachings of Paul, whom, they insisted, had "perverted" the teachings of Christ and made this Christian religion out of his ideas.

Kenyon was in evangelistic work in northern Maine when the state secretary of the Baptist Association met him on the train one day. Kenyon had noticed him in meetings in various places, as this gentleman traveled constantly and made it a point to hear Kenyon when possible. He was a very suave and cultured gentleman, Kenyon reported, and he dropped down into the seat next to Essek. Then he spoke and said, "Brother Kenyon, I have been listening to you lately and been reading your articles in your magazine."

Kenyon said, "yes."

He continued, "You have a wonderful personality."

At this point Kenyon knew "he was getting ready to swallow me, because he was not the kind of man to give me a compliment."

The secretary went on, "Mr. Kenyon, if you will give up your notions of the first three chapters of Genesis, your Johanian theology

[theology derived from the apostle John's writings], and your Pauline theology [derived from the apostle Paul's writings], I will open all the large churches to you."

Kenyon replied, "Doctor, if I should give up what I believe about Genesis, the gospel of John, and Paul's revelation, I would be as useless and powerless as you are."[19]

Suffice it to say the secretary didn't open any doors for Kenyon!

A VORACIOUS READER

As is obvious from the tremendous amount of documentable influences in the formation of Kenyon's theology, he read many, many books.[20] He said, "Just give me the Bible and some good books written by godly men, and let me get alone for an hour to meditate and pray. There is where God reveals Himself to me. As I wait there before Him, in quiet and meditation, things unfold, His glorious truths are opened to me."[21]

Essek was interested in what others were saying and how their ideas related to the gospel. He also enjoyed poetry and classical literature. At one period in his life he read Homer's *Iliad* and the *Odyssey* every year. As a young boy he read the Stoic philosophers, whom he felt contributed to his personal determination to never quit. When he was converted, he channeled that determination toward pleasing God, winning the lost, and becoming an educator. He would attribute his success to the grace of God, however, not Stoic philosophy. Essek also read and enjoyed Shakespeare very much.

Kenyon read many authors with whom he disagreed. While he was studying the mind of Jesus for his book on the deity of Christ, he investigated the writings of many supposedly great intellects of the day. He examined the writings of the champion of atheism of the day, Robert Ingersoll. He read Huxley, Spencer, and Darwin—all defenders of the theory of evolution. Spencer's definition of God, Kenyon remarked, "is an absolute absurdity. There are two distinct contradictions in his own statement."[22]

He examined Confucius and said that intellectually "he labors and struggles." Jesus, Kenyon said, "speaks as God. All other men argue." He examined the "masterly arguments" of Daniel Webster, whom he considered to be "the second or third great intellect of America." He read Jonathan Edwards, whom he considered to be the greatest intellect in America's history.

Kenyon read Oswald Spengler's *The Decline of the West* and was troubled by Spengler's analysis of a nation in decline and how the description fit America. He also quoted historian Will Durant in some of his sermons. He greatly enjoyed Joseph Cook's *Boston Monday Lectures.* Cook, who defended orthodox Christianity against all the "isms" of the day in the last quarter of the nineteenth century, also articulated the doctrine of the Trinity in the clearest terms, in Kenyon's opinion, of anyone he had ever heard. Kenyon also read his lectures—part of the same series mentioned above—on conscience. This series of lectures stimulated much of Kenyon's thought on the human spirit as expressed in his book *The Hidden Man.*

While he was in Southern California he published tracts refuting the metaphysical cults, quoting their own literature. He marshaled statements from their own writings and compared the statements with the gospel. Ironically, he said they presented "another Jesus," not the Jesus of Paul and John. Someone else accused Kenyon of the same thing![23]

Kenyon was very concerned about the influence of Communism on American culture. He always pointed out the superiority of the gospel and the church's responsibility to model an answer to the inferior philosophies of what Kenyon termed the "world-mind."

He was aware of the philosophy of Friedrich Nietzsche, whose thoughts later fueled the Nazi regime. Nietzsche's "superman" concepts—the supposed racial and national superiority of some people—caused Kenyon to reflect on God's "superman," the new creation man or woman who walks in the fullness of his or her redemptive rights and privileges in Christ. This was God's intended super race—men and women from all races, tongues, and tribes who matured into the image of Christ and revealed to the world the power of a supernatural gospel.

Kenyon's Praise of His Mentors

Kenyon left a tribute to one of his favorite authors that reveals some fascinating insights into Kenyon's philosophy of life. He greatly admired and appreciated the devotional writer S. D. Gordon. Gordon, (not to be confused with A. J. Gordon whom we quoted earlier in this book), wrote some twenty books, all of which were called *Quiet Talks.* Kenyon expressed his thoughts about Gordon by saying that "S. D. Gordon is a sporadic outburst of divine grace. He is unusual, as are all of God's rare tools. He is eccentric, as are all of those who walk according to the Spirit instead of reason. He will be called, on the one hand, a genius; on the other hand, unbalanced. He is unbalanced, as far as reason is concerned, but he is perfectly balanced in the Word and in the Spirit."

Continuing to express what made Gordon such a blessing to him, Kenyon added, "He is a genius in that he has beaten out a path all his own. He hasn't followed the footprints of others . . . He represents that rare but vanishing class of spiritually minded men of the last generation."[24] Kenyon then mentioned the "rare spiritual genius" of F. B. Meyer, G. Campbell Morgan, Andrew Murray, H. W. Webb-Peploe, and A. J. Gordon.

In this revealing tribute, Kenyon suggested that the need of the hour was another voice to rise up and rally God's people. "There must be a new message," he said, "an emphasis placed where it has never been before." What will this new emphasis be? "It will be Jesus. It can't be anything else. It will be the Word. There isn't anything else. It will be the Holy Spirit's ministry. We haven't any other. It will be an answer to the heart cry of hungry men and women, and this can only come as we pray."[25]

Kenyon felt deeply the spiritual peril of our nation. He felt that godly leadership for God's people was critically needed.

> This isn't a time for us to think of our own spiritual problems. It is a problem of a nation. It is a problem of the world. Every one of us have been so exercised as to our own spiritual condition that we have forgotten that there was a world need, and ours [our need] is but a symptom of that world need.

What would he think if he were alive today? He would probably have the same passion about the same issues as he did in his own time. "Only God," Kenyon wrote, "can meet that need, and He will only meet it through someone with His message for this age."

Kenyon wrote this tribute to Gordon in the late 1920s or early 1930s. Later in his life I believe Kenyon felt strongly that his "message of faith" was at least part of God's answer to that great need that he perceived. At this point, however, he hoped Gordon could provide such a message and leadership. "Pray," he exhorted his readers, "that S. D. Gordon's books will meet the heart cry of the multitude."[26]

We gain a fascinating insight into Kenyon's character in this tribute. We see his tremendous respect for those he admired and his belief in their message. We also see that Kenyon, like Gordon, chose not to "follow the footprints of others." In all the material that Kenyon wrote over his fifty-some years of ministry, S. D. Gordon is only mentioned one other time that I have found. Kenyon assimilated Gordon's teaching and restated what he absorbed in his own language. Had I not found this tribute, I would not have known of Gordon's influence or investigated Gordon's writings at all.

This brings to mind an aspect of Kenyon that is also interesting. He wanted his ministry to hold forth a pure message that pointed to the Word, not to himself. He showed this when he wrote *Jesus the Healer.* Unlike most authors writing on divine healing, especially those like Kenyon who had seen scores of people healed, he put no testimonies whatsoever in the book. He wrote the book, he said, "that people might see their deliverance in Christ from oppression and sickness, that they might see their complete redemption already purchased for them. We feel that if they were to read of the physical manifestations in others' lives, they would unconsciously look to the other person's healing and not see their own deliverance already accomplished." He concluded, "We want you to look to the Word for your healing."[27]

Near the end of my research I made another discovery of a primary influence that does not show up anywhere else in his writings. Jessie Penn-Lewis, whose writings on identification and the work of the cross I had read previously and thought were remarkably similar in many respects to Kenyon, was also very influential on Kenyon. In the *Herald of Life* in 1945, Kenyon wrote, "For many years I was entranced by the teaching of a very spiritually minded woman of England [actually she was Welsh]. Twenty-five years ago her name, among the spiritually minded of this country, was almost a household word."[28] This "woman" could only be Jessie Penn-Lewis.

Kenyon shared in the article mentioned above that he eventually abandoned his fascination with her because he felt the victory was not centered in the cross, but in the throne. It was the triumph of the Resurrection and Christ's seating at the Father's right hand, for Kenyon, that was the completed victory. "Our victory in not the victory of the cross, but it is the victory of the seated Christ," Kenyon concluded.

Yet Penn-Lewis's influence on Kenyon is quite significant. She taught much on spirit, soul, and body and the need to have the human spirit rule over soul and body. Her ideas are strikingly similar to those Kenyon expressed in his early days, reflecting her influence. A comparison of her teachings with the metaphysical cults makes clear which of the two really influenced E. W. Kenyon.

It doesn't seem as if Kenyon desired to hide his influences. On many occasions he credited those who had influenced him. He constantly read other godly authors. Yet in some cases he hardly mentioned authors (like S. D. Gordon and Jessie Penn-Lewis) who had a profound affect on him. It might be truly said that E. W. Kenyon was a voice and not an echo.

Like his mentor S. D. Gordon, E. W. Kenyon "has beaten out a path all his own."

CHAPTER 12

KENYON'S BIBLE SCHOOL

Bethel is not the place for those who put worldly knowledge, or even spiritual knowledge, before daily living the Word of God. Bethel is not the place for those who, having the theory, are content without the practice. Bethel Christianity is self-abnegation, simple and entire. We have no other to offer you, for we see no other in the Word of God.

—E. W. Kenyon, 1901[1]

Nothing illustrates Kenyon's dual emphasis on evangelism and Bible teaching as clearly as his Bible school. From roughly 1900 to 1923 Kenyon was the guiding light of Bethel Bible Institute. Both Kenyon's giftings—evangelist and teacher—were highly developed during these years.

In this chapter we'll examine his quarter century of nurturing this school, its students, and its teachers. Nearly all of the money Kenyon raised in crusades was poured into the school, which required no tuition of its students (and guaranteed no salary to its teachers!). At times the school teetered on the brink of disaster and at other times rose up to the sublime.

WHY A BIBLE SCHOOL?

Having no training in the foundational teachings of the Scriptures after his powerful conversion, Kenyon had lost out with the Lord for a few years. Therefore, Kenyon knew the necessity of grounding the new convert in the Word. He did not want to see the zeal that comes at the new birth stolen by a lack of biblical understanding.[2] "Great enthusiasm and joy comes at the new birth," Kenyon wrote, "but unless that is cared for and fed by the mind being renewed through feeding on the Word and practicing it, that joy will die out."[3]

Kenyon's Bible school grew out of his desire to see many trained to bring in the harvest of lost souls at home and overseas. Foreign and home missions had been a highly esteemed part of his life as a Free Will Baptist. Missions was also a burden Kenyon shared with Frank Sandford and Moody's warriors.

Bethel Bible Institute began with the Kenyons' practice of bringing people into their home in order to disciple them. For around twenty-three years Bethel would be the center around which Kenyon's evangelistic efforts would orbit. This was personally expensive to the Kenyons, but Essek felt it was the cost of discipleship that they had opted to pay.

> I remember distinctly when the day came for me to become a disciple; I was a preacher; it was about the time I received the Holy Spirit. [He received the Holy Spirit in February 1897.] I learned this truth, then for about a year and a half I fooled about [with] the thing. One day I found out what it meant to be a disciple. I never told any other man that he had to do it, but for me personally to be a disciple, this was what I had to do. I had to give up my own home; I had to take into my home people who did not have a home, and the privacy of my house ceased. Then I had to give my property over to other people and let them have the use of it.
>
> I remember the furniture I had purchased, and the Father only knows how hard it was for me to pay for after I began to preach for four hundred dollars a year. [Kenyon had been making about ten times that amount before he returned to the ministry.] It was no easy matter. I did not believe it was right for a sinner to be in debt, and certainly not for a Christian. I had paid for that furniture, and had paid for it out of blood money; when I saw that furniture broken up by the boys that I was taking care of, it was hard. It was like sleighing when the snow is gone.
>
> I had some dishes. If any man likes pretty china, I think I do. I had some good dishes. I had a hard fight to pay for them, and saw

the gilt washed off them. I saw them broken, one by one.

Discipleship meant business with me. Then everything else went until my library became public property. Now, it may not mean to you that you give up your home, but it may mean that your home is no longer to be yours alone, but the home of any one whom the Holy Spirit may send there.[4]

Kenyon also decided that the money he received for his ministry in evangelism would not be for his personal use. He poured the offerings from his crusades into Bethel to keep the school afloat. Many converted under his ministry would find their way to the school for training.

A FAITH WORK

E. W. Kenyon, emulating his mentors Charles Cullis and George Müller, and following his Lord, insisted that "a work of faith . . . Bethel must always be. . . ."[5] The needs of the school were not publicized, but, following the pattern of Cullis and Müller, reports of the gifts received were mentioned. Occasional requests for prayerful consideration of supporting the school were also voiced in the ministry's publications. No salaries were paid to the teachers and no tuition was required of the students. The students were asked to work on the farm to help support the school, however.

The early years of the school brought many challenges. Making ends meet was a constant fight of faith. Sometimes it looked like the good ship Bethel was going to sink. Kenyon, teachers, and students were constantly praying and looking to the Lord for provision. When times were especially tight, Kenyon would gather everyone for prayer and ask, "Do you know why the money has stopped coming?" Many times this would lead to a confession of sin from one or more of the students. When things were right spiritually, the money and provision would flow in again.[6] A demanding way to live, for sure.

The pressure of this life of faith and the necessity of Kenyon's constant traveling brought considerable strain upon his marriage. This new lifestyle was quite a change for Kenyon's wife, Evva, who had been raised in an atmosphere that had demanded little of her. Physical frailness exacerbated the problem, and at times she felt overwhelmed. As in any marriage, the stress brought forth personal issues about their relationship that needed to be resolved.

Through all this, Bethel might have remained open without interruption, but a tragic event occurred in 1902. An unstable student committed suicide by hanging himself. The press took full advantage of this event, sensationalizing the tragedy with the tasteless headline "Resident at Kenyon Bible School Swings into Eternity."[7] To make matters worse, the young man was the stepson of the family that had contributed the farm to the school, and this family was quite visible in the community.

Bethel Bible Institute had to be closed for a season (summer 1902 through summer 1904), but Kenyon persevered. The school reopened in September 1904, having received a fresh injection of life from the success of Kenyon's evangelistic ministry and the founding of the Reality Publishing Company, which enlisted many to purchase its stock. Bethel rose again to become strong and influential. Kenyon fought the good fight of faith, and his determination paid off. His burden to see young people trained and released was not extinguished.

THE VISION FOR BETHEL

Kenyon articulated his vision for Bethel Bible Institute in a 1912 article titled, "Concerning the Opening of the Bible School," Kenyon declared:

> We believe that the Father has made it possible for us to give the best preparation for evangelistic, pastoral, and mission work of any school with which we are acquainted. This is not saying aught in disparagement of any other school.
>
> We desire our friends to lay our school, its teachers, and all its helpers daily before the Lord; also praying that the spirit of evangelism and a real cry for the lost shall be upon every one connected with this work.
>
> The one yearning of our hearts above everything else is that there shall be such a consciousness of God in this place that every student will have an abiding sense of His presence. We want them to be touched by a peculiar energy that will make them absolutely restless for souls.
>
> Oh, for companies of young men and women who will go out, abandoned to God, utterly careless of what men say or think of

> them, utterly indifferent as to whether they receive money or not
> as long as they can see souls saved and Christians built up in the
> knowledge of the Truth.[8]

It would be hard to find a better statement of the passion of E. W.
Kenyon's heart—the evangelist and teacher.

In 1912 Kenyon wrote, "The faith fight is so different from any
other fight that only those who have fought its battles can really understand it, only those who have seen its victories can tell its joys or know
its mighty tests." Kenyon felt the school existed only to show the
reality of God and His faithfulness, emulating Müller's passion.
Kenyon wrote, "Bethel stands alone amid the hundreds of schools in
the land, as an institution that wishes and purposes to live the New
Testament, to read and then practice what it reads, to profess then practice it, to live the Word of God, to act out the principles of the sermon
on the mount."

This vision was certainly idealistic, and Kenyon was aware that they
fell short of the mark. "We do not do it yet," he admitted, "but we are
aiming at the mark of the high calling. Bethel has but one reason for
existence, when she surrenders that she has no ground for longer life
among the schools of the land, that is, to show forth the reality of God
in daily life."[9]

The life of faith, the life of total abandonment to God and His Word,
was the foundation of the school and all that Kenyon exemplified. God
as a Father, Jesus as Lord, and the Holy Spirit as an indwelling Person
were for Kenyon the *realities* he called others to know and experience.

SPIRITUAL LIFE AT BETHEL

Although Kenyon was frequently out on evangelistic trips, he greatly
enjoyed the time he could spend at Bethel with the students. Seeking
God together and studying the Scriptures were a part of the spiritual
life of Bethel. Kenyon reported having a few exceptionally brilliant
students with whom he sometimes studied into the early hours of the
morning, searching out a deeper understanding of the truths of
redemption.

Kenyon boasted of one young man who "possessed a keen, legal
intellect, and he would come blazing out with many new truths" as
they searched the Scriptures. Unafraid to investigate the truths of

redemption from different perspectives, Kenyon shared, "We just broke loose from the old orthodox fields of thought into liberty and freedom and saw a mighty drama in which God and Jesus were the chief actors. Satan was the bad actor."[10]

What did Kenyon mean by saying he broke loose from the "orthodox field"? Did Kenyon and his students leave orthodox teachings and wander into metaphysics? Hardly. Rather, they were rejoicing in scriptural truth that much of the church had forgotten. It was the drama of Christ's death and victorious resurrection that gripped Kenyon and his students.

> We saw it step by step. We saw the Man hanging in defeat on the cross, carrying out the demands of justice. We saw Him go down into hell bearing the torments of the damned until all hell shouted with glee. But out of the depths He arose and stood triumphant over death, hell, and the grave.
>
> Brethren, talk about dramas! Sinai—Calvary—here is no drama equal to the Great Resurrection Day.[11]

Kenyon, teachers, and students fellowshiped around the Word in the time not consumed by their rigorous schedules. Kenyon and the students loved these rich seasons of digging into the Word and seeking to understand the mysteries of the Scriptures, particularly Paul's revelation.

THE MIRACULOUS AT BETHEL

Times of dramatic manifestation of God's healing power also touched the students when Kenyon was ministering. On one occasion, among those attending a meeting at the school, there were about thirty young people who wore glasses. God's healing power so came and confirmed the Word Kenyon was preaching that after the meeting Kenyon reported "not one of them could use the glasses."[12]

Kenyon reported a "series of continual manifestations of divine power" at Bethel. "We have seen some blessed cases of healing instantaneously, the power of sickness broken suddenly, pain and inflammation and fever instantly leave the body," he testified. "A few cases have been stubborn," he admitted, "requiring battle again and again, but permanent deliverance came."[13]

One time they had almost no flour left and sixty people to feed. When Kenyon heard this from Mother Shelton, who did the cooking, he responded, "We will just have to trust the Lord." She kept taking flour out of the barrel until there was enough to feed all sixty!

On another occasion during a snowy season they ran out of coal at Bethel. "There was no coal in the bin. God filled it. It was snowing and there were no tracks in the snow. We knew it was from God. He never leaves tracks."[14]

PRAYER AT BETHEL

Because they were dependent on the Lord for all their needs, all those connected with the school were highly motivated toward prayer. Prayer took a central place at Bethel among the teachers as well as the students. Kenyon observed, "Bethel has a striking history; our students learn to pray long before they can preach. We feel that Bethel's prayer life is recorded in heaven. It is true that many of our students are stronger on their knees than on their feet."

"Bethel . . . was born in prayer and has been maintained by prayer. Its great battles are prayer battles; its great victories are victories won on bended knee." The environment at Bethel necessitated a life of prayer. "Here, young men and women learn to depend on God. Every barrel of flour and piece of meat comes in answer to prayer; to lower the standard means to go hungry."[15] No answered prayer, no food!

Aside from provision for their needs, a major prayer emphasis at Bethel was to petition God for a great revival in America. In 1903 Kenyon reported "a National Convocation for Prayer under the auspices of what is known as the 'Modern Holiness movement.'" The convocation was to "covenant together to cry out to God day and night, for more of the spirit of prayer and supplication and intercession for the accomplishment of His will in this respect, and to be greatly used of God in bringing about a deep, thorough, and general revival of pure and undefiled religion." S. B. Shaw of Chicago, a leader in the Holiness movement, was overseeing this effort.[16] Kenyon supported all efforts toward intercession for revival.

TEACHERS AT BETHEL

The teaching staff at Bethel all felt a calling to lay down their lives for the kingdom of God. Kenyon mused on this in an article titled "Trial of Faith."

> Think of it, these teachers come here without a salary or a promise of a dollar for their work. They are in the prime of their life, have all given up fine positions, simply because the love of the Christ has gripped them. They count it the greatest work in the world to fit men for the ministry, so they are glad that He counts them worthy to fill such an exalted office.[17]

The fact that these teachers would give up good positions and come to Bethel is an indication of the dramatic effect of Kenyon's ministry on those who heard him and came to know him. His proclamation of the finished work of Christ (more about this later) gripped many highly trained individuals with its fresh presentation of the plan of redemption. To rally around Kenyon was to rally around his message. Let's look at some of the people who joined with him at Bethel.

In 1907 a long-time friend of Kenyon's, Francis Bernauer, accepted the position of president of Bethel, which he held for two years. Bernauer had attended Emerson College of Oratory with Kenyon and had considerable academic credentials. Bernauer held a B.A. from the University of Rochester and a B.D. from Rochester Theological Seminary.

Bernauer embraced Kenyon's understanding of the finished work of Christ, and they traveled and taught together during these years. Their work was so successful that Bernauer eventually resigned in order to pastor the many converts their work together had gathered in the Chicago area.

Bernauer wrote one of the two forewords to the original edition of *The Father and His Family* in 1916, expressing his admiration for Kenyon and his belief that if the truths contained in that book had been widely seminated a few years earlier, Christian Science and other metaphysical cults could never have found such a ready audience.

During the years of Bernauer's presidency, Kenyon also traveled widely by himself, and his success in evangelism brought the school into prosperity and needed stability. When visiting the West Coast, Kenyon investigated the blossoming Pentecostal movement and interacted with some of the leaders. (More about this later.)

For seven years (1904–1911), the principal of Bethel was Amy C.

Ridge, a graduate of A. J. Gordon's Missionary Training School. She also taught synthetic Bible courses. The pastor of the Spencer Baptist Church, Matthew Francis, was on the faculty. His brother James A. Francis was the pastor of the Clarendon Street Baptist church, a position that had been held by A. J. Gordon until his death.

J. H. Hartman became the vice-president of Bethel in 1912. He enjoyed a relationship with Kenyon previous to assuming this position. During the summers, Hartman taught at A. B. Simpson's Nyack Summer School in New York. In 1915 Hartman accepted a position as the principal of Boydton Institute in Boydton, Virginia. Charles Cullis, father of the Faith-Cure movement, had founded the school, which after his death had come under the control of the Education Committee of the Board of the Christian and Missionary Alliance.[18]

Many other men and women were part of the staff at Bethel over the years. Most of them were well educated and well qualified to instruct the students both in spirituality and academics.

KENYON RESIGNS

In the early 1920s the school needed more room to accommodate its student body. Kenyon, the staff, and students had been praying for a new location. They took an opportunity to move from Spencer to Dudley, Massachusetts, and lease Nichols Academy, which allowed for needed expansion. The school's name was changed to Dudley Bible Institute and successfully relocated. While Kenyon considered this opportunity an answer to prayer, he was troubled that many desired to abandon the life of faith on which the school had been established.

According to Kenyon's daughter Ruth, a problem arose regarding the financial operation of the school. Kenyon had insisted that the school should always be run after the model of George Müller and Charles Cullis, without tuition or salaries. But the trustees and teachers decided to pay salaries and charge tuition. So in April 1924 Kenyon officially resigned from his superintendency. According to the local paper his resignation was accepted with deep regret, and the trustees immediately voted Essek W. Kenyon president emeritus of the Dudley Bible Institute.[19]

WHATEVER HAPPENED TO BETHEL BIBLE INSTITUTE?

After Kenyon's resignation, Crawford O. Smith was elected president. Smith resigned in February 1925, and Paul Rader was unanimously voted in as president. Rader had succeeded A. B. Simpson as president of the Christian and Missionary Alliance and had been the pastor of the Moody Tabernacle.[20] In September 1926 Howard W. Ferrin succeeded Rader as president.

In 1929 the school was moved to Providence, Rhode Island, and the name changed to Providence Bible Institute. Eventually it became known as Barrington College. The school kept its doors open for decades. To continue its story, let me recount a letter that was received by Kenyon's daughter, Ruth, in February 1966. It was from a Leonard E. Smith at Barrington College. At that time he was the assistant-to-the-president and regional representative in New England.

> I doubt very much if you will remember me, so let me introduce myself. I am Leonard E. Smith, an alumnus of the class of '24 and one of the original five that went from Bethel Bible Institute in Spencer, Massachusetts, to Dudley to take over the Conant property . . .
>
> . . . I am writing for certain information preparatory to the writing of the history of the school. We need to know certain facts concerning your dear father, whose portrait, done in oil, now hangs in the reception hall in the main building of the college.
>
> Your father was without exception the greatest Bible expositor I have ever heard, and I've heard some good ones. He left us all a golden heritage of a life well lived and a ministry that was constructive in every way.[21]

Smith's letter gives us a feel for the attitude that the students had for E. W. Kenyon. The letter was written more than forty years after his association with Kenyon.

Sixty years after Kenyon's resignation, another poignant event occurred in relation to the college he founded. In October 1984 plans were announced to merge Barrington College with Gordon College, which was founded by one of Kenyon's mentors, A. J. Gordon. In September 1985 the merger between Barrington and Gordon was completed, and classes began on the campus of Wenham, Massachusetts,

127

and continue to this day. A history written for the centennial celebration of Gordon College included a chapter on Bethel and Kenyon's founding work.

We shall see in a later chapter that the vision for a Bible school never left Kenyon. In his later years he would again start a school known as the Seattle Bible Institute. It is sweetly ironic that Kenyon's beloved Bethel should eventually marry Gordon College, the school begun by one of Kenyon's most important mentors.

CHAPTER 13

PENTECOSTALISM

I cannot see that those with tongues have any more power in testimony or preaching than many Spirit-indwelt people I know. But the joy that comes into the soul and the ecstasy that thrills it is worth the effort that some seem to display to get the gift. Of course there is a wave of fanaticism following the real gift.
—E. W. Kenyon, May 1907[1]

There is somewhat of a mystery surrounding Kenyon's relationship to the Pentecostal movement. While his writings have been embraced by Pentecostals and charismatics more than any other segment of the body of Christ, Kenyon's opinion of the Pentecostal movement has been questioned. Did he embrace it or reject it?

In this chapter we'll see that Kenyon was very open to the Pentecostal movement, because he was anticipating a worldwide revival. His initial exposure to tongues included a visit to Azusa Street, and he became a friend and influence on many Pentecostal leaders, including William Durham, Finis Yoakum, and Maria Woodworth-Etter. Kenyon's teaching on sanctification had a major effect on the Pentecostal movement. At the end of his life he could clearly articulate where he agreed and disagreed with the Pentecostals.

ANTICIPATION OF REVIVAL

At the time the Pentecostal movement was forming, E. W. Kenyon was

129

looking for, praying for, and expecting a great revival. Kenyon kept in touch with what God was doing around the world through the various Holiness and Higher Life periodicals that were abundant in those days. There are articles and quotes from many of these periodicals in *Reality.*[2]

As he learned of areas where revival broke out, he eagerly examined them and reported them to the readers of *Reality.* In March 1905 *Reality* carried a report of revival in Wales and England and a call to prayer for revival in America.

> In view of the remarkable work of grace going on under Dr. Torrey in England, and the mighty awakening in all parts of Wales, it would seem that the worldwide revival which has been prayed for so long has really begun.
>
> Already we are encouraged that our prayers are being answered as we hear of the work in Denver and Schenectady and in other places in the West. But as yet we see no general awakening in New England.
>
> We invite all the readers of *Reality* to join the Bethel Prayer Circle in praying that during this year the work so graciously begun in England and Wales may sweep over our States.[3]

Kenyon saw evidence that worldwide revival was manifesting in various locations around the globe. Seven months later in the November issue of *Reality* he indicated that the prayers of Bethel were evidencing revival power in his own meetings in Maine.

> The mighty awakening in Wales is another manifestation of the Spirit's power. The work that has been going on in Aroostook County, Maine, is yet another example of the loosing of God's power among people.
>
> What a need there is that men lay themselves prostrate before God and plead for the outpouring of the Holy Spirit.[4]

Kenyon's excitement bubbles through the pages of his periodical. He was longing for America to experience a revival. His evangelistic burden, which motivated all that Kenyon did, was thrilled with the thought a great outpouring of the Spirit.[5]

Kenyon encountered this awaited outpouring and discovered it was accompanied by a manifestation he had not previously seen–the gift of tongues.

KENYON AND THE GIFT OF TONGUES

In May 1907 Kenyon held a series of meetings in Chicago where he saw many who had experienced the Pentecostal infilling and were speaking in tongues. In an article entitled *The Gift of Tongues,* he asked, "Has the gift of tongues been restored to the church?" That question, Kenyon related, "confronted the editor [Kenyon] several months ago. For years he has been looking for it, felt that it would be [restored] before the Lord returns . . ."

Kenyon went on to describe the meetings in Chicago where he saw many people speak in tongues. "They all praise God and Jesus. I never heard sweeter praise in my life. Sometimes they sing in an unknown tongue, several at a time, a real heavenly chorus." Kenyon observed that the Rev. William Durham of Chicago "seems to represent the highest and most scriptural type I have met, so far, among the leaders . . . "

Essek acknowledged that what he witnessed in Chicago was the real gift of tongues restored to the church. He then encouraged his readers to seek the Lord and "see if this gift is for you; if it is, seek it."[6] Kenyon had seen fanaticism about receiving the Holy Spirit at some of the Holiness meetings, but he had also seen the opposite—spiritual dryness—in other parts of the church. So he wrote, "Of course there is a wave of fanaticism following the real gift." But he concluded, "There are dangers in it, but no greater than the danger of dying of dry rot as most Christians are doing now."[7]

Kenyon, while looking for and desirous of an outpouring of the Spirit, was drawn to Durham because he, like Kenyon, insisted that everything be soundly scriptural. Kenyon was delighted to see tongues restored but was wary of experience not held in balance by the Word.

Another preacher living in Chicago at this time may also have influenced Kenyon positively about tongues—F. F. Bosworth. Bosworth worked with John Alexander Dowie for many years before entering into a very successful divine healing ministry. He embraced Pentecostalism in meetings with Pentecostal pioneer Charles Parham in Chicago in September 1906.[8]

With a little detective work we can determine that Bosworth may have told Kenyon about his Pentecostal experience. According to Kenyon's daughter Ruth, Kenyon met Bosworth and Dowie during a trip to Chicago. Dowie died in early 1907, so the meeting had to have taken place earlier than Kenyon's crusade in Chicago in May 1907. It is possible that Bosworth and Kenyon renewed their acquaintance in May 1907, and Bosworth could have told Kenyon about his recent Pentecostal experience.

Bosworth would become a controversial figure among Pentecostals due to his quiet withdrawal from the Assemblies of God in 1918. He could not endorse the initial evidence doctrine. He did not believe that speaking in tongues was the *only* evidence that one was baptized in the Holy Spirit, although he received tongues when he was baptized in the Spirit under Parham's ministry. He and Kenyon proved to be like-minded on this issue. They were already extremely like-minded on healing and faith.

KENYON VISITS THE AZUSA STREET REVIVAL

Let's look closer at what attracted Kenyon to William Durham and how their relationship developed. Just two months before Kenyon met him in Chicago, Durham had visited Los Angeles and received the Pentecostal experience.[9] Durham later became a key figure in the theological development of the Pentecostal movement.

A pastor who visited Durham's North Avenue Mission made this observation:

> The glory of God filled the place. Brother Durham rose to preach, but was unable to begin his sermon. He himself was so under the power of God, he could scarcely speak in the English language. Messages in tongues and interpretation [came] by Sister Aimee Semple-McPherson. I was spellbound and took hold at once.[10]

Another wrote that at times "a thick haze . . . like blue smoke" filled the upper region of the sanctuary. The people entering the building "would fall down in the aisles. Some never got to sit in the pews. Many came through to the baptism or received divine healing."[11]

E. W. Kenyon, his spiritual appetite apparently whetted by his contact with Durham and those experiencing the Pentecostal blessing, arranged a trip to Los Angeles in 1908 where he visited the revival in

Los Angeles at Azusa Street. While in Los Angeles he met and prayed with George B. Studd. Studd (1859–1945), who was the brother of the famous C. T. Studd who gave up a career as a star cricket player in England to give his life to mission work in China.

George Studd, who helped build Peniel Hall (a Holiness church in Los Angeles), had accepted the Pentecostal message by 1907. Studd taught daily, five days a week, at the Upper Room Mission in Los Angeles as well as frequenting the Azusa Street meetings. Studd's diary, which is preserved from these years, speaks of Kenyon. (The original is in the Assembly of God Archives in Springfield, Missouri.)

> May 11, 1908: Very good prayer meetings at Mrs. Hupp's—Rev. Morrill and Coleman were present—at night to Mrs. Hopkison to meet Evangelist E. Kenyon.
>
> May 13—. . . Essek Kenyon came to see me—had a good visit and prayer.
>
> May 14—Another visit from E. Kenyon—God is dealing with him.
>
> May 15—Yet another visit and prayer with Kenyon in the morning.

Clearly, Kenyon desired to receive anything fresh from God. He had been looking for the restoration of tongues and through William Durham and his own observations knew it to be of God.

Did he receive tongues at this time? It isn't completely clear. He encouraged the readers of *Reality* to seek God and find out if tongues was for them. Surely he followed his own counsel. We do know that either at this time or sometime later Kenyon did speak in tongues.

The strongest evidence that Kenyon actually spoke in tongues is his application for credentials with the Assemblies of God. On the application the question is asked, "Do you speak in tongues?" In Kenyon's unmistakable handwriting is written "yes." He would later, for reasons we will discuss, downplay tongues and Pentecostalism. But E. W. Kenyon definitely spoke in tongues and identified himself with the Pentecostal movement to some degree, at least.

KENYON'S INFLUENCE ON PENTECOSTALISM

Few people realize that Kenyon's teaching dramatically shaped the developing Pentecostal movement. Kenyon's ideas entered into Pentecostal circles through William Durham. In 1908 Kenyon spent an extended time in the Chicago area holding tent meetings and probably developing further his relationship with Durham. Articles from Durham's periodical *The Pentecostal Testimony* began appearing in *Reality.* While in Chicago Kenyon taught on the finished work of Christ. Durham was apparently gripped by Kenyon's teaching and made a dramatic shift in his own teaching about sanctification.

Durham wrote a series of articles in *The Pentecostal Testimony* on the biblical reasons why he had rejected the second-work-of-grace teaching and embraced the finished-work concept. The teaching is strikingly similar to Kenyon's. Durham objected strongly to reducing regeneration to the forgiveness of sins—which was one of Kenyon's strongest objections to second-work-of-grace teaching as well.

Durham first publicly declared his acceptance of the finished work of Christ teaching at a Pentecostal convention in Chicago in 1910. Incidentally, this was the same convention where Aimee Semple-McPherson was healed. The following year Durham took the message to Los Angeles amid much controversy. Durham wrote concerning Peter's preaching on the day of Pentecost:

> He preached the finished work of Christ which brought men into a place that they could be filled with the Holy Spirit. He did not teach, as men are teaching today, that men are partly saved in conversion, and that it takes a second work of grace to complete the job.
>
> It seems to me that when a man is born again is when his nature is changed . . . In conversion both the state and nature of a man is changed. In conversion a man is changed from a state of sin to a state of righteousness. He is made a new creature, not partly new. He is changed from a state of condemnation and death to a state of life and peace. He is changed from a state of sin and uncleanness to a state of purity and holiness, from a child of Satan to a child of God. Conversion is the great experience that works a complete change in the life of a man.[12]

Shortly after Durham began to teach "the finished work," he resigned, moved to Los Angeles, and pioneered a work there emphasizing the finished-work teaching. Kenyon acknowledged Durham's actions in the April 1912 edition of *Reality*.

> One of the brightest signs of the times is the new movement that
> is breaking out in the West among the Pentecostal people, begin-
> ning with Brother Durham, formerly of North Avenue, Chicago,
> who is now in Los Angeles, and which is now rapidly spreading
> through the northwest. These brethren have always held to the
> Wesleyan second-work-of-grace theory, but recently they have
> seen the finished work of Christ.
>
> It has revolutionized their ministry. The writer can't tell how
> happy he is to see the new light that is breaking in upon them.
> With characteristic zeal and fiery eloquence, with voice and pen
> they are assailing the old dogmas.
>
> We trust that they will go on, and not only accept these first
> principles, but come to understand the deeper nature of the suffer-
> ings of Christ, the teachings of the blood covenant, and a clear
> conception of the family teaching of the Scriptures, giving the
> Father His rightful place.[13]

Kenyon saw Durham as having embraced the rudiments of the revelation that God had given to Kenyon. He hoped that Durham and the
other Pentecostal leaders who embraced the finished-work teaching
would press on to see the other revelations that Kenyon was teaching.
In Durham's case, we will never know if he would have or not. Just a
couple months later, Durham died of pneumonia.

Dale Simmons, a researcher who appears to be the first to note
Kenyon's influence on Durham and therefore on the Pentecostal movement in general, stated, "The fact that Durham's presentation of the
finished-work teaching is virtually identical to Kenyon's offers com-
pelling evidence that Durham's 'truly unique' presentation of
sanctification was indeed taken from E. W. Kenyon."[14] Durham is nor-
mally cited as the source of the "revolutionary" teaching on the
finished-work of Christ that so impacted the young Pentecostal movement, creating its first major split. The finished-work teaching spread
like wildfire through the Pentecostal movement, eventually become
the dominant view of sanctification. Durham was considered the
source, but in reality (no pun intended) it was E. W. Kenyon who lit the
fire.

KENYON'S PENTECOSTAL FRIENDS

Kenyon associated with and preached for many other notable Pentecostal figures in the years to follow. The next year, as the finished-work teaching he had proclaimed swept through the Pentecostal movement, he ministered with another Pentecostal minister and close friend of Carrie Judd Montgomery's, Dr. Finis E. Yoakum.

Yoakum (1851–1920) was a medical doctor who discovered divine healing when he was prayed for by Missionary Alliance leader W. C. Stevens in 1895 and experienced a remarkable recovery. Shortly after his healing Yoakum had a vision of opening a mission for the needy. He built a tabernacle in Arroyo Seco between Los Angeles and Pasadena where he carried out his vision.

While in the Los Angeles area, he associated with Holiness churches, frequently speaking on divine healing at their camp meetings and annual gatherings. When the Azusa Street revival broke out he visited the mission. He, however, had spoken in tongues as early as 1902, and wrote of his continuing experience in 1911.[15] Yoakum called his center *Pisgah.*

In 1907 Yoakum began to travel and minister to a wider circle. In the summer of 1912, Kenyon ministered with Yoakum at Montwait, Syracuse, Schenectady, and Boston.[16] After Kenyon moved to the West Coast, he would minister for Yoakum at Pisgah. In an unpublished sermon, Kenyon reported getting to his hotel at four o'clock in the afternoon after having preached at Pisgah.[17] Kenyon also quoted Yoakum in the later publication *The Kenyon Herald,* referring to him as though his readers would no doubt know of Yoakum.

Carrie Judd Montgomery credited Yoakum's prayer for her as greatly helping her recovery when the enemy attacked her body early in 1911.[18] George and Carrie Judd Montgomery were among a group of Pentecostal believers in divine healing with whom Kenyon fellowshiped closely after he moved to the West Coast. These relationships will be examined in a later chapter.

In August 1913 Kenyon became involved in a now-famous arrest of the noted Pentecostal evangelist and minister of divine healing, Maria (pronounced muh-RI-uh) Woodworth-Etter. Kenyon attended and supported a series of her meetings in Montwait, Massachusetts. Reporters from Boston (twenty miles away) came and took photos of all the people "slain in the Spirit." People heard the reports and a great revival broke out. Many miracles of healing were reported and testified to.

Mrs. Woodworth-Etter and two of her co-laborers, Earl W. Clark and Cyrus B. Fockler, were arrested and charged with obtaining money under false pretenses. They were accused of hypnotizing the people. The trial lasted for four days, and about thirty-five witnesses testified of their remarkable healings and blessings and to the falsity of the claims against the defendants. The judge ruled in favor of Woodworth-Etter and company.[19]

Among the many witnesses called to testify on behalf of Mrs. Woodworth-Etter was a "professor in a theological school," one E. W. Kenyon! Responding to the charge that Mrs. Woodworth-Etter was practicing hypnotism, the *Boston Globe* reported, "E. W. Kenyon of Spencer, professor in a theological school, said he did not believe hypnotism has been practiced at Montwait. He said hypnotism is condemned by the Bible and that, in his belief, the leaders at Montwait depended on God for their healings.[20]

The *Framingham Daily Tribune* reported that "Mr. Kenyon, Spencer, Massachusetts, principal of a theological school testified that he had attended several meetings and had sat upon the platform but never had sat in the chair provided for patients. Had often attended camp meetings, but never had seen a exhibition of hypnotism but understood something of it." When Kenyon was cross examined he testified, "Hypnotism as we understand it from a Biblical point of view is condemned by the Bible. It is not a work of God, and for that reason is not practiced by these people at Montwait." Kenyon added that he "had heard healers at Montwait publicly deny on the platform that hypnotism was used on them."[21]

Kenyon's association with Mrs. Woodworth-Etter was another relationship with one who, like Kenyon, was contending for an empowered Christianity that reflected the New Testament vision. Mrs. Woodworth-Etter had held meetings the previous year in Dallas, Texas, with another acquaintance of Kenyon's, F. F. Bosworth (who had relocated from Chicago). Mr. and Mrs. Montgomery had attended the Dallas meetings as well. Carrie Judd reported their power and success in her *Triumphs of Faith.*

Although Kenyon disdained any overemphasis on experience that undervalued the Word, he had no tension with Pentecostalism per se. He would continue his associations with any who contended for miraculous Christianity that was thoroughly biblical. As the Pentecostal movement progressed, however, Kenyon became more and more unhappy with the emphasis on tongues and experiences. For him this was a repeat of what he had observed among the Holiness people. Kenyon's message of faith emphasized the objective truth of the Word of God while embracing any and all biblically warranted experience. But the Word must always be first, Kenyon insisted.

Kenyon's Matured Views on the Holy Spirit

In 1940 Kenyon reflected on his own journey regarding the Holy Spirit. "So many religious teachers have built a wall about the Holy Spirit and about the sweet experiences of His indwelling that it has confused most of us," he lamented. "For years I sought the Spirit. I read every book I could find about Him." But the more he read, Kenyon shared, the more confused he became. "One told me that if He came in there would be great physical manifestations, that unless I had these manifestations (and they were all physical, of sense evidence) I could not be sure I had received the Holy Spirit." (Remember, Kenyon is reminiscing back to 1896–1897 when he was under the influence of the Holiness movement).

After a Sunday of frustrating labor among God's people that seemed to him to be all in vain, he turned in despair to Luke 11:13: "How much more will your heavenly Father give the Holy Spirit to them that ask him?" In his desperate state he "simply asked Him to give me the Holy Spirit. When I did, He came in. He did not come in to display Himself. He did not come in to entertain people with physical manifestations. He came into my body to unveil the Father and the Son."

Kenyon often met people who testified to a great experience and resulting manifestations. Yet he observed that they weren't intimate with the Father and didn't know the realities of their redemption. He said that the Holy Spirit came "to guide me into the reality of the redemptive work of Christ," not for outward display. Kenyon's appreciation of the Spirit's ministry was profound. "All these years," he said, "He has been functioning in my body. It is He who has unveiled Jesus in such a marvelous manner. It is He who has taken the things of the Father and made them realities in my life and ministry."[22]

Kenyon had watched with interest the birthing of the Pentecostal movement. He recognized it as a true move of God, yet he had learned

138

his lessons well in regard to the danger of walking and living by experiences and not the Word. He contended that the Holy Spirit had come to unveil the Father and the Son and to reveal our great redemption so we could grow up into the image of Christ. This would mean a real walk in love. The outpouring of unselfish giving was the greatest miracle of the Day of Pentecost in Kenyon's sight—the tremendous love that gripped the hearts of the early church. He observed, "The principle manifestations on the day of Pentecost was *love*. It is the love that we have lost." He went on to describe the Pentecostal movement. "There was a great outpouring of the Holy Spirit twenty-five years ago [writing in 1937], all up and down the Coast and through the East, and the thing that marked it was love."

"After awhile love died out, and all that was left was speaking in tongues in the assembly. They could speak in tongues and interpret, but love was gone."[23] Kenyon went on to share his observation that it was the love in the early Pentecostal outpouring that had attracted the hungry-hearted men and women in the denominational churches who rushed to them when the revival first started. Kenyon told his readers that in his early days he had thought that great knowledge would take the place of love, that if he could know the Bible as few men knew it, then he would have power. But he had come to the conclusion that the only way to maintain God's power was to seek love, and the Holy Spirit would lead us to know Jesus in reality, because He is love and the source of love.[24]

So in his later years Kenyon downplayed the importance of speaking in tongues. He was never against speaking in tongues any more than he was against true manifestations of the Spirit. But Kenyon knew we were to live by faith in God's Word, with or without confirming manifestations. He would leave the manifestations with God, enjoy them when they came, but trust only in God's written Word. This was his message of faith. His view was,

> There is a genuine speaking in tongues from the Holy Spirit. But speaking in tongues is not the evidence of having received the Holy Spirit. The evidence is the Word of God.

CHAPTER 14

TRIUMPH AND TRAGEDY IN SOUTHERN CALIFORNIA

Mountains and valleys, one after another, have all worked together to make the teacher [Kenyon] what he is today.[1]

Kenyon decided to move his base of operations from Massachusetts to Southern California in 1923. The reasons for this were probably many, but the burgeoning Pentecostal movement and its receptivity to Kenyon's message on the finished work of Christ seemed to be a large factor. Another factor was his resignation from the presidency of Bethel Bible Institute due to his disappointment with the direction the school had taken (see chapter 12.)

Kenyon's years in Southern California were some of the most productive years of his life. He pastored a number of churches, founded the church that would represent his vision and gifts most clearly, wrote his second book, *The Wonderful Name of Jesus,* and developed relationships with many Pentecostal leaders, especially those who taught divine healing. He encountered the cults in Los Angeles just as he had in New England and taught against them. His time in California ended with his divorce in 1930. Let's look at these years in detail.

STARTING OUT IN CALIFORNIA

Kenyon began his years on the West Coast by holding a series of meetings in San Jose. He eventually settled in Oakland where he lived until 1925. In Oakland he spent much time with a couple who were extremely like-minded: George and Carrie Judd Montgomery. It is not clear whether Kenyon had met the Montgomerys on one of their trips back East where Carrie ministered in Christian Missionary Alliance conferences for A. B. Simpson or if their association began in Oakland. Carrie must have known of Kenyon as early as 1914, because she published one of his articles in her magazine. At any rate, this was a close friendship, and Kenyon felt particularly close with George. He mentioned attending conferences and sitting with "my great friend George."[2]

The Montgomerys were part of a network of ministries Kenyon would move among while in California—Dr. Finis Yoakum, Maria Woodworth-Etter, F. F. Bosworth, Aimee Semple-McPherson, Lillian B. Yeomans, Cornelia Nuzum, and a host of others. Kenyon preached for many Pentecostals in the area, including McPherson. Another notable teacher at McPherson's church was the British healing evangelist Smith Wigglesworth, who preached to a capacity crowd.[3] Wigglesworth, who taught faith and divine healing much like Kenyon, was close friends with the Montgomerys and may have met Kenyon during one of his trips to California.

Kenyon preached many different places throughout Southern California. These included

- Glad Tidings Temple and Bible Institute in San Francisco, led by Assemblies of God pastor Robert J. Craig. It was a thriving ministry by 1920.[4]
- A crusade in San Jose, October 1925. In a notebook Kenyon recorded the expenses and offerings for what appears to be about three weeks of meetings. The notebook does not indicate where the meetings were held, however. One of his messages during this crusade was "The Place of Miracles in Christianity."
- Bethel Temple in Los Angeles, for at least five weeks in December 1925–January 1926. The church was pastored by George Eldridge (1847–1930), a former Methodist pastor who received the Pentecostal experience at the Azusa Street revival.

Kenyon apparently was fond of Eldridge and Bethel Temple, according to the texts of the many sermons he preached there. Eldridge was enthusiastic about Kenyon and his message and paid for many newspaper advertisements for his meetings at Bethel. An ad in the *Los Angeles Times* on January 2, 1926, read:

> A Great Day Sunday. A treat to hear Dr. E. W. Kenyon, of Massachusetts, for years a Baptist clergyman; 25 years President Bible Training School; a great man with a great message. Bring your Bible, but don't come unless you can come again, once will never satisfy. He is speaking Sunday, Jan. 3, at 11 A.M., 3 P.M., and 7 P.M., also every day next week except Monday, at 11 A.M. and 7 P.M. at Bethel Temple.

The church continued to run notices of Kenyon's meetings. On January 9, 1926, the ad read: "New Oil Well Discovered in Los Angeles. A gusher of love is Dr. E. W. Kenyon of Massachusetts, hear him on Sunday." Kenyon preached that Sunday at 11 A.M., 3 P.M. and 7:30 P.M.. His messages were "Psalm 23," "The Need of the Holy Spirit," and "Why Jesus Is a Perfect Saviour."[5]

Kenyon apparently felt he wasn't keeping busy enough, however. In between the meetings at Bethel he spoke at least one morning for Dr. Finis Yoakum at Pisgah![6]

A new fact recently came to light regarding Kenyon's time in California. He is listed in the Oakland telephone directory for 1925 as the pastor of Plymouth Congregational Church, but little is known about this church or Kenyon's time there.[7]

KENYON'S RECEPTION IN LOS ANGELES

E. W. Kenyon's ministry was warmly received in Southern California. Many pastors and preachers came out to hear this "gusher of love." A respected local pastor who had been associated with A. B. Simpson's ministry on the East Coast, a Dr. Frederic Farr, attended some of Kenyon's meetings. Undoubtedly Kenyon was greatly encouraged when Dr. Farr, then the pastor of Calvary Baptist Church in Los Angeles commented on the meetings at Bethel, "Mr. Kenyon, these five weeks have made the profoundest impression upon theologians and Christians of Los Angeles of anything that has happened in all the twelve years I have been here."[8] Kenyon said he was moved to tears.[9]

Dr. Farr was probably taken by Kenyon's frankness. Speaking in a noted Assemblies of God church, Kenyon was quite outspoken about the weaknesses of the Pentecostal movement.

> Why did you come out of other denominations? Because you wanted to get rid of some things. Then I beseech of you to leave off more things, and don't take them on into this move. They don't belong to this movement.
>
> I have a conviction that there will rise up under this teaching [Kenyon was teaching on the authority of the name of Jesus] a new kind of faith, and there will rise up men and women who are not bound by false conceptions of Jesus and faith and prayer, a new order of things, and men and women will walk right out in Pentecostal power and do the things that Jesus did. This is a mighty job I have got, but you men and women have to follow on to know the deep things of God and get ready for these things, and your graveclothes will drop off, and you will stand in the power of the risen Christ.[10]

We see, in the above quote, Kenyon's vision and hope for the Pentecostal movement. He also seemed to feel that the message that God had given him—his message of faith—was the needed thing to keep the young movement from missing God's best and becoming sidetracked.

In another message at the same church he grieved over the pitiable condition of the major denominations and told his listeners that the theological schools were turning out skeptics and unbelieving ministers. Seminary attendance destroyed the faith of many young men, he complained.

> Dwight L. Moody saw it, and the Bible schools sprung up, and out of the Pentecostal movement Pentecostal Bible Schools sprung up; but they had not the real standard [of education that old theological schools held before they became liberal] and decided that they were a kind of makeshift, and there are men rising up and saying we don't want educated men. God never filled the mouth of an ignorant, lazy man yet, and never will. God fills the mouth of a man that is willing to dig, and pray, and study,

143

and who will walk with Him . . . You can't have a mind too trained for God to use.

It will be the greatest miracle that ever happened if we can have a professional evangelism. There are two things that will bring it to pass. First, a type of preachers that will bring together a company of people really trained in the Word of God; and second, that there come to them [the lost] the Word of God, absolutely showing them the condition of the sinner and his position as a sinner. The Pentecostal people are being honeycombed with false teaching, the New Issue, New Thought, etc., which teachings release all the forces of the air.[11]

In light of all the criticism of Kenyon, isn't it ironic he was concerned that *New Thought* was infiltrating the *Pentecostal* movement! He also mentioned the New Issue, which was the teaching known as *Oneness* or *Jesus Only.* Kenyon defended the trinitarian view of the Godhead. Kenyon maintained that New Thought and the New Issue opened the church to the forces of darkness (which he called the "forces of the air").

These were strong statements to make at one of the leading Assemblies of God churches in Southern California, yet the message was well received by the Assemblies leaders in Southern California. Since Kenyon offered an analysis of the Pentecostal movement, it appears that he felt he was a part of this new move of God.

While Kenyon lived in Oakland (1923–1925) he made application to the Assemblies of God for licensing. On his application he indicated that he could accept and endorse the statement of fundamental truths, which included the distinctive of the denomination: speaking in tongues as the initial evidence of the receiving of the Holy Spirit. In answer to the question, "Have you an experimental knowledge of salvation and the baptism of the Holy Spirit with speaking in tongues?" Kenyon wrote "yes."[12] Yet for reasons we will now discuss, Kenyon decided not to follow up this application.

THE FUTURE OF THE PENTECOSTAL MOVEMENT

While living in Los Angeles, Kenyon developed a relationship with John G. Lake (1870–1935), the legendary missionary to Africa who had established a dramatic healing ministry in Spokane, Washington.

144

Lake spoke at least once at Kenyon's church in 1927. (He was accompanied by Gordon Lindsay, who later founded Christ for the Nations in Dallas, Texas.)

Lake, who was originally a Methodist and had experienced a definite second work of grace in sanctification, embraced the revelation that God had given to Kenyon. Lake's son-in-law, Wilford Reidt, reported that Lake's favorite book other than the Bible was Kenyon's *The Father and His Family.*[13] An examination of Lake's writings will reveal that his theology is basically Kenyon's theology.

Both Lake and Kenyon took part in 1927 in some informal gatherings of Pentecostal leaders who were concerned about the direction the movement was taking. Lake wrote a letter to Charles Parham, who was considered to be the main spokesman for the Pentecostal movement. His letter reveals the concerns that probably contributed to Kenyon's withdrawing his application to the Assemblies of God.

> What I am anxious to talk over with you is your vision of the future of the Pentecostal movement; and whether any of us have sufficient light from God to know what His purpose is for this hour . . .
>
> While at San Diego, I was in the habit of meeting with a few of the brethren in Los Angeles, Dr. Kenyon, Cannon, Wallace, myself, and others. We would get together once in a while and talk things over. We did not discuss just the interests of the Pentecostal movement only, but whether or not there was anything that a group of sane men could do that would be of real value to the Christian institution. The consensus of opinion was that what the Christian world is suffering for more than anything else is a lack of the ideal of Christianity. The world does not know what real Christianity is. Pentecost[alism] should have exemplified it. In that, it has failed in my judgment about 93 percent. However, it has done this much: It has demonstrated that there is such a thing as the baptism of the Holy Ghost. That men may enter into God if they will. That some have to a slight degree.[14]

Lake went on in this letter to voice his disappointment with the institutionalization and denominalization of the Pentecostal movement and its various expressions. He then related how thirty years of strenuous ministry had necessitated him slowing way down and that for three years he had been moving at a "snail's pace." But, he said:

> The thing has wrought a marvel in me. With the quiet and semi-rest, even though forced upon me, there has come an expanding vision, and a profound conviction that somehow if this is real Pentecost there must come out of it eventually the thing that Pentecost produced in the early church, and that was the real body of Christ . . . a group of Holy Ghost baptized souls in which dwell and through which is manifest the life of the Lord.

As his letter demonstrates, Lake shared with Kenyon a desire to proclaim and demonstrate what he termed the "ideal" of Christianity—Christ really seen in the lives of men. A Christianity with demonstrable power to heal and deliver. Apparently many Pentecostal leaders were concerned that the original power of the Pentecostal outpouring was waning and being channeled into denominational structures.

I think this answers the question as to why Kenyon did not follow up on his application to the Assemblies of God. Many of his good friends were in that movement, but Kenyon (and Lake) seemed to feel that the Pentecostal movement in general (including the Assemblies of God) was heading away from the place God wanted it to go: showing forth a demonstration of the power and glory of the early church.

Kenyon was a man of uncompromising vision. The churches he previously pastored either let him preach and practice everything he saw in the Bible, or Kenyon handed in his resignation. Kenyon must have soberly weighed whether the Pentecostal movement was going to become bogged down in denominationalism or not and then decided it was safest for him to remain independent.

KENYON'S CHURCH IN LOS ANGELES

Following the death of his first wife Evva in 1914 from an undisclosed illness, Kenyon married Alice M. Whitney in November 1914. Essek Jr. was born in 1916, and Ruth followed in 1918.[15] Sometime in 1926 Kenyon, his wife Alice, and his two young children moved to Los Angeles. Soon he founded a nondenominational church there. The *Los Angeles Examiner* for September 27, 1926, reported:

> They have no church organization; they have no church building.

They have numbers and faith and enthusiasm—this congregation of a few months under the leadership of Dr. Essek W. Kenyon . . . Soon it will move into still larger quarters and will become, undoubtedly within the near future, one of the leading interdenominational churches of Los Angeles.

Dr. Kenyon, a Baptist clergyman, has had a long and worthy career as a Bible teacher and full-gospel preacher. For twenty-five years he was at the head of the Bethel Bible Institute in Spencer, Massachusetts . . . Such men as Dr. A. Gordon MacLennan, pastor of "The John Wanamaker Church" in Philadelphia, and Jaen Buijse, the well-known missionary to Africa, have been numbered among his students . . . Dr. Kenyon conducted a service yesterday morning which was remarkable I thought in its spirit of genuine consecration.

In this article the church is referred to as Immanuel Church. In a publication produced by Kenyon's ministry in 1929, known as *Living Messages,* the beginnings of the work are shared with the readers:

A small group of folks who were sincerely desirous of reaching into the deeper things of God happened to come in contact with Dr. Kenyon during one of his campaigns in this city. These few attracted others until at last they succeeded in getting Dr. Kenyon to adopt them as a permanent family.[16]

By October 1927 the name had been changed to *The Church of the Living Word,* and a publication was instituted known as the *Kenyon Herald.* In an article entitled "What We Believe," we have a sketch of the church's doctrinal position. This article gives an excellent synopsis of Kenyon's fundamental beliefs.

If a creed should be written, and we go on walking with the Lord, it would have to be left open at the top, and on all sides, that new thoughts might be added as the Lord opened the Word . . .
We stand for the whole Bible as the whole revelation of God in Christ, and that what God revealed in Christ is every true believer's heritage.
We believe in the finished work of Christ.
We believe in the Holy Spirit, and His indwelling presence.
We believe in the gifts of the Holy Spirit.

We believe that healing is for us.

We believe that the miracles of the Book of Acts are to be perpetuated.

We believe in the new kind of love that Jesus brought to be the law of
the brethren and we believe that we are to walk in that love . . .

We believe in the great commission . . .

We believe in the second coming of our Lord.[17]

The church also eventually published a concise booklet of their declaration of faith. In it, the question of tongues was addressed more specifically. It states, "We believe that speaking in tongues, when God-given, is a legitimate and visible evidence of the indwelling of the Holy Spirit, but we encourage believers to look for and earnestly desire the Holy Spirit rather than to watch for manifestations and signs."[18]

Two things might be noted here. First, Kenyon does not say that tongues are *the* evidence of the indwelling Holy Spirit, rather he says *a legitimate and visible* evidence. He had backed away from the Assemblies of God position. Second, for the church to accept tongues as a legitimate gift would immediately classify them as Pentecostal. In later years Kenyon identified less with the Pentecostals, but in this period in Southern California he was comfortable with Pentecostalism.

Within a year the church had found a location with a large seating capacity which they weren't filling yet but were hopeful they soon would. "Our auditorium provides a seating capacity of seventeen hundred. Needless to say, we have not yet filled the building, but each week sees us growing to that end."[19]

By November 1927 a decision was made to identify themselves as Baptists. Kenyon's only ordination had been among the Free Will Baptists. He was always comfortable with the basic doctrines of the Baptists and although not rejecting tongues or Pentecostalism in general, he may have been moving away from his identification with Pentecostals.

> Last Wednesday night we organized an Independent Baptist Church, feeling that there were many people in the city who longed for a church organized on sane and scriptural lines, where the deep teachings of the Word as well as the simple Gospel of Salvation was taught.[20]

The new name of the church was Figueroa Baptist Church. This name reflected the new location at Ninth and Figueroa streets in Los Angeles. Although using the name *Baptist,* the church was actually unaffiliated with an organization.

Essek liked to keep busy for God. A man of untiring zeal, he soon developed a rigorous schedule of teaching and preaching. A Sunday school class at 9:30 A.M., main service at 11 A.M., a teaching service at 2:30 P.M.and an evening address at 7 P.M. Tuesdays at 10 A.M., he taught on divine healing, Wednesday evenings after a lecture on soul-winning by one of the other brothers, Kenyon led the prayer meeting. Fridays featured a 7 P.M. lecture on soul-winning followed by expository teaching through Leviticus. The series was called "Seeing Christ Anew in the Book of Leviticus."

Kenyon's burden for equipping the flock for evangelism and establishing them in the Scriptures was well expressed at Figueroa Baptist Church. An examination of the program for summer of 1928 demonstrates his commitment to this vision.

> The Tuesday night class was finishing up an exposition of the first eight chapters of Romans. Next will be taken up the Book of Ephesians. Two classes on Wednesday night, one in expression; the art of telling the truth beautifully and effectively . . . the art of public speaking; the art of personal contact . . . [reflecting his time at Emerson].[21]
>
> The second period is a study in homiletics: how to lead meetings; how to make Jesus attractive; how to prepare a message; how to lead a song service, a testimony meeting, or a prayer meeting; and, how to become a soul winner. On Fridays, the pastor is giving a series of addresses on the neglected teachings of the Word.

Kenyon's writings major on the revelation given to the apostle Paul. He felt strongly that the neglect of Paul's teachings had opened the door to the metaphysical cults. Kenyon maintained that the spiritual vacuum in the church, which the cults had sought to fill, would be satisfied if believers understood and entered into Paul's revelation. Whenever Kenyon pastored, however, he always taught through various books of the Bible. Kenyon felt that expository preaching and teaching was a great safeguard against error. While he definitely encouraged people to meditate deeply on Paul's revelation, he felt that his congregations and his Bible school students needed a thorough grasp of the whole Bible.

Kenyon also began his radio ministry during these years. In 1930 he began broadcasting regularly over KNX in Los Angeles every Tuesday and Friday morning at eight. The messages were recorded and rebroadcast on stations throughout the country. His newsletter grew from a four-page leaflet to a very nicely done fifty-page magazine.[22]

ADDRESSING THE CULTS

Kenyon had observed the rise of the metaphysical cults in New England. He had sought to teach a New Testament Christianity that would establish believers solidly in Christ and keep them from the seductive power of these cults. When he moved to Southern California, however, he found the metaphysical cults flourishing, especially Christian Science. This undoubtedly troubled him. Unity, which was more an expression of New Thought than Christian Science, was also quite popular. Kenyon saw signs that New Thought was invading Pentecostalism and this concerned him.

Kenyon felt that these metaphysical cults represented a most serious threat to the church. His opening article in the *Living Messages* for February 1928 was entitled "Is God a Person?". He began, "The church is passing through a crisis of which the great body of Christian people are ignorant." Kenyon, having witnessed the effect of these cults in New England, was not ignorant. He shared with his readers that there was "a wide-spread theory, sponsored by enthusiastic propagandists, that is absolutely destroying the church; that is capturing many of the finest intellects of the day" and this "new propaganda holds as its basic principle that God is not a person."

Kenyon proceeded to quote a Unity author who insisted that God is a principle and not a person. Kenyon showed the folly of this belief and then exposed the underpinnings of this error.

> Their declarations of belief in the substitutionary sacrifice of Jesus are absolutely misleading. They have used the language of the Bible to express an error more deadly to faith and life than has ever been expressed in words . . . They take the language of the Bible to clothe that which the Bible absolutely refutes from

Genesis 1:1 to the close of Revelation.

God is Person.

This religion is in the final analysis, simple and pure worship of *"self."* It is exalting man to the place of God.[23]

What stronger language could one use to condemn these cults? Self worship that exalts man to the place of God—that is Kenyon's appraisal of these metaphysical groups. Hardly very sympathetic! It is interesting in the light of these statements made by Kenyon, to note the similarity between Kenyon's assessment of the cults and Kenyon's critics' assessment of him! As I have stated from the beginning of this book, Kenyon was not sympathetic to the cults and considered them to be a demonic seduction of the church.

The next article in that issue of *Living Messages* was "God Is a Person." Kenyon considered these articles important enough to publish them as tracts and make them available to his readership. Continuing in this vein, his lead article the next month was even more hard-hitting. It was called "Another Jesus." In it, Kenyon informed his readers that:

There are several Jesus' today whose advocates are challenging us to worship. The Jesus of the various cults has very little resemblance to the Jesus of the apostle Paul.

There is the Jesus of Unity, who did not have a pre-existence as a person; who was not conceived of the Holy Spirit, though he was born of the virgin Mary. He did not die an actual physical death, and his soul and spirit did not go into the place of anguish, a suffering for our sins. He didn't satisfy the claims of justice and did not set man right with God on the ground of justice. He is not the Lord Jesus Christ of whom Paul tells us. He is a metaphysical Jesus . . .

The Jesus of Christian Science is practically identical with the Jesus of Unity. They have emasculated Him. They have taken away my Lord, and have given me a philosophical lithograph in His place.

The Unitarian has a Jesus, but He is not the Jesus of John, or Matthew or Mark or Luke. He is not the Jesus of the apostle Paul. He is the Jesus of the unregenerate human mind. They begat him in their own counsel. They created their Jesus themselves. He had no beginning, and when Unitarianism is done there will be no future for their Jesus.[24]

These articles, written some thirty-five years after Kenyon's time in Boston, condemn Christian Science, Unity (which is basically New Thought), and Unitarianism. These are three teachings toward which Kenyon was supposedly sympathetic due to his time in Boston.

In another unpublished sermon Kenyon complained that the denominational churches lacked any real message for the hour and suggested that the cults had sought to fill this void with teachings that were the "products of the natural hearts, seeking release from the burdens."

> They have sought by a system of humanly evolved philosophies to negate disease and say that it isn't. They seek to negate pain and say that it isn't. They seek to negate Satan and say that he isn't. They seek to negate evil and deny its very presence.
>
> In order to do it, their philosophy demanded that they should negate God and say that He is not, that He is but a principle, and that every man is the fountain of God, and that the only real God is in man. This glorifies man in his ignorance, but it doesn't solve the problem.
>
> Disease is! Tuberculosis is! Cancers are! Pneumonia is still slaying one-tenth of those who die.[25]

Ironically, one researcher suggests that "the cultic elements" in Kenyon's teachings "grew considerably in his later writings."[26] But Kenyon actually became more outspoken against these heresies in his later years (1930s–1940s). Kenyon indicted the cults for promoting an atheistic religion of "self," yet Kenyon's critics seek to charge him with the same thing!

PERSONAL TRAGEDY

Kenyon was pastoring a successful church of over a thousand members, enjoying the fruit of a respected radio ministry. His two books were selling well, and he was publishing a popular teaching periodical known as the *Living Messages*. He seemed to be at the height of his career. There was, however, tragedy just ahead.

A business meeting was held at the Figueroa Independent Baptist Church on Wednesday evening, November 19, 1930. At this meeting Kenyon offered his resignation as pastor. It was accepted with "much regret and reluctance, but feeling it is God's will that he enter a larger field of service." Kenyon was designated pastor emeritus, and it was resolved, "We have the utmost love, confidence, and trust in Dr. Kenyon as a true and faithful preacher of the blessed Gospel of our Lord and Saviour Jesus Christ, and also as a true man of God, a faithful friend, father, husband, and loyal citizen."

They further resolved, "We cheerfully recommend Dr. Kenyon to all Assemblies and churches who need a faithful, fearless Spirit-filled man of God to assist them in special services, or in any other Christian capacity, or to bring them the deeper teachings of God's Word."

There was also a note in the same bulletin from the supply pastor who is not named, but was most likely George Hunter. Hunter was a Bethel graduate and had preached for Kenyon at Figueroa on occasion. He lived in the area, overseeing the Scofield Correspondence Course for the Bible Institute of Los Angeles (BIOLA). It read:

This church has been having an unusual ministry under the leadership of Dr. E. W. Kenyon. No man that we know of has such a gift as a teacher. We all wonder at him, but let us remember the price he has had to pay.

I have seen Dr. Kenyon suffer as few men have suffered.

During those early days at the Bible School, the things I saw him pass through are almost unbelievable. I saw him suffer persecution from brethren. I remember the early struggles against false teachings. I saw him suffer financial loss and misunderstanding. I saw the work of false friends. I saw those he helped, turn traitor. I knew of heartaches unknown to the crowds. Then I saw sickness and death come and take his mate [she died in 1914]. I stood at the graveside with him. I saw men rob him of all that he had labored for. Lies, abuse, and insults were heaped upon him, and in the midst of it all he walked like a king, and God gave him victory in his soul.

I have also seen him enjoy happy days and prosperity, without losing his head.

I remember the high spots in his life; when a great Bible School was in full swing; when evangelistic tours were winning thousands; when the country was praising him; when he again took a bride to himself and had a happy home; when he enjoyed the love of a great body of young ministers whom he had trained.

Mountains and valleys, one after another, have all worked

together to make the teacher what he is today.
Are we also willing to pay such a price?
After all, it is worthwhile. Isn't it?[27]

This glowing tribute may have been addressing an issue that was about to become public. Kenyon's wife, Alice, would, in less than three weeks from the time of his resignation, file divorce charges against Essek, accusing him of making advances toward other women. She stated that he treated her in a "cruel and inhuman" manner.

How much truth there was in the accusations is hard to say. Mrs. Kenyon's tone in the record of the trial shows a real alienation from him. Oddly, although she named a number of women toward whom she states Kenyon made advances, no one came forward to testify on Alice's behalf at the hearing.

In an article in *Living Messages* some months after the divorce he made a comment on marital relationships that probably described his relationship to Alice.

> A wife unconsciously robs herself of her privileges in her hus-
> band's life by entertaining doubts and criticism of him in her heart.
> If she criticizes him before others, she unconsciously closes her
> own life against him. She may want, she may crave fellowship with
> him, but entertaining a critical spirit has unconsciously robbed her
> of the capacity to inspire him to give his confidence to her.[28]

According to the court records, the Kenyons had been separated since June. There is no record of Kenyon appearing in court. He apparently did not respond to the accusations.

Alice believed Kenyon was obtaining "great sums of money" through his ministry. After investigation the court found that he did not make the amount of money she claimed he did, and rewarded her less than she had asked.

In those days the divorce of a minister was absolutely scandalous. The newspapers "went to town" with the story. It was headline material. Kenyon, either by his own wrongdoing, by the anger of a neglected wife, or both, faced yet another season of humiliation and suffering.

I haven't found any record of Kenyon addressing the issue of his divorce directly. He continued to teach that *agape* love would never end up in the divorce court. In his own life, the ideals of his teaching clashed bitterly with the realities of human frailty, whether his own or Alice's.

In a notebook of sermons and other odds and ends from this period of his life, Kenyon left one of his poems. It read,

> Memories hold me a prisoner tonight;
> They bind me foot and hand.
> My heart is dead, my feet as lead,
> Refuse is this barren land;
> The ragged rocks in the desert of life,
> The starless gloom where hope has died,
> They hold me, they hold me tonight!
>
> I cannot die, for others this lonely way
> I must force my unwilling feet to tread.
> The light faded when her love died;
> No one sings or walks by my side.
>
> I know the High Road, I know the Low;
> I know dead griefs, under the sod;
> I know living ones, as onward we plod;
> Their only casket will be my own.
>
> —Heading North

His reputation in shambles, Kenyon left Southern California and headed for the state of Washington. He would start over again at the age of sixty-three and rebuild his life and ministry. Interestingly, his former wife soon followed him up to Washington. There is not much known about his relationship with Alice while in Washington, but her relocation to be near him speaks volumes.

In his latter years, at least, their relationship must have been cordial. He spent the last three months of his life at the home of his ex-wife and daughter Ruth. The three of them dined together regularly until the day he went home to be with the Lord.

CHAPTER 15

THE FRUITFUL NORTHWEST YEARS

God will not leave us broken there,
In failure's deadly gloom;
But mend our wrecked and shattered faith,
Once more life's hope will bloom.

—E. W. Kenyon[1]

After the crushing blow and public humiliation of his divorce in 1930, Kenyon left Los Angeles and headed to Washington state. He lived in the Northwest until his death in 1948. Down, but definitely not out, Essek entered into what were to be his most fruitful years. Kenyon proclaimed a loving and forgiving Father whose abundant mercy would meet us in any calamity. He had known the comfort of his God when he was unjustly accused in his early days. Now he came to know the comfort of God in what may have been his personal failure. Whatever the truth about his divorce may have been, Kenyon found, in his God, the courage and strength to begin again.

In 1931 Kenyon arrived in Washington. He settled first in Olympia, then in Tacoma, and finally settled permanently in Seattle. He was listed in the Tacoma phone book in 1932, and in the Seattle book by 1934.

RADIO MINISTRY

He began his radio ministry, *Kenyon's Church of the Air,* on KVI in Tacoma on October 11, 1931. Having pioneered in radio while still in Southern California, Kenyon knew it was an effective tool to reach the lost and untaught. For him to have no expression of his evangelist heart and teaching ministry would be a denial of his life breath. Radio gave vent to the vision that drove him. He was broadcasting *Kenyon's Church of the Air* on KJR in Seattle by September 5, 1933.[2]

The popular radio broadcasts won many people to the Lord, who then became interested in Kenyon's teachings. Kenyon began offering daily Bible studies through the mail to his listeners around 1935. Eventually this evolved into the Bible study courses that are still available through Kenyon's Gospel Publishing Society. They now are known as the *Basic Bible Study Course* and the *Advanced Bible Study Course.* The society also offers a *Personal Evangelism* course.

A NEW BIBLE SCHOOL

Kenyon's ministry found its feet again, and people gathered around him to learn his message of faith. In a scenario reminiscent of the past, many were requesting instruction and equipping for ministry. This, of course, struck a chord with a man who had led a Bible school for nearly twenty-five years.

In September 1935 Kenyon opened his second Bible school, the Seattle Bible Institute. The fifty enthusiastic students met in Ballard, a suburb of Seattle.[3] Three nights a week were devoted to Bible study. In the first year the school offered the following courses: Jewish History, Church History, Natural Man's Search for God, The Study of the Bible in the Light of Our Redemption, Synthetic Study of the New Testament, and Personal Evangelism. The teachers were Kenyon, Dorothy Goodman, and Lee Hofmo.

At the end of the first year the accolades from the students were impressive. Some of these students continued to work with Kenyon for many years. He obviously won their hearts. Wesley Alloway, who would become one of the associate pastors with Kenyon, wrote after his first year:

The Bible School has meant a transformation of my outlook on life and an absolutely new vision of God's eternal purposes in me . . . It has meant victory in my life where defeat reigned as king. I have been introduced into a vast storehouse of riches to which I have perfect access. I know Him in a newer, richer way through having attended this Bible School.

Jack Mitchell, who would also become part of the pastoral team in Kenyon's church in Seattle, testified after the first year:

The Bible School has completely altered the course of my life. The knowledge of the Living Word of God that I have received brought me into a relationship with my Heavenly Father that has made my life rich, full, and guarantees success. God's Word in my life has brought quiet confidence and peace that cannot be obtained by any other means.

Many other glowing testimonies of changed lives were included in the announcement of the end of the first year of studies from which these quotes are taken.[4]

A NEW PERIODICAL

Shortly after opening the institute, Kenyon began to publish a paper which he dubbed *Kenyon's Herald of Life*. This paper became quite influential, reaching into twenty thousand homes at the time of his death in 1948. It was in every state and province in the United States and Canada, in addition to fifty-seven foreign nations.[5] Many of his books were compiled from the articles first published in the *Herald*. The *Herald of Life* was literally filled with constant testimonies of dramatic healings.

Kenyon also for a season put systematic Bible studies in the *Herald* before he developed his correspondence courses. Many testimonies like the ones above from the Bible school were printed in the *Herald* as people studied with Kenyon through the mail and on the radio.

In November 1942 a new name appeared in the paper as assistant to the editor: Ruth Kenyon. From this time until her death in December 1993, Ruth would be deeply involved in her father's work. She faithfully managed Kenyon's Gospel Publishing Society and published her father's books after his death in 1948. The Society is now managed by

Bonnie Dofelmier, who worked with Ruth for twenty-five years before the latter's death.

A NEW CHURCH

Another addition to the list of new things for Kenyon in the early 1930s was a new church. It was originally called Kenyon's Church of the Air. Shortly afterwards the name was changed to the Church of the Open Door. In the *Herald* for October 1935 he invited his readers to attend services.

> How we wish you could have been with us in our services here at the church this last week. They have been utterly unusual. In almost every service there have been persons healed. Others have come into a new experience in Christ. Some have been born again. Plan to come to our Bible class and Sunday school at 10:00 on Sunday.
>
> At 11:00 our great redemption is being unveiled by the Spirit in a thrilling way.
>
> At 3 o'clock we have a healing service. These are unusual. The Spirit Himself is illuminating His own Word. Men and women are seeing their privileges as never before. Many are being healed in this service.
>
> At 6 o'clock the most unusual messages are being given by young people. These messages are making a profound effect upon old believers. They cannot understand how young people should have such a vision, such a message, such liberty in Christ.
>
> At 7:30 o'clock, which is our crowning service, we have an evangelistic service. Every Sunday evening souls are being saved.[6]

The church's name was later changed to New Covenant Baptist Church—Kenyon always thinking of himself primarily as a Baptist. By January 1940 the church boasted a membership of more than four hundred and fifty. Wesley Alloway and Jack Mitchell had been ordained to the ministry and were associate pastors. Kenyon would eventually turn the church over to these two men. Kenyon reported regarding his parishioners:

> We have now quite a large group of both men and women who are

capable of going into the pulpit and ministering in the Word. Many are going into homes and ministering to the sick . . .

Dorothy Goodman is holding evangelistic meetings in the East. Douglas Saxby and Robert Cheek have held meetings in Everett and Everson.[7]

"This [1939] has been the most outstanding year of this ministry," Kenyon gushed. Past his seventieth year, Essek was still full of excitement and fire.

NEW BOOKS

With things going well, Kenyon set about to revise and reprint his two previously published books, *Father and His Family* (1916) and *The Wonderful Name of Jesus* (1927).

In February 1937 Kenyon announced the new English edition of *The Father and His Family.* He wrote, "We are revising this book that has caused so much controversy in the past. It has gone through three editions [actually printings, not editions]. We are now enlarging it."[8] Three chapters were added and a new introduction. It came off the press in time for the July 1937 edition of the *Herald* to announce it.

During 1934 Kenyon spent considerable time dictating articles for the many books he desired to publish. After revising and printing *Father and His Family* and *The Wonderful Name of Jesus,* he put the finishing touches on some of these manuscripts.

The Two Kinds of Knowledge and *Sign Posts on the Road to Success* were made available in 1938. The former was Kenyon's statement of the distinction between what he termed *sense knowledge* and *revelation knowledge.* Kenyon, in this book, gave fresh terminology to concepts that the Faith-Cure movement had taught all along. Part of Kenyon's vision was to recapture the imagination of the church by stating in a new way truths that had lost their hold on the church. Unfortunately, some have failed to grasp his reasoning and have seen his restatements as metaphysically influenced.

Sign Posts was a series of success talks Kenyon had given over the radio that had created a demand for something in book form. Kenyon always related to men in the business world and wanted to encourage them to use their faith and the name of Jesus to succeed wherever they were called.

The first edition of *Kenyon's Living Poems* was released in 1939 and revised in 1945. Kenyon loved poetry and wrote a multitude of poems when he wasn't writing prose. There are boxes full of notes and poetry that never were published. He referred to himself during these years as "the lone poet of the Olympics."

Kenyon published his first book devoted entirely to the subject of divine healing in June 1940. *Jesus the Healer* placed healing in the light of the finished work of Christ as one of the privileges of the redeemed. It was revised and enlarged in 1943, with material on confession added.

Kenyon's books were well received judging by the response in the *Herald of Life*. Encouraged by this, Kenyon diligently compiled more of his writings. In 1941 he released the book *Identification*. This small book expounded on the believer's identification with Christ in His death, burial, and resurrection, and the implications of identification in the believer's daily walk.

Later that year another book was birthed, *The New Kind of Love*. This important book stated Kenyon's conviction that living for self was a sure way to cut off all the blessings of God. We were to follow the Master's example in laying down our lives for the will of God and the needs of mankind. In many ways this was the pinnacle of Kenyon's revelation. He saw failure to receive from God in faith—whether it be healing or something else—rooted in a neglect of consistently walking in love.

Kenyon saw that through his books he could leave a legacy to the next generation. He diligently brought together his ideas to print more books. Two more titles came in 1942—*The Two Kinds of Faith* and *The Two Kinds of Righteousness*. In the first book Kenyon contrasted real Bible faith that needed no other evidence other than the Word of God with what he termed *sense-knowledge* faith, the kind of faith that must have physical evidence before it believes.

The Two Kinds of Righteousness was Kenyon's restatement of the doctrine of justification by faith. Rather than stating the doctrine in only forensic, or legal, terms, Kenyon saw our justification as both legal and vital. We were legally justified in the finished work of Christ. But, Kenyon taught, we were vitally justified in the new creation by receiving a righteous, new nature. The new birth was a change from a sin nature to a righteous nature in Kenyon's thought.

During the next two years, Kenyon released two more of his larger works: *The Two Kinds of Life* and his work on prayer, *In His Presence.* The first book expressed his understanding of the difference between natural human life and eternal life received by the believer in the new birth. Kenyon saw eternal life as the life and nature of God received by man.

In His Presence, a book that has changed the prayer life of many, showed that prayer was primarily the privilege of the sons and daughters of God to enter their Father's presence and enjoy fellowship with Him. Out of that relationship and fellowship they could labor with Him through their petitions and requests.

The next two years, 1944–45, brought another two of his larger works into being. *New Creation Realities* and *What Happened from the Cross to the Throne?* hit the presses and were eagerly received by those who had come to delight in Kenyon's written ministry.

What Happened was his larger work devoted to expounding the cross and resurrection (*Identification* being the smaller one). He felt that this book should have been written four hundred years earlier. Kenyon always maintained that the sufferings of Christ in His substitutionary death were the strongest motive for total surrender to the will of God.

After her father's death in 1948, Kenyon's daughter Ruth published his teachings on the *Blood Covenant,* which remains his best-selling book. In 1955 she published the book Kenyon had been working on the last two years of his life, *The Hidden Man of the Heart,* his teaching on the recreated human spirit.

All of these titles, as well as the three Bible study courses mentioned earlier, are still available from Kenyon's Gospel Publishing Society in Lynnwood, Washington. Kenyon's dream of a written legacy became a reality.

FOREIGN BOOK TRANSLATIONS

During his lifetime Kenyon was pleased to see that several of his books were translated into foreign languages.

In May 1936 the *Herald* announced that *The Wonderful Name* had been translated into Chinese. The article stated, "A few months ago we were greatly honored with a visit of Rev. Andrew Ghi of Shanghai, who had a deep impression upon our people. After reading 'The Wonderful Name of Jesus' he offered to translate it into Chinese. Last week a dozen copies came to us of the translation."

Kenyon's ministry was supporting Brother Ghi's Bethel mission in prayer and finances. Articles about the work in China were frequently featured in the *Herald*.

W. W. Simpson (1869–1961), a pioneer missionary to China affiliated with the Assemblies of God, also arranged to have forty thousand copies of Kenyon's book *Father and His Family* printed in Chinese and distributed.[9] Kenyon was delighted and wanted to contribute, with the help of his readership, as much as he could to the publishing costs.[10]

Kenyon's materials and periodicals were being translated and distributed in many other nations, including India, Nigeria, Italy, Holland, and Colombia, South America. It was interesting to note that the individual translating Kenyon's material into Dutch was a "Miss Corrie ten Boom" the noted author and Holocaust survivor.[11]

NEW TEACHING: THE TWO KINDS OF KNOWLEDGE

One area of truth that Kenyon had always articulated had to do with the two kinds of knowledge. This teaching crystallized for him in these years in the Northwest. When he revised *Father and His Family* one of the additions to the new edition was a teaching on the two kinds of knowledge. He clearly felt this was an important truth.

For Kenyon there was a necessary distinction between what we could know by faith and what our senses could confirm to us. This distinction had been articulated by all the Faith-Cure people in one form or another, but Kenyon sought to "capture the imagination" of his readers, something he felt modern theology had failed to do.

Kenyon felt the knowledge we received from the Bible by the illumination of the Holy Spirit was a necessary addition to the knowledge that could be gained by the senses. The knowledge of spiritual things, the things of God, and the realities of Christ's finished work, could not be gained by the senses. As a student of Paul's writings, Kenyon noted that "the natural man does not receive the things of the Spirit of God, for they are foolishness to him" (1 Cor. 2:14).

Kenyon's critics have misrepresented him horribly on this point, suggesting he taught a kind of "Gnostic dualism." Astoundingly, one author stated that "[Mary Baker] Eddy's dualistic understanding of knowledge is almost exactly the same as Kenyon's."

Kenyon's thought was a reflection of the apostle Paul's thought, who tells us:

Our light affliction, which is but for a moment, is working for us a far more exceeding and eternal weight of glory, while we do not look at the things which are seen, but at the things which are not seen. For the things which are seen are temporary, but the things which are not seen are eternal (2 Cor. 4:17–18, NKJV).

Paul here contrasts two realities, seen and unseen, temporary and eternal. Paul taught the "superiority" of the eternal order over the temporary. Our walk by "faith and not by sight" was based on the unchanging realities of the truth of God's promises (2 Cor. 5:7, NKJV). Paul did not deny the reality of the temporal—and neither did Kenyon—but Paul maintained that our stability was in clinging to the unseen while we walked through this life.

As a student of Paul, Kenyon observed that the Holy Spirit was given to us that "we might know the things that are freely given to us of God" (1 Cor. 2:12, NKJV). The vast majority of what Paul knew and taught about Jesus came to him by revelation rather than by observation or interaction with the other disciples. It was the Spirit's light on the Old Testament Scriptures (Rom. 16:25–26) and the Lord's personal visitations with him (Gal. 1:11–12, 15–16) that unveiled to Paul what he termed *his* gospel (Rom. 2:16).

Having observed the metaphysical cults, the advocates of the Higher Criticism, and the growing liberal and Unitarian thought that had infected the seminaries, Kenyon concluded that men could take the Scriptures without the help of the Holy Spirit and come up with very damaging ideas. The antagonism of the scholarly world to the miraculous was an evidence to Kenyon of this mental approach to the Word.

He advocated prayerful meditation in the Word, depending on the Holy Spirit to illuminate its truths. This is hardly a radical idea. In accusing Kenyon of "anti-rationalism" his critics ignore the vast amount of teaching in his books on the renewing of the mind. One critic understands Kenyon to teach that "the human spirit has little or nothing to do with the intellect, which can only process sense knowledge." He also accuses him of fideism, which suggests that one can accept by faith that which has no rational basis.[12] (For more about these accusations, see Appendix One.)

As we will show in a later chapter, Kenyon taught just the opposite about the relationship between the spirit and the mind. Kenyon taught that the knowledge of divine things flows in the following order: from the Holy Spirit to the human spirit to the mind. Kenyon taught that the senses could not "discover or know" the things of God without "assistance from this revelation knowledge."[13] This was a common teaching in the Keswick/Higher Life branch of the church. Radical dualism just isn't present in Kenyon's writings.

Kenyon believed that the believer must have a rational basis for his faith and that faith can't function beyond knowledge. For Kenyon, the clear teaching of the Word of God *was* the rational basis for faith. But Kenyon also insisted that the Holy Spirit must illuminate the Word for us to intelligently act upon it. For Kenyon, faith was acting on the Word (James 1:25). "Faith is acting upon what you know . . . Faith is the product of personal knowledge, a personal unfolding of the character and nature of the infinite God," Kenyon held.[14]

Kenyon talked much about "mental assent," the giving of intellectual acknowledgment to the facts of Scripture. He said the *mind* could agree to the truth of Scripture, but that it was with the *heart* (or spirit) that man believed (Rom. 10:10). Others have described this same distinction as *head faith* and *heart faith.*

When Kenyon published *The Two Kinds of Knowledge,* He told his readers:

> It has been my privilege during the later years of ministry to give what is known as new material to the church. But I have never made the contribution that I feel will mean so much as this little book.
> It will be a revelation to many of you.[15]

Kenyon felt he was putting a tool into the hands of the saints that would help them in the "good fight of faith." Many have found it to be just that in their personal experience.

NEW TRAVELS

It seems as if Kenyon's heart never quite left Southern California. In November 1940 Kenyon returned to Los Angeles to conduct a crusade. The meetings were successful with many salvations and many healings. By December Kenyon was broadcasting on thirty-one stations reaching nine million people from Canada to Mexico. The program was broadcast from 8:30 to 9:00 on Sunday mornings.

His voice was heard throughout Southern California, so those attracted to his broadcast went to hear him in person.[16] Over the next months Kenyon frequently returned to Southern California and held extended meetings.

In the summer of 1943 Kenyon held meetings in Santa Barbara, a small town adjacent to Los Angeles. They were well received, and it was reported that two individuals were healed of cancer as they simply *listened* to the teaching! Kenyon said, "It was one of the most delightful experiences of my life."[17]

Kenyon preached for many others during these years, never taking much time out for rest. He preached in Portland, Oregon, for Willard H. Pope at his Trinity Tabernacle. Pope became a close friend, eventually writing articles for the *Herald*. Pope's son also contributed teachings.

William Booth-Clibborn, who pastored Immanuel Temple in Portland, also had Kenyon minister for him. The church advertised him as "a man whose unique gift has given him a widely recognized ministry in divine healing." Kenyon and Booth-Clibborn also worked together on other occasions, according to another minister who pastored in Vancouver, British Columbia, Canada.[18]

Kenyon again left for California in May 1944 to hold more meetings. Still in Los Angeles in December 1944, Kenyon was holding Sunday morning services at the Embassy Hotel. The *Herald* notes that these services were continuing in March 1945.

By June the growing meetings included a 9:30 A.M.Bible class followed by a 10:30 A.M. service. During the week Kenyon kept busy holding meetings Tuesdays in San Gabriel, Thursdays in Pasadena, and Fridays in Long Beach.

It seems pretty clear that Kenyon was establishing a new work in Los Angeles. By October Kenyon stated, "The Father has very graciously brought together a fine body of Christian men and women in Los Angeles, California . . . We are asking the Father to give us a suitable building . . . Our work in Pasadena is growing . . . Many other doors are opening which we are unable to fill at the present."[19]

Kenyon continued to labor in California but did make it back to Seattle to celebrate his seventy-ninth birthday. The people in Seattle rejoiced to see him, honoring him with a special dinner. Kenyon reported that there were now four separate groups meeting under his leadership in and around Los Angeles.

One year later in October 1946 the *Herald* reported that Wesley Alloway, former co-pastor of the New Covenant Church of Seattle, had been studying with the New Tribes Mission in Chicago and had recently returned to Seattle. The report noted that Alloway then joined Kenyon in Los Angeles.

The next month it was reported that Kenyon was back in Seattle to preach along with his friend Willard Pope. The February 1947 *Herald* invited the readership out to hear Kenyon at services in Seattle and mentioned the ministry in song by Miss Ruth Kenyon. Kenyon was ministering and traveling vigorously up until the last few months of his life.

A Controversial Homegoing

Some controversy has surrounded the death of E. W. Kenyon, which I will attempt to clear up. His "homegoing" has been reported in glowing terms. These reports, though exaggerated by some, are based on details which were supplied by Kenyon's daughter Ruth, who was with him when he died.

One example of an accurate report is from Kenneth E. Hagin's book *The Name of Jesus.*

> Kenyon, too, went home to be with the Lord without sickness and disease at the age of nearly eighty-one. He was holding Bible classes in Southern California shortly before his death, teaching several times a day. (His daughter Ruth Housworth, who keeps his ministry and writings going stronger today than ever, said that the young people in the team which traveled with him had a difficult time keeping up with his pace.) He had just finished writing *The Hidden Man of the Heart*. And he came home to rest for a while. One morning his wife and daughter asked what he would like for breakfast. He replied, "You girls go ahead and eat. I don't believe I will eat right now." A short time later he was home with the Lord. He went home the Bible way without sickness or disease.[20]

In 1991 a man from England wrote to Ruth Housworth concerning some information that he had received that indicated that Kenyon had died of cancer. He was questioning Kenneth Hagin's report of the details of Kenyon's death. Ruth responded:

> In answer to your questions concerning Kenneth Hagin's statements about my dad, Kenneth Hagin is quoting facts which he received directly from me. There have been many stories about my dad's passing and I don't know how they all started. My dad never received any treatment for cancer. He simply died of old age.
> There are malicious rumors being said about my dad and other faith teachers today, and it is truly sad.[21]

This gentleman then sent to Ruth a copy of Kenyon's death certificate that he had obtained from a ministry critical of Kenyon. The death certificate said under cause of death: Malignancy, probably lymphoid. The certificate also indicated that the doctor had attended Kenyon from April 10, 1947, to March 19, 1948, the day of his death.

So how are we to put these seemingly contradictory stories together? I will attempt to bring the sequence of events into what I believe to be their true unfolding.

THE STORY UNFOLDS

The story of Kenyon's homegoing begins in October 1946 when Wesley Alloway was summoned to Southern California to help Kenyon with the work. Word had come up from the workers in California that Kenyon was weak and struggling physically. Kenyon continued to preach for a while in Los Angeles but eventually agreed to return to the Northwest with Alloway. *After* Kenyon's death it was rumored that he had cancer. The source of these rumors will be discussed shortly.

Kenyon continued to hold meetings when he returned to the Northwest. Ruth, his daughter, ministered with him. He apparently showed no signs of serious sickness and continued to minister accompanied by Ruth. Surely, if he showed any signs of being "seriously ill" Ruth would have noticed. She reported him to be strong and busy until his last few months. Yet the evidence suggests that he was fighting for his health.

Though he continued to minister, Kenyon himself may have

recognized that his body, by reason of age, was wearing out. He was near his eightieth year. This would be a factor in his thinking if he were battling against disease or just plain wearing out. The notes from a December 24, 1946, message may give us a glimpse behind the scenes as Kenyon preached a sermon that he was very possibly living out in his own life. It was titled *Sickness Does Not Affect Our Relationship or Our Legal Rights*. If he were fighting sickness in his body it was most likely an unknown battle to those around him. His sermon notes stated:

> God is still our Father. It [sickness] does not annul our righteousness . . . Does not take the name from us, [the] Holy Spirit does not leave us! Cannot rob us of the Living Word! Does not break our fellowship! Does not rob us of His Love; sickness is war in the senses! We are healed, senses deny it! Healing is a spirit fact, senses repudiate it. By His stripes I am healed, God did it, [the] Word declares it, I know it. So I contradict the message of the senses and stand by the Word.[22]

Another message Kenyon preached the same day was entitled *Some Facts About Sickness.*

> Sickness is of the devil, comes through ignorance, overwork, or eating. The more you are important or useful in Christ, the more he hates you. You are in his way. Spiritual condemnation hits you like an avalanche. It upsets you, leaves you defeated. Now Satan rides you, accuses you, slanders you, some actually in secret rejoice to see you ill, your good health has condemned them . . .
>
> Don't yield, keep a solid front, God is for you, you are a victor. Samson a prisoner, eye[s] destroyed, was a blood covenant man, he won in the final bout. You are a New Covenant man, Jesus is interceding for you, you are a victor, nothing can separate you from his love . . .
>
> You are the object of Satan's hatred! He has turned his heavy guns on you! Isaiah 41:10 is yours. [Kenyon then lists a number of Scriptures—1 John 5:4–5; Isaiah 53; Col. 1:12–14; Rom. 6:14; Phil. 2:13; 4:13, and went on to say] Satan can't lord it over me. He [Jesus] bore these pains, put them away! He healed me! I am well, disease is gone!

Kenyon added a little poetry (or maybe it was a chorus) to his message, writing:

> His Word has triumphed over the senses!
> And from pain at last I'm free.
> Faith has captured Satan's stronghold;
> Thank God my spirit's free.

Then he concluded that page with, "Satan may mar, even break your fellowship, but can't touch your relationship, only the Father could sever that." Then he added his note of victory, "Nay in all these things we are more than conquerors." Kenyon continued to preach into March 1947, which is evidenced by his various dated teaching outlines. On March 5 he brought a message entitled "Why I Am a Victor."

While on a ministry trip sometime before April 1947 Kenyon fell from a hammock and injured his back. He went to stay with his son, Essek, Jr., and Essek's wife, Jerry. Jerry took care of Kenyon, and she insisted that her doctor, a Dr. Williams from the Mason Clinic in Seattle, look at Kenyon's back. At this time (as a result of his fall) Kenyon's back was such a problem that he could not move around without help. Kenyon agreed to an examination.

According to Jerry Kenyon, while examining his back, the doctor said he discovered a tumor of quite a large size. This was his opinion—no tests or x-rays were performed.

The doctor told Jerry Kenyon that the tumor (which he assumed was cancerous) was not causing Kenyon any apparent problems and that nothing should be done about it. The doctor did not mention this diagnosis to Kenyon, nor was Ruth informed of it. Jerry Kenyon said all the medicine he ever took was a half an aspirin.

Kenyon was down, but not for long. Jerry Kenyon told me that Kenyon was miraculously healed of his back injury. She described it as a broken back, and indicated that they were shocked when he was up and around.

A letter written by Ruth Kenyon in 1992 has a similar description of her father's fall. Ruth also told about the circumstances of her father's death.

> My father fell from a hammock and injured his back on an evangelistic trip. My brother's wife insisted he go to her doctor to treat

his back. He did, and this is the only time to my knowledge that he went to him. [This would be the April 10, 1947, visit. Actually, the doctor visited Kenyon at Essek and Jerry's house]. He was at home with my mother and myself until he passed away. He still had some weakness in his back, but he was not under the doctor's care, and at no time did the doctor ever tell us he had cancer and certainly did not treat him for it. We had no doctor, so I called the doctor who had treated his back when we saw he was in a coma. As far as we knew, his body just wore out.[23]

So Dr. Williams saw Kenyon twice—once when Kenyon first injured his back and a second time to confirm Kenyon's death. There is a possibility this doctor saw Kenyon one other time after his initial consultation, but the records are not clear. What is clear is that Kenyon did not receive cancer treatment from this doctor and was never x-rayed or examined regarding the suspected cancer. No surgery or autopsy was performed, so there is no way to state positively one way or another if the suspected tumor was actually there when he died.

Jerry Kenyon insists that Kenyon died of heart failure rather than cancer. "We don't know what became of the cancer," she reported.[24]

KENYON'S ATTITUDE

What was Kenyon thinking at the time the doctor examined him? I believe Kenyon knew he had a battle to fight. It was not the first time he had been seriously ill. Kenyon had been raised up from a death bed (peritonitis, see chapter 6) in 1897. In 1938 he wrote:

When I awaken in the morning [at the age of 71] I am as fresh as a boy. I haven't an ache or a pain. I awaken at four or five in the morning, ready for a long day of grueling work. And at night I am still fresh.

I have passed the seventieth milestone, and I am as vigorous today as ever in my life.

And I believe you can be as healthy as I am.

I have been given up for dead twice; I have heard the nurse count me out, saying, "He is dying," but I have refused to die, refused to stay sick.

I refused to be sick; I have refused to be laid aside.[25]

It isn't clear when Kenyon's second brush with death took place or the nature of the sickness. But I believe he made a reference to this illness in an article published in 1942 in which he wrote, "I had been praying, struggling, and crying to God for healing. That old chronic difficulty had me in bondage for more than three years."[26] It is possible that the incident being described was his first healing in 1897, but the phrase "old, chronic" suggests something later in his ministry. He also went on to say that in receiving his healing in this case he discovered that his healing was an accomplished fact of his redemption. This discovery came later in his ministry, long after he was already praying successfully for the sick.

The fact that he would share that struggle openly in his publication suggests that he didn't find an extended battle with sickness contrary to his understanding of our redemption and the fight of faith for healing. Kenyon clearly believed that divine health was God's perfect will, yet he didn't feel that it was a contradiction to face some serious battles with disease.

Having successfully faced death by disease twice previously, we can easily imagine what Kenyon's attitude would be if faced with another battle with sickness. He had seen many people healed of every kind of disease in his ministry. He would undoubtedly determine to stand on the Word of God and fight.

Having stated this, Kenyon also surely recognized that he was wearing out physically. He was now over eighty. The thought of going to be with his Lord was certainly not an unappealing possibility. The man who wrote . . .

> As I dictate, it seems to me as though the Master were here, and if I should open my eyes I would see Him standing before us. I long to throw my arms about His feet and kiss the scars where the nails once held Him to the Cross. My Lord! My wonderful Risen Lord![27]

. . . would not find going to be with his Master an unappealing thought.

Ruth Housworth said that her father recognized that his death could be imminent.

Shortly before his passing, he had a premonition that he would

172

not be here long, and he called me and said he felt I was the one to carry on his work. He said, "Ruth, dear, I have a feeling I won't be with you much longer. This work must go on. It is up to you now, you have been looking after it all these years, and with the help of the Lord, I know you can carry on." I promised I would.[28]

Kenyon took some other steps that may indicate he knew his time on earth was coming to a close. The June issue of the *Herald* announced the forming of the New Covenant Fellowship Foundation. It had come into being within the last twelve months "under the direction and guiding hand of Dr. E. W. Kenyon. The foundation existed to "inspire by every means possible a rebirth of allegiance to the fundamentals of historical New Covenant redemption truth." The foundation was formed to continue the spread of Kenyon's message and the distribution of his books. Willard Pope of Portland was among the founding members.

Around January 1948 Kenyon went to stay with Alice (his ex-wife) and Ruth. In an article in the *Herald* in February 1948, Ruth announced that her father "now in his eighty-first year has felt it necessary to retire from active service." Kenyon spent the last three months of his life with Alice and Ruth. Ruth described these last months to another inquirer:

> I took care of him the last few months that he was alive as he was having back problems and was weak. The doctor that had seen him once or twice never made any mention that he had cancer.[29]

It is interesting to note that there were no obvious evidences of cancer in Kenyon's behavior. He got up every morning and had breakfast with Alice and Ruth until the morning he died. Ruth described that morning:

> Dad was very tired the day he went home to be with the Lord. He did not get out of bed that morning, and he told Mother and I to go ahead and eat our breakfast without him. About nine o'clock I was ready to walk out the front door, but I heard Dad breathing and it was very heavy. When I went into his room to check on him, he had already gone into a coma. He was in a coma from nine till about noon, and I was holding his hand when he went

home. Dad was not sick, just old and tired.[30]

Ruth believed her father died of old age, without sickness or disease. His body had just worn out. Certainly one caring for a person the last three months of his life is in a position to state whether or not he are suffering from a serious disease. Ruth was shocked to hear the rumors that her father had died of cancer. There is no good reason to question her testimony.

A LAST NOTE OF TRIUMPH

A few months before he died, E. W. Kenyon wrote a poetic article for the *Herald* that surveyed the previous year. It was titled *The Old Year.*

> Genius had three friends: a broken heart, hard work, and a vision.
> When the crash comes, and they lie bleeding amid the ruins of the work of years, when hope turns down the light, and ambitions fail to awaken the broken spirit, then truly great souls cry, "Thank God! I am at last identified with the great throbbing human heart."
> Failures lift the true soul into purer light, success leads the real man to feel for the one who fails.
> As I sit and look back over the year I cry, "Old Year, you have left scars and unhealed wounds, but I love you.
> "Goodbye, Old Year, my tears have made rivers flow across your face. There have been days with no sun, nights with no stars, deserts with no oasis, riverbeds with no water, couches with no rest, yet I love you."
> But as I look back there are mountain peaks that catch the sun and throw it back upon the clouds and fill all the past with a radiance that no artist's brush could paint.
> I hear ripples of laughter pealing from the joy-days of the past, I hear music, it is the chimes of the bells of the past, there is no discord, distance has mellowed every note. I weep tonight, but it is not in sorrow. I turn my heart and face the newborn year and ask,
> "Can you give me as much?"[31]

Essek William Kenyon—a man of never-ending vision—died the following month.

CHAPTER 16

THE SUFFERINGS OF CHRIST

*I believe His suffering was spiritual. I believe in substitu-
tion . . . I believe the Book teaches that Jesus actually went to
hell, that he actually suffered seventy-two hours in hell, until the
demands of justice against the human race were fully satisfied.
How can this be? Because the suffering of Deity for one hour is
more than the sufferings of the human race for an eternity.*

—E. W. Kenyon[1]

The idea of Christ having experienced spiritual sufferings (as
well as physical) in the work of the atonement is not an inven-
tion of Kenyon. It has a long history in the church, and since the
Reformation it has been taught by many. Because it is not widely
taught today (except in the Faith movement) it is often considered
strange, and some have called it heretical.

It is held by those who teach this idea that in His work of substitutionary sin-bearing, Christ suffered not only physical death, but also
something beyond physical death—spiritual separation from His
Father, or *spiritual death*. It is held that Christ endured the "cup" of
God's wrath in the place of the sinner.[2]

In this chapter you will learn why some people believe Christ died
spiritually and how Kenyon taught on this subject. In the following
chapter there is an overview of the many teachers in Kenyon's day
who also taught about the spiritual sufferings of Christ.

175

KENYON'S TEACHING

Kenyon taught that from the time that Jesus cried, "My God, My God, why have You forsaken Me?" on the cross, until the Spirit raised Him from the dead after three days and three nights (Matt. 27:46, 12:39–40, NKJV), Christ was separated from God the Father. At this time Christ also experienced the wrath of God that the sinner deserved. He continued to suffer until the *claims of justice* were met. This idea of the claims of justice is a key concept in Kenyon's understanding of the work of Christ.

In his book *Identification* Kenyon wrote:

> In the great drama of our Redemption, as soon as Christ was nailed to the cross, with His crown of thorns, and with the howling mob that surrounded Him, justice began to do its awful work behind the scenes.
>
> Sense-knowledge men and women who surrounded the cross could only see the physical man, Jesus, hanging there.
>
> God could see His spirit.
>
> Angels could see His spirit.
>
> Demons could see the real man, hidden in that body.
>
> Then came the dreadful hour when 2 Corinthians 5:21 was fulfilled. "He hath made him to be sin for us, who knew no sin; that we might be made the righteousness of God in him."
>
> "He was wounded for our transgressions, he was bruised for our iniquities: the chastisement of our peace was upon him; and with his stripes we are healed. All we like sheep have gone astray; we have turned every one to his own way; and the Lord hath laid on him the iniquity of us all" (Isaiah 53:5–6).
>
> On that awful cross, He not only became sin, but He became a curse, for in Galatians 3:13 it tells us, "Christ hath redeemed us from the curse of the law, being made a curse for us: for it is written, Cursed is every one that hangeth on a tree."[3]

Kenyon believed this spiritual suffering was the heart of Christ's substitutionary sacrifice. This was the ultimate outpouring of Christ's love. This gripped Kenyon deeply. He felt that if the lost heard it preached they would be unable to resist the drawing power of such a demonstration of love. His ministry in evangelism would seem to confirm the accuracy of this idea. We will examine Kenyon's evangelistic fruit in a later chapter. Suffice it to say that Kenyon's evangelistic ministry was very effective.

Seven years after he was restored to the Lord, Kenyon wrote an article on Christ's sacrifice in which he revealed the place he felt these sufferings have in the ministry of evangelism.

> For God so loved the world, is the key of evangelistic effort; the man who best understands the extent of that love will be able to tell others of it in such a manner as to win them.
>
> The greater the knowledge of that Almighty love, the greater the results.
>
> The object of this article is to show the love that constrained the mighty Saul of Tarsus to the greatest work and suffering of any man since Jesus of Nazareth. Some statements will be startling to the reader, they were to the writer when the Word was opened to him by the Spirit.
>
> The writer has been convinced for some time that the suffering of Christ in redemption should be the one plea to move men to give up sin, to stir their sensibilities, win their judgment, and take captive their wills.[4]

Kenyon did not believe that the physical or mental sufferings of Christ, as dreadful as they were, were dramatic enough to capture the sinner's heart. He felt that the spiritual sufferings of Christ held the greatest appeal to the lost in that they revealed such a tremendous love for mankind. This theme is found in most of his books in a place of foundational emphasis.

Kenyon clearly felt that the apostle Paul was gripped by this revelation of Christ's love, and it motivated him to endure all that he did for the cause of Christ. Kenyon identified himself with Paul and his revelation, being himself motivated and captured by the love expressed in Christ's spiritual sufferings.

Because of his strong emphasis on the spiritual sufferings of Christ, some of Kenyon's critics have implied that he didn't value Christ's physical sufferings. This is not the case. Near the end of his life Kenyon wrote:

> As I dictate, it seems to me as though the Master were here, and if

I should open my eyes I would see Him standing before us.

I long to throw my arms about His feet and kiss the scars where the nails once held Him to the cross.[5]

Hardly the words of a man who doesn't value the physical sufferings of Christ! Yet undoubtedly the spiritual sufferings gripped him in even a more profound way.

He commented elsewhere:

If you and I can find out that Jesus of Nazareth, that His soul, went to hell and there suffered what was our penalty to suffer, if there He bore the judgment that was against us, if there He suffered the torments that should have fallen upon us, it will stir our hearts to a heroism and love for Him and fellowship in His sufferings and work that will change our whole lives . . .

I believe if we understand what it meant to God, what it meant to Jesus Christ, to redeem us, our redemption will be of such a value that it will take hold of our lives and will produce character in our lives.[6]

E. W. Kenyon was a man gripped by the reality of Christ's sufferings. Motivated and captured by the love expressed in Christ's spiritual sufferings, Kenyon was, like Paul, constrained by the love of Christ (2 Cor. 5:14).

THE THEOLOGICAL JOURNEY

Kenyon's understanding of Christ's spiritual sufferings took a central place in his developing theology. Perhaps this was the theme of the message Kenyon heard when he rededicated his life to Christ at A. J. Gordon's church. The horror of Christ being made sin may have taken Kenyon beyond the physical sufferings of Christ and deeply touched him with the tremendous love Jesus demonstrated at the cross. Something he heard that night at Gordon's church broke through his unbelief and rebellion and brought him to his knees. The evidence suggests it was this truth that gripped him that night.

Through some of Kenyon's comments we can surmise that he started research on Christ's sufferings immediately after he rededicated his life.

I was possessed with a peculiar temperament. I hunted for seven years for a scripture I knew must be in the Word. I knew that Jesus died twice on the cross. He died spiritually when He was made sin and died physically after that.[7]

Kenyon rededicated his life to the Lord in 1893. He wrote his first article on the spiritual sufferings of Christ in 1900. So that seven-year search took place between his rededication and the writing of this article. Then he discovered Isaiah 53:9.

Jesus died twice on the cross. I knew this for many years, but I had no scriptural evidence. One day I discovered Isaiah 53:9, the answer to my long search: "And he made his grave with the wicked, and with the rich in his death." The word "death" is plural in the Hebrew. Many of you who have Bibles with marginal renderings will notice it. That is, Jesus died two deaths on the cross: He died spiritually before He died physically.[8]

Notice he said the Spirit opened the Word to him (apparently not long before writing the article in 1900), but his revelation of this truth preceded the Spirit's opening of the Word by many years. Though Kenyon stated that it was revealed to him by the Spirit, he searched the Scriptures to verify its accuracy before he began to teach it.[9]

By the time he wrote the article in 1900, he had applied his seven-fold test to the teaching. He found the death of Adam and Eve in Genesis 2:17, the type in Leviticus 16:8; Christ's soul in hades/Sheol in Psalm 16, Christ's soul an offering for sin in Isaiah 53; Christ's soul in the heart of the earth in the Gospels in Matthew 12:40; Peter preaches Psalm 16 in Acts 2:24–31; and in Paul's epistles 2 Corinthians 5:21 and Galatians 3:13; in Romans 10:7 Christ is made sin and a curse and descends into and is raised from the abyss.

THE BLOOD OF JESUS

Because of his strong emphasis on the spiritual sufferings of Christ, some of Kenyon's critics have also implied that he didn't value Christ's blood. This, too, misses the mark. Kenyon had powerful teachings on Jesus' blood, not to mention the fact that he wrote a book titled *The Blood Covenant*.

Kenyon's teaching on the atonement gave due respect to the Old Testament types as explained in the Book of Hebrews. He asserted that Jesus fulfilled the type of the Day of Atonement in His substitutionary sacrifice. Christ was both the priest and the sacrifice.

Following is a description of the ritual on the Day of Atonement. In the tabernacle of Moses (and in the temple of Solomon) the priest killed the sacrifice and the offered its blood to God. The priest slayed the sacrificial victim at the bronze altar, which was located in the outer court and visible to the people (at least at the tabernacle of Moses). Then the priest took the blood and went into the holy of holies and presented that blood to God by sprinkling it on the mercy seat. If the blood was accepted, the priest would then pronounce the blessing of the atonement being accomplished and the sins of Israel forgiven.

The atonement was not accomplished until the blood was accepted by God. The letter to the Hebrews indicates that Christ fulfilled the type by bringing His own blood into the heavenly holy of holies and presenting it to the Father. (See Heb. 8–10.) The believer has access to the Father because the blood is in heaven!

Kenyon's critics, seeking rightly to honor the sacrificial death in the "outer court" (His physical dying), do away with his priestly ministry in the heavenly holy of holies. Perhaps this is not their intention, but to insist that the atonement was accomplished by Christ's physical death alone is to say that the work was totally finished when Christ died. They insist that the atonement was accomplished entirely in the "outer court," so to speak.

Kenyon, recognizing the necessity of fulfilling these types (in the Book of Hebrews) insisted that our redemption was not *fully* accomplished until the blood entered heaven and was accepted by the Father. (See Lev. 16.)

> As the High Priest, He took His own blood and carried it up to the Heavenly holy of holies and there presented it to God. It was accepted, and that red seal is upon the document of our redemption. The blood of Jesus, God's Son, is the eternal witness of His finished work for us, of our legal right to eternal life, and sonship with all its privileges.
>
> On the basis of that blood, we are more than conquerors. Satan has no dominion over us. His dominion is utterly broken. The tokens of that victory are continually before the Father.

If you are in grave danger, or Satan is pressing hard upon you, you call the Father's attention to your rights that are guaranteed on the ground of that blood.[10]

Hebrew scholars agree that the sprinkling of the blood was essential for atonement. In his book *The Temple, Its Ministry and Service,* respected Hebrew Christian scholar Alfred Edersheim (1825–1889) wrote:

For the death of the sacrifice was only a means toward an end, that end being the shedding and sprinkling of the blood, by which the atonement was really made.[11]

The high priest did not sprinkle the blood until it was taken behind the second veil into the holy of holies. In his book *The Blood Covenant,* Kenyon spoke of the value of Christ's blood presented to the Father in heaven as described in Hebrews 9:21–24. He wrote, "As we come to value the blood of Christ as God values it, then the problem of our standing and relationship never enters our minds."[12]

Another type that foreshadows this same truth is the Year of Jubilee. The pronouncement of debts dissolved, inheritance restored, and slaves being set free, came on the Day of Atonement when—*after the high priest had presented the blood behind the second veil*—he came out and announced that the Year of Jubilee had begun.

This is why when Kenyon wrote a book on the work of the cross, he called it *From the Cross to the Throne.* After Jesus presented His blood and it was accepted, He sat down on His throne. Christ moved from becoming the Sacrifice, to becoming the Priest, to sitting down as the King.

From the Cross to the Throne is Kenyon's larger exposition of Christ's finished work. A smaller exposition of his understanding appears in *Identification,* which focused on Paul's teaching about our participation with Christ in His sacrifice. I believe that Kenyon's study of our identification with Christ led to his change in belief about sanctification. Sanctification, he found, was in the finished work, not a second work.

Kenyon gloried in the cross, but he didn't see the work of the cross end with Christ's death. For him, the physical sufferings, the separation from the Father, the three days and nights in hades, the glorious resurrection with its defeat of Satan and the hosts of Hell, the entrance with His own blood into the heavenly Holy of Holies, His Father's acceptance of that blood, and finally His seating at His Father's right hand were all involved in the finished work of Christ. This is why he called his book on the finished work *From the Cross to the Throne.* Kenyon also taught much on the ministry of Christ at the Father's right hand as Mediator, Intercessor, Advocate, and High Priest.

At the beginning of this chapter I mentioned that many people since the Reformation had taught about the spiritual sufferings of Christ. Because few people are aware of this widespread teaching, the next chapter will be devoted to an overview of some of the major teachers who articulated this concept. Their similarity to Kenyon's teaching may be shocking to those who thought Kenyon's teachings were unusual or unique!

CHAPTER 17

CONCURRING VOICES ON THE SUFFERINGS OF CHRIST

"The physical suffering of Jesus Christ was not the real suffering. Many men before Him had died. Many men had become martyrs. The awful suffering of Jesus Christ was His spiritual death. He reached the final issue of sin, fathomed the deepest sorrow, when God turned His back and hid His face so that He cried, "My God, why hast Thou forsaken me?" Alone in the supreme hour of mankind's history Christ uttered these words!"
—Billy Graham[1]

This chapter contains many quotes from respected figures of the past who articulated their understanding of Christ's sufferings. May I encourage the reader to persevere through these deep waters? Some of the authors quoted do not write with the greatest of simplicity or clarity, yet their ideas shaped nineteenth century Christianity. Their voices were listened to by the ministry of Kenyon's day. For this reason they are quite important to Kenyon's story.

Although Kenyon first saw this truth of Christ dying spiritually by revelation of the Holy Spirit, this was a fairly widely taught concept in the circles in which Kenyon moved. Many of his favorite Bible teachers taught it. They did not always see it quite the same as Kenyon, but the essential idea—that Christ's sufferings were more than physical in the work of the atonement—was not an uncommon teaching at all.[2]

J. N. DARBY

John Nelson Darby (1800–1882) was a very influential teacher in the Brethren movement, whom all of Moody's warriors acknowledged as an inspiration. Kenyon acknowledged his debt to Darby and other Brethren authors in 1902. "The teaching of the Brethren through J. N. Darby, C. H. M. [MacIntosh], and others is the real foundation of all advanced Bible study."[3] Darby believed that Christ suffered spiritually as part of His paying the price for our sins and wrote:

> We cannot have too deep a sense of the depth of the Lord's suffering in His atoning work . . . Divine judgment against sin, and the being made a curse, really felt and truly felt *in the soul* of One who, by His perfect holiness and love to God and sense of God's love in its infinite value, could know what the forsaking of God was, and what it was to be made sin before God (italics added).[4]

He continued a little later in his argument:

> No divinely taught mind . . . will . . . fail to distinguish from all else the reality of *Christ's own soul as made sin for us,* exposed to and enduring God's righteous dealing with sin and being forsaken of Him (italics added).[5]

Darby was graphic in his teaching of God's wrath poured out on Jesus.

> All that God was in His nature, He was necessarily against sin; for, though He was love, love has no place in its wrath against sin, and the withdrawal of the sense of it, consciousness in the soul of the privation of God, is the most dreadful of all sufferings—the most terrible horror to him who knows it: but Christ knew it infinitely. But God's divine majesty, His holiness, His righteousness, His truth, all in their nature bore against Christ as made sin for us. All that God was, was against sin, and Christ was made sin. No comfort of love enfeebled wrath here.[6]

Darby distinguished between the physical sufferings of Christ brought upon him by man and the spiritual sufferings endured as God's wrath against sin was borne by Christ as our substitute. Darby considered the latter to be the real heart of the atonement. Remember, J. N. Darby was one of the most influential expositors of Scripture in late nineteenth-century America.

Kenyon, it appears, arrived at his conclusions independently, but Darby would have been for Kenyon a highly regarded confirmation of this truth.

Ironically, this teaching got Darby into trouble with some other leaders in his own movement. H. A. Ironside (1876–1951), who pastored the Moody Memorial Church in Chicago from 1930–1948, reported:

> A breach occurred between Mr. Darby himself and some of his most intimate friends, over his matured views on the sufferings of Christ . . . the extent and nature of Christ's sufferings had been more or less to the fore in the teachings of the Brethren . . . [Some of the Brethren] insisted that he had taught that atonement was made by "wrath-bearing" rather than by "blood-shedding."[7]

Ironside commented on Darby's critics:

> As to the charge that he taught atonement by wrath-bearing and apart from blood-shedding it seems plain to me that only one who overlooked the great mass of his writings on the subject could ever make such a claim.
>
> One might almost as well declare the same of Isaiah because in his great atonement chapter (the 53rd) it is the truth of Christ's soul being "made an offering for sin" that is dwelt on and nothing mentioned about the actual shedding of blood.
>
> . . . But as the years have passed and Mr. Darby's views on this much-discussed and most sacred subject have become better understood there are few indeed of those who really investigate the matter who do not see in it precious truth to be accepted with reverence and adoring love rather than dangerous error as [Darby's critics] thought.[8]

Kenyon's critics might well heed Ironside's comments. They, too, have failed to recognize Kenyon's appreciation of the blood of Christ and of Christ's physical sufferings. Like Darby's critics, Kenyon's detractors have "overlooked the great mass of his writings" that deal with the blood and physical sufferings of Christ. Kenyon honored both the blood and the physical sufferings of Christ, but for him the spiritual sufferings were central.

H. A. Ironside himself also believed the spiritual sufferings were central. In a sermon entitled *The Sinless One Made Sin,* he wrote:

> It was not simply the physical sufferings which our blessed Lord endured upon the cross that made expiation for our iniquity. It was what He suffered in His holy, spotless soul, in His sinless being, when the judgment that our sins deserved fell on Him. . . .
>
> Then it was that He was made to be sin for us. In some way our finite minds can not now understand, the pent-up wrath of the centuries fell upon Him, and He sank in deep mire where there was no standing, as he endured *in His inmost being* what you and I would have had to endure through all eternity, had it not been for His mighty sacrifice (italics added). [9]

JOHN CALVIN

New England, where Kenyon spent the first fifty-six years of his life, was historically Calvinist. From Jonathan Edwards (1745–1801) onward the commonly accepted view of the death of Christ was seen as primarily affecting God. This view—often referred to as the substitutionary penal view—emphasized that by his death Christ paid the penalty for sin to which humans were liable.[10] This was considered the orthodox view that other views of the atonement were judged by.

Darby was a Calvinist (from Great Britain) as were many of Moody's associates such as R. A. Torrey, A. T. Pierson, James M. Gray, A. J. Gordon and A. B. Simpson. Many of them, no doubt, were familiar with John Calvin's (1509–1564) *Institutes of the Christian Religion,* one of his major works.

In this book, Calvin wrote:

> If Christ had merely died a corporeal [physical] death, no end would have been accomplished by it; it was requisite, also, that he should feel the severity of the divine vengeance, in order to appease the wrath of God, and satisfy his justice. Hence it was

186

necessary for him to contend with the powers of hell and the horror of eternal death.

... For the relation of those sufferings of Christ, which were visible to men, is very properly followed by that invisible and incomprehensible vengeance which he suffered from the hand of God; in order to assure us that not only the body of Christ was given as the price of our redemption, but that there was another greater and more excellent ransom, since he suffered in his soul the dreadful torments of a person condemned and irretrievably lost.[11]

Here, John Calvin, one of the greatest voices of the Reformation, articulated the necessity of Christ's soul experiencing the wrath of God. He spoke of the suffering of Christ's *soul,* as the "greater and more excellent ransom" than the physical sufferings of Christ. "Not only the body of Christ was given as the price of our redemption," he wrote.

Calvin certainly did not deny or undervalue Christ's blood because he maintained the importance of the spiritual sufferings of Christ. Calvin also affirmed the necessity of satisfying divine justice, as did Kenyon. Kenyon read Calvin and knew his position, referring to it in one of his sermons.

Calvin stated that if Christ had merely died a physical death, nothing would have been accomplished by it. This statement is shocking to some of today's evangelicals, and they have labeled Kenyon a heretic for this belief. I'm sure they would be shocked at the list of those throughout history who also held this belief.[12]

One researcher stated concerning Kenyon's teaching on identification and the necessity of Christ's spiritual death: "The most overtly heretical aspect of identification [is] the denial of atonement by physical death."[13] A like-minded fellow critic also wrote, "All the Biblical evidence indicates that Jesus never died spiritually, and that His physical death paid the price for humanity's sin."[14]

As you read through this chapter, you might like to note how many other "heretics" believed that Christ's spiritual sufferings were necessary to pay the price for sin.

Charles Haddon Spurgeon

Spurgeon (1834–1892) was one of the most popular and influential preachers of his day. His sermons are still in print and considered masterpieces of sound, biblical exposition. In his sermon *Christ Made Sin,* he stated:

> "He hath made *him to be sin for us.*" Do not fritter that away by putting in the word "offering" and saying "sin-offering." The word stands in apposition—what if I say opposition?—to the word "righteousness" in the other part of the text. He made Him to be as much sin as He makes us to be righteousness; that is to say, He makes Him to be sin by imputation, as He makes us to be righteous by imputation.
>
> On Him, who never was a sinner, who never could be a sinner, our sin was laid. Consider how His holy soul must have shrunk back from being made sin, and yet, I pray you, do not fritter away the words of the prophet Isaiah, "The Lord hath laid on him the iniquity of us all."
>
> Do you know what it means for Christ to be made sin? You do not, but you can form some guess of what it involves; for, when He was made sin, God treated Him as if He had been a sinner, which He never was, and never could be. God left Him as He would have left a sinner, till He cried out, "My God, My God, why hast thou forsaken me?" God smote Him as He would have smitten a sinner, till His soul was "exceedingly sorrowful, even unto death."
>
> That which was due from His people for sin, or an equivalent to that, was literally exacted at the hands of Jesus Christ, the Son of God . . . When justice came to smite the sinner, it found Him in the sinner's place, and smote Him without relenting, laying to the full the whole weight upon Him which had otherwise crushed all mankind forever into the lowermost hell.[15]

In another sermon he added:

> Truly did one say that, "the sufferings of Christ's soul were the soul of His sufferings."[16]

In yet another of his messages on the cross he touched this theme:

> The Holy God treated Him as if He were one of us: "It pleased the
> Father to bruise him; he hath put him to grief." God not only
> turned His back on transgressors, but He turned His back upon
> His Son, who was numbered with them. God can never forsake
> the perfectly innocent, yet He who was perfectly innocent said,
> "My God, My God, why hast thou forsaken me?" Sinking and
> anguish of spirit, even to soul-death, cannot come to a man who is
> numbered with the perfectly righteous. It was because Jesus vol-
> untarily put Himself into the sinner's place that He had to bear the
> sinner's doom; and He being numbered with the transgressors,
> the justice which smites sin smote Him.[17]

"Anguish of spirit, even to soul-death," he said. Spurgeon saw the
spiritual sufferings as the heart of Christ's substitution. He also saw the
atonement in the light of satisfying God's justice as did Calvin (and
Kenyon).

In another of his sermons, he reflected on Martin Luther's attempts
to articulate the depth of Christ's spiritual sufferings. Referring to
Luther's "wonderful book on Galatians," he said:

> In that book he says plainly, but be assured he did not mean what
> he said to be literally understood, that Jesus was the greatest
> sinner that ever lived; that all the sins of men were so laid upon
> Christ that He became all the thieves, and murderers, and adul-
> terers that ever were, in one; and such language teaches that truth
> very plainly; but, Luther, like in his boisterousness, he overshoots
> his mark, and leaves room for the censure that he has almost
> spoken blasphemy against the blessed person of our Lord.[18]

Spurgeon here, recognizing the passion that gripped Luther in
regard to the tremendous love revealed in Christ's substitution, was
willing to overlook the extreme statements Luther made to express the
reality of Christ being made sin. He saw these statements as the frailty
of Luther's humanity attempting to express the inexpressible.

We could learn something from Spurgeon in relation to some of
Kenyon's strong statements about Christ being made sin for us. In his
zeal, describing our Lord's tormented state while under the burden of

our sin, Kenyon may have, like Luther, left room for censure from his critics. These critics, unfortunately, have not been as merciful as Spurgeon. Some of them have suggested that Kenyon has "spoken blasphemy against the blessed person of our Lord." They have not like Spurgeon understood Kenyon's passion regarding the death of his Lord.

Lutheran scholar Paul Althaus, in his *The Theology of Martin Luther,* pointed out that Luther believed:

> Christ really was forsaken by God; he was removed from the experience of his fatherly closeness, and in its stead he was surrendered to the experience of wrath and hell.
>
> According to Isaiah 53, God strikes him because of our sins and punishes him with our punishment. This, however, does not consist only in physical death but "also in the anxiety and terror of a terrified conscience, which feels God's eternal wrath as though it would be forsaken and rejected by God for all eternity."
>
> ... Whoever does not take this completely seriously— because he finds it unbearable to say that Christ has borne our punishment and our curse—robs us of the sweetest comfort.
>
> Christ has thus fully endured the horror of the anxiety of death, of being forsaken by God, and of being under God's wrath . . .
>
> Thus he is forsaken by God and suffers God's wrath in our place. He takes our sins upon himself as though they were his own. In this way, he stands before God as a sinner among sinners and God treats him as such. *Our salvation depends on Christ's thus taking our sins upon himself* (italics added).[19]

Clearly the great reformer held to the importance of the spiritual sufferings of Christ as essential to His redeeming work. He even suggested that our salvation is dependent on the spiritual sufferings of Christ, not the physical sufferings.

R. W. DALE

If Kenyon were to have inquired among his friends in the ministry as to what works on the atonement he could read that held to an orthodox view, what would they have recommended? R. W. Dale's work, *The Atonement,* written in 1875, would be a likely candidate.

Dale (1829–1895) a respected British theologian and Congregationalist pastor and preacher, defended the penal sufferings of Christ as necessary to the accomplishment of our redemption. Many theologians were offering other explanations of the atonement or denying the need of Christ's substitutionary sacrifice altogether.

One of Dale's statements regarding Christ's work is a good reminder to us all to make a distinction between the *fact* of the atonement and our particular view of the atonement.

> It is not the theory of the death of Christ that constitutes the ground on which sins are forgiven, but the death itself; and the faith, which is the condition on our side of receiving "redemption through His blood," is trust in Christ Himself as the Son of God and Savior of men, not the acceptance of any doctrine which explains how it is that salvation comes to us through Him.[20]

It might be noted that Kenyon never suggested that one's salvation depended on accepting his understanding of the atonement. He saw his teaching as a deeper unveiling of the work of the cross to more powerfully reveal God's tremendous love for us.

Dale had much to say about the spiritual sufferings of Christ. In considering Jesus' cry on the cross (Matt. 27:46; Mark 15:34), Dale stated:

> I cannot believe that His terror was caused by His anticipation of the physical tortures of crucifixion . . . There came another and still more appalling sorrow. His fellowship with the Father had been intimate and unbroken . . . The light of God's presence is lost, He is left in awful isolation, and He cries, "My God, My God, why hast Thou forsaken Me?" In the "hour of great darkness" which had fallen upon Him He still clings to the Father with an invincible trust and an immeasurable love, and the agony of being deserted of God is more than He can bear.
>
> He knew that He was to die the awful death; that He was to be forsaken of God in His last hours . . .
>
> Surely this supreme anguish must have a unique relation to the redemption of mankind.
>
> When I try to discover the meaning of the sorrow of Christ on the cross, I cannot escape the conclusion that He is somehow involved in this deep and dreadful darkness by the sins of the race whose nature He had assumed.[21]

Elsewhere Dale offered:

> But Christ not only felt and confessed the justice of God's punishment for sin, He actually submitted to death, and, what was more terrible than physical death, the loss of the consciousness of God's presence, and this spiritual agony appears to have been the immediate cause of His death. Having become man, He submitted, though sinless Himself, to these dreadful consequences of sin.[22]

Dale saw the physical death of Christ as the result of the spiritual death of Christ. This was exactly the teaching of Kenyon (as well as others whom we will mention). Notice, also, that Dale sees Christ acknowledging the justice of God's punishment of sin, a common idea among the defenders of the penal substitution (or satisfaction) theory of the atonement.[23]

In a book published in 1949 titled *The Atonement: Modern Theories of the Doctrine,* author Thomas Hywel Hughes explained why he included an "old" book by R. W. Dale. He wrote, "Dr. Dale's work on *The Atonement* has been so influential and still carries such weight with a large number of scholars, that it was found imperative to include it."[24]

HENRY C. MABIE

Henry C. Mabie was a close personal friend of A. J. Gordon's. They were roommates in Bible school and shared a common vision and passion for world missions. Mabie spoke regularly for both Moody at Northfield and A. B. Simpson at Old Orchard, Maine. During Kenyon's theologically formative years (1894–1897), Mabie spoke at Northfield annually.

Mabie wrote three books on the atonement and was conversant with all the theories and debates of the time. He wrote *The Meaning and Message of the Cross* (1906), *How Does the Death of Christ Save Us?* (1908), and *The Divine Reason of the Cross* (1911).

In one of his sermons Kenyon said Mabie "was considered one of the greatest teachers of the Bible in America."[25] In this same sermon he acknowledged reading *How Does the Death of Christ Save Us?* Mabie had a chapter on the spiritual death of Christ in the book.

It is difficult to say how much Mabie influenced Kenyon. Mabie's books were written some years after Kenyon was already teaching these ideas. In the sermon just referred to, Kenyon seemed to be unclear about Mabie's position. Mabie actually agreed with Kenyon much more than Kenyon seemed to be aware. Mabie was, at any rate, highly influential, particularly in New England, and his books and teaching about the atonement were well respected.

Mabie's teachings on the atonement influenced the Higher Life movement notably. As early as 1910, Jesse Penn-Lewis, the Welsh devotional writer who taught much on identification with Christ, recommended Mabie's books in her publication *The Overcomer.* (Kenyon said he was "entranced with her writings" for many years.) She quoted Mabie in several of her books.

Mabie wrote:

> The term "death" as applied to the nature of Christ's vicarious sufferings for man constituting Him the redeemer, has a meaning in the New Testament altogether unique. That death was more than mortal dying, although mortal dying was linked with it. This would seem to be morally requisite, if a man is to be saved from his real woes. The sentence which was pronounced upon the race at its fall in Eden was something deeper than mere physical death. The Hebrew reads, "To die thou shalt die." The death which our first parents in the garden died involved more than mere mortal dissolution, the separation of soul and body. Such a separation indeed was entailed, but sin in itself effects spiritual death, soul-death; not annihilation but a perversion of the functions normal to personality, eventuating in moral unlikeness to God and separation from Him. Such a separation in fellowship between the soul and its God, *itself is death* in the profoundest sense: it is the destruction of the very possibility of God-likeness resulting in malformation and reprobacy of spiritual being. All this and vastly more is involved in spiritual death.

It is worth the time and effort to read carefully the description of spiritual death expressed by Mabie in this quote. Mabie felt that Jesus experienced spiritual death in His substitution. His language and his understanding are strikingly similar to Kenyon.

At this point in the book (quoted above), Mabie footnoted Alexander MacLaren, the famous "prince of expository preachers" from Manchester, England. Commenting on this deep subject, MacLaren declared:

> We are not to set the physical sufferings of Christ in separation from, or contrast with, the spiritual agonies, but let us not suppose that the physical death was the atonement, apart from the spiritual death of separation from the Father, which is witnessed by that cry of despair mingled with trust that broke the darkness.[26]

Mabie then continued:

> The death for which Christ came into the world, that in its elements He might taste it, and then by resurrection be saved out of it, was chiefly a profound non-physical, psychical experience, inseparably connected with the sin-principle: a death of which the crucifiers of Jesus had no conception whatever.
>
> Doubtless the spiritual death which Christ experienced, was itself the cause of the cessation of His mortal life on the cross. That death brought on His mortal dying long before His executioners expected to see Him expire.
>
> Surely no less a death than that spiritual one which I have represented Christ as experiencing, could have power to "bring to nought" such an adversary, as declared to have had "the power of death."
>
> As by sin came death, and so by death the bond of Satan was cast about all mankind; so through death—death of an infinitely profound sort—Jesus has destroyed even him that had the power of death, and potentially set free all his intended victims. No less a death than that we have attributed to Christ could thus avail . . . Thus, it was that self-imposed death—the voluntary tasting of spiritual separation from God—which constituted the reconciliation.[27]

Notice that the death that Mabie saw Christ suffering continued until He was saved out of it *by resurrection*. Although Mabie doesn't elaborate upon this fact, he seemed to be in agreement with Kenyon that Christ wasn't restored to fellowship with the Father until He was raised from the dead. Mabie also suggested that the spiritual death of Christ was the cause of His physical death. R. W. Dale and E. W. Kenyon would agree.

194

Many more quotes from Mabie could be given about the spiritual nature of the atonement and the power of this truth on the conscience of the sinner. Mabie saw the death of Christ as a powerful evangelical tool to bring deep conviction on the unbeliever. Kenyon, as previously mentioned, was like-minded about the power of Christ's sacrifice to bring conviction to the lost.

G. CAMPBELL MORGAN

G. Campbell Morgan (1863–1945) was another favorite Bible teacher of Kenyon's. Morgan, who eventually became the pastor of the famous Westminster Chapel in London (from 1904–1917), was a popular and respected Bible expositor. Like E. W. Kenyon, he was without academic training, but he eventually became the president of a Bible school (Chestnut College, Cambridge, 1911–1914). His many books are still popular today, especially among preachers and teachers.

As mentioned earlier, Kenyon believed that Jesus suffered in hades until the time of the resurrection. Morgan also believed and taught this. In one of his most respected works, *The Crises of the Christ,* he asked:

> Why did this Holy One pass into hades?
>
> As the Lamb of God He had made Himself responsible for the sin of the world, and the issue of that responsibility was death, essential death, the separation of the spirit from God, and death expressed in the separation of the spirit from the body. To that issue the perfect One who had assumed the responsibility of all human guilt, passed by the way of the cross. In the deep and unfathomable mystery of the cross, His Spirit was separated from God, and that Spirit separated from the body passed down into hades . . . One Who . . . has taken upon Himself the responsibility of the sin of a race, and in those solemn hours between the passing of the Spirit of Christ on the Cross, and the resurrection morning, the holy body of the Man lies in the tomb. His Spirit has passed into hell, the place of lost spirits. Now hear His words, "Thou wilt not leave My soul unto hades."[28]

Mabie and Morgan may not have embraced everything Kenyon taught about Christ's substitutionary work. Perhaps they would have. But clearly they held to the basic outline of Kenyon's understanding and they were not considered heretical for their positions.

CHARLES CUTHBERT HALL

Charles Cuthbert Hall was the author of *Does God Send Trouble?*, a book that was popular particularly among the Faith-Cure movement. F. F. Bosworth quoted Hall in his own book *Christ the Healer.* Hall defended the idea that God doesn't send sickness and trouble upon us. His contention was that God cannot punish us for our sin and punish Jesus as well.

> There is but one place on earth where man obtains a glimpse of what the punishment of sin is as a crime against God. That place is the hill of Calvary, where stands the cross of Jesus Christ. When we can look into the secret anguish of that sacred heart; when we can comprehend the horror and misery that rent His soul; when we can understand the hideous sense of alienation from all good which surged over Him in that frightful darkness, wringing from His lips the shriek, "Forsaken"; when we rise to the point of grasping that—then, and not until then, may we think we comprehend what the *punishment of sin* is.
>
> And when I think of the nameless horror of His punishment, the only uninspired language which approaches a description of it is that clause in the creed (which some tell us we ought to reject as unscriptural), *"He descended into hell."* I cannot reject these words from the creed. Ah! When that shriek, *"Forsaken,"* burst from the pallid lips of Jesus Christ, was He not descending into hell?
>
> His sufferings have redeemed the world.
>
> The alternative is this: to meet the future alone, because *forsaken,* or to be saved in Him, Who was "forsaken" that all men might be forgiven; who descended into hell that all men might ascend into heaven; who was separated in darkness from His Father's face that all men might behold that face in righteousness and peace forever and ever.[29]

These ideas regarding the work of the cross were not obscure or unusual among the evangelical churches of Kenyon's day. This is evidenced by the fact that Kenyon's school, which taught these truths, was well respected. Kenyon spoke for A. B. Simpson at his New York Tabernacle during the years that Bethel Bible Institute was at Spencer. Surely, if these ideas were considered heretical, Kenyon would have been "banned in Boston" and throughout New England.

In the next chapter we will examine another teaching that emerged from his studies: The Finished Work of Christ.

CHAPTER 18

THE FINISHED WORK
OF CHRIST

We live under the dominion of the adversary, continually con-
fessing sickness, want, fear, weakness, and doubts in the face of
this revelation from God of our redemption, of the substitutionary
sacrifice of Christ, and the fact that He is now seated at the right
hand of God having finished a work that perfectly satisfies the
demands of justice and meets the needs of humanity.
—E. W. Kenyon[1]

Kenyon's entire teaching ministry revolved around the cross.
Few ministers have centered their focus more completely on
the work of Jesus. He felt called and compelled to preach and teach
what he referred to as the finished work of Christ. What did he mean
by this concept? We will attempt to gain some understanding of
Kenyon's idea of the finished work in this chapter.

In his first periodical, the *Tabernacle Trumpet,* he wrote in October
1900:

> The fall of man was complete; it took in the whole man—body,
> soul, and spirit; his redemption must cover all that was lost.
> Our redeemer must redeem us from all three of these.
> In order to redeem us from sin, "He was made to be sin on our

behalf, that we might become the righteousness of God in Him" [See 2 Cor. 5:21].

In order to redeem us from sickness, "yet it pleased the Lord to bruise Him; He hath made Him sick. Surely He hath borne our sicknesses and carried our diseases," that we might be healed.

In order to redeem us from death "He tasted (experienced) death for every man, that whosoever believeth on Him should never die."

Kenyon went on to explain the necessity of Christ's spiritual as well as physical sufferings to purchase this three-fold redemption.

He did not have redemption for them [the spirits in prison of 1 Pet. 3:18–22; 4:6] until He was resurrected . . .

There is no ground for salvation through Christ unless he actually took the sinners' place, became sin, voluntarily suffered the extreme penalty of the wrath of God against sin; which is conscious incarceration in hades. This alone satisfies divine justice.[2]

The Protestant Reformation had taught that Christ purchased justification for us. The Holiness movement proclaimed complete sanctification was also ours because of Christ's finished work. The Faith-Cure movement had announced the availability of healing because of the atonement. Kenyon saw all three of these things (justification, sanctification, and healing) as belonging to the believer because of what Christ had done.

Although many were seeing (and teaching) these same truths, often it was in the context of a second blessing or crisis of consecration. Kenyon, after diligent study, motivated it seems by personal need and exposure to Moody's warriors, rejected the second work of grace (or second blessing) concept.

He came to believe that conversion—the new birth, the new creation—gave us all that Christ accomplished in His finished work. After conversion the believer was to receive the Holy Spirit. The Holy Spirit would teach the believer what belonged to him in Christ and empower him to walk in those realities.

It was a finished work—not a second work of grace.

This teaching set him somewhat at odds with much of the Holiness movement. He was always gracious in his presentation, but he felt it necessary to challenge what he believed were unbiblical concepts.

Moody's warriors had already challenged the second work of grace concept and proposed a less radical view. This was the dual nature teaching. ("Dual nature" is the idea that the believer receives a new nature in salvation, but also maintains an "old nature" or "sin nature.") Although a great admirer of Moody's warriors (particularly A. J. Gordon, A. T. Pierson, and many of the teachers from Keswick), Kenyon also felt the dual nature teaching that the majority of them (and the Brethren) embraced could not be validated from Scripture.[3]

Kenyon went on to describe the second work of grace teaching and the failure that even Wesley himself recorded in his journal. In the same periodical in which the earlier quote appeared, Kenyon also indicated his reasons for rejecting the dual nature teaching that was taught by many in the Keswick movement.

Kenyon continued to voice his admiration for his mentors, both in the Holiness and Keswick movements, printing articles and quotes from them in his periodical *Reality*. He did, however, challenge their teachings and offer his own perspective. His life had been changed by what he discovered personally, and he passed it on to his students and those who heard him. The other teachings had failed to bring Kenyon lasting victory.

For Kenyon, the finished work meant man was a new creation. Man only had one nature, not two natures. As a new creation the old nature had passed away (2 Cor. 5:17). Man had become—through the new birth—righteous and holy (Eph. 4:24). The believer didn't need a second work of grace to eradicate indwelling sin (as the Holiness people taught). It was taken out at the new birth when man became, in reality, a new creature.

The believer's needs after conversion were to submit to the lordship of Christ, receive the Holy Spirit, and renew his mind. A genuine submission of all to Christ's lordship and a humbling of the mind to be taught by the Holy Spirit were a more biblical approach to sanctification in Kenyon's perspective.[4]

The above quote gives a pretty good picture of Kenyon's matured view of the new birth and his concept of spiritual growth. The Holy Spirit's purpose, seen through the Word, is to build Christ into us until we reflect Christ to the world. Spiritual growth, then, is the unveiling of the realities purchased by Christ in His finished work, followed by the Spirit's enabling us to walk in those realities.

Kenyon emphasized the fact that the Fall meant partaking of the nature of Satan. He reasoned that if a believer still maintained his old nature as well as the new one, he was now a horrible creature—a house divided—who was partaking of the divine nature and the satanic nature at the same time. For him that was unthinkable. The church had, by and large, Kenyon felt, failed to appreciate the reality of the new creation—what Christ had actually purchased for them through the tremendous suffering He endured.

A. J. Gordon and Identification

As Kenyon examined Paul's epistles, he discovered that Paul saw the believer involved (or identified) with the sacrifice of Christ. We were crucified, we had died, we had been buried, we were made alive, we were raised, and were now seated with Christ, Paul taught. E. W. Kenyon sought to articulate these liberating truths from Paul's epistles. Focusing on this theme was not original to Kenyon, although he had a definite slant on it that gave his teaching a unique quality. One of Kenyon's favorite teachers, A. J. Gordon, had written a book on the subject in 1872!

Gordon wrote "No words of Scripture, if we except those, 'God manifest in the flesh,' hold within themselves a deeper mystery than this simple formula of the Christian life, '*in Christ.*'" In words that sound familiar to readers of Kenyon's works, Gordon continued "Indeed, God's taking upon Himself humanity, and yet remaining God, is hardly more inexplicable to human thought than man's becoming a 'partaker of the divine nature,' and yet remaining man." Yet, Gordon maintained "great as is the mystery of these words, they are the key to the whole system of doctrinal mysteries." He reasoned:

> If one is in Christ, he must have regeneration; for how can the head be alive, and the members dead? If one is in Christ, he must be justified; for how can God approve the head, and condemn the members? If one is in Christ, he must have sanctification; for how can the spotlessly holy One remain in vital connection with one that is unholy? If one is in Christ, he must have redemption; for how can the Son of God be in glory, while that which He has made a part of His body lies abandoned in the grave of eternal death?[5]

A reading of Gordon's book, along with the knowledge of Kenyon's deep regard for Gordon, easily convinces one that this book deeply impacted Kenyon. A few more statements from the book may be helpful: "This truth [of our identification with Christ in His resurrection] is most strikingly told again in those words of the Apostle, 'Who was delivered for our offenses, and raised again for our justification,'—literally, 'delivered *because* of our offenses, and raised *because* of our justification.'"

Gordon saw Christ completely identified with us in our sin and death. He stated, "So enwrapped was He in our sins that were upon Him, that he could not escape death. But when justification of us who are in Him had been accomplished, He could not be detained by death. And so because our justification was completed, He was raised again." In language that Kenyon would echo throughout his entire ministry, Gordon continued, "Opener of the prison doors to them that are bound, He yet waits till the last demand of justice has been satisfied before He comes through the gate of the grave to lead them out."[6]

"So enwrapped was He in our sins that were upon Him . . . He could not escape death . . . so because our justification was completed, He was raised again." Gordon saw Jesus so identified with us in our death that He could not be resurrected until we could be justified. This was precisely Kenyon's teaching. He may well have been struck for the first time with this idea as he read Gordon's book. He may even have picked it up the night he rededicated his life to the Lord in Gordon's church. Observe that Gordon saw Christ continuing to suffer under the punishment of our sins until the resurrection. This was precisely Kenyon's teaching.

Notice also these words: "the last demand of justice has been satisfied." Kenyon often used this phrase. Gordon also used another descriptive term about Christ that has brought Kenyon much criticism: "[Jesus] joined to His people that He might carry them with Him through the pains and penalties of death, He now in the same gracious partnership of being brings them up again from the dead. He spreads the mighty miracle of His own regeneration from the dead, along the whole line of history. He repeats it in every true believer."[7]

Gordon here spoke of the "regeneration" of Christ and the believers' participation in it. Kenyon's critics have mercilessly rebuked him for suggesting that after having been made sin with our sin, Jesus experienced a regeneration—or was "born again." A. J. Gordon apparently—in seeking to understand Paul's teachings on the believer's identification with Christ—came to the same conclusion.

A. T. PIERSON AND CHRIST'S REGENERATION

A good friend of Gordon's, and a respected mentor for Kenyon, A. T. Pierson also wrote along these lines. While the interim pastor for Charles H. Spurgeon in London, Pierson preached a sermon titled *The Attestation of the Son of God; or, Hope Through the Resurrection.* Commenting on Acts 13:33, he said, "the reference in the second Psalm, 'This day have I begotten Thee,' is to the resurrection of Jesus Christ from the dead. The death is figuratively treated in Scripture as His *ceasing to be*—as though God had, on the day of His crucifixion, lost His only begotten Son—and His resurrection is correspondingly treated in the Word of God as a *re-begetting* of Christ from the dead, as though that tomb which had never before received a human body, a sepulchre in which no man had yet been laid—that virgin tomb—had become, on the third day, a virgin womb, out of which Christ was reborn to die no more."

Pierson exhorts his listeners to "bear in mind this startling and majestic metaphor. The resurrection of Christ is held up before us, in the Scriptures, as a re-begetting of Christ, so that He became the first born or first begotten from the dead, coming out of the grave as one that is born again, or begins life anew."[8] The "firstborn of many brethren" as the apostle Paul put it in Romans 8:29 and as Kenyon quoted frequently.

Kenyon saw this truth of Christ experiencing a new birth out of death as being necessitated by Paul's statements of our "being made alive together with Him" (Eph. 2:5; Col. 2:13) after having been made sin (2 Cor. 5:21), and being made a curse (Gal. 3:13). It would be hard to deny that Gordon and Pierson understood Christ to have undergone some kind of new birth out of death in His resurrection. Acts 13:33 became a favorite of Kenyon's in showing Christ being "born again."

PARTAKERS OF THE DIVINE NATURE

E. W. Kenyon has been criticized for suggesting that every believer is an incarnation. What did Kenyon mean by this? If he meant we are all equally God with Jesus, as his critics seem to understand him to mean, then he is guilty of serious error. But is this what he meant? Let's consider some statements that his mentors made that could have easily influenced his thinking.

A. J. Gordon wrote in *Grace and Glory* (1880): "But now God comes with the veritable promise that they shall, through faith, be made godlike, sharers of His nature and conformed to His image." Noting that the believer possesses everlasting life, he explained that "this means not simply that our natural life shall be prolonged into endless duration; but that we shall be endowed with a supernatural life; that God's own immortal nature and being shall be communicated to us through regeneration."

Gordon continued "He has it, that is, the instant he believes, by the new birth from above, by the communication of the divine nature."[9] A little later in the same chapter he offered "regeneration is the same process . . . the holy nature of God weaving itself into our being, and making us one with the Father and the Son. It is the spirit of Christ in us, lifting us up into union with the personal Christ upon the throne . . . "

Relating our new birth to the physical birth of Jesus, he wrote "Each heart that opens itself to His entrance becomes a manger for Jesus; there the miracle of the incarnation is repeated, the Holy Ghost again brings God and man into union in the same person, and one who was born from beneath in his human nature is now born from above with a divine nature. He has Christ in him now as the power for attaining unto the likeness of Christ without him—a divine spirit to mould him to the divine person."[10]

Gordon said that "God's own immortal nature and being shall be communicated" to the believer, and "the miracle of incarnation is repeated"! The idea of the believer being an incarnation because he is partaking of the divine nature—through being indwelt by Christ—was a popular theme among Kenyon's mentors. They were apparently unconcerned that someone would misunderstand them and accuse them of heresy. Assuming that in today's church would not be wise.

Notice also that Gordon's concept of eternal life was "being endowed with a supernatural life . . . God's own immortal nature and being . . . communicated to us." Kenyon spoke frequently of eternal life being the receiving of the life and nature of God. It is quite likely that he was influenced by A. J. Gordon in this area.

A. T. Pierson wrote along these lines: "The Lord Jesus submitted to certain limitations of His and our humanity, and was therefore, while in the flesh, not practically omnipresent. Whereas the Holy Spirit, not having assumed a human body as His mode of incarnation, is equally everywhere resident in and abiding with every believer. In them He so incarnates Himself that through them He works upon others, so that by the indwelling Holy Spirit they become, like Him, teachers . . . witnesses."[11]

In studying the literature of the day, it seems that the dramatic realization that the Holy Spirit, who is God, had condescended to indwell human nature, to "incarnate" Himself in man, was so striking that many in this period of evangelical history (last quarter of the nineteenth century) used the language of *the* incarnation to describe the wonder of the Holy Spirit's indwelling redeemed man.

A. B. Simpson, another contemporary and influential voice in Kenyon's life, said the "truth of the indwelling of Christ is no vague figure of speech, this is no dream of Pantheism, of New Theology, or of the Divine Immanence, but it is a great supernatural fact which marks a crisis in every Christian's life when the son of God becomes incarnate in the believer, just as truly as He became incarnate in the Christ of Judea and Galilee." Simpson carefully distinguishes between what he is teaching and the pantheism of the cults and the transcendentalism that was rampant in the more liberal parts of the church. Yet he used the language of incarnation to describe the believer. "The mystery of the incarnation is repeated every time a soul is created anew in Christ Jesus."[12]

A. B. Simpson maintained that the "man who apprehends this truth" goes forth to fight the battle of life no longer fighting "even with divine assistance, but is a Christ-man, an anointed soul, a dual life with two persons united in everlasting bonds, one, the lowly disciple, the other, the living Christ, and these two henceforth forever one, 'Not I, but Christ who liveth in me.'"[13] For Simpson, the union of life with the indwelling Christ was central to all he preached. He even taught that divine healing was an outflow of the resurrection life of the Son of God brought into the physical dimension through this union.

To those who have read much of E. W. Kenyon, the similarity of thought between him and the above-quoted mentors should be striking. Because these men were very visible leaders, spoke frequently in conferences in New England, contributed to many periodicals (in addition to their own periodicals), and authored many books, Simpson, Pierson, and Gordon were quite influential on Kenyon.[14]

Simpson distinguished between Christianity as an imitation of Christ and the reality of His indwelling. In *The Christ Life* he explained that "Christ life is a vital and divine experience through the union of the soul with the living Christ Himself. Christian life may be an honest attempt to imitate Christ and follow His teachings and commandments, but Christ life is the incarnation of Jesus Himself in your own life. It is the Christ reliving His life in you and enabling you to be and to do what, in your own strength, you never could accomplish."[15]

A. B. Simpson had his own unique view of sanctification that was not easily classified. He believed in a definite second "crisis" experience, but it didn't fit the Holiness model. This crisis, for Simpson, was more often described in terms of receiving Christ as one's "indwelling life." Kenyon used similar language to Simpson but usually put it the framework of the new birth. Although Kenyon definitely rejected the theology of a second work of grace, he didn't disdain a definite crisis of consecration. He viewed it more as a total submitting to the lordship of Christ.

KENYON ON THE BELIEVER AS AN INCARNATION

In Kenyon's first book *The Father and His Family* (1916), he spoke in language very similar to some of his mentors—language his critics have used to misrepresent his teaching. He wrote, "Every false religion that denies the incarnation of Jesus of Nazareth has attempted to provide a theory of universal incarnation in order to stimulate to a higher moral or spiritual life. Theosophy tries to make us believe that all men have the nature of deity. The same thing is held by practically all our modern liberal theological teachers and preachers! That so-called 'Spark of divinity' dwells in all men, that the new birth is simply the awakening, the blowing-into-a-flame, or this spark of divinity."

In his book Kenyon obviously disagreed with such modern, liberal theology. He wrote "If man had a spark of deity or any part of deity abiding in him, then man was already God Incarnate. We know that this whole theory is fallacious, for man has experimentally proven it false. The entire New Testament contradicts it." No "spark of divinity" in man apart from the new birth in Kenyon's thinking.

But Kenyon did draw the same conclusion as his mentors from the dramatic reality of the Lord's incarnation. "The Incarnation of Jesus of Nazareth is no more difficult to believe nor to understand than the creation of the first man or the birth of a child. If God is Almighty, he had the power to beget a child in the womb of the Virgin Mary." Here we see his view of Christ's incarnation. Kenyon, like his mentors, concluded that, "If Jesus was incarnate, man and God can become united; God can dwell in these human bodies of ours; God can impart His own life and nature to our spirits, and we may have God's life in these human bodies."

Then he stated the implication of Christ's incarnation: "Every man who has been *born again* is an incarnation, and Christianity is a miracle. The believer is as much an Incarnation as was Jesus of Nazareth."[16] Kenyon did not mean that man is an incarnation in the same sense that Jesus was. He meant that because man and God can become united, as is proven by our Lord's incarnation, then "God can dwell in these human bodies of ours." Men can become the dwelling place of God by the indwelling of the Holy Spirit. Men do not become "gods," but the living God comes and dwells in man.

The last part of the above quotation (The believer is as much an incarnation. . . .) has been taken out of its context and has been frequently used by Kenyon's detractors to suggest that he taught we could develop into "gods." One wrote that Kenyon taught "that [there is] just such a 'divine element' within man, and [it] could, indeed, be developed to the point of man becoming a god."[17]

He then footnotes two of Kenyon's books so we may see where he teaches this heresy. The first quote is from *The Hidden Man,* a book Kenyon was working on when he died and which was published posthumously by his daughter. Here's the quote:

> The third kind of spirituality [Kenyon has just discussed the false spirituality of the metaphysical cults and spiritualism] is that of the new creation spirit, for a man becomes a new creation by receiving the life and nature of God.
>
> The Holy Spirit makes His home in the physical body and dominates the human spirit that has been recreated. As this is cultured and developed through the Word, there is no limit to its possibilities.[18]

As he did in all his books where he mentioned the metaphysical cults, he contrasted them negatively with the superiority of the new birth and the biblical gospel. The indwelling Holy Spirit and the Word are the reason there is "no limit to its [the human spirit's] development." This hardly describes man developing into a "god." Actually, Kenyon was encouraging his readers to recognize that the Holy Spirit could dominate the human spirit and form Christ in them.

The second piece of evidence (?) used to suggest that Kenyon taught we could develop into gods was in Kenyon's book *The Two Kinds of Life*. Discussing the superiority of the benefits of Christ's sacrifice compared to the Old Covenant sacrifices that "covered" sin, he pointed out that in the New Covenant a new kind of life—eternal life—had come to the believer. Referring to Jesus' statement that He had come to bring abundant life, Kenyon remarked that believers "were to become partakers of the divine nature, the very essence and substance of deity."[19]

I think you can see that Kenyon is saying nothing about men developing into "gods." Unless, of course, we interpret Peter (2 Pet. 1:4) as teaching that idea when he tells us that through the "exceedingly great and precious promises" we may be "partakers of the divine nature." This was one of E. W. Kenyon's favorite verses.

When Kenyon revised his first book, *The Father and His Family*, around 1936, he chose a quote from A. J. Gordon to introduce the chapter on the new birth. Gordon said:

> The new birth therefore is not a change of nature as it is sometimes defined; it is rather the communication of the divine nature . . .
>
> Regeneration is not our natural life carried up to its highest point of attainment, but the divine life brought down to its lowest point of condescension, even to the heart of fallen man . . . It has been the constant dream and delusion of men that they could rise to heaven by development and improvement of their natural life. Jesus by one stroke of revelation destroys this hope, telling His believers that unless he has been begotten of God who is above, as truly as he has been begotten of his father on earth, that he cannot see the kingdom of God.[20]

If Kenyon believed we could develop into gods, he certainly made an odd choice in this quotation from Gordon. It should be noted that the revision of *Father and His Family* came out in 1937, just eleven years before Kenyon died. It is in this period (1937–45) that most of his other books were published. It has been claimed that it was in his latter years that Kenyon became heretical and started to teach that we could develop into "gods." Again, the evidence doesn't at all justify such an accusation.

As you can see from the quotes above, many of Kenyon's contemporaries used similar language to describe receiving eternal life, the new birth or the indwelling of the Spirit. Some may question the wisdom of using language that so easily lends itself to misunderstanding. This may be a valid criticism. However, it is also possible that these men were so well-known and respected as men of sound doctrine that their orthodoxy wasn't questioned, and they were given the benefit of the doubt. Kenyon saw himself aligned with these men of God.

Kenyon described an overview of his thoughts on the new birth in an article in the *Bethel Trumpet* in 1901.

> The first thing the sinner needs is imputed righteousness. Our substitute Jesus had all the graces that God demanded of us, and when we accept Him as our Saviour God, all of His graces become ours, they are reckoned as ours by God. Our first need is something that will enable us to stand uncondemned in God's presence, as Adam did before the fall; this the sinner has in Jesus.
>
> The first benefit he receives is remission of sins and imputed righteousness . . .
>
> When a son receives this mighty Spirit into his heart, He brings the righteousness of the Christ into our very being, and we then actually become "partakers of his holiness" [Heb.12:10], of "his divine nature" [2 Pet.1:4], of "the Holy Spirit" [Heb.6:4]; that is God becomes incarnated in us, in a manner almost beyond conception, and "we become the righteousness of God in him" [2 Cor. 5:21].
>
> Oh that in some way I could by the Spirit show you that what you want, is not an experience or blessing, but simply *Jesus*. If you will take Him to be your righteousness up there before God, then take the Holy Spirit to dwell in you and make real to you all that Christ is for you; and trust the Spirit to finish all that God has begun in you, to make His righteousness a reality in you; you will

never need another anxious seat, or seek after another man, for "Christ will be all in all" to you and satisfy your every longing.[21]

In this early quote it is easy to see that Kenyon believed in justification and sanctification, but he also wanted people to get their focus on the Person of Jesus as heavenly Mediator and the Person of the Holy Spirit as the indwelling One.

Kenyon's teaching on the finished work of Christ revolved around our identification with Christ in His death, burial, and resurrection. He took very seriously the new creation and the dramatic change that the new birth brought us. For him, the reality of the internal change was central to our new identity as sons of God. Righteousness was experiential and a part of the new man, not merely judicial or legal. He valued the importance of what was done *for* us, but felt we needed the Holy Spirit to reveal to us what was done *in* us. These truths, suggested by the teachings of many of his mentors, had liberated Kenyon from a life of defeat. He felt compelled to expound them and readily found an audience for his message of faith.

CHAPTER 19

REVELATION KNOWLEDGE

You had to take time to learn your algebra, your mathematics,
your history, and your geography. Now you must take time to sit
with His Word and let the Spirit unveil his Word to your spirit.
—E.W. Kenyon[1]

O f all that Kenyon taught, his views on the nature of man have
been subjected to the greatest misrepresentation. In some
cases, all of his Christian influences have been overlooked, even
though their teaching on the nature of man was almost identical to
Kenyon's.

In this chapter we'll compare Kenyon's view of the nature of man to
the cultic view. Then we'll review quotes from the many Christian
leaders of Kenyon's day who believed that man is spirit, soul, and body.

THE METAPHYSICAL VIEW

Kenyon believed that man is primarily a spiritual being and that sickness has its origin in the unseen realm of spirit. Some cults in his day
also believed man is spiritual and sickness had a spiritual source.
Because of these similarities, some have claimed Kenyon's teaching
was drawn from these cults. This is not the case and it is relatively easy
to demonstrate why.

The metaphysical cults point to the spirit realm as the realm of perfection. Christian Science teaches the perfection of the spirit realm and

denies the existence of matter all together, while Unity (which is for the most part the heir of New Thought teachings) doesn't deny matter but clings to the concept of a perfect Universal Mind.

Metaphysical teachers maintain that the spiritual realm governs the physical and that sickness is either an "error of mortal mind" (in Christian Science sickness is not considered real) or the result of wrong thinking (in Unity and New Thought sickness is considered real but its source is not physical). These cults generally agree that the spiritual realm must be accessed to attain healing.

For Kenyon, the ideal spiritual realm was not an impersonal Perfect Mind, but rather the grace of God provided through the finished work of Christ which existed in the "unseen realm of spiritual reality," (as evangelical scholar John R.W. Stott put it). (See Ephesians 1:3; 2 Peter 1:3.)[2] This grace was administered by the Holy Spirit through the written Word of God. The atonement of Christ was Kenyon's only basis for obtaining healing. This healing was received by faith in God through prayer from its source (God) in the spiritual realm—in the heavenly place in Christ—and then manifested in the physical realm.

When Kenyon said the source of sickness was spiritual, not physical, he was referring to sickness's roots in Satan, sin, and the Fall. This is totally contrary to the understanding expressed by the cults when they suggest healing is primarily spiritual. They uniformly deny the existence of Satan and the Fall. (Some acknowledge something they call "sin," but it falls short of the biblical definition.)

Because Kenyon believed in Satan, sin, and the Fall, the spirit realm was not an ideal realm of perfection, but rather the realm of spiritual conflict. Receiving healing involved spiritual warfare against Satan and demons. The ideal realm for Kenyon was "every spiritual blessing in the heavenlies in Christ" (Eph.1:3), "far above all principalities and powers" (Eph. 1:21). The realm of perfection was in Christ alone. This is the apostle Paul's teaching, not the metaphysical cults. Physical healing, in Kenyon's thought, was among the things God had provided for us in Christ. This doesn't resemble the metaphysical concept at all.

Kenyon chastised the metaphysical cults for developing their minds and performing mental healing and not the true spiritual healing (or divine healing) that the Bible teaches. In *Jesus the Healer* he wrote:

> You must have seen as you have studied this book that healing is spiritual.

212

It is not mental as Christian Science and Unity and other metaphysical teachers claim. Neither is it physical as the medical world teaches. When God heals, He heals through the spirit.[3]

Kenyon believed that healing was received by faith from God the Father into the spirit of man, then manifested in the body. The part of our being that "touched" God was the human spirit; therefore, faith was receiving from God, Spirit to spirit. Kenyon insisted that faith was spiritual, not mental.

THE REAL MAN IS SPIRIT

Kenyon saw the spirit man as the real man. Though, as we shall see, this was a typical belief among Christians of his day, some say that this aspect of Kenyon's teaching was cultic. One author commented on this belief, "Anyone vaguely familiar with metaphysics will recognize the cultic nature of the Faith view of man. All the metaphysical cults teach the pantheistic idea that because God is in everything, everything is God."[4]

What is the "Faith view of man?" Kenyon and the modern Faith movement have taught that man is a spirit, just as God is a spirit. They say that the human spirit can become a partaker of the divine nature (2 Pet. 1:4). After being born of God (John 3:5; Heb. 12:9), the human spirit can serve as the dwelling place of the Holy Spirit, who *is* God. These ideas fall quite a distance short of pantheism—saying that God is in everything and everything is God. The above-mentioned author took an amazing leap of logic, to say the least.

KENYON'S BELIEFS SUMMARIZED

Much of Kenyon's teaching on the nature of man is summarized in the following quote. Read this quote carefully because you will notice later that it sounds nearly identical to the teaching of several of Kenyon's mentors.

We know that man is a spirit.
He is in the same class as God.
We know that God is a spirit and that He became a man and took on a man's body, and when He did it He was no less God than He was before He took the physical body.

213

We know that man, at death, leaves his physical body and is no less man than he was when he had his physical body.

We know that man cannot know God through Sense Knowledge.

God is only revealed to man through the spirit.

It is the spirit of man that contacts God.

We know that spiritual things are just as real as material things.

God is just as real a person as though He had a physical body.

Jesus, with His physical body now in Heaven, is no more real than the Holy Spirit or the Father.

The real man is spirit.

He has a body and a soul.

The soul contacts the intellectual realm, the physical body contacts the physical realm, and the spirit, the spiritual realm.

The Holy Spirit cannot communicate directly with our minds, but He must communicate with our spirit which reaches and influences our intellectual processes.[5]

Kenyon believed man was a trichotomy, that is, man consists of spirit, soul, and body. Man is a spirit, he has a soul, and he lives in a body—this would be the often-used terminology. Many, if not most, of Kenyon's mentors held to the trichotomist view, and would not have been troubled by Kenyon's view of the nature of man at all.

Kenyon's teaching echoed many others of his day who thrilled at the prospect of a personal relationship with God through the Holy Spirit and rejected the dead formalism of much of the rest of the church. It has been said that Kenyon derived his view of the nature of man from the cults, but this is speculation, not fact.

VOICES IN THE CHURCH

There is no evidence that Kenyon arrived at the view that man is primarily a spirit from the cults, but it is easy to see how he picked it up from the church. S.D. Gordon, many of whose books Kenyon read, wrote in his classic, *Quiet Talks on Prayer* (1904):

Man is a spirit being; an embodied spirit being. He has a body and a mind. He is a spirit. His real conflicts are of the spirit sort; in the spirit realm, with other spirit beings.[6]

Gordon's books remain popular to this day. Though Gordon believed man was primarily a spirit being, as far as I know, no one has accused him of being influenced by the metaphysical cults.

Another respected contemporary of Kenyon's, G. Campbell Morgan, also saw man as primarily spirit. In his 1908 book *Christian Principles,* (the chapters were originally given as a series of lectures in New York, which Kenyon may well have attended), Morgan said,"Man is made in the image and likeness of God. God is Spirit, and man therefore essentially is not material, but spiritual . . . "

Morgan saw the essence of man as the human spirit reflecting the likeness of God. He further avows that "the supreme truth of human life, according to the teaching of the Word of God, is that as God is a Spirit, man is also a spirit."[7]

Morgan believed with Kenyon that the human spirit is the essential man—the real man. The "supreme truth" of human life is that God and man are essentially spirit, Morgan claimed. In this book, Morgan also expressed an idea that Kenyon often voiced in his writings: that our spiritual life is determined by whether the human spirit or the body is in ascendancy.

Kenyon wrote:

> In the beginning, man's spirit was the dominant force in the world; when he sinned, his mind became dominant—sin dethroned the spirit and crowned the intellect; but grace is restoring the spirit to its place of dominion, and when man comes to recognize the dominance of the spirit, he will live in the realm of the supernatural without effort.[8]

In this teaching of the primacy of the human spirit, there is no blurring of the distinction between the Creator and the created.[9] This is not pantheism. Yet, wrote Morgan, "The first business of human life is the culture of the spirit," a statement with which Kenyon was in hearty agreement.[10]

In language that finds many parallels in Kenyon's teaching about the nature of man and spirituality, G. Campbell Morgan further stated:

> If the spirit be the central thing in our lives, then the mental and the physical are concentric, and where this is so, there is perfect harmony. But if we make the physical central in life, or if we

make the mental the central, we become eccentric.[11]

Kenyon has been criticized for making an artificial distinction between mind and spirit. This distinction was upheld by many of Kenyon's mentors who were the orthodox Christian leaders of his day. The apostle Paul makes this distinction in 1 Cor. 14:14 where he stated:

> For if I pray in a tongue, my spirit prays, but my understanding [the Greek word for *understanding* is *nous,* usually translated *mind*] is unfruitful.

LINES OF COMMUNICATION

A.T. Pierson, another Kenyon favorite, used the following metaphor to show the lines of communication between spirit, soul, and body.

> The soul is the natural man, that does not see or know the things of God, and the spirit is the highest part of the man, capable of direct communication with God, enlightened and illuminated by the Holy Spirit.
> Such passages [1 Thess. 5:23; 1 Cor.2; Heb. 4:12] . . . suggest a three-storied house, the upper story, an observatory, with the skylights and majestic windows that look out on celestial prospects; the body, the lowest story, with its five senses—sight, hearing, taste, touch and smell, opening out into the external universe, like doors and windows, through which to gather information about things without, and report to the soul, which is like the second story of the building, shut in darkness, but getting by way of the body, through the avenues of the senses, knowledge with regard to the external world.

Pierson proceeded to describe the human spirit and the means by which the soul receives its knowledge.

> The topmost story, the spirit, the highest of all, is alone capable of direct knowledge of God, and an intimate communion and fellowship with Him. The soul seems to be that part of man's complex being which may thus derive its information with regard

216

to the world without, through the senses; or of higher truth, through the intuitions of the spirit, which gets its knowledge not through the body or soul only, but through intuition and direct revelation from God.[12]

Those familiar with Kenyon's concepts of sense knowledge and revelation knowledge will notice a striking parallel in Pierson's teaching here. The soul—or mind—Pierson asserted, can receive its input from either the body or the spirit. The former Kenyon would call sense knowledge, the latter, revelation knowledge.[13]

Pierson's stature and influence during Kenyon's years in the East (until 1923) should not be underestimated. Although he died in 1911, he was highly respected and admired and his many books remained popular. His opinions were esteemed of great value and worth. Kenyon's teaching was strikingly similar to Pierson's on this important theme.

One critic stated that Kenyon's "doctrine of Revelation Knowledge exhibits the radical dualism of the metaphysical cults."[14] He interpreted Kenyon to mean that all knowledge comes to one or the other of two mutually exclusive sources: the spirit or the mind. He further stated his understanding of Kenyon as teaching that the "knowledge from one realm is of no value to the other."[15] This is not what Kenyon taught. Kenyon believed that the Holy Spirit touched the human spirit which then illuminated the mind. Kenyon wrote:

He [God the Father], being a spirit, can only reveal Himself to spirits. He can reveal Himself to our spirits through the Word.

For instance, we hear someone read the Word of God. The thing that is read is weighed and measured by our intellect, but in some way, which is inexplicable to reason, if affects our spirits. It answers a need. By listening to the Word, it changes our spirit.[16]

A little later in the same book he added:

Originally the spirit dominated the physical body and dominated the avenues through which the mind received its knowledge. In the beginning the human spirit governed the human reasoning faculties.[17]

E.W. Kenyon did not see the mind as incapable of receiving spiritual understanding. He, like A.T. Pierson, saw the necessity of the mind becoming subject to the human spirit in order to obtain revelation from God. Kenyon constantly taught the necessity of a renewed mind to walk in faith. In *In His Presence* Kenyon wrote:

> As soon as he is Recreated, the Father begins the beautiful process of Renewing his mind . . .
>
> The renewing of the mind will be a transfiguration of our minds.
>
> No one can overestimate this wonderful fact.
>
> These minds of ours have been dominated by the Senses, so that all the knowledge that we have had has been Sense Knowledge.
>
> This mind is going to be renewed by the Spirit, and by our meditation in the Word and practicing the Word, until our mind is in perfect fellowship with our recreated spirit and with the Word.
>
> The renewed mind, coming into this deep, rich fellowship with the Father through the Word, is able to appreciate and understand the wealth of the Redemptive work that was wrought in Christ.[18]

Kenyon highly valued the believer's mind, seeing the mind as an ally to the human spirit. Mind and spirit were to come into perfect fellowship as the mind was renewed. He understood, however, the necessity of submitting the mind to the ministry of the Holy Spirit. The Holy Spirit illuminated the human spirit through the Word, resulting in the mind being renewed. In Kenyon's thought (following Paul's teaching in Rom. 12:1-2), this renewing of the mind was the key to transformation.

When one of Kenyon's detractors suggested that he taught "the human spirit has little or nothing to do with intellect, which can process only Sense Knowledge," we see how Kenyon's teaching on this subject has been misunderstood and therefore misrepresented.[19]

Kenyon wrote:

> Before we were Born Again, our minds were in harmony with our unregenerate spirit.
>
> Now that our spirit has been recreated, our minds become renewed by the Word.

Now the two, our spirit and our mind, are brought into har-mony.[20]

Your mind, which has been dominated by the Senses, receiving all of its knowledge through the nerve centers, is being renewed through the Word so that it is coming into fellowship with your recreated spirit.[21]

Kenyon saw a harmony and fellowship between the mind and spirit to be the desired goal.

SIMPSON'S POINT OF VIEW

A.B. Simpson, whose influence on Kenyon was dramatic, also commented on the distinct nature of the spirit of man. Answering the question *What is the spirit?* he offered, "In a word it may be said that it is the divine element in man, or perhaps more correctly, that which is cognizant of God. It is not the intellectual or mental or aesthetic or sensational part of man but the spiritual, the higher nature, that which recognizes and holds converse with the heavenly and divine."

Simpson's basic agreement with Kenyon's perspective is shown in this quote. Simpson proceeded to say, "It [the human spirit] is that in us which knows God, which directly and immediately is conscious of the divine presence and can hold fellowship with Him, hearing His voice, beholding His glory, receiving intuitively the impression of His touch and conviction of His will, understanding and worshipping His character and attributes, speaking to Him in the spirit and language of prayer and praise and heavenly communion."

In language that resembles Kenyon and their (Simpson and Kenyon's) biblical inspiration, the apostle Paul, he continued, "It is that which resembles God, the new man created in righteousness and true holiness after His image."[22]

Simpson believed the human spirit in the believer to be the new man—the new creation—created in righteousness and holiness. Kenyon would heartily agree.

Simpson acknowledged the human spirit as the "higher and divine element" in man, but, he felt, " . . . He needs our mind as well as our spirit to use as the instrument and organ of His high and holy service." Not content to have access to our human spirit only, "The Holy Spirit is a quickening force to the consecrated intellect" as well.[23]

Kenyon in his teaching on this theme, has simply restated in his own unique style and language, that which his many mentors (Simpson among them) were teaching.

DUALISM

All of the above-quoted authors saw the human spirit as the essential man, the new creation. And they all recognized the difference between the human spirit and the intellect. In various ways they tell us that the human spirit receives from the Holy Spirit and informs our intellect. The knowledge of God and spiritual things comes to the spirit and then to the intellect. This was Kenyon's teaching precisely.

While it should be fairly obvious from the quotes above that Kenyon did not necessarily have any influence from the cults to develop his ideas about sense knowledge and revelation knowledge, some still insist he did. One wrote:

> Kenyon believed that to know God, one must transcend sensory and scientific knowledge in order to act upon the knowledge of the Bible. [This author is describing what Kenyon termed *revelation knowledge.*]
>
> The Faith theology [rooted in Kenyon's teaching] teaches the Gnostic view that "man is a spirit being" who just happens to have a body. Only the "spirit man" has the capacity to receive revelation directly from the Holy Spirit . . . This view of revelation reflects the Gnostic spirit-matter dualism that Kenyon learned from the metaphysical cults.[24]

The evidence suggests a different conclusion. As I have been pointing out in this book, Kenyon drew his ideas from the Higher Life movement and the Keswick movement. F.B. Meyer, a respected Keswick teacher whom Kenyon heard at Moody's Northfield conferences, also commented on the human spirit. In *The Message of Keswick and Its Meaning,* Meyer is quoted as saying:

> It is in the *spirit* that the birth from above takes place. "The Spirit itself beareth witness with our spirit, that we are children of God" (Rom. 6:16).
>
> It is through the spirit that we come in touch with the Saviour.

220

It is with the spirit we welcome the Lord, who stands and knocks. It is by the spirit that we pray and meditate and grow in grace. It is by the eyes of the heart (another name for the organ of the spirit) that we come to know what is the hope of His calling, the riches of the glory of His inheritance, and the exceeding greatness of His power to usward who believe! (Eph. 1:18–19, italics in original).[25]

Meyer clearly held the view that the human spirit was the faculty for receiving the knowledge of spiritual things. Meyer also equated the heart with the human spirit as did Kenyon. Neither Kenyon nor any of these men whose statements we have examined disdained the mind or embraced the dualism that the above-quoted critic claimed Kenyon espoused.

A.T. Pierson also commented on the human spirit's capacity to fellowship with God and receive revelation. In *Lessons in the School of Prayer* (1895) he wrote:

God is a Spirit, and must be worshipped in the spirit. Invisible to the eye, inaudible to the ear, intangible to the touch, He cannot be tested by the senses. They utterly fail us as channels of impression or communication. His subtle essence evades all carnal approach or analysis. He must be otherwise known, if at all: the spirit alone has the higher senses which, being exercised to discern good and evil, can enable us to perceive God and hold communication with Him.

Pierson, here, expressed what Kenyon would have referred to as the "utter failure of sense knowledge" to reveal God. Pierson continued:

When a devout disciple takes God's Word in his hands, for studious and thoughtful meditation, he naturally lifts his heart to Him who alone can unveil the eyes of his understanding to behold wondrous things out of His law. As he reads and searches, meditating therein, the same Spirit who first inspired the Word, illumines his mind. New light is thrown upon the sacred page, so that what was obscure or hidden, becomes visible and legible; and new clearness of sight and insight is given to the spiritual organ of vision, so that it becomes more capable of seeing, more keen-sighted and far-sighted.[26]

To meditate on God's words introduces us to the secret chambers of God's thoughts, and imparts insight into God's character.

This is one of the closed mysteries, a stumbling-block of mysticism, or the foolishness of fanaticism, to the unbelieving; but to him whose experience has been enriched by it, an open mystery, a fact as indisputable as anything in the realm of matter.[27]

Pierson was well educated and exhibited a fine intellect. What he was expressing was that the Holy Spirit had to make real the things of God through the human spirit and then illuminate the mind. God could and would reveal himself to the human spirit.

In *The Father and His Family* Kenyon wrote:

It is the privilege of every member of the Father's Family to have a little time with Him every day in the Holy of Holies of his own nature, where his spirit fellowships with the Great Father Spirit, a place, where we sit and lean against His breast, look into His face, and draw inspiration from His love and greatness and power, until we finally become imitators of the living Father in our conduct with men.[28]

In *The Two Kinds of Life* Kenyon wrote:

Now you see the necessity of your taking time to meditate in the Word, to get quiet with the Lord.

You had to take time to learn your algebra, your mathematics, your history, and your geography.

Now you must take time to sit with His Word and let the Spirit unveil his Word to your spirit.

If you will, you will know Him in reality.

I am learning to do this. I become quiet and say: "Blessed Spirit, now make the Word a living thing in my spirit; open it to me."

I go over the passage I want unveiled to me. I meditate on it. After a bit the clamor of my mind is gone. The noise it makes is gone. You can become as noisy in your intellect as you become noisy with your hands and feet.

I grow quiet. Then in a single minute, or a half-minute there will be an unveiling of the Word of God such as I have never seen before. It does not take Him more than a moment to unveil the Word, to throw upon the screen a message that will take you hours to write.

Eternal Life has come into your spirit. Now let God have freedom to lead you into the realities of His Revelation in the Word.[29]

Henry C. Mabie, a respected and prominent voice in New England, made some comments that describe Kenyon's concept of revelation knowledge quite well. He wrote:

> The redemption of Christ is grounded in the deepest *realities* of the universe of which we are a part. The use of this term "reality' in its deepest sense needs to be restored to Christian thought and vocabulary. Alas! much of the religious thought of our day is confined to the mere realm of speculative dogmatic opinion, or so-called "beliefs."
>
> It is now recognized by the great teachers that if truth is to be really apprehended, it is not enough to bring the intellect merely to bear upon it.
>
> No man ever touches reality by exercising the speculative understanding merely. Such an one stands outside the truth; he merely patronizes it; he cannot grasp it until he has personally surrendered to its authority, and is held captive by it.
>
> The words with which John concludes the epistle truly rendered read thus," And we know that the Son of God has come, and has given us insight—a through-knowledge—that we may understand Him that is *real,* and we are in Him that is *real,* even in His Son Jesus Christ; this is the *real* God and eternal life." To know thus, is to stand in an entirely different realm from that occupied by mere dogmatic opinion.[30]

THE THEOLOGICAL CLIMATE

Rather than being influenced by the metaphysical cults into a "Gnostic spirit-matter dualism" view of knowledge (as the critic quoted above attempted to categorize Kenyon), Kenyon was touched by deeply spiritual men who were calling the Church to go beyond the dead, dry formalism of the day and really experience Christ and the realities of redemption on a spiritual level and not merely on an intellectual level.

Many of the orthodox leaders and theologians of Kenyon's day, were defenders of the historic creeds and their particular denomination's understanding of scripture. Many of them, unfortunately, saw the emphasis on holiness, personal experience with the Holy Spirit and divine healing as "strange, new doctrines."

E.W. Kenyon, emulating his many mentors who reacted against this formalism, contended for a deeper experience with God and spiritual realities. He desired to do this without going into the ditch on one side by departing from the written Word or on the other side by teaching spiritual experiences as doctrine. He contended for valid, spiritual experience which submitted to the authority of the written Word of God.

On the other hand, some of the leaders and theological instructors of Kenyon's day had embraced, to a great degree, Higher Criticism, the approach to the Scriptures dominating the European theological scene. This way of viewing Scripture rejected to a large degree, the authority of the Word, and subjected the Bible to man's intellectual analysis. Consequently, much of Scripture was rejected as authoritative and a resultant low view of inspiration was embraced. Kenyon saw himself as one of the voices proclaiming a alternative to these two views.[31]

Many solidly evangelical Bible teachers were advocating concepts of spiritual life and development similar to Kenyon's. Kenyon sought to develop a unique, striking terminology for these concepts because he felt the church had lost it grip on the imagination of the age.

Given his environment, none of the concepts were all that radical or different from his contemporaries. Many in this day have failed to realize how similar Kenyon's teachings really are to those of his day. This failure to appreciate Kenyon's true mentors has caused them to look to the similarities in the teachings of the metaphysical cults. This is unfortunate, to say the least. And, I might add, a misrepresentation of the man and his teachings.

CHAPTER 20

THE METAPHYSICAL CULTS

We are dealing, not in terms of psychology nor human religion,
we are dealing not with negatives; we accept the fact that Satan
is, that sin is, that disease is. But we come against disease as
Jesus came against it, not denying its reality, but driving it out as
the Master did, healing it, the health and life of the Son of God
displacing it. It is not error to say disease is; it is the truth,
acknowledge it. It takes faith to destroy it.

—E. W. Kenyon, 1934[1]

Anyone teaching divine healing in the latter part of the nine-teenth-century faced the inevitable comparison with Christian Science and the other metaphysical cults. Unfortunately, many leaders in the orthodox church who were opposed to healing in general failed to distinguish any significant difference between the two approaches to healing.

In 1886 a prominent New York Methodist preacher wrote an article entitled "Faith-Healing and Kindred Phenomena" for a popular magazine. This clergyman lumped all the cults together with those teaching divine healing, considering them all to be false doctrine.[2] His article sparked a debate in print between himself and A. B. Simpson.

In this climate, divine healing teachers had to be able to show the differences between biblical healing and metaphysical healing. This was done through many books and tracts that surfaced in the years preceding and following this debate.

The relevance of these differences in the teaching of divine healing and metaphysical healing in the study of E. W. Kenyon's life is therefore quite significant. In this chapter I want to establish the following:

- The Faith-Cure movement predated the metaphysical cults by a number of years.
- The practices of the Faith-Cure movement were established before the metaphysical cults were visible as distinct movements.
- The Faith-Cure movement, which was rooted in the evangelical church, had distinctly different teachings than the cults.
- E. W. Kenyon's teachings are in the Faith-Cure tradition.

CHRISTIAN SCIENCE AND THE METAPHYSICAL CULTS

Christian Science was the first and best known of the cults of healing, but it was followed by other groups, the most notable being New Thought and Unity. The teachings of Christian Science were also more extreme than the other groups mentioned. Its founder, Mary Baker Eddy, even denied the existence of matter!

There were many metaphysical healers in New England teaching similar concepts to those popularized by Mary Baker Eddy and Christian Science. Mrs. Eddy, however, had the organizational skills necessary to create a recognized movement gathered around metaphysical ideas of healing. None of her predecessors did.

New Thought historian Charles S. Braden noted:

> The first really to organize a healing ministry was Mary Baker Eddy, and it must be recognized that it was her organizing activity which produced, either directly or indirectly, both Christian Science and what may be termed the whole "Metaphysical movement," of which both Christian Science and New Thought are component parts.[3]

In 1885 a correspondent for the London *Times* reported from Boston:

> Clergymen of all denominations are seriously considering how to deal with what they regard as the most dangerous innovation that has threatened the Christian church in this region for many years.

Scores of the most valued church members are joining the Christian Science branch of the metaphysical organization, and it has thus far been impossible to check the defection.[4]

Christian Science exploded in the 1890s. The movement grew from seven congregations in 1890 to more than eleven hundred in 1910. By 1900 there were almost fifty thousand members; ten years later there were over eighty-five thousand.[5] It was certainly understandable that the orthodox churches were concerned.

EVANGELICAL RESPONSE

In 1913 the popular evangelical publisher Fleming H. Revell (D. L. Moody's brother-in-law) published a book that sought to clarify the difference between the cults and divine healing. It was written by E. L. House, a pastor who had been educated at Harvard and Boston Universities. (Kenyon refers to this book in one of his own books).

House compared the two approaches to healing by contrasting their views on six important areas of truth. Here's a summary of his points.

1. *Supreme authority.* For Christians it is the Bible. For Christian Science, Mary Baker Eddy's textbook *Science and Health.* New Thought used the Bible but considered all "scriptures" (from every religion) equally inspired.
2. *The nature of God.* For Christians God is most definitely a person. Christian Science and New Thought (and later Unity School of Christianity) all deny the personhood of God.
3. *Sin.* Christians defined it as "a transgression of the law of God." Christian Science called sin "an illusion with no basis in fact." New Thought called it "a lack of knowledge."
4. *Atonement.* Divine healing makes Christ an atoning Savior; both Christian Science and New Thought deny or avoid any clarity in this area. Mrs. Eddy wrote, "One sacrifice, however great, is insufficient to pay the debt of sin."
5. *Prayer.* Mary Baker Eddy said the only value of prayer was on the individual's mind. Physical sickness was an "error of mortal mind" in Christian Science. In New

Thought teaching it was an absence of harmony, the result of a broken law of the mind. For the Christian, prayer was personal contact with a personal God. Petitioning God for healing was advocated by divine healing ministers, rejected by the metaphysical teachers.

6. *Disease.* In Christian Science the reality of the disease was denied. New Thought, while not denying the reality of sickness, saw its cause in the mind of man. Divine healing advocates affirmed the reality of sickness, sin, and Satan. For them, sickness was the result of the Fall, sin, and Satan. The metaphysical cults recognize no personal devil or demons, no biblical Fall of humanity.

KENYON'S FAITH-CURE ROOTS

Kenyon would be in agreement with E. L. House point for point on biblical divine healing as expressed above, and against all the concepts embraced by Christian Science and New Thought.

As I pointed out in an earlier chapter, Kenyon did read some philosophy and metaphysical literature while he was away from the Lord. There is, however, no evidence whatsoever that he ever practiced metaphysical healing. Kenyon did not discover healing until ten years after he was saved. In 1909 he wrote, "I knew Him first as my Savior, and never knew Him as anything else but Savior for ten years of my Christian life. Then I learned to know Him as my Healer."[6]

Kenyon met the Lord in January 1885, so his discovery of Jesus as healer would have been around 1895. That was a few years after he was restored to the Lord. He said he had partially embraced divine healing among the Free Will Baptists with whom he aligned in 1894 (see chapter 7). When he was restored to the Lord, he completely abandoned any metaphysical teachings, referring to them as "reason darkness." He saw their source to be the minds of men without the help of the Holy Spirit.

FAITH-CURE OPPOSITION TO CHRISTIAN SCIENCE

The Faith-Cure movement developed from Holiness roots and the influences of European divine healing ministers. The timing of the beginning of the Faith-Cure movement under Charles Cullis is important.

Cullis began his healing ministry in Boston following the healing of Lucy Drake in 1870. He made his call to heal the sick public in 1873.[7] In early 1873 he took a four-month trip to Europe in which he and William Boardman visited the faith works of Dorothea Truedel, Johann Blumhardt, and George Müller.[8] Cullis began annual faith conventions later that same year at Framingham, Massachusetts, and Old Orchard, Maine. These were Holiness-style conventions, but they added teaching about divine healing and prayer for the sick.

Divine healing historian Paul Chappell reported that these conventions "did more to focus attention on the message of divine healing throughout America than any single event. The outpouring of articles from both secular and religious presses across the country on the faith conventions and on divine healing in general was extraordinary, considering that the topic had seldom appeared in the news media before this date."[9]

Make note of the fact that Cullis was having Holiness and healing conventions in 1873 while Mary Baker Eddy did not publish her textbook on Christian Science until 1875. (New Thought, as a movement, developed even later.) A history of Christian Science written in 1907–1908 noted that even after the publication of the book, the movement's notoriety did not extend outside of its county.

> At the beginning of 1877, her seventh year as a teacher in Lynn [Massachusetts], Mrs. Eddy and her Science were little known outside of Essex County, though her first edition of *Science and Health* had been published more than a year before[10]

In 1880 the movement still had not gained momentum. Mrs. Eddy's group met in people's homes in Lynn and in Boston, with six to ten people in attendance. By September 1880 the attendance had risen to twenty-two.[11] Christian Science would eventually grow rapidly and become a serious threat to orthodoxy, but in 1880 it was still a small, little-known movement.

The point I wish to make is that the Faith-Cure movement was drawing national (and international) attention when Christian Science was in its infancy. Cullis's faith work was the center of the divine healing movement in America. By 1885 there was an international convention held in London around the topics of holiness and divine healing. By the time Mrs. Eddy moved her headquarters to Boston,

Boston was already a center for the propagation of orthodox divine healing.

So successful was the healing ministry of Charles Cullis in Boston that after Mrs. Eddy relocated to Boston, she had to address Cullis's success in one of her books. Apparently her followers were asking her why the Faith-Cure movement was getting better results than her practitioners! In 1891 Eddy wrote:

> It is often asked, "Why are faith-cures sometimes more speedy than some of the cures wrought through the Christian Scientist?" Because faith is belief and not understanding; and it is easier to believe, than to understand spiritual truth. It demands less cross-bearing, self-renunciation, and divine Science to admit the claims of the corporeal senses and appeal to God for relief through a humanized conception of His power, than to deny these claims and learn the divine way.[12]

She complained essentially that the Faith-Cure advocates were petitioning a personal God in faith rather than the Christian Science "truth" of denying that sickness existed. The Faith-Cure movement did not deny the reality of the sickness but saw Christ's atonement as a basis for petitioning God for healing. Mrs. Eddy is quite clear on the difference between Christian Science and divine healing among orthodox Christians. Too bad some of today's observers can't see the difference!

JOSEPH COOK

In Boston two men led the attack against Christian Science teachings: Flavius Josephus Cook and A. J. Gordon. They created quite a stir, and the newspapers reported the ongoing debates.

Flavius Josephus Cook (1838–1901), educated at Harvard, Yale, and Andover Seminary, was a Congregationalist lecturer who was catapulted into international prominence in the 1870s as a spokesman for the concerns of American Protestantism. Cook had stood against Unitarianism, Transcendentalism, and Darwinism and many other attacks against orthodoxy. Kenyon felt he was a "most brilliant intellect."[13] Cook's Boston Monday lectures were considered an institutional fixture for almost a quarter of a century.

Cook's lectures were held at Tremont Temple in Boston and were quite popular and well attended by the clergy. In 1885 he read aloud at Tremont Temple a letter from A. J. Gordon regarding Christian Science which informed the audience, "One only has to open the published volumes of its lady apostle in this city to find such a creed of pantheism and blasphemy as has been rarely compounded."[14]

Gordon observed that in Christian Science "evil is not; sin, sickness and death are unreal; matter and the mortal body are nothing but a belief and illusion. Dispel the belief of sickness and cast out the illusion of matter and you heal the disease."

Its platform, Gordon continued, opens with the astounding declaration "that there is neither a personal deity, a personal devil, nor a personal man." Gordon referred to Mrs. Eddy's textbook *Science and Health* as "a work of lies." He added, "Seeing on almost every page its connection revealed with Theosophy, esoteric Buddhism, Kabalism and Pantheism, and yet the roots of these doctrines so artlessly entwined with devout and reverent exposition of Scripture as to deceive the very elect."

Gordon concluded, "It will hardly be necessary after what has been said, to distinguish 'Christian Science' from the 'prayer of faith,' which is said in the Scripture to 'save the sick.'"

Pointing out that no one among the Faith-Cure advocates ever felt that divine healing "depends upon the action of mind upon mind," he further stated that "all who credit 'faith-cures,' as they are sometimes called, hold that they are the result of God's direct and supernatural action upon the body of the sufferer. Christian Science pointedly denies the efficacy of prayer for the recovery of the sick."[15]

For A. J. Gordon the lines were clearly drawn quite early regarding the errors of Christian Science. His analysis of this cult would be similar to the thinking of most of those who taught divine healing in his day. Although both Christian Science and the Faith-Cure movement talked about healing the body, there the similarity ended. Gordon published a tract against Christian Science that was first published in the *Congregationalist* and later distributed in many editions.

Gordon, as we pointed out earlier, was one of a handful of men who shaped Kenyon's thinking profoundly. As a teacher of divine healing, Kenyon would have read this respected mentor's thoughts on the differences between divine healing and metaphysical healing and found himself in complete agreement.

A. B. SIMPSON AND CHRISTIAN SCIENCE

Another Kenyon favorite who violently opposed Christian Science and boldly proclaimed Christ as healer was A. B. Simpson. Simpson was good friends with both Gordon and Cullis. After Charles Cullis died in 1892 and A. J. Gordon in 1895, A. B. Simpson became the central figure in the defense of divine healing and in opposition to Christian Science.

Simpson came to emphasize the centrality of Christ's finished work as the basis for healing. This was certainly true of Kenyon as well. Seeing the diseases of mankind borne by our Substitute was the foundation for all of Kenyon's teaching on divine healing. In his 1886 book, *The Gospel of Healing,* Simpson wrote:

> Many persons strangely confound this strange anti-Christian error with divine healing . . . This philosophy denies that Jesus Christ has come in the flesh. It denies the reality of Christ's body; therefore it is anti-Christian in its teaching. This is *not* divine healing. There is no fellowship between the two.

A. B. Simpson maintained that he would rather die a horrible death than be healed by Christian Science. Like his good friend, A. J. Gordon, Simpson was repelled by its blasphemies.

> It is the most fatal infidelity. It does entirely away with the atonement, for as there is no sin there can be no redemption. I would rather be sick all my life with every form of physical torment, than be healed by such a lie.[16]

Simpson, in language that would be echoed by E. W. Kenyon in his analysis of the metaphysical cults, observed:

> It puts knowledge and intellect, or the mind of man in the place of God. It is not healing by remedies, but by mental force . . . a theology which is atheistic and infidel. The basis of it is that the material world is not real . . . It has captivated hundreds of thousands of people in this country.[17]

In this vein, Kenyon wrote:

Christian Science says that disease is mental. So Mrs. Eddy became the most outstanding mental healer that the world has ever seen. Jesus brings us into contact with spiritual things, not mental.[18]

Simpson, writing around 1915, indicated the tremendous growth (hundreds of thousands) the cult had experienced. As the influence of Christian Science grew it would become more and more necessary in New England to be knowledgeable and address the errors of this cult, particularly if you were a teacher of divine healing.

In December 1907 *Reality* published a sermon of Kenyon's in which he said:
Every believer should understand the fundamental principles of Christianity. Lack of this knowledge explains why whole churches have been swept into Christian Science, Dowieism, and other isms. Believers who understand the principles of redemption are fortified against every delusion of Satan.[19]

One of the principles of redemption that Kenyon referred to is the satisfaction of divine justice at the cross. God, Kenyon observed, had taken responsibility for the sin of mankind and had judged that sin in His Son. The tremendous love demonstrated at the cross should grip the heart with a sense of the reality of God and of Christ. In other words, when the cross is not preached, people are open to the deception of the cults.

Kenyon recommended a tract he had come across entitled *How the Lord Miraculously Delivered Me from Christian Science* in his periodical *Reality* in 1910 and then commented, "In view of the dangerous character of the errors of Christian Science and the injury they are doing the church, we are glad to recommend to our readers any book which will expose them."[20]

The next year Kenyon indicted Christian Science and other groups again.

Every false religion is based upon some theory of incarnation. Christian Science, Theosophy, New Thought, and Modern Unitarianism, teach, consciously, or unconsciously, the incarnation of the human family, that is, they teach that every man has

233

God in him. If a man has God in him then he and God are in union, if united, incarnated.[21]

Kenyon did believe that through the new birth and receiving the Person of the Holy Spirit, the believer was an "incarnation." God did actually dwell in the believer who was His temple. This didn't turn man into God, but it did make man the temple of God. But the cults, Kenyon pointed out, believed man was an incarnation without being born again or receiving the Holy Spirit.

From the beginning of his ministry until his last years, Kenyon held to the same opinion about the metaphysical cults. He believed them to be dangerous, delusive, and heretical. How some could postulate that he was secretly sympathetic to them is a mystery. One person even suggested that he introduced a form of "baptized Christian Science" into the church.[22] This suggestion fails to recognize the dramatic differences between Kenyon's teaching and Christian Science that we have been pointing out in this chapter.

THE CHURCH INDICTED

Many of the leaders of the day felt that a lack of biblical teaching on divine healing had left the door open for Mary Baker Eddy and her movement. R. A. Torrey declared:

> The Gospel of Christ has salvation for the body as well as the soul. It is the church's forgetting this and not teaching this that left an opening for Mrs. Eddy and for a host of other pretenders. There are thousands today entangled in the destructive errors of Christian Science who would never have become so entangled if they had been taught what the Bible teaches about Divine Healing.[23]

Torrey, a central figure among evangelicals at the turn of the century, discovered divine healing around 1887 and for thirty-five or more years experienced God's healing power in his own body and observed the healing of many others. "I know," wrote Torrey, "God performs miracles of healing today."[24]

R. L. Marsh wrote a graduate thesis for the faculty of Yale Theological Seminary on the topic of healing. He later published it as a book, *Faith Healing: a Defense, or, the Lord Thy Healer,* in 1889. He compared divine healing to Christian Science this way:

> Divine healing is by some discredited because they suppose that it does not differ materially from Christian Science and kindred theories. But that it has nothing in common with such theories can very readily be seen by an examination of the principles on which they rest. Of all mere theories of healing, Christian Science makes the most extravagant claims, and is most widely spread; and that this theory and divine healing stand fundamentally opposed to each other appears at once upon comparison.

Marsh contended that "if the doctrine of divine healing is true, there is nothing improbable or unreasonable in the supposition that the Christian Science theory and practice are a direct effort of the devil to discredit the works of Christ in this generation and time."[25]

Marsh saw the rise of Christian Science as an attempt by Satan to discredit the Faith-Cure movement. This is a reasonable idea. Isn't it odd that Mary Baker Eddy moved her base of operations to Boston and established the First Church of Christian Science in the same city where the central voices of the Faith-Cure movement were proclaiming a healing Christ? She began publishing her *Christian Science Monitor* in the city that was home to the only publisher of divine healing literature at that time. Is it a coincidence that Mary Baker Eddy brought her message of metaphysical healing to the very city where Charles Cullis and A. J. Gordon were already teaching biblical divine healing?

The sad success of this strategy is shown by the fact that most evangelical Christians think of divine healing as primarily a Pentecostal/charismatic doctrine and for the most part have never heard of the Faith-Cure movement. Many evangelicals are totally unaware that many of the bright lights of early fundamentalism were also teachers of divine healing.

James M. Gray, who succeeded R. A. Torrey as president of Moody Bible Institute, also wrote a book about Christian Science in 1907. It was titled *The Antidote to Christian Science.* He believed, like R. A. Torrey, that if the church had faithfully taught divine healing, it would have limited, if not destroyed altogether, the influence of Christian Science.

Referring to the "indictment of Christian Science against the church" brought about by the claims of Christian Science to heal as Christ commanded His church to do, he asked if these cultists had "never heard of David Brainerd and Dorothea Truedel, and pastors Blumhardt and Stockmayer, and Charles Cullis, and A. J. Gordon and A. B. Simpson, and a host of others in the last century and this, too numerous to even name?"

Gray then pointed out that he could "tell of the cure of rheumatism, of pneumonia, of abscess, of cancer, of deafness, of paralysis in cases pronounced by reputable physicians as incurable; and he can tell of prayer meetings over which he has regularly presided where such testimonies were too common to excite any particular remark."[26]

Kenyon dictated an article around 1934, in which he described why he thought the metaphysical cults prospered. He maintained this view from his early days until his death in 1948. He stated:

> Faith demands a sweet fellowship with God, an abandonment to His Word, a recognition of His Lordship, and a walk in love.
>
> When faith dies, Philosophy flourishes.
>
> A living Christ and a living Father God perfectly satisfies, and we need no philosophy; we need no metaphysics.
>
> It is when we lose Christ out of our daily life that we turn to metaphysics and philosophical theories that have no place in the life of faith.[27]

Kenyon, like most of his contemporaries, was concerned about the many who were being seduced into the cults. He sought to answer what he perceived to be the needs of the people to which the cults made their appeal. One of the reasons he wrote *The Two Kinds of Faith* was to address this issue. In his introduction he wrote:

> Unanswered prayers stand between the individual and a faith life.
>
> Some have lost faith altogether. Many have turned to philosophical and metaphysical cults because their prayer lives were failures.
>
> If we should ask the individual what he believes to be his greatest difficulty in his Christian walk, I believe invariably his answer would be, "I haven't enough faith. I know it is not God's fault. I know the promises are there in the Word. I have simply

failed to get faith. I have prayed for it; I have fasted for it; but I don't know how to get it."

This is the reason for this book. We have written it to answer the faith problem for thinking men and women.[28]

Kenyon greatly believed in the superiority of the gospel over the cults but lamented the fact that much of what was preached in the church was powerless and did not grip the hearts of the people. Kenyon felt the church needed the miraculous. People craved the supernatural and desired miracles.

Kenyon moved to Southern California in 1923, where the cults were flourishing. In 1927 he wrote:

We cannot ignore the amazing growth of Christian Science, Unity, New Thought, and Spiritism.

The people who are flocking to them are not the ignorant masses, but the most cultured and wealthy of the land, and their strongest appeal is the supernatural element of their so-called religions—the testimonies of healings by their followers are their strongest asset.

We cannot close our eyes to the fact that in many of our cities on the Pacific Coast, Mrs. Eddy has a stronger following today and a larger attendance at her churches than have the old line denominations; and the largest percentage of her followers have at one time been worshipers in the denominations—they have left them because they believe they are receiving more help from Mrs. Eddy's teaching than from the preachers.

They will tell you how they were healed and how they were helped in their spiritual life by this strange cult. This is a libel upon the modern church—it is not only a libel but a challenge. Christian Science could not have grown to the place where it is dominating many of our larger cities unless there had been a demand in the heart of the people for a supernatural religion.

The Pentecostal movement could not have risen with the power it has, had not the heart of the people been craving a new, fresh vision of Christ.[29]

Kenyon's comments and burden sound quite similar to Torrey and Gray. This should not be surprising. He was voicing the opinion of many of the day who were concerned about the cults and knew the superiority of the gospel of Christ the Healer.

It should be pointed out that Kenyon's last statement (in the above quote) should not be construed as putting the Pentecostal movement in the same class with Christian Science. Kenyon was a part of the Pentecostal movement for the most part. His point is that both movements offer the supernatural as part of their appeal. Pentecostalism made this appeal within the bounds of orthodoxy; Christian Science, outside of orthodoxy.

In an unpublished article that Kenyon dictated on April 6, 1934, *The Limitlessness of Faith,* he described the differences between divine healing and metaphysics.

> We are dealing, not in the terms of psychology nor human religion, we are dealing not with negatives; we accept the fact that Satan is, that sin is, that disease is.
>
> But we come against disease as Jesus came against it, not denying its reality, but driving it out as the Master did, healing it, the health and life of the Son of God displacing it. It is not error to say disease is; it is the truth, acknowledge it.
>
> It takes faith to destroy it.

This late statement shows Kenyon clearly still in agreement with his roots in the Faith-Cure movement in regard to the reality of sickness and the basis of healing. In this quote he makes the same distinction that all the orthodox teachers of divine healing made when their teaching was compared with Christian Science.

SENSORY DENIAL?

Kenyon and the modern Faith movement have been accused of practicing sensory denial, that is, that they deny the reality of sickness. This is thought to be the same practice as the metaphysical cults. The metaphysical cults, particularly Christian Science, deny the reality of matter which includes sickness, disease, and death. They affirm the reality of a supposed perfect spiritual mind or principle and seek to bring their "patients" into harmony with this principle by having them deny the existence of the sickness.

The Faith-Cure movement, today's Faith movement, and Kenyon

operate on an entirely different principle. They see the healing already accomplished in Christ's finished work and available to be appropriated by a living faith.

R. A. Torrey illustrated this in his first experience of divine healing. He prayed for a young man in his congregation who was in the last stages of typhoid fever. He was told that the crisis was past and that there was no hope of recovery.

> As I sat there an impulse came to me to kneel and pray to God that He would heal the young man. I did this, and as I prayed a great assurance came into my heart that God had heard my prayer. I arose and said to the doctor, who was a backslider, "He will get well." The doctor smiled and replied, "Well, Mr. Torrey, that is all very well from your standpoint, but he cannot get well. The crisis is past and has passed the wrong way, and he will die." I replied, "Doctor, that is all right from your standpoint, but God has heard my prayer. The man will not die, he cannot die at this time, he will get well."
>
> A short time afterward they came up to tell me the young man was dying, that he was doing certain things that only one dying would do. I replied to them, "He is not dying, he cannot die now, he will get well." And get well he did, and as far as I know is living still, though that was over forty years ago.[30]

This story perfectly illustrates the marked difference between healing by faith and metaphysical healing. Torrey prayed and received from God a great assurance that God had heard his prayer. Torrey expressed this belief in a positive confession, saying, "He will get well." This confession was based entirely on Torrey's assurance that God had heard his prayer, not on any change in the one who had received the prayer.

When the patient took a turn for the worse, Torrey was unmoved. In spite of the doctor's insistence that the man was dying, Torrey "held fast to the confession of his faith" and said the man would not, could not, die. This was based on the assurance that God had heard his prayer and nothing else.

This is faith in God, not metaphysics. The symptoms weren't denied, the assurance of being heard by God was considered more authoritative than the condition of the boy's body. Torrey, who would hardly be considered a teacher of positive confession, nevertheless spoke what he believed in the face of contrary evidence. "Out of the abundance of the heart the mouth speaketh," Jesus said (Matt. 12:34).

A. B. Simpson affirmed the same principle in his teaching on healing.

> Our faith itself is nothing but simply taking His free gift of grace. Thus come and claim His promise; and having done so, believe according to His Word that you have received it.
>
> ... Be careful not to begin to watch the result or look at the symptoms, or see if you stand. You must ignore all symptoms, and see only Him there before you, almighty to sustain you and save you from falling.
>
> Be prepared for trials of faith. Do not look always for the immediate removal of the symptoms. Do not think of them. Simply ignore them and press forward, claiming the reality behind all symptoms. Be the symptoms what they may, we must steadily believe that back of all symptoms God is working out His own great restoration.[31]

Carrie Judd Montgomery taught about sensory evidence this way:

> Before we have the evidence of our senses in regard to the matter, we accept the evidence of faith.
>
> Having faith in God is believing His word without looking at probabilities or possibilities, as humanly viewed; without regarding natural circumstances; without considering any apparent obstacles in the way of His keeping His promises. ...It is faith not to be staggered at any complication of adverse circumstances.
>
> Our faith in God must be so steadfast that even if the evidence of all our senses should deny His word, we must consider them as deceiving us, and still continue to uphold His faithfulness. Such faith as that *never* fails to remove, sooner or later, the mountain of difficulty or doubt (her italics).[32]

Those familiar with Kenyon's teaching on faith will be struck by the similarities between Carrie Judd Montgomery's teaching and his. She describes the "war" between what our senses tell us and the promise of God. Or, in Kenyon's terminology, the war between sense knowledge and revelation knowledge.

Consider the words of another divine healing minister, evangelist Maria Woodworth-Etter.

> In seeking healing for our bodies, we are so apt to look at feelings, or symptoms; and believe we are healed just in proportion to the amount we see and feel. When in reality we are healed when we believe. "What things soever ye desire, when ye pray, believe that ye received them, and ye shall have them." The work was all finished on Calvary. On Calvary's tree the remedy is found that will heal all sicknesses and diseases of the soul and body . . . Sometimes it is instantly realized in the body, but more often it is a gradual deliverance, requiring us to step out in faith before we see any signs of having it.
>
> Faith looks away from the natural, from the things of the senses, and sees the fulfillment of the promise, through Christ's complete work on Calvary. It sees every need supplied through the atonement . . . We must cling to the promises of Jesus instead of looking at our feelings, or go by them, for our senses are false witness unto us when we step out in faith.
>
> If we are looking and going by our feelings, we are believing them instead of believing God.[33]

Andrew Murray, another respected mentor of Kenyon's, also commented on symptoms and our attitude toward them after we pray the prayer of faith.

> Divine healing . . . calls us to turn our attention away from the body, abandoning ourselves—soul and body—to the Lord's care, occupying ourselves with Him alone.
>
> The first thing to learn is to cease to be anxious about the state of your body. You have trusted it to the Lord, and He has taken the responsibility. If you do not see a rapid improvement immediately, but on the contrary symptoms appear to be more serious, remember that you have entered on a path of faith, and therefore you should not consider your body, but cling only to the living God.
>
> To consider the body gives birth to doubts, while clinging to the promise of God and being occupied with Him alone gives entrance into the way of faith, the way of divine healing, which glorifies God.[34]

Another preacher of divine healing who wrote a book that would become a classic statement of this teaching was F. F. Bosworth. In his original 1924 edition, he wrote:

> To the extent that we base faith on our improvement, or are affected by what we see or feel, instead of by the word of God alone, just to that extent ours is not real faith. To be occupied with what we see or feel is to exactly reverse the condition God lays down for us to follow. "Every one that looketh at it shall live," simply means that every one who, like Abraham, so occupies himself with God's promise that he is no longer affected by symptoms, "shall recover." It means, the word of God (not what we see or feel) shall be the basis of our faith. Our "looking unto the promise of God" is to be kept up until we are healed.[35]

Now let's look at a quote from Kenyon and see how similar it sounds to the quotes we have just read from R. A. Torrey, A. B. Simpson, Carrie Judd Montgomery, Maria Woodworth-Etter, Andrew Murray, and F. F. Bosworth.

> We should not need the evidence of the senses. Let us rest on the Word. Faith holds fast to the confession of the Word. Sense knowledge holds fast to the confession of physical evidence. If I accept physical evidence over against the Word of God, I nullify the Word as far as I am concerned.[36]

E. W. Kenyon's teachings on divine healing are clearly consistent with these other early Faith-Cure advocates. That is quite understandable given the fact that these were his stated influences.

It might be pointed out that all of the teachers of divine healing of Kenyon's day (and Kenyon himself) assumed that those they taught were dedicated Christians seeking holiness and consecration of their lives to God and His will. This was the foundation upon which they offered the added benefit of divine healing. Healing was a part of the deeper life teachings.

AFFIRMATIONS

Kenyon believed strongly in the value of affirming God's word as a means of building faith. The metaphysical cults also use affirmations. I will examine Kenyon's teachings about affirmations in chapter 21, but for now I do want to mention how Kenyon perceived the difference between what he taught and what the cults taught.

In one of the many notebooks of teaching outlines that Kenyon left behind, he had a teaching about affirmations. It dates from about 1934. Under the heading "Affirmation—versus—Negations" he wrote:

> I know Satan is—But he is defeated.
> I know sin is—But for me it is put away.
> Satan has power—But it is broken.
> Diseases are—But by His stripes I have been healed.
> Weakness is—But He is our strength.
> Ignorance is—But He is our wisdom.
> Spiritual death is—But He is our LIFE.
>
> Human reason cannot know Him—We know Him through Revelation. Science denies His presence because it cannot find Him or know Him. Senses can't register spirit.
>
> Genesis 1:1 stands through ages of denial—It solves mysteries of creation.
> An affirmation cannot change error to truth.
> A negation cannot make truth an error.
> God performs all miracles of creation.
> Calling Him a principle does not destroy fact.
> God is a Person who created the universe.

In Kenyon's book, *The Hidden Man,* he commented further on the difference between his concept of affirmations and Christian Science.

> There are two types of affirmations that I wish you to notice. First, there is the affirmation with nothing behind it but my own will to make it good. It is based on a philosophy born of sense knowledge. That sense knowledge is a product of my own mind. If it be in regard to sin, I deny the existence of it. If it be in regard to sickness, I deny the sickness has any existence. We see this in Christian Science.
>
> All that I have to make these affirmations good is something

that I am, or have, of myself. The Word of God has no place in this affirmation. I cannot say that greater am I than disease, or greater am I than this demand upon me, consequently, my affirmation becomes a failure.

The second type of affirmation is based on the Word of God.

In this quote, Kenyon is making the point that based on God's Word, we *can* affirm that "greater is He that is in me" than this disease or demand upon me. Our confidence is in an indwelling Holy Spirit, not in something in and of ourselves, as the cults imply.

Kenyon continued:

You see the vast difference between an affirmation based upon your own will or philosophy and an affirmation backed up by God Himself.

The affirmations based upon sense knowledge philosophy have no more value or ability to make good than is in the will and mind of the maker of the affirmation. But the affirmation that is based upon the living Word has God back of it to make it good.[37]

Kenyon used affirmations in the same way R. A. Torrey did in affirming that the sick boy would recover. Out of the assurance in his heart that God was faithful and would keep His promises, Kenyon affirmed God's faithfulness in the face of all contrary circumstances. His affirmations were based on the character of God, the finished work of Christ, and the promises of Scripture.

Surely every Christian should continually affirm these things.

CHAPTER 21

POSITIVE CONFESSION

Jesus' bold and continual confession is our example. We are what He made us to be. Jesus confessed what He was. Sense knowledge could not understand it. We are to confess what we are in Christ. Men of the senses will not understand us.

—E. W. Kenyon[1]

By far the most controversial aspect of Kenyon's teaching is his strong emphasis on positive confession. This teaching has been said to have been derived from the metaphysical cults and to have therefore compromised Christianity. It's amazing to think that such furor could arise over suggesting that we should speak God's promises and the facts of God's Word aloud!

In this chapter I will examine the emphasis that Kenyon put on this teaching and where and how it came to be a major part of his thought. In chapter 6 we established that the Holiness and Higher Life movements both stressed the necessity of public testimony or confession in regard to obtaining and maintaining sanctification. Affirming the Scriptures was also taught. Kenyon was documentably influenced by these movements as we showed in that chapter.

But what about the command of faith and holding fast to one's confession? Were these ideas taken from the cults? Or did Kenyon draw them from his own study or some other source? We will attempt to let Kenyon and his mentors answer these questions for us.

Testimony and Confession

From his early days when he was influenced by the Holiness movement, Kenyon always emphasized the importance of testimony. It was a common practice for him to encourage those who had received Christ in his evangelistic meetings to publicly testify to their experience.

Kenyon would increasingly emphasize the spoken word more in his later years of ministry. I believe he did this, in part, to counteract the waning influence of the Holiness and Higher Life movements, which emphasized the importance of testimony quite strongly.

Let us see how Kenyon's concept of testimony eventually developed into his teaching regarding confession.

A report of Kenyon's meeting in Arlington Heights in 1904 declared, "Those who were saved gave very clear testimonies."[2] The concept of a *clear testimony* dates at least as far back as Phoebe Palmer's writings in Holiness circles, if not before her time. A clear testimony would be a bold, definite statement of what God had done for an individual.

Referring to the devastating effects of broken fellowship with the Father, Kenyon noted that, "Our boldness in testimony is gone."[3] Kenyon assumed that a clear testimony would accompany any life rightly related to the Father.

After his report on Arlington Heights, Kenyon described what he felt was an appropriate testimony and what was not.

> How often we sit in prayer meetings and listen to people giving what is called a testimony when they are not witnessing of Christ. They are witnessing of their own doubts and fears, or perhaps their own fancies or some hobby, rather than witnessing the saving power of the work of Christ and of the joy they have in communion and fellowship with the Father through the Spirit.
>
> Just a word in regard to testifying. The very word *testify* gives us an inkling. We are on the witness stand and are going to say something that will glorify our Lord; we want to win the case for Him. We want the unsaved people that hear to accept Him as their Savior, and we desire that the words that we speak shall encourage weaker believers to abandon themselves more entirely to His care.

I cannot believe that we should testify because it is our duty, but our witness should flow from a heart filled with a desire to do it because He has been so good to us.

We should not eulogize ourselves, but Him of whom we witness.

I was in a meeting recently where the young converts testified. One after another would arise with Bibles or New Testaments in hand and read some appropriate verse in connection with the subject on which the leader had spoken, and then as they wove their witness, testimony, or experience around these words, it left a very inspiring impression.

The Lord has had an opportunity to work through His own Word and the workers have given their testimony and experience and have also sent forth the word that "will not return unto Him void."[4]

In this quote from a young E. W. Kenyon we see the background for his later teaching on confession. He saw public confession as giving a Scripture-based testimony in order to glorify the Lord. He also felt it was giving voice to God's Word that would not return void. In other words, God could use the testimony to convict or encourage those who heard it.

Notice also that he discouraged and criticized the habit of giving voice to doubts, fears, or pet doctrines. His concern was, What will the listener think of God as he listens to my testimony? What effect will my words have on the hearer? Will they want to trust in God having heard me testify? His foundational concern was whether or not God would be glorified through the testimony. Continuing in this same vein, he stated:

Yes, we must witness for Him first with our lives, but we must witness for Him with our mouths as well, for "with the mouth confession is made unto salvation," and "whosoever therefore shall confess me before men, him will I confess also before my Father which is in heaven."

If you want to develop the spiritual power that is within you, speak out what you have to say in and of your own self. It will do you more good to give a stumbling, halting testimony that is all your own than to read the most flowery thing ever written by any other man . . . People wish to hear real testimonies from the children of God who are on fire for Him . . .

People say of me that I am all right until I get to talking about my friends, and then they say I am apt to become a little enthusiastic. Get into that spirit in regard to your Father and your Savior and you will never have any trouble giving a testimony that is your own, one that is alive and to which men and God will listen.[5]

Testimony was an important part of Kenyon's early Methodist-influenced services, a significant enough part that Kenyon felt it was important to encourage and offer instruction to his readers. This would be true throughout his entire ministry. Two years later Essek wrote about the purpose of testimony—to magnify God.

God wants us to witness in our daily life with men, telling them how good and real He is to us . . . He desires us, through a simple confession in prayer meetings, to say we are Christians. He wishes to be highly spoken of.

He wants us to magnify Him in our testimony.[6]

This concept of magnifying the Lord is further expressed in a later issue of *Reality* where Kenyon said, "Testimony is the pleasure afforded him to speak well of the One whom he loves, and to whom he owes all he has and hopes for."[7] Testimony, confession, and witnessing were synonymous concepts for Kenyon. They all meant to speak out boldly for God and His gospel. Kenyon believed strongly that our testimony—our confession—should bring glory to God by exalting Him and the finished work of Christ. Glorifying God in our bold witness for Him could lead others to salvation.

The Command of Faith

Another area of controversy associated with Kenyon and the modern Faith movement is the "command of faith" or "speaking to the mountain" ("the mountain" meaning the problem, sickness, or circumstance).

The idea that "you can have what you say" is actually derived from the words of Jesus in Mark 11:23. Jesus also taught this concept in Matthew 17:20 and Luke 17:6. These scriptures are not three different synoptic authors reporting the same event, but rather three different incidents where Jesus taught the same truth.

A survey of the healing and deliverance ministry of Jesus in the four Gospels shows that the command of faith is the primary way that Jesus ministered—not the only way, but the primary way.

Those who pray for the sick and afflicted often examine the ministry of Jesus for the model of ministry to emulate. Those who do not pray for the sick often overlook the methodology of Jesus. Consequently, when today's ministers imitate that model, their critics don't relate it to Jesus' teaching or example. This is unfortunate.

So, were any of Kenyon's early mentors teaching about the command of faith? Yes, definitely. I am now going to give you some of the teaching on the command of faith from the leading evangelical teachers of Kenyon's day. As you read you may think, "This sounds like a modern Faith teacher." But remember, these quotes are one hundred years old, and many are from prominent evangelical leaders of the day. I have devoted a lot of space to these quotes, partly to make my point and partly because they are so good.

A. T. Pierson

In his 1895 book *Lessons in the School of Prayer,* A. T. Pierson wrote:

> Our Lord therefore says, "Have faith in God"—literally, Have *the faith of God.*
>
> Faith is mighty, not because it is small, but because it is the hiding place of God's power. It is the seed of God—having in it God's life, and where it lodges there is growth, motion, expansion, reproduction; so far as it is genuine and Godlike—the faith of God—it exercises the Power of God and is irresistible.
>
> That, however, which is most marked in this lesson on faith is the *authority* conceded to faith and with which faith is clothed . . .
>
> In all these cases it's not "pray" but "say," not the word of petition but of direction, not as of a suppliant but as a sovereign.
>
> This we regard as the central, vital heart of this great lesson of faith. The Master of all girds the servant with His own power and intrusts him with authority to command. Faith claims not only the blessing but power to bless. This lesson is at first sight so astounding as to seem incredible—it passes all understanding, and faith itself staggers at such promises.

Let us reverently seek to take in the marvelous thought. Faith in God so unites us to God that it passes beyond the privilege of *asking* to the power of *commanding*. This language of Christ is not that of a *request*, however bold, but of *fiat*. God said, "Be light! And light was! Such is the sublime announcement in Genesis. And He says to His disciples, Concerning the work of My hand, *Command ye Me!*

And so—marvelous fact! The child of God laying hold by faith of the power of the Omnipotent One, issues his fiat: "Be thou removed!" "Be thou plucked up by the roots!" and it is so.

Pierson recognized the command of faith in the teaching of Jesus. Notice that Pierson used God's fiat in creation—Light, be!—as the example of the faith of God. He tells his readers that they are to follow God's example and command in faith like God!

We have only to regard and observe those laws and limits within which the Spirit acts, and we find even His blessed power placed at our disposal: in other words, it is still divinely true: Obey the law of the power and the power obeys you.

Conform to the laws and modes of the Spirit's operations, and in the work of God's hands you may command the Spirit's power.[8]

It is important to note that Pierson felt he was expounding Jesus' teaching on faith and prayer. He spoke of laws of the spirit realm: "In the spiritual realm there is one all-subduing, all-controlling force, power, or energy: *The Holy Spirit of God.*" Unfortunately, if Pierson were alive today he would most likely find himself labeled as a heretic attempting to bring metaphysics into the church.

Charles H. Pridgeon

Another man who headed a Bible institute in Pittsburgh and was known to Kenyon was Charles Pridgeon. A former Christian and Missionary Alliance associate and friend of A. B. Simpson, he received the Holy Spirit in the early days of Pentecostalism and established a Pentecostal church in Pittsburgh, Pennsylvania. He was well educated in Greek and Hebrew. His meetings on divine healing filled some of the largest downtown theatres in the city.[9]

Pridgeon wrote a book entitled *Faith and Prayer.* In his chapter "The Law of Faith" he stated:

> When we say, "law of faith," it would be almost synonymous if we said, "force of faith." . . . Our thesis is: *Faith is a force.*
>
> What is the dynamic of prayer, or the dynamic of the Christian life? We would say, It is the law, or force, of faith. The literal Greek in the passage in Mark [11:22] is, "Have God's faith," not your own faith, but God's faith.
>
> It is the faith of God and His own impartation. It is not a faith that believes a thing is so just because you want to believe it is so; nor a faith that is not grounded properly upon the Word of God; but the faith that is the gift of God; that is inwrought by the living God; the faith that believes on the authority of God's Word; and is wrought in the heart by the power of the Holy Ghost—the faith that "cometh by hearing, and hearing by the Word of God."
>
> It is uttered. It "calleth those things which be not" . . . Many fail there; they will not say that they believe God. They believe, but they will not say so . . . Get down before God, believe His promises and tell Him so; and the very act of telling God will increase your faith. This makes invisible faith incarnate and puts a seal upon it.[10]

Jessie Penn-Lewis had printed an article by Pridgeon in her *Overcomer* magazine as early as 1910 on this subject. She introduced Pridgeon's article by saying:

> We give in our present issue a striking message by Rev. C. H. Pridgeon on prayer in the aspect of "He shall have what *he saith,*" [her italics] which can only be the very faith of God Himself operating through our inner man.[11]

In his article, Pridgeon wrote:

> So many Christians have faith away down in their hearts, and do not dare to confess it. If you have the faith of a grain of mustard seed, you will be able to *say* unto the mountain, "Be removed," or to the fig tree, "Be withered." Any mountain of difficulty will

remove, no matter where it is placed, either in body, soul, or spirit.[12]

Here we see the well-educated head of a Bible institute plainly teaching the command of faith and the necessity of confession. All are free to disagree with these men's interpretations of Christ's words. But to suggest that the teaching is derived from metaphysics is another matter.

GEORGE B. PECK

Another amazing book from these early days that is quite rare today is *Throne-Life, or The Highest Christian Life* by George B. Peck. Peck lived in Boston and was friends with A. J. Gordon, A. B. Simpson, and George and Carrie Judd Montgomery. He was also associated with Frank Sandford for a season and could have been known personally to Kenyon through Sandford.

Throne-Life was published in 1888 by the Watchword Publishing Company, Gordon's publishing company. The book's language and teaching is very much in the vein of Kenyon's later expressions. Peck wrote concerning the exercise of "throne-power."

> We are to enquire respecting the exhibition of throne-power by the mode of language. Its modes of speech are two: the *prayer* of faith, and, in its highest energy, the *command* of faith.
>
> Mark the following points in evidence of the matter in question.
>
> First, in the command, "Have faith in God," it is evidently throne-faith they are bidden to possess. For they had just witnessed the fig tree withered by a word of command . . . Then, again, the language literally is, "Have faith *of* God." That is, as [Bible scholar John] Bengel remarks, "Such as those should have, who have God;" and such as our Lord Himself had just exercised.
>
> Secondly, the privilege of *commanding* in faith is as fully accorded here to the possible experience of the apostles, as the privilege of *praying* in faith. The promises as to the certainty of results to follow these utterances of faith, are equally definite.
>
> And if we do not falter at this point in the application, as to believing when we *pray*—as most Christians do not—then why need we stagger, through any dazed amazement, at a further

application, that is, as to the allied encouragement to believe when we *command?*[13]

Carrie Judd Montgomery mentioned meeting Peck while visiting with Charles Cullis in Boston. She called Peck's book "that remarkable book" and went on to say that she and her husband became deeply interested in Dr. Peck and his writings, and that he paid them a lovely visit at their home in Oakland.[14]

A. B. SIMPSON

Another well-respected contemporary who also wrote about the "faith of God" was A. B. Simpson. Simpson mentioned the concept in many of his books, but, coincidentally, I received a periodical in the mail while working on this book that had an article in it by Simpson entitled, "The Faith of God." I contacted the publishers to find the source of the article, and they said it was from a tract published in China! Simpson wrote:

> This simple faith is a stupendous power, for it takes everything from God. It is one of the two omnipotences to which "all things are possible." The other is God. This faith, simple as it is, is divine too. It comes from God and is the "faith of God" (Mark 11:22).
> This reading, which the margin gives us, is most valuable, and teaches us a precious and most practical truth, that our faith must come to us from God, and that we may come to Him for it even as we come in the name of Jesus for every other grace.
> We may lower God's standard, and bring it down to the level of our unbelief. Or we may bring our faith up to the great and glorious standard of His mighty promises, His own mighty and proffered faith. With such promises for faith to rest on, such performances to encourage it, such powers and possibilities presented to us, such awful need of it in the world today, and such a fountain from which to draw it, let us hear the Master saying to us as never before, *"Have the faith of God."*[15]

Other examples could be cited, but I trust these will convince the reader that the "faith of God" operating in and through the believer was a widely taught concept many years ago. The similarities between what these men taught and what Kenyon and the Faith teachers of today have taught should be obvious. One difference that is note-worthy, however, is that most of the above-mentioned men were well taught in Greek.

Carrie Judd Montgomery

Another teacher of divine healing who saw this concept and was a friend of E. W. Kenyon was Carrie Judd Montgomery. She wrote of "commanding faith" in her journal, *Triumphs of Faith*. In an article entitled "The Power of Praise and Testimony" she shared:

> He [Jesus] not only comes to live in our hearts, but He gives us "the word of faith" in our mouth. We read in the eleventh verse, "Whosoever believeth on Him, shall not be ashamed," and if we truly believe on the Lord Jesus Christ, we shall not be ashamed of Him, but shall be glad to confess Him with our mouth. Here we see again the wonderful part that our testimony has in relation to salvation.
>
> Now we will read Matt. 21:21: "Jesus answered and said unto them, Verily I say unto you, If ye have faith, and doubt not, ye shall not only do this which is done to the fig tree, but also if ye shall say unto this mountain, Be thou removed, and be thou cast into the sea; it shall be done." Here we see again the power of the word of faith. If we doubt not in our heart we may say to this mountain, "Be removed and cast into the sea." There are moun-tains of difficulty and trouble that come into our lives, and God wants us to speak to those mountains in faith, and command them to be removed and cast into the sea . . . This is commanding faith, the Lord Jesus Himself speaking through us with great authority. It is not only faith which is spoken of here, but it is the authority which causes us to *say* to the mountain, "be thou removed."

Carrie Judd Montgomery then went on to relate an incident when she and her husband faced a "mountain of difficulty."

> We agreed together in faith, and then spoke to the mountain of difficulty in the name of the Lord Jesus Christ and commanded it

to be removed and cast into the sea. We said further to this mountain, "you *do* obey us because Jesus said that you would; we refuse to doubt in our heart and we shall have *whatsoever we say.*" We quoted that passage in Mark 11:23, "For verily I say unto you, That whosoever shall say unto this mountain, Be thou removed, and be thou cast into the sea; and shall not doubt in his heart, but shall believe that those things which he saith shall come to pass; *He shall have whatsoever he saith.*" This meant not only thinking about it, but saying it and saying it in faith.

Beloved, you may have a mountain today, but if you will feed much upon the Word, and hide it away in your heart, you will be able to command the mountains to be removed.

We must not read a verse of Scripture and merely wish it was true, but confess that it is true, because it is the Word of the living God which cannot be broken. We may not feel it, but we must say it, because God says it. You will find great power in getting hold of a promise and saying it over and over until it becomes a part of your very being.[16]

George Montgomery (husband of Carrie Judd), although he was not the Bible teacher of the Montgomery household, occasionally brought a message at the chapel adjoining their Home of Peace. A few found their way into the *Triumphs of Faith.* One article, entitled "Standing on God's Word," tells of his personal test of faith for physical healing.

After I was healed I was having a time of testing, and the enemy said, "Now it won't do any good for you to get up and testify when you are not feeling strong and well. Wait until you are well and then testify." I did not know the tactics of the enemy then as well as I know them now, and I stopped testifying. In a little while I found that I was losing the wonderful healing that I had received. A dear Christian doctor, who was a friend of mine, said to me, "I have not heard you say lately what the Lord is doing for you." I told him I was waiting until I felt perfectly strong and well before I testified any more. He answered me, "If you do that, you will lose it all."

After that I got up and testified every opportunity I had, and the life of the Lord increased in me and I became strong and well. The Word says, "He shall have whatsoever he saith." You can take your stand on that word and say whatsoever God says. The Word cannot fail, and the symptoms and feelings and everything must fall into line with the Word of God. Abraham called the things that be not as though they were, and he was a great favorite with God.[17]

Carrie and her fellow workers at the Home of Peace had stood in prayer and faith with George. He had contracted malaria while in Mexico. She reported, "We had no physician but the Lord Jesus Christ, for my dear husband had known him as his Physician for about twenty-five years [this was in 1914]."[18] As they continued their prayer vigil, she reported:

God made me understand that I must press him to personal testimony even when from a human standpoint it seemed cruel to make him exert himself when too weak to speak a word, or hardly to understand what I was saying to him.[19]

The same principles of faith and declaration (or testimony) were obviously practiced by the Montgomerys in the area of healing of physical sickness and other mountains.

FAITH OF GOD OR GOD-KIND OF FAITH?

We've established that many respected Christian leaders of Kenyon's day taught about the "faith of God" and its meaning for the believer. However, one may still ask, What if they were sincerely wrong? Is there really a basis in the Greek of Mark 11:22 for translating it "the faith of God?"

One author quoted some Greek scholars to prove that the faith teachers are teaching "a truth that has escaped the notice of orthodox Christian scholars for the last two thousand years."[20] He began his discussion of scholarly opinion with a man he described as "almost universally accepted as the final word on Greek grammar." The man is A. T. Robertson.

He told us of Robertson's findings and assured us that no Greek scholars accept the "faith of God" idea. In his footnote he even cited Robertson's highly respected work *A Grammar of the Greek New Testament in the Light of Historical Research,* page 500, where he quoted Robertson as saying "we rightly translate [Mark 11:22] have faith *in* God."[21]

Now here is the irony. Robertson was quoted correctly, but incompletely. The whole quote was not given because it would prove embarrassing to the argument. Here is the whole statement from Robertson:

> Here again we must appeal to the root idea of the genitive [*genitive* is the name of one of eight Greek cases that show word relationships] as the case of genus or kind. The resultant idea is due to the context and one must not suppose that the Greek genitive means all the different English prepositions used to translate the resultant idea. Thus in Mark 11:22 [he then gives the Greek phrase] we rightly translate 'have faith in God, *though the genitive does not mean 'in,' but only the God kind of faith.*"[22]

This is amazing! The scholar who is being quoted to disprove the "faith of God" is actually the source of that very phrase that has drawn tremendous criticism to the Faith movement, "Have the God kind of faith." And this critic quoted *part* of the very sentence in which Robertson said it, and yet argued that "these perversions find no basis in the original Greek."[23]

Also notice that Robertson describes the Greek case used in Mark 11:22 as the case that indicates "genus or kind." That is why the following seven sources of Greek scholarship also say the phrase could be understood as referring to the faith *of* God.

Albert Barnes, J. A. Alexander, and Adam Clarke each say that Mark 11:22 is literally, "Have the faith of God."[24][5] *The Numeric New Testament, The Bible in Basic English,* and Godbey's translation all say, "Have God's faith." Douay-Rheims and Worrell give us "Have the faith of God," and *Young's Literal Translation* offers "Have faith of God." The above-mentioned author told us that this idea is "a truth that has escaped the notice of orthodox scholars for the last two thousand years"!

It's not my intention to "prove" which is the right interpretation of Mark 11:22. I simply want to make it plain that credible Greek scholars have held to the interpretation suggested by the Faith teachers. Too many people have been persuaded otherwise due to scholarly-sounding quotes from experts.

I call this heresy hunting technique "smiting by scholarship." Most people have a great respect for scholarship and if enough scholars are quoted they will believe whatever is proposed. There are many divergent views among scholars. A little charity in these matters would seem called for. We are all entitled to our opinion and to do our own research. But it is not right to cry "heresy" when someone disagrees with our understanding and then to validate our accusations with one-sided documentation.

Writing this book has brought me into contact with the sad realities of apologetics in the church today. Some who call themselves researchers have mastered the ability to quote out of context and to paint a warped view of what others in the body of Christ teach. They can search through vast amounts of orthodox materials and find a sentence or phrase which, quoted out of context and placed side-by-side with a similar sounding phrase from a known heretic, makes the author of the first quote sound like a heretic. Kenyon's writings have been treated in just this manner.[25] (These things should not be so, my brethren, as the apostle Paul said [James 3:10].)

HOLDING FAST TO ONE'S CONFESSION

Kenyon was always looking for biblical truth that would make his life more like Jesus. He really believed that God was serious when He said we were predestined "to be conformed to the image of His Son" (Rom. 8:29). One influence in the direction of holding fast to a confession of faith was Kenyon's good friend in Pasadena, John S. Norvell.

Not much is known about Norvell. He pastored in Pasadena, and he and Essek frequently exchanged pulpits. He was an admirer of D. L. Moody, and attended meetings where Moody ministered. He had some association with John Alexander Dowie's ministry at some point and was good friends with the Eldridges, preaching at Bethel Temple on many occasions. Kenyon's daughter Ruth named Norvell as Kenyon's closest ministry friend.

Kenyon spoke of Norvell and the value of a strong confession of faith in an issue of the *Herald of Life.*

> I used to read the gospels and wonder why Jesus continually and persistently confessed what He was. Then I came in contact with brother John Norvell in Pasadena and I noticed that in every service he made a certain confession.

258

It was that God had healed him years before, and that Satan had no ability to put any disease upon him. He denied that Satan had any authority to put any calamity, any sickness upon him whatever. This confession made him a wonder to folks. But it kept him well.

The secret lay in his continual confession of the absolute faithfulness of God and the ability of God to overcome every adverse circumstance. Christianity is a confession of our faith in Christ, of our faith in our relationship as sons and daughters. It is our faith in God's ability in us.

We continually confess that God is our sufficiency in every circumstance and condition.[26]

When Kenyon came into contact with Norvell in Pasadena in the mid-to-late 1920s, Norvell constantly affirmed the faithfulness of God and God's ability to keep him healthy. This obviously made an impression on Kenyon. It struck Kenyon that Norvell was doing the same thing as Jesus did—constantly affirming who he was because of his calling and relationship with the Father.

Apparently this sent Kenyon on a quest to understand the importance of constantly affirming our redemption and who we are as sons and daughters of God. He tells us more of this quest in *Jesus the Healer*.

For a long time I was confused over the fact that in my own life and in the lives of others there was a continual sense of defeat and failure. I prayed for the sick. I knew the Bible was true, and I searched diligently to find the leakage. One day I saw Hebrews 4:14, that we are to hold fast to our *confession*. I asked myself, "What confession am I to hold fast?"

I am to hold fast to my confession of the absolute integrity of the Bible.

I am to hold fast to the confession of the redemptive work of Christ.

I am to hold fast to my confession of the new creation, of receiving the life and nature of God.

I am to hold fast to the confession that God is the strength of my life.

I am to hold fast to the confession that, surely He hath borne my sicknesses and carried my diseases, and that by His stripes I am healed.

> I found it very difficult to hold fast to the confession of perfect healing when I had pain in my body.[27]

Holding fast to a positive confession for Kenyon was continuing to affirm God's faithfulness and the reliability of the promises and statements of Scripture no matter what contrary circumstances or symptoms may appear. This was consistent with his understanding of a God-honoring testimony. He continued:

> Many believers have failed when things became difficult because they lost their confession. While the sun was shining brightly, their confessions were vigorous, strong, and clear. But when the storms came, the testings came, and the adversary was taking advantage of them, they gave up their testimony.[28]

The issue for Kenyon, in the teaching of positive confession, was to honor God by every word of our mouths by holding fast, in the face of all the trials of life, to our testimony of God's faithfulness and His Word's truthfulness.

Certainly this is an honorable idea. Instead of complaining and talking like the world, we are to maintain a testimony to the goodness and faithfulness of God. Israel was overthrown in the wilderness because of their complaining and unbelief. Yet today, to suggest that we should keep our testimony positive even when our God promises "that all things work together for good to them that love God, to them who are the called according to his purpose," may bring a cry of "heresy" to your doorstep!

In 1941, near the end of his life, Kenyon wrote:

> I can remember when I dared not confess what God says I am. And my faith came to the level of my confession.
>
> If I dared not say I was the righteousness of God, Satan took advantage of my confession.
>
> If I dared not say that my body was perfectly well and that Satan had no dominion over it, disease and pain followed my negation.
>
> Since I have learned to know Him and to know His redemptive ability, and to know our ability in Christ, I have been able to maintain a testimony, a confession of the completeness of the

finished work of Christ, of the utter reality of the new birth.[29]

It can be seen here that holding fast to one's confession was maintaining a good testimony no matter what circumstances confronted the child of God. Kenyon saw a confession (or testimony) of faith as a way to honor God and uphold the victory of Christ's finished work.

As he practiced maintaining a consistent confession Kenyon noticed the effect of speaking God's Word on his own heart. This led him to discover that speaking God's Word aloud was also a way to *build* faith. "Faith cometh by hearing, and hearing by the word of God" (Rom.10:17).

AFFIRMATIONS

To affirm something is to make a positive statement of fact or to assert with confidence a belief. The metaphysical cults use affirmations to develop a positive mental attitude and to appropriate healing or prosperity. They do this with no faith in the God of the Bible or trust in the atonement of Christ. They have no regard for the will of God for their lives as they are still unregenerate.

Near the end of his life Kenyon wrote, "There are two types of affirmations I wish you to notice." One type, he wrote, has nothing behind it but "my own will to make it good." He said this type of affirmation may be found in Christian Science. In this type of affirmation "I affirm with all my might" that I can do whatever it is I determine to do. There is nothing behind it but the person making the affirmation.[30]

But an affirmation made by a New Testament believer who is quoting the Word of God in dependence on the Holy Spirit, is "backed up by God Himself," not just human will. The Christian is looking to God and the finished work of Christ as the power and provision, not to some impersonal force or universal mind.

Influenced by John Norvell and his study of the Word, Kenyon came to accept the value of constantly affirming the truth of Scripture. In 1930 he wrote:

> I once doubted the efficacy of affirmations, but when I read in the first five books of Moses the expression "I am Jehovah" occurring more than twenty-five hundred times, then I knew the value of affirming; reiterating; confessing the fullness of Jesus Christ and of His finished work in the presence of my weaknesses; in the

presence of my enemies; in the presence of hell.

I would suggest that the reader constantly affirm to his own soul, the great outstanding facts of Redemption. They may not mean much the first time you repeat them, but you constantly reaffirm them. By and by the Spirit will illumine them and your souls will be flooded with light and joy.

Every time I repeat what God has said about the church, about Himself, and about me as an individual, these truths reach down deep into my inner being with strength and joy and victory.[31]

Notice Kenyon acknowledges the believer's dependence upon the Holy Spirit to illuminate the Scriptures that are being affirmed. Again I want to emphasize that this is not some technique used independently of God. Rather it is something done in dependence upon God, expecting the Holy Spirit to make the truths real in the heart of the believer.

In an article written a little later in 1930, Kenyon added:

Only recently have I seen with clearness the infinite value of con-
tinually affirming, not only to our inner man, our own soul and spirit, but to the world. Our spiritual life depends upon our constantly affirming what God has declared, and what God is in Christ, and what we are before the Father in Christ.

The thing that made Methodism so mighty in its early days, was a continual confession of the things for which Mr. Wesley stood. When they stopped affirming, faith stopped growing, and believing or acting upon the Word became more and more difficult.[32]

It should be clear that for Kenyon affirmations were not a technique to get what you want in life, but rather a means of building the truths of God's Word into the life and consciousness of the believer in dependence on the Holy Spirit.

Notice that Kenyon related the idea back to his Methodist roots. Affirming the truth of God was what Kenyon felt had made Methodism strong. Once he saw that affirmations were another way of using testimony and confession to encourage our faith in God, he wholeheartedly embraced the idea. And he found it extremely helpful in his own walk with God as have thousands of others who daily affirm the Word of God in their devotional life.

The use of confession and affirmations had other advocates in the Christian community. One was Cornelia Nuzum, who ministered with the Montgomerys and wrote a book that is still in print called *The Life of Faith.* She may have been personally acquainted with Kenyon through the Montgomerys.[33] Nuzum wrote:

> Your own mouth can hasten the victory greatly. God says in Mark 11:23, you shall have whatever you say if you do not doubt. Say, "I refuse to have this sickness," no matter how much Satan tries to make you feel or see it. Ephesians 4:27 says, "Neither *give* place to the devil." God means here that the devil cannot get a place to put sins, pain, or disease upon you if you resist him all the time by the blood, the word of your testimony, and faith. If we thus refuse Satan a place in us or on us, he cannot *take* a place for himself.
>
> Never say, "I have pain, disease, doubt, or other evil." Say, "I will not have it. I will not let Satan put it on me. I refuse to accept it or recognize it or own it." Continue to say, "I am delivered, no matter how I feel or look." Praise hastens victory. Believe the thing is *done,* praise and rejoice, not because it is going to be done, but because it is done, even though you cannot see it or feel it.[34]

Another teacher of divine healing, Lillian B. Yeomans (1861–1942), echoed this emphasis on the spoken word. Yeomans was delivered from a morphine addiction after prayer from John Alexander Dowie (sometime before Dowie went into error). She and her sister eventually opened up a healing home for desperate cases. She exhorted her patients:

> Now repeat with me, "Christ hath redeemed me from the curse of the law, of which curse consumption [tuberculosis] is a part, so Christ hath redeemed me from consumption." And the seeker obeys; and repeatedly, with the Bible open before us at Deuteronomy 28:22 and Galatians 3:13, we say together, "Christ hath redeemed me from consumption." And faith cometh by hearing the Word of God, and the mountain is cast into the sea.[35]

Notice the importance of God's Word being *spoken* is emphasized by Yeomans. Kenyon was one of many who saw the truth of the importance and power of speaking God's Word to build faith for healing.

This truth was not derived from the cults but rather from the Bible. The true roots of this teaching, hopefully, are clearly seen.

An examination of Kenyon's writings on confession will reveal another interesting fact. He saw this truth modeled most distinctly in Jesus. Jesus only spoke the words the Father gave Him. Jesus' tongue was under the control of the Holy Spirit. Jesus used His words powerfully and carefully. His words were spirit and life. Jesus healed the sick and cast out demons with words. Kenyon sought to emulate Jesus in the use of his tongue and encouraged others to follow Jesus' example.

WERE THEY ALL LYING?

Everyone quoted in this chapter claimed that the Bible was their source for this teaching of faith and confession. Are they all lying? Or have Kenyon's critics misrepresented him? These people are documentable friends or influences of Kenyon. He was accepted among them and quite highly respected, for that matter. The similarity in their teachings is obviously not coincidental.

Kenyon's Methodist roots gave him an appreciation for testimony. He saw a consistent testimony or confession as a means of glorifying God in the early days of his ministry. Many of his contemporaries in the early days taught on the command of faith and the power of our words. The quotes in this chapter demonstrate that fact.

As time went on, Kenyon discovered the importance of holding fast to his confession. He then discovered the value of affirming the Word of God as an expression of praise to God, and as a means of faith-building. The dramatic effect this had on his life compelled him to teach others as well.

Kenyon's critics have misunderstood and misrepresented him. Neither have they honestly evaluated the modern Faith movement. Questionable scholarship has given a caricature of both the source of the teachings and the teachings themselves.

You have just read the evidence. I believe you can see clearly both the historical roots of the teaching and the biblical foundation for it.

CHAPTER 22

THE BELIEVER'S AUTHORITY

*You have been delivered out of the authority of Satan. Satan
has no authority or legal right to reign over you. You are the
absolute master of satanic forces in the name of Jesus.*
                                                    —E. W. Kenyon[1]

When the Spirit is poured out in revival, believers aggressively
take hold of the promises of God in a fresh way. The Holy
Spirit, the Author of the Word, quickens (or illuminates) them and
motivates them to believe. Mental assent to doctrine is transformed
into a living faith.

The status quo of that generation's (the one experiencing revival)
thinking about prayer and faith is often challenged. People who are content with their spiritual understanding and experience are threatened
by forward movement in the things of God. Revival upsets the status quo.

The status quo of Kenyon's day were challenged by teaching
about the believer's authority. In this chapter you will learn: 1) how
nineteenth-century teachers taught that healing fell within the sphere
of the believer's authority, 2) the basis for Kenyon's teaching on the
believer's authority and 3) Kenyon's beliefs about the deity of Christ,
which for him was an essential element in the believer's authority and
the use of Jesus' name.

GOD'S SOVEREIGNTY

In the latter part of the nineteenth century the renewed emphasis on faith, prayer, and divine healing prompted an investigation into the believer's authority. George Müller claimed that God answered all his prayers, which caused many theologians to accuse him of denying God's sovereignty. Charles Spurgeon, however, argued that God's sovereignty was not compromised by a believer's standing on God's promises. Spurgeon explained:

> Before He pledged His word He was free to do as it pleased Him; but after He has made a promise, His truth and honor bind Him to do as He said. To Him, indeed, this is no limiting of His liberty; for the promise is always the declaration of His sovereign will and good pleasure, and it is ever His delight to act according to His word.[2]

Despite the understanding demonstrated by Müller and Spurgeon, many nineteenth-century Christians used the sovereignty of God as justification for their unbelief and lack of results. Similarly, many today accuse E. W. Kenyon and others of challenging God's sovereignty by claiming God's promises in faith. They disagree with Spurgeon's statement that God's "truth and honor bind Him to do as He said." Teaching on the believer's authority is characterized as "demanding" God to do what they (the critics) perceive God to be reluctant to do.[3]

Let's look how this conflict is played out in the doctrine of healing. Some maintain that sickness in the believer's life is an expression of God's sovereignty and that healing is also at His sovereign discretion. To demand healing is to "give orders" to God. Others understand the atonement of Christ to cover sickness as well as sin; therefore, they believe God wants to heal everyone. But they do not demand healing of God. Rather they demand that the devil remove his demonic affliction. In this approach, they imitate the ministry of Jesus.

Most of the Faith-Cure advocates believed God wanted to heal all, but were certainly aware that not all were healed. Many insisted, however, that the failure to be healed was not necessarily an expression of God's sovereignty, but rather the result of some other known or unknown hindrance to healing. A. J. Gordon spoke of those who . . .

... bore so hard upon the divine sovereignty as practically to deny man's freedom to ask or expect miraculous healing. More than this, indeed, they seemed to have pushed the sovereignty of God into an iron fixedness, where even the Almighty is not at liberty to work miracles any longer, as though under bonds to restrain this office of his omnipotence since the apostolic age.[4]

Though Gordon allowed that God might withhold healing in some cases, Gordon said it was more often the unbelief of the church. Why aren't there more healings? Gordon thoughtfully remarked that the reason healing was so rare was "probably because the prayer of faith itself is so rare, and especially because when found it receives almost no support in the church as a whole."[5]

In 1888 Gordon published a book by George Peck titled, *Throne Life; or the Highest Christian Life,* which expounded on the believer's privilege of participating in the authority of the throne. Peck's teaching was well received among the Higher Life movement, and his book was much discussed. Peck wrote:

This believer [who recognizes his identification with Christ in His death and resurrection] will necessarily discern in the resurrection of Christ's physical body, not only the pledge and likeness of his own future glorified body, but also the privilege now made available to his faith in view of his present identification with Christ's glorified body of realizing in the midst of infirmity, or disease, or wearisome Christian service, a divine renewal of his physical strength . . . the life of Christ may become operative not only in his "inner man," but also in his "outer man," in the very "mortal flesh" of his "mortal body."[6]

Victory over guilt, sin, and sickness, Peck maintained, were part of the atonement's provision for the believer's walking in his authority in Christ.[7] Peck was for a season closely associated with Frank Sandford, with whom the Kenyons were in close relationship with for a time, and they were very likely aware of Peck's writings. The teaching in Peck's book is very similar to Kenyon's theology. Let us now take a look at Kenyon's much-criticized teaching on the believer's authority through the name of Jesus.

Kenyon's Revelation of the Name of Jesus

Kenyon saw the believer, because of his identification with Christ, raised up and seated with Christ (Eph. 2:5–6; Col. 3:1–3). As a new creation in Christ the believer had been delivered out of the authority of darkness. Kenyon focused his teaching on the practical application of the believer's authority around the use of the name of Jesus. In 1927 he released his second book, *The Wonderful Name of Jesus,* which was Kenyon's teaching on the believer's authority. Kenyon believed our right to the use of the name of Jesus was the key to New Testament authority for the church.

His first gleam of light on this truth occurred while he was listening to R. A. Torrey preach when Torrey was pastoring Moody's church in Chicago. (Kenyon must have heard Torrey preach this sermon before 1902 because Torrey left the pastorate of Moody's church in 1902 to begin a worldwide evangelistic tour.) Kenyon wrote:

> I was in Moody's church listening to one of Dr. Torrey's sermons when I caught that scripture [John 16:23]. Like a flash I saw it. Up to that time I had never asked anything in His name, I had prayed to Jesus. I had prayed to the Father; but I had never intelligently prayed in that name.

Kenyon had been seeking God for power. He had received the Holy Spirit and was surprised that he still lacked power. As he heard about the name of Jesus he caught a glimpse of fresh light. "Then I saw that the power I had sought was in the name of Jesus. It wasn't in the Holy Spirit. It would be the Holy Spirit giving me ability to use that name."[8]

Kenyon had some dramatic experiences that compelled him to respect the use of the name of Jesus. One such event he described in a sermon preached in 1928.

> The night which caused me to write that song, "We Have Victory in Jesus' Name," was a fearful night. All day it had stormed. The wind whipped up into a fury and the snow had piled up in great drifts. It stormed as only it can storm on that fearful eastern coast.
>
> The crowd had come. Conviction was so great that it seemed like nothing could keep the folks away. Drifts were high. They had to wade through the snow to get there. Oh, how the wind

268

shrieked and howled that night. A voice could scarcely be heard above the noise of the elements. It seemed like the fury of hell was let loose around us.

I turned to a young man who travelled with me, and who was mighty in prayer, and said, "Theodore, will you pray?" He got up and tried to pray, but the wind drowned out his voice, and in a moment he broke down, and gave up.

Then I turned to his wife who also was mighty in prayer and asked her to lead and she broke, too.

All the demons of hell seemed to be let loose on us. There were spiritualists and uni-nothings [Kenyon's derogatory term for Unitarians] in that audience that night.

I was walking the platform when Nellie was trying to pray, and when she gave up, I stepped forward and charged the elements in the name of Jesus to cease. I rebuked the storm.

In a moment it became calm. It wasn't the dying down of the wind. It wasn't the gradual subsiding. It had seemed I couldn't raise my voice above the tumult, and when the storm ceased, before I finished praying, I found that I was actually yelling. I became quiet. The audience became hushed and awed in the presence of the power of that name.

It was in the name of Jesus.[9]

This was not the only time Kenyon used the name of Jesus to take authority over the natural order. During the years at Bethel another example of the power of the name occurred. Kenyon wrote:

Few people know that most of the insects that afflict man are evidently governed by the adversary. Again and again I have come into contact with those who have learned this secret. We learned it years ago at the school. An old house was given to us for a dormitory and it was full of insect trouble for us. We tried everything, until finally in our desperation we turned to the Lord and in that name we commanded them to leave. The house was instantly rid of them, and so far as I know we were never again troubled with them. We learned our lesson.[10]

Not only insects, but rodents too were subject to the name of Jesus. Kenyon wrote, "When rats and mice became a pest, we knew how to get rid of them. In Jesus' name we drove them out."[11]

As early as March 1902 Kenyon wrote about this great authority in the name of Jesus. In the *Bethel Trumpet* Kenyon stated:

> In this *name* lies the very essence of Christianity; it is the one thing that differentiates it from all other religions. We have salvation, power over demons, healing, absolute assurance of answer to prayer; all in the name of the man Christ Jesus.
>
> Men are seeking power—they call it Pentecostal power; they seek it in all directions but the right one. It is in *the name*. Seek it there. If you learn to use that name according to the Word, in the power of the Spirit, you have the secret which shook the world through the apostles.[12]

In language that sounds strikingly similar to Kenyon's teaching on the use of the name, A. T. Pierson had written:

> To ask in the name of Jesus is not simply to ask "for His sake," but it is to ask in the power of my union with Him as my redeemer; it is to ask in His stead; it is to ask because I belong to Him and He belongs to me; and this union is my authority in the request . . .
>
> When I ask a favor in another's name it is not I that am the suppliant, but the Man whose name I use. I simply present the request which He makes through me. And reverently let me say, when, in the name of Jesus, I present my request to the Father, not I but Jesus Christ is the suppliant. And therefore I have the assurance that I shall be heard.[13]

In *The Wonderful Name of Jesus* Kenyon wrote:

> Jesus says, "You do the asking and I will do the doing; you ask of the Father in My name; I will endorse that, and the Father will give it to you."
>
> This puts prayer on a purely legal basis, for He has given us the legal right to use His name.
>
> As we take our privileges, and rights, in the New Covenant and pray in Jesus' name, it passes out of our hands into the hands of Jesus; He then assumes the responsibility of that prayer, and we know that He said, "Father, I thank Thee that Thou hearest Me,

and I know that Thou hearest Me always."

In other words, we know that the Father always hears Jesus, and when we pray in Jesus' name, it is as though Jesus Himself were doing the praying—He takes our place.[14]

Another important development in the unveiling of this teaching about the name of Jesus occurred for Kenyon while on a preaching tour. "Several years ago I was holding meetings in a city in Tennessee," Kenyon wrote. "One afternoon, while giving an address on 'The Name of Jesus,' a lawyer interrupted me, asking: 'Do you mean to tell us that Jesus gave us the *power of attorney,* the legal right to use His name?'"

Kenyon, recognizing his limitations in matters of law responded, "Brother, you are a lawyer, and I am a layman. Tell me—did Jesus give us the power of attorney?"

The attorney replied, "If language means anything, then Jesus gave to the church the power of attorney."

This motivated Essek to a renewed search of the Scriptures. "Then I began my search," he wrote, "to find out how much power and authority Jesus had."[15]

The Wonderful Name of Jesus is a thorough study of the New Testament's teaching on the use of the name by the early church. Kenyon saw our right to use the name of Jesus as God giving us the authority of Christ over Satan and all his works. The name was given to us (the church) for prayers, and petition toward God, and to use in our conflicts with demons and sickness. Every knee must bow to the name of Jesus, Kenyon concluded, when that name was used through the believer's lips in faith.

THE DEITY OF CHRIST

Kenyon saw that the authority of the name of Jesus was linked to another important truth. They stood or fell together. That truth was the deity of Christ. While he was preparing his book on the name he was also studying deeply the deity of Jesus. *In The Wonderful Name of Jesus* Kenyon stated:

There has never been a more intense battle over the deity of the man of Galilee than is being waged today. The great body of the church do not see—as they never have seen—the issue squarely; neither have they realized the result of this struggle. The deity of the man of Galilee is the crux of Christianity. If that can be successfully challenged, then Christianity has lost its heart, and it will cease to function; it will become a dead religion.[16]

Kenyon was deeply moved by the reality of this struggle over Christ's deity.

E. W. Kenyon had faced his own struggles with the truth of Christ's deity and had satisfied his heart and mind. He understood the importance of challenges to this fundamental doctrine. He saw this truth as a tremendous deterrent to keep Christians from being seduced into Christian Science and the other cults. He wrote, "Could Christian Science have made such inroads if the people had been rooted and grounded in the truth of the deity of Jesus? You never knew a man or woman to go into Christian Science except they were ignorant of the Word of God."[17] Kenyon felt if people were properly grounded in the knowledge of Christ's deity they would be protected from the errors of Christian Science.

Kenyon himself had struggled with the question of Christ's deity shortly after he was restored to the Lord in 1893. He recalled, "When I went into the ministry, I went in with a lot of doubts. There came an hour in my living when I faced the great problem of the deity of Jesus."[18] For Kenyon, the question of Christ's deity was tied to the question of His resurrection. "I used to say, 'If He was actually raised from the dead, then His deity and His substitutionary work are realities.'"[19] This was clearly an intellectual battle because Kenyon had responded to the Spirit of God and dedicated his life back to God by this time. Earlier we referred to the battle that Kenyon faced with skepticism. This was part of that battle.

In a sermon preached at Bethel Temple in 1925 on the deity of Christ, Kenyon related his own arrival at the assurance of the truth of the deity of Christ. After describing his walking with the disciples Peter and John as they came to the tomb after Christ's resurrection— Kenyon was meditating on John 20—he saw himself (with the disciples) coming to view the graveclothes. Knowing the graveclothes would have been hardened due to the hot climate into a kind of solid casing, Kenyon saw that the graveclothes were empty! He related:

When I saw that, I slid off my chair on my knees and buried my face in my hands and cried, "Lord, I believe Thou didst arise from the dead." Then I saw another miracle. That napkin had been folded up and laid in a place by itself. That man had come out of the graveclothes, left them intact; then He stopped and took the napkin, and just as He said to His disciples to pick up the fragments that nothing be lost, He put it by itself, so that it might be a witness to the world. When I saw that, every doubt of His resurrection died. I knew that the man of Galilee rose from the dead![20]

As he meditated in the Word, the Holy Spirit made real to him what Peter and John experienced that day in the tomb. This most likely took place in the first six months after his rededication to the Lord, between June, 1893 and his ordination with the Free Will Baptists in early 1894. He was required to acknowledge a complete faith in the deity of Christ in order to be ordained.

Having settled this issue of Jesus' deity, Kenyon set himself to defend and proclaim the twin truths of His deity and His resurrection. He preached on these truths often. In his old Bible, given to him by the Sunday school department of his church in Springville, New York, in November 1896, Kenyon had saved a notice of his preaching for A. B. Simpson at Simpson's Gospel Tabernacle in New York. The ad read:

Interdenominational Gospel Tabernacle
44th St. and 8th Ave.
Rev. A. B. Simpson, Pastor.
Special Easter Services 10:45 A.M. and 7:30 P.M.
(Special baptismal service at 4 o'clock)
Evangelist E. W. Kenyon
of Spencer, Massachusetts
will preach morning and evening
Morning topic: "Resurrection"
Evening topic: "Deity of Christ"

The time of this event would have been during Kenyon's years at Bethel Bible Institute (that was when he lived in Spencer) and before Simpson's death in 1919. The fact that Simpson allowed Kenyon to preach at his church is significant. Simpson also had one of instructors from Bethel Bible Institute, J. H. Hartman, teach during the summers at Nyack training center (Simpson's school). Simpson would not have endorsed Kenyon and his school if there was something questionable about his character, teaching, or practice. Simpson readily condemned Frank Sandford when Sandford went into error.

The deity of Christ was such an important doctrine to Kenyon that he spent considerable time working on his book on the subject. In the back of the original edition of *The Wonderful Name of Jesus,* three forthcoming books are mentioned. The third one mentioned is *The Deity of Jesus.* It is stated:

> Still a third feast is promised to those of you who have followed the ministry and teaching of Dr. E. W. Kenyon. In this you will find the most convincing array of evidences that have ever been given on this subject. Years of research and study have brought about this masterful work concerning the deity of our Lord Jesus Christ. Watch for the announcement of its publication.[21]

Although this book was never published, it probably represented one of Kenyon's sincerest attempts to address the issues he felt were of great concern to the church. As previously mentioned, he felt that knowledge of Christ's deity would stem the tide of the metaphysical cults. But he also knew it was the real issue underlying the debates with the Higher Criticism and Unitarianism. If Jesus is deity, Kenyon reasoned, then the doctrine of the Trinity is secure.

Kenyon was also concerned about how the attacks on Christ's deity had infected the seminaries with unbelief. Without His deity and the supernatural nature of His birth, all that was left were the ethical teachings of Jesus, who was merely the greatest product of humanity. To this dwarfing of Jesus, Kenyon attributed the moral decline of the nation.

Kenyon wrote about twenty chapters of the book but apparently was never quite satisfied with it. It was never published. The unpublished manuscript, with some unfinished chapters, remains among the things that Kenyon left.

As mentioned in an earlier chapter, Kenyon had a dramatic encounter with the Lord as he studied the person of Christ. This encounter with the Lord was one of a handful of powerful life-changing milestones in Kenyon's life. As the Lord manifested Himself to Kenyon, all of Kenyon's knowledge of Scripture seemed to melt in significance. The Lord Himself was far greater than any knowledge about Him. This manifestation of the Lord to Kenyon led to a passion to defend His deity and to a desire to more fully imitate Him in all things. One effect of his encounter which we discussed was that it produced in Kenyon the desire to speak only God's Word as Jesus did.

Jesus was very real for E. W. Kenyon. His use of the name of Jesus in healing and prayer was far from mechanical. Walking in intimate fellowship with the Father and the Son, Kenyon was empowered to use John 14:13 to do the works of Jesus. As he translated it: "Whatever you demand in My name that will I do, that the Father may be glorified in the Son." Many sitting under Kenyon's ministry were saved, received the Holy Spirit, and were healed and delivered from demonic bondage as he used the name of Jesus.

The name of Jesus, intimately tied to the truth of Christ's deity, was for E. W. Kenyon a truth that released him "do the works of Jesus" (John 14:12).

CHAPTER 23

THE FATHER AND HIS FAMILY

Reader, allow me to be frank with you. I believe the time has come for a restatement of the plan of redemption in language the common people can understand.

—E. W. Kenyon[1]

Most of the writings critical of E. W. Kenyon focus on what are perceived to be the controversial aspects of his teaching (positive confession, healing, and the atonement) and, unfortunately, present a caricature of the man's teachings. All that Kenyon taught came from the heart of an evangelist. He passionately wanted to reach people for Jesus Christ. While pastoring, if a month went by without a soul being won, he would seek the Lord diligently to find out what the problem was. This passion for the lost was the motivation for all that he did and taught.

Kenyon's evangelistic passion, however, was nourished by a hidden stream that found expression in his first book *The Father and His Family*. Using this book as a guide, this chapter will explore the true heart of Kenyon's doctrine. We will begin by showing Kenyon's motives for writing *The Father and His Family*. In the rest of the chapter we'll examine the major truths that were expressed in Kenyon's first book—fellowship with God the Father, desiring God's will, the lordship of Christ, confession of Christ's lordship, the justice of God, eternal punishment and eternal life, the new birth. It will be important to note that these assumptions undergird everything else

Kenyon taught throughout his entire ministry. This book was his "systematic theology for laymen."

KENYON'S MOTIVES

In his early days Kenyon's evangelistic fire went out when he lost his fellowship with the Father. Unfortunately, he didn't know how to restore it. He spent between two and three years out of fellowship with the Lord. He thought he was lost again because he had sinned, and that he needed to be justified and sanctified again. In his thinking, he was consistent with the popular Holiness teaching of the day. With his fellowship broken, his love for the lost was diverted into the "sales game" and a desire to pursue a career in acting.

So the knowledge of the Father heart of God and the way to maintain a rich, deep fellowship with Him became the hallmarks of E. W. Kenyon's ministry. Kenyon's message of faith expressed the truths he believed would reach the unsaved, and the truths he personally discovered that stabilized and empowered him to maintain his zeal in reaching out to a lost world. He saw the absolute necessity of grounding new believers in the Word so they too could be consistent fruit bearers. Kenyon's discovery that we were either in one family or the other—God's or Satan's—was an important, stabilizing truth for him. He wrote:

> Satan is unable to affect my relationship. He may destroy my joy, rob me of my liberty in testimony, drag me into darkness, and keep me from my privileges, but it is a very difficult thing for him to affect in any way my relationship with my Father. I was born into the family of God, and I am His child.
>
> Now the fact that I am a child does not necessarily give me joy. There is a measure of joy in it, but the real joy of the Christian life lies purely in the degree of fellowship and communion with my Father in the Holy Spirit.
>
> The trouble with the great body of believers is that they do not know the difference between union and communion, fellowship and relationship, a child in fellowship and a child out of fellowship.
>
> When we sin we grieve the Holy Spirit. He can no longer have fellowship with us. He is obliged to withdraw His fellowship

from us. We also lose the sense of the presence of the Father and
the freedom of prayer. Our boldness in testimony is gone, and the
joy is gone out of the study of the Word.[2]

Shortly after his rededication to the Lord, Kenyon began a diligent
study of the Scriptures for himself. He had previously relied on the
opinion of others, to his own hurt. Being of a skeptical mind and
having wandered into the byways of an agnostic unbelief for a season,
he had some work to do in answering some of his own questions.
Essek acknowledged that in the time immediately following his
restoration he had questioned the authority of the Bible, the deity and
resurrection of Christ, the reality of eternal punishment, and the justice
of God. He had read some philosophy and metaphysics during his time
away from the Lord. So it is important to note that his first book dealt
with all of these issues, directly or indirectly.

The great majority of the above issues were thoroughly dealt with
on a personal level by Kenyon shortly after his restoration to the Lord,
while he was in Springville, New York (1894–1897). It was during
1897 that he received the Holy Spirit, surrendered fully to Christ's
lordship, and discovered the Father heart of God. Having personally
met and overcome the doctrinal questions that faced him, however,
Kenyon wanted to help others who may, like himself, need answers.

In addition to dealing with his questions, truths about God's Father
heart, the lordship of Christ, and receiving the Holy Spirit were being
cultivated and developed in Kenyon's heart for almost two decades
before finding expression in his first book. In many places in later
writings he made reference to the time in February 1897 when he submitted to Christ's lordship, received the Spirit, and came to know God
as Father. It was of major importance to his spiritual life.

In the book Kenyon also clarified his scriptural understanding of the
nature of man, our privileges in prayer, the authority of the believer,
who we were in Christ, and sanctification. *The Father and His Family*
was the foundational statement of his theology, and he based all his
other writings on the truths articulated in this book. When Kenyon
revised the book in 1936, he eliminated the two introductions and
added an author's preface on the two kinds of knowledge, which was a
teaching that developed in his later years. He also added three chapters
on themes that were important to him and quotes to the beginning
pages of each chapter. A. J. Gordon and G. Campbell Morgan are

among those quoted. But this revision did not significantly alter his teachings.

In one of his publications Kenyon acknowledged that he at one time endeavored to write a new systematic theology, likely with the assistance of his teachers at Bethel. He abandoned this project in favor of *The Father and His Family.*

A SCHOLAR'S OPINION

Francis S. Bernauer, who was a fellow classmate at Emerson College with Kenyon, also had a Bachelor of Arts degree from the University of Rochester and a Bachelor of Divinity degree from Rochester Theological Seminary. Bernauer, who taught at Bethel and was for a few years its president, wrote one of the two introductions to the first edition of *The Father and His Family.* In his introduction he lamented the lack of clear, doctrinal teaching available to the layman in understandable language. He wrote, "Within the past twenty years various cults, such as Christian Science, New Thought in all its ramifications, and Millennial Dawnism have gained a tremendous following, which has been drafted almost entirely from the nominal membership of our protestant churches."[3]

Bernauer believed that a lack of sound doctrine was the root problem for most of God's people. He felt Kenyon's book was an answer to the problem.

> We venture the assertion that had this book been published twenty-five years ago with the financial and advertising facilities to give it worldwide dissemination, that Russellism and Eddyism [Christian Science] would have died of a congestive chill in infancy with no monuments reared to their honor; such cults can only thrive in the dark atmosphere of ignorance or the dark soil of superstition.

Praising Kenyon's soundness as regards orthodoxy and his willingness to investigate new areas of Bible teaching, Bernauer stated, "[A] careful reading of the book will demonstrate the fact that he [Kenyon] is a mighty defender of the old landmarks, as well as a pioneer in his search for truth."[4]

It is significant to note that Francis Bernauer, who attended

Emerson College with Kenyon, felt that *The Father and His Family* was an antidote to New Thought and Christian Science. Bernauer claimed that Kenyon's teachings would have stopped these cults from taking root had they been disseminated years earlier. Note that both Kenyon and Bernauer had attended Emerson College, yet both opposed New Thought and Christian Science bitterly, seeing them as true enemies of the church. How ironic that Kenyon should be perceived today as *importing* Christian Science and New Thought ideas into the church when one reason for writing his first book was to refute and uproot them!

Kenyon believed that no one who saw clearly the love of God demonstrated by Christ's sacrifice to satisfy justice and offer man redemption could be misled by the metaphysical cults. It was a lack of the availability of this teaching stated for the layman that motivated him to put his teachings in print. The finished work of Christ, which took Christ from the cross to the throne, would always be a central truth in Kenyon's proclamation of the gospel.

Kenyon also felt that a spirit of unrest had seized the heart of Christendom due to the Higher Criticism. This attack on the integrity of the Bible had, Kenyon believed, a devastating effect on the church. The faith of millions had been shattered and the ministry was overwhelmed with unbelief.[5] *The Father and His Family* was a response to the pressing need of the church to take the Bible literally and seriously in that it offered the only real answers to man's need of a purpose and destiny in life.

Because of his background in the experience-oriented Holiness movement, he deeply longed to see people strong in doctrine. It was the unfolding of the Scriptures through his many doctrinally strong mentors and his personal study that enabled Kenyon to find stability and peace. His life-long passion was to teach people to live by faith in God's Word and not on the shifting sand of experiences, however biblical. His message of faith was a message of the integrity and reliability of the Word of God.

FELLOWSHIP WITH GOD AS FATHER

The *Father fact* and the *Family fact* were Essek's descriptive terms for what he felt were the true and needed foundational concepts for a healthy walk with God. In 1897, not long after he discovered the depth of fellowship with the Father that was available, Kenyon read Müller's *Life of Trust*. Besides challenging Kenyon to begin to trust God for all his finances, Müller's book pointed to another truth that had recently touched Kenyon's life. Müller wrote regarding fellowship with the Father,

> The believer in the Lord Jesus does not only obtain forgiveness of all his sins, as he does through the shedding of the blood of Jesus, by faith in his name; does not only become a righteous one before God, through the righteousness of the Lord Jesus by faith in his name: is not only begotten again, born of God, and partaker of the divine nature, and therefore a child of God and an heir of God; but he is also in fellowship or partnership with God.

Müller went on to speak of "an *experimental* fellowship, or partnership with the Father and with the Son," by which the blessings of redemption are "brought down into our daily life . . . enjoyed, experienced, and used." This experimental (the word was used as we would use *experiential*) fellowship, Müller maintained, determined what we received in accordance with "the measure in which faith is in exercise . . . " Müller considered this fellowship to be unlimited and that we could "draw by prayer and faith out of the inexhaustible fullness which there is in God."[6] Essek's hunger for more of God was surely stirred by Müller's words.

Kenyon discovered Müller shortly after the season when he was desperately seeking sanctification and desiring to receive the Holy Spirit, which was during most of 1896. By February 1897 he had received the Holy Spirit, surrendered to the lordship of Christ in a covenant of consecration, and was dramatically healed. This period also marked his discovery of God as his Father.

Kenyon published the entire section from the *Life of Trust* from which a portion is quoted above, in *Reality* in March 1909. The themes of *relationship* and *fellowship* would become of major importance to Kenyon.

It is not surprising, then, that he wrote much about this problem of broken fellowship and sought to bring what he felt was biblical clarity to the issue. In December 1904 he wrote an article titled "Relationship and Fellowship," which said in part:

Why is it that the majority of those who accept Christ as their Savior in evangelistic meetings lapse back into the old life, and why is it in organized work, such as missions and The Salvation Army, that there are always a large number in the congregation who are continually going forward and then going back again into the world?

Essek felt the same thing was true of those who attended the Holiness conventions and camp meetings. The people were "losing their experiences, their liberty in testimony and prayer, and are unable to help themselves or to get back into fellowship with God without the assistance of an altar or a convention," he observed. Both his personal experience and his observations of the church of his day convinced Kenyon that the popular teaching must not be sound. In distinguishing between relationship and fellowship, Kenyon found a key which gave him—and those he instructed—a measure of stability he found lacking in the lives of many believers.

In December of the next year (1905), Kenyon again touched on this theme in an article called "Broken Fellowship." He shared about a woman he met in one of his meetings where "the power of God was on the meeting; scores had been swept into the kingdom in the last few evenings." As he talked with this discouraged one who thought she had lost her salvation, his heart ached for her. Kenyon encouraging her by explaining, "If you were ever a child, you are one now are you not? All that has happened is that you have lost fellowship with the Father; you have wandered into sin."

It became an important part of Kenyon's ministry to teach believers how to restore their fellowship if it was lost or broken. His heart broke for the "thousands scattered everywhere" throughout the churches who at one time knew they were born of the Spirit and enjoyed fellowship with the Father. Then something had happened and they didn't know how to be restored. "We know that the secret of joy in the Christian life is in the child's fellowship and communion with the Father," he wrote. "If this be true, our chief ambition and first care should be that this fellowship grow richer, deeper, and stronger as the years go by, that nothing be permitted to mar or break it."[7]

Here we see the essence of the type of Christianity Kenyon advocated. Christianity for Kenyon was a simple thing: *The Father and His Family.* Maintaining and deepening this fellowship with God the

Father was at the heart of everything Kenyon taught. To suggest that he advocated the use of impersonal spiritual laws like the metaphysical cults, as his critics have suggested, is to totally misunderstand him. Few Bible teachers emphasize more than Kenyon the importance of close fellowship with the Father in the life of faith. This deep, rich fellowship with the Father was the heart of Kenyon's message of faith.

Kenyon saw the works that we were to do flowing out of this rich fellowship with the Father. He believed that this was the secret of Jesus' ministry. He explained that Jesus' "example in His relationship with His Father is the true example. What He did for men was but the result of His fellowship with the Father. So if we are to take Him as an example it must be in this respect."

DESIRING GOD'S WILL

Out of this deep fellowship with the Father, Kenyon found that the individual's desires were changed from seeking to have the believer's plans blessed by the Father, to having a desire to do only the will of the Father. He continued, "Here we see the hidden source of that power he exercised over men. His meat was to do the will of Him that sent Him." Kenyon understood the source of power in the ministry of Jesus to be His dedication to do only the Father's will. This is a significant observation.

Sharing his own failure to grasp this secret in his earlier days of ministry, he shared that he mistakenly thought that service was what God wanted from him. But, Kenyon discovered, "in reality he wanted my heart and fellowship. He wanted me lost in the folds of His will, enwrapped in its mighty love for men." But, in those early days, Kenyon said, "I had plans of my own for Him to bless!"

Kenyon gave up all his plans and abandoned them to the will of the Father. Jesus was his example. "Most of the unhappiness in our lives is the result of thwarted self-will," he explained. Real happiness came in following the example of Jesus. "There was no room for that [self-will] in the heart of the Son of God, so His joy was always overflowing."[8] Kenyon taught that true happiness was only available when we do the Father's will.[9]

In another of his reminiscences, Kenyon shared further on his discovery of his Father. He recalled that "as a young man, I was afraid of the Father. I did not know Him then as Father, I only knew Him as God." Not comprehending God as his Father caused Kenyon to hesitate to let Him have complete control of his life. "I was afraid to let Him come into my life and take me over. I was afraid to yield unconditionally to the lordship of Christ. I had ambitions that I longed to achieve, and for a year I fought letting Him become the Head of my life."

The day came during this year of battling with the Lord when Essek heard a voice saying, "I love you more than you love yourself. I am more interested in your success than you are. I know what is best for you, and I know how to enable you to achieve it." The tender love of the Lord for Kenyon melted away the last of his resistance. He could no longer hold out anything in rebellion against this lordship of love. He admitted, "This utterly unarmed me. I could go no farther. I took Him as my Head and Lord."[10] I wonder how many in the church today need to know their Father in this way?

For E. W. Kenyon, though he definitely believed that "faith comes by hearing, hearing by the word of God" (Rom. 10:17), he felt that ultimately, faith came from a rich fellowship with the Father. The Word of God became the living voice of God to the heart in intimate fellowship with the Father and the Master. In his book on prayer, *In His Presence* (written in 1944, just a few years before his death), in the chapter on "Relationship and Fellowship," Kenyon wrote: "The new birth and righteousness are to one end: That we may enjoy the sweetest fellowship with the Father and with the Son." We are born again and justified so we can enjoy fellowship with the Father, he believed. This fellowship, Kenyon said, "is the parent of real faith. If you find someone whose faith is weak, you may know that his fellowship has been broken, or it is of a low type." The life of faith revolves around the level of one's fellowship, Essek insisted.

Most of the problems in the Christian life were the result of weak or broken fellowship. "This broken fellowship does not break your relationship, but it mars it and robs that relationship of its richest blessings and benefits. All low-grade faith comes from a low grade of fellowship." The source of joy and zeal was unhindered fellowship. "Fellowship in its fullness is the joy life with the throttle wide open on a downgrade. Fellowship in its fullness is the soil out of which living faith grows to fruition. Faith dies on a low type of fellowship."[11]

E. W. Kenyon's message of faith was a message about the call to intimate fellowship with the Father. A strong faith life was rooted in this deep fellowship with the Father. Any analysis of Kenyon's teachings about spiritual laws or positive confession must keep in mind that he understood these things in the light of this rich fellowship with God and the empowerment of the Spirit. The message of faith that was proclaimed by E. W. Kenyon was rooted in the joy of unhindered fellowship with the Father and the Master.

THE LORDSHIP OF CHRIST

In the same season he discovered God as Father, Kenyon discovered another life-transforming truth for him. It was the lordship of Christ. Kenyon, having been introduced to Christianity in the Holiness movement, had fallen away from God in part because of the teaching (or lack of teaching) in that environment. It was commonly taught in the Holiness movement that conversion only brought forgiveness of sins and justification. It took a second work of grace, a crisis of consecration to remove your sin nature and bring you into "entire sanctification."

The truth of Christ's lordship was part of a newly emerging doctrinal understanding for Kenyon that would replace second-work-of-grace Holiness teaching in his life. Kenyon wrote: "Some of us know what it means to have had a time somewhere in our lives when we spent a great deal of time trying to consecrate ourselves to the Lord; what it means to have humbled ourselves and cried before God trying to surrender ourselves to Him . . . I cannot tell you how many times I personally tried to do this."

Kenyon came to understand that attempts to consecrate oneself to the Lord meant that "we attempt to do something that only God can do. We attempt to do something which the new birth has already done. The new birth has put us into the family of God, and if we are in the family, then we are God's. We may not fully recognize our relationship, may not fully recognize our responsibility, but we are children nevertheless."

Kenyon observed that the Greek word for *Lord* meant, "owner, possessor, one who rules, one who controls." The significance of this meaning hit Kenyon profoundly. "The lordship of Christ means Jesus Christ's right to rule in everything connected with our life on this earth. When a man recognizes the lordship of Jesus over his life, there is no place for consecration."

How could one consecrate to someone something that did not belong to him? If Jesus was Lord, He already owned the believer, and *conversion,* not a second work of grace, was the point of surrender to the new Lord. "When a man recognizes the right of Jesus Christ over him as Master and Ruler, that [means] he has no right to enter into an occupation, accept a position, do any labor, do anything, without getting consent of his Lord." Confessing Christ as Lord, meant that "the thought of surrender and of consecration will have no place in [one's] life."[12]

This truth gripped Kenyon and was a part of his preaching from the time he recognized the lordship of Christ in his own life. When the implications of Christ's lordship manifested in Kenyon's life, he began to practice the Word with a renewed understanding that Christ's lordship meant unquestioning obedience to the Bible. "As I practiced the Word, there came an unveiling of the Master such as I had never seen before. His very heart seemed to be uncovered. I came to know Him with a spiritual intimacy that I had never realized possible."[13] Kenyon is describing the season of his life after settling the question of Christ's lordship. This would be the late 1890s.

Compelled by the loving lordship of his Master, Kenyon realized the necessity of becoming a disciple of Christ in the totality of his life. In an article on discipleship Kenyon wrote:

> The real disciple who loves Him, and who has laid his crown down at the feet of Jesus, says, "Here, Lord Jesus, I recognize that I cannot make myself happy or anyone else happy; neither can I bring joy and glory to Thee except as I place the reins of authority of my life in Thy loving hands. So, here, now, I recognize Thy lordship of my spirit, soul, and body.
>
> I recognize Thy right to rule and to make of my life what will please Thee. I do this of my own volition; I do it after mature meditation; I do it in the face of my own failure; I do it for Thy glory. Now, Lord Jesus, I give to Thee the remainder of my life to be used as seemeth best to Thee. I do not ask for position, power, or money. The only favor I crave today is to know that I am pleasing Thee."[14]

Notice the similarity between this prayer of dedication published in 1912 and the prayer Kenyon himself prayed in 1897 when he surrendered to Christ's lordship. (See chapter 4.)

OTHERS EMBRACE KENYON'S TEACHING ON LORDSHIP

Essek was wonderfully blessed when he found that others appreciated this emphasis on Christ's lordship. The Brethren, whom Kenyon greatly respected, had followers in Massachusetts. When the Brethren in Massachusetts read the articles Kenyon wrote in *Reality* about the lordship of Christ, they responded enthusiastically. One leader wrote to Kenyon, "I want to tell you that you have uncovered a new vein of teaching. It is new to us. We are rejoicing in it." The author of the letter then wrote a long article called "The Lordship of Christ" in the Brethren's periodical.

This, of course, greatly blessed and encouraged Kenyon. He then sent the articles he had written to one of his favorite Bible teachers in Britain: G. Campbell Morgan. Imagine Kenyon's delight when Morgan came to Northfield the next year and brought a series of messages on the lordship of Christ![15]

CONFESSING CHRIST'S LORDSHIP

Kenyon began to see the confession of the lordship of Christ in a new light. Rather than "receiving Christ as Savior," or "being justified," Kenyon began to preach the lordship of Christ to the lost. The lost person was not *getting converted* but rather *being called to surrender all to a new Lord.* After explaining the lordship of Christ and its implications and demands, Kenyon had the new convert publicly testify to his new Lord as a regular part of evangelistic services.

One church worker, describing Kenyon's ministry to his Baptist church in Elizabethton, Tennessee, wrote that he had never heard a man with a more profound knowledge of the Scriptures, or who "taught the sovereignty of God, the lordship of Christ, and the work of the Holy Spirit in a clearer and more concise way." Kenyon, he said, "attracts his hearers by his masterful arguments in favor of the deity of Jesus, the inspiration of the Scriptures from Genesis to Revelation, the mediation of Christ for the sinner, and His advocacy for the Christian."

Kenyon, line upon line, unveiled the plan of redemption to his hearers, bringing them to the necessary point of decision. The clerk went on to remark, "His sermons on the deity of Jesus, the rejection of Him as Savior, judgment, hell, and the devil made a profound impression upon his hearers, showing very plainly that there is a literal hell, and all who reject Jesus will be cast into the bottomless pit with the devil and his angels."

But there is one other significant point that deserves notice and comment. This church clerk was apparently struck by a noticeable distinctive of Kenyon's ministry. "One remarkable thing about the converts," he observed, "is that they arise and testify, and we have never seen a meeting where this formed so important a feature."[16] For E. W. Kenyon, the first and most significant event in the Christian life is sealed by a positive confession of the lordship of Christ.

The confession of the lordship of Christ and publicly testifying to that lordship came to be an important part of Kenyon's evangelistic ministry. In this practice, Kenyon had given a new application to the principle of public testimony for entering into and maintaining a biblical experience that he learned among the Holiness people. Instead of applying public testimony to a *second* work of grace, he used it in the *first* work of grace. This is an important foundation stone in his developing understanding of positive confession.

A report of a convention in an area where Kenyon had been holding evangelistic services for some months is informative. Nearly a thousand new converts or individuals restored to fellowship through Kenyon's ministry gathered together. The report stated, "Their testimonies of salvation from sin and 'all their enemies' including Satan, death, and habits of drink, tobacco, and profanity, gave positive proof that God had recreated them in Christ Jesus."

The report then gave a good overview of the systematic teachings of Kenyon used in one of his evangelistic crusades. First, he taught about the new birth "as a new creation and its once-for-all deliverance from Satanic union." Then Kenyon explained "the lordship of Christ and obedience to His loving rule." He led the people to see "the Holy Spirit as the One who must sojourn in the tabernacle newly created in the believer's life." And, not surprisingly, he expounded on "the privileges of the believer in fellowship with the Father and the brethren in prayer, in study of the Word."

Because Kenyon taught such a strong message about the lordship of Christ, confessing Christ's lordship represented a real repentance in those he led to Christ. No need to emphasize a second work of grace if the first one was taught correctly, he reasoned. He stressed this idea of Christ's lordship in *The Father and His Family.*[17]

This also explains why Kenyon taught receiving the Holy Spirit in the manner he did. Having emphasized the lordship of Christ and the new birth as a new creation—a real change of nature—he then invited people to receive the Holy Spirit as a gift of grace without struggle or trying to be worthy.

He encouraged them to receive the Spirit in the same manner as they had invited Jesus into their lives—by receiving *a Person* to indwell the newly sanctified temple prepared for Him by the new birth. After he gained light on the restoration of the gift of tongues (around 1908), he encouraged those receiving the Holy Spirit to seek God and see whether He wanted to give them that gift. At least in these early days, Kenyon did not believe tongues were the initial evidence of receiving the Holy Spirit.

THE JUSTICE OF GOD

Two important issues, doctrinally speaking, confronted Kenyon after his restoration to the Lord: the justice of God and the reality of hell (or eternal punishment). He heard a respected preacher question whether God was just in creating man, knowing that man would fall. As a young, untaught minister, Kenyon had no answer to that question. How could God be just?

It's not surprising, then, that this question is addressed in Kenyon's first book. In the chapter, "How Can God be Just?," he observed, "Man is ever accusing God of injustice in dealing with the human race, and has declared that He had no right to create man in the face of the fact that He knew man would fall." Kenyon knew that many questioned not only God's right to create man knowing he would fall, but also his right to judge the human race and send it to hell. Kenyon believed he had found the answer to his dilemma.

He reasoned, "If God should assume the liabilities of man's fall and pay man's penalty independent of man, then God will have answered the criticism of man against His justice." How would this transpire? If God's Son would "become incarnate, and God should lay upon Him the entire guilt of the human race, and He should go to hell and suffer in man's stead so that no human would be obliged to suffer, then God would have vindicated Himself."

God would have answered this accusation against His character, and, as a result, "God stands acquitted before the tribunal of universal human consciousness in that He did not leave man after his treason without means of salvation."[18] In Kenyon's thought, because God assumed responsibility for the Fall, man had no ground to question His justice.

ETERNAL PUNISHMENT AND ETERNAL LIFE

Under the influence of an older minister, the young E. W. Kenyon had once embraced annihilationism. *Annihilationism* is the belief that the wicked do not suffer eternal punishment, but rather cease to exist. Not surprisingly, Kenyon also dealt with this subject in his first book.

It was his study of the substitutionary sacrifice of Christ that brought him to the conclusion that hell was a reality. While studying the substitutionary sacrifice of Christ, Kenyon discovered that Christ's soul was not left in hades (Acts 2:27, 31). "If he [Jesus] went to hades while dead, then the theory of the sleep of the dead falls flat. The idea of annihilation of the dead is false . . . if death means extinction, then our Lord must have become extinct or annihilated for us."[19] Kenyon, by a thorough study of the Scriptures, had rejected this false teaching that he had earlier embraced.

Not surprisingly, since Kenyon was initially unaware of the reality of eternal punishment, he was also uninformed about the reality of eternal life. "One of the great days of my life was when I discovered the fact that I had eternal life, the very nature of the Father God, and that I had become a Christian because I received eternal life." For Kenyon, the fact of receiving eternal life was of tremendous importance. While still among the Holiness people he had sought the prescribed experiences. At that time he thought "all there was to becoming a Christian was having a series of remarkable experiences and blessings." The realization of actually receiving eternal life was a great blessing to E. W. Kenyon.[20]

Partaking of the divine nature (2 Pet. 1:4) was an amazing fact of the grace of God to him. Much of his later teaching revolved around the fact of God's life being in us. He would later dedicate an entire book to this subject, *The Two Kinds of Life*. For Kenyon, the receiving of eternal life was the essence of the new birth. Receiving eternal life changed the nature of man, which for Kenyon was far more significant that only having our sins forgiven. Eternal life made man a new creation.

THE NEW BIRTH

"The new birth is the heart of Christianity," wrote Kenyon in *The Father and His Family*. "Man's interpretation of the new birth determines his whole Christian experience."[21] As Kenyon explained his view of the new birth he contrasted it with both the Holiness view and the Keswick view, showing his complete grasp of both views. Under the influence of the Brethren and his more doctrinally-oriented mentors (Gordon, Pierson, Simpson, Penn-Lewis), Kenyon moved away from Holiness theology in the direction of the Reformed Higher Life or Keswick view.[22] This is important because one of Kenyon's critics reasoned that because Kenyon did not teach second-work-of-grace Holiness, he was not a part of that movement or unfamiliar with that tradition; therefore, he *must have* embraced metaphysics.[23] This is clearly not the case.

But Kenyon wasn't entirely comfortable with the Keswick view, either. Most of the Keswick teachers believed that the old nature was suppressed in sanctification, rather than eradicated, as the Holiness movement taught. They did have a much stronger teaching on the new birth and receiving eternal life. This emphasis, Essek found very helpful, but he was still convinced that something wasn't quite fully biblical.

As he studied the Scriptures, he became convinced that even these respected teachers had failed to appreciate the full reality of the new birth. In seeking to understand the new birth, Kenyon, reading the apostle Paul, began to feel that it needed to be viewed from two perspectives: the legal side and the vital side. God did something *for us* in the past at the cross. God does something *in us* in regeneration and receiving the Holy Spirit.

Commenting on the church of his day he observed that one part of the church had emphasized the legal, or the objective, (the Reformed or Calvinist churches) and one part of the church, the vital, or subjective, (the Holiness or Methodist churches). Kenyon attempted a synthesis of the two aspects into one system that he felt incorporated all the biblical data.

From the legal perspective, once the sinner had accepted Christ and confessed Him as Lord, "that starts the legal machine in the courthouse in Heaven." Then, "his sins are remitted, wiped out as though they had never been . . . he is legally justified or set right with

God . . . his name is written in the Book of Life . . . he is legally adopted into the family . . . Jesus publicly confesses him before the Father and the holy angels . . . " and "he is legally reconciled to the Father."

This legal work in the heavenly courtroom gave the new convert certain rights. Kenyon mentioned "a legal right to his Father's protection . . . [a right to] Jesus' intercession . . . legal right to the advocacy of Christ, the great family lawyer . . . a legal right to the gift of the Holy Spirit . . . a legal right to a son's place in the Royal Family . . . a legal right to a son's inheritance."

This was very important to Kenyon. He observed that when "you overlook the legal side of the new birth you are rearing an experimental superstructure [a foundation built on the shifting sand of personal experience] without a foundation and the building will surely fall. Here is the reason that so many who teach only the experimental [read *experiential*] side of the new birth have so many backsliders," he concluded.

Though Kenyon felt all believers needed to understand the legal side of salvation, he did not say that the experiential side wasn't valid and important. Kenyon explained the vital [or experiential] side this way: "This is the work the Holy Spirit does in the believer when he publicly confesses Christ as Savior and Lord. First, the Holy Spirit overshadows him. He is immersed in the Spirit and this is the real baptism of the Holy Spirit. The receiving of the Holy Spirit into his body comes later." (As pointed out earlier, the *baptism* of the Holy Spirit was, for Kenyon, the new birth. *Receiving* the Holy Spirit was subsequent).

He continued, "the Holy Spirit imparts to his spirit the nature of God, eternal life. This make him alive in Christ . . . the peace of God that passeth all understanding floods his soul . . . the Holy Spirit witnesses with his spirit that he is a child of God . . . the love of God is shed abroad in his heart by the Holy Spirit, and he knows he has passed from death into life because he loves the brethren. Joy fills his heart and he cries, 'Abba, Father,' and he knows he is a child of God, joint-heir with Jesus Christ the Lord."[24]

Kenyon spent the rest of the chapter explaining why the dual-nature theory of the Calvinists [the Keswick view] and the second-work-of-grace theory of the Methodists both fall short of the biblical teaching of the new creation.

Anyone reading *The Father and His Family* could not help but notice Kenyon was entirely familiar with both Holiness and Higher Life/Keswick teaching. Strange that there is no mention of these discussions by Kenyon of sanctification teachings in the critic's book. Particularly when this book—*The Father and His Family*—is the first and the foundational book for Kenyon's entire ministry.

E. W. Kenyon loved the Father that had graciously revealed Himself to him. He embraced the lordship of his Master Jesus. He was aflame with love for the lost and lived for the delight of seeing people saved. He was also passionate in his desire to see believers established in both sound doctrine and solidly biblical experience. *The Father and His Family* makes these truths obvious.

E. W. Kenyon was a man who loved God and passionately desired to see the lost come to know Jesus. He defended the deity of Christ and His Resurrection from the dead. The Bible was for Kenyon the living voice of God, and he vigorously defended it's inspiration. A pioneer in divine healing, he proclaimed the right to healing for the believer because of Christ's sufferings. His dedication to the Lord reflected his love for Jesus in response to the deep suffering that Christ endured on our behalf in His substitution. His teachings, though in many ways unique, fit easily into the late nineteenth-century evangelical movement. His many documentable mentors show this quite clearly. Kenyon is one of a few remarkable links between that late nineteenth century and the twentieth century Pentecostal movement. It is my desire that as a result of this book, many will evaluate Kenyon's contributions without the cloud of suspicion created by his detractors, and objectively consider the merits of his message of faith.

Epilogue

E W. Kenyon was an evangelist, teacher, pastor, poet, and song-writer. He is best known today as an author. His writings have encouraged thousands in the body of Christ. Through his books, many have discovered the father heart of God, who they were in Christ, the life of faith and the truth of divine healing. In this book I have sought to present a portrait of the real E. W. Kenyon in contrast to the carica-ture painted by his critics.

Let me sum up some of the observations I have made in this book regarding Kenyon's theological development.

- His burden for the lost was the consuming passion of his life. Kenyon's life and ministry demonstrated his devotion to God the Father and the Lord Jesus Christ. He brought thousands of men and women to Christ through his evangelistic ministry. He desired to teach those converted under his ministry to walk in the fullness of God's provision for them in Christ so they would remain stable and become fruitful in their walk with the Master.
- Theologically, he was a fundamentalist, identifying himself mostly with the Baptists. His only ordination (other than as an exhorter among the Methodists) was with the Free Will Baptists, who were a very conservative group, doctrinally speaking. At one time he applied to the Assemblies of God for ordination but didn't follow through on it. The Assemblies are also a theologically con-servative denomination.

- He greatly desired to establish new converts in the Word. This was a burden that developed out of his own experience. After his conversion, he fell away from the Lord. He attributed his falling away to not being established in the truth of God's Word after his conversion and not having received the Holy Spirit. He personally received no discipling as a young convert. He didn't want others to experience the grief that befell him as a young believer.
- Kenyon's true mentors and their influence in his life are clear and documentable. Yet while his respect for these mentors is unquestionable, he insisted that the Bible must be the final court of appeal in all matters of doctrine. He put all questions of doctrine to a Genesis-to-Revelation test before embracing them, and rejected what he felt to be unbiblical even if this put him at odds with some that he greatly respected.
- While gladly embracing all biblically warranted experiences, he refused to build doctrine on experience. His tension with both the Holiness and Pentecostal movements was not with their experiences. It was with those who looked to an experience rather than the teaching of the Word. His message of faith demanded that the Word of God be given the proper place in the believer's life.
- He wanted to express a supernatural yet completely biblical Christianity in language that would grip the imagination of the people of his day. He felt the traditional churches had lost their hold on the imagination of the people.

KENYON'S INFLUENCES

Documenting Kenyon's true influences was a primary focus of this book. This was necessitated by the numerous attempts made by some to align him with metaphysical cults. Because Kenyon's teaching does not easily fit into the Holiness or Pentecostal framework, some have attempted to paint him into a metaphysical corner. Let's review his actual influences.

When Kenyon was forming his theology, there were a number of movements influencing the church. The Holiness movement, which expanded beyond its Methodist roots, evolved into the Higher Life movement. Both of these movements greatly influenced Kenyon. Kenyon was converted in a revival meeting in a Methodist church. His first few years as a Christian were among the Holiness people.

The Free Will Baptists, with whom Kenyon aligned during his most significant formative years, had embraced and aligned with the Holiness movement with its emphasis on the second work of grace. Out of the Higher Life movement, which was the name given to the Holiness movement as it broadened its influence among the various denominations, sprang a movement which became known as the Faith-Cure movement. This was a movement of divine healing that historically preceded the metaphysical cults and New Thought. Kenyon was greatly influenced by this movement, and his teaching reflects that influence. The Keswick movement from Great Britain also strongly influenced Kenyon.

New England was the center for these movements as well as the location of D. L. Moody's Northfield conferences, where thousands gathered for the deepening of the spiritual life. Moody's desire was that Northfield would become the American Keswick. Keswick is a city in the Lake District of northern England which held an annual teaching conference for the deepening of the spiritual life. Kenyon attended conferences at Northfield and sat under many internationally known Bible teachers such as Andrew Murray, F. B. Meyer, G. Campbell Morgan, A. T. Pierson, A. J. Gordon, R. A. Torrey, and many others.

The very influential Welsh devotional writer, Jessie Penn-Lewis was also an acknowledged mentor. The Plymouth Brethren also significantly influenced Kenyon.

Kenyon's doctrine of positive confession, for example, is firmly rooted in the Holiness movement. This was documented in this book. His teaching on faith, healing, and the atonement also find their roots in the teaching of the above-mentioned teachers (and some others mentioned in the book)—soundly in the evangelical wing of the church. These people are respected in the church for their tremendous contributions. To indict Kenyon is to indict them.

This is not to say that Kenyon's teachings do not have ideas that are unique to him. The particular truths he emphasized, such as positive confession and the spiritual death of Christ, were not emphasized in the ministry of his mentors to the degree that Kenyon emphasized them. But these ideas were clearly and documentably present in Kenyon's orthodox influences. They were not strange or unusual ideas, and certainly not considered heretical. Kenyon's teaching on faith was not significantly different from Ethan O. Allen, A. B. Simpson or

Carrie Judd Montgomery, just to cite a few examples from the Faith-Cure movement.

Looking at the larger picture of the various movements of the day and the people Kenyon actually mentioned as his mentors (and what those mentors were teaching as Kenyon's ministry was maturing) paints a very different picture than his critics have painted. In this book I have attempted to tell the true story of E. W. Kenyon's message of faith.

The true story deserved to be told.

When I Am Gone

My work will not be finished
When this form you've laid to rest;
I'll be living in my writings,
I'll be doing then my best.

I'll be in the books I've written;
In their words I'll live again.
I'll be breathing out my passion
To help the sons of men.

You will feel me though I'm hidden;
I'll be speaking to your heart;
Will be driving you to study
In life to do your part.

To be living is my craving;
To help you find life's best.
When my name they have forgotten,
You'll be working while I rest.

—By E. W. Kenyon

Appendix One

A RESPONSE TO *A DIFFERENT GOSPEL*

M uch of the current misunderstanding of E. W. Kenyon's theology is due to the publication of D. R. McConnell's book *A Different Gospel*. McConnell is undoubtedly a sincere scholar, yet I disagree strongly with his book.

In his book McConnell states that he believes he has "treated the historical evidence in a fair fashion" and that his findings will bear "the scrutiny of historical analysis." But, he admitted, his intent was not to report his findings in the "placid manner of a professional historian. I have used my historical findings as the basis of a theological polemic against the Faith theology, something a true historian would never do" (p.xi).

I believe Kenyon was McConnell's scapegoat. If McConnell could establish that Kenyon was bringing metaphysics into his theology then he could successfully attack the Faith movement. He stated his thesis in the third chapter: *Our thesis is that in his attempt to help the church respond to the "challenge" of the cults, Kenyon "absorbed" metaphysical concepts in order to restore the healing ministry to the church (p.30).*

In building his case, McConnell informed us about the use of "evidence." "The best evidence," he wrote, "is always firsthand. In seeking to establish the facts of a given case, evidence that comes from an original source, such as a signed confession, is considered the most authoritative. The next best thing to a signed confession would be eyewitnesses who saw the accused commit the crime, or else, heard him admit to it. A final form of evidence would be what is referred to as 'circumstantial evidence.'"

McConnell continued, "In evaluating the evidence for the Kenyon Connection, we do not have any written (McConnell's emphasis) confession by Kenyon in which he admits to having formed his theology from cultic sources. But we do have witnesses who heard him make a verbal admission of doing so" (p.25).

I will take a look at those eyewitnesses in the next appendix. In this appendix I want to examine sixteen specific accusations of heresy that McConnell levels against Kenyon.

McConnell did acknowledge, "The direct statements of Kenyon regarding the metaphysical cults do not betray any conscious acceptance on his part of their ideas. In fact, in his earlier writings, Kenyon is occasionally hostile toward these cults, describing them as 'hellism' and 'devilism'" (p.43).

After reviewing a number of quotes in which Kenyon explained the difference between what he taught and the inferior idea of the metaphysical cults—Kenyon's written convessions of his repudiation of the metaphysical cults and their teachings—McConnell informed us that Kenyon's disclaimers were the "classic ploys of the modern day cultists, who use them to confuse and disarm the intellectual defenses of those whom they are indoctrinating into their cult" (p.45).

So, if Kenyon admits to metaphysical influence, it's a signed confession. If he denies and refutes the cultists, it's a classic ploy of a cultist attempting to indoctrinate his victims! Kenyon's fifty years of consistent refutation of the metaphysical cults do not constitute a written confession for McConnell, but if he had admitted in writing even once that he drew from the cults, that would be a written confession! Hmmm . . .

So much for treating the historical evidence in a fair fashion! But it doesn't get better. McConnell accused Kenyon of more things than most cultists are ever accused of.

I've come to call this heresy hunting technique Name Calling. The idea seems to be if a critic calls somebody enough negative descriptive terms, some of it is bound to stick, whether there is any truth in it or not. If they're theological or philosophical terms that many people don't understand anyway, those untrained in these ideas will often take the word of the critic, assuming he knows what he is talking about.

For the rest of this essay, I'll list the accusations with comments of my own. My intention is to supply those who read McConnell's book with a balancing viewpoint.

Deism

Deism is the view that the world is governed by impersonal, spiritual laws rather than by a personal, sovereign God (p.45). This is an interesting accusation to make against a man whose ministry revolved around intimacy with God as Father as the basis of the faith life.

Deification

Deification, according to McConnell, is the metaphysical view that salvation entails man becoming a god (p.45). Kenyon taught that we were "incarnations," that in regeneration and the indwelling of the Holy Spirit, who *is* God, we become temples of God. Man is not a god, God—the Holy Spirit—dwells in man. Kenyon did teach that we become "partakers of the divine nature" (2 Pet. 1:4). His understanding of that concept is not unorthodox.

Kenyon (and many of his orthodox contemporaries) could be faulted for using the term *incarnation* in a sense other than the uniqueness of God the Son becoming man. This was possibly too easy to misunderstand. But Kenyon and his contemporaries certainly did not mean what Kenyon's critics have implied.

Gnosticism

This accusation by McConnell focuses on Kenyon's understanding of revelation knowledge. (See p. 109.) The Gnostics (a second-century heretical group) believed salvation came by receiving a spiritual experience of hidden knowledge. Spirit was good, matter was evil. But, in contrast to Gnostic teaching, Kenyon held that revelation knowledge was Holy Spirit-revealed understanding of the Scriptures rather than a mere intellectual understanding of doctrine. "Blessed are you, Simon, Bar-Jonah, for flesh and blood has not revealed this to you, but My Father who is in heaven" (Matt. 16:17). The things of God must be revealed by the Spirit of God, was Kenyon's contention.

Dualism

McConnell thought Kenyon's concept of revelation knowledge was dualistic. He says, "The Gnostics taught that the knowledge of God is absolutely distinct from and mutually exclusive from all other kinds of knowledge" (p.109). Kenyon taught that the knowledge of spiritual things came first to the spirit by means of the Holy Spirit. Then the human spirit illuminated the mind. Then the body could act on that knowledge. Kenyon distinguished between the Spirit-taught mind and the theologically-taught mind. Renewing the mind is one of Kenyon's major teachings.

Sensory Denial(p. 106)

McConnell discusses this on pages 106, 152–156. Like all the teachers of divine healing quoted in this book, Kenyon believed you could receive when you pray (Mark 11:24) and a period of time elapse before the answer was discernible to the senses. Kenyon, as I have shown throughout this book, never taught denying the reality of sickness, but rather claiming the healing Christ's finished work had purchased.

Denial of the Blood Atonement

McConnell discussed this on pages 128–130. Kenyon taught that the work of the cross was not completed until Jesus presented His blood to the Father in the heavenly Holy of Holies, fulfilling the type of the Old Testament Day of Atonement. This is clearly taught in the Book of Hebrews. In order to present His blood, Jesus first had to be bodily resurrected. McConnell maintains that atonement was by the physical death of Christ. McConnell is not alone in his view, But I don't understand how this is reconciled with the Book of Hebrews.

Repudiation of God's Sovereignty

Kenyon believed in the authority of the believer and our right to claim God's promises (p. 56.). Whenever an aggressive claiming of

God's promises is taught, someone raises the objection that God's sovereignty is being challenged. George Müller faced this criticism when he maintained that all of his prayers were answered. How can God's sovereignty be in conflict with His promises? His promises are an *expression* of his sovereignty. This tension has always existed when divine healing and aggressive faith has been taught, because it challenges the status quo.

Fideism

Fideism is the idea that faith doesn't need a rational basis (p. 105). Kenyon consistently taught that faith is not a "leap in the dark" but rather a "step into the light" of the love of a caring, heavenly Father whose Word was absolutely reliable. Kenyon insisted that accurate knowledge (of the Word) *must* precede faith. Faith, to be biblical faith, must be based upon knowledge of God's will and God's Word. It goes without saying that the Bible is a "rational basis" for faith.

Metaphysical Concept of Man

McConnell insisted that Kenyon's belief that man is primarily a spirit being was a metaphysically derived concept (p. 118, 123). As we have demonstrated in this book, the primacy of the human spirit was widely taught among evangelicals who were documentable mentors for Kenyon.

Pantheism

McConnell accused Kenyon of espousing pantheism, the idea that God is in everything and everything is God because of Kenyon's belief that man is primarily spirit (p. 118). Kenyon certainly didn't believe everything was God and he didn't believe the human spirit was God. He believed that man could partake of the divine nature and be indwelt by the Holy Spirit. This is a far cry from pantheism.

Ironically, Kenyon is accused by McConnell of espousing deism, which teaches that God created the world and then left it and is no longer personally involved with it, and pantheism, which sees God in everything and everything as a manifestation of God. It would be a little difficult to embrace both of these ideas simultaneously!

Spiritual Laws

The concept of spiritual laws in the evangelical wing of the church was not the same as in the metaphysical cults (p. 139). Kenyon believed you could teach someone to meet certain conditions to receive the Holy Spirit, for example, and if the conditions were met, God would respond *every time*. This was a common teaching at least from the time of Phoebe Palmer. This is not the same as espousing impersonal laws that operate independently of God at man's whim, but rather intelligent cooperation with the Word *and* the Holy Spirit.

Unitarianism

McConnell cited Kenyon's attendance at some Unitarian services while he was out of fellowship with the Lord as evidence of his sympathies with this theological position (p. 43). In the context of the actual quote, Kenyon was *refuting* what he heard the man say. Kenyon referred to Unitarians as "uni-nothings," hardly sounding very sympathetic!

Spiritual Resurrection

McConnell implies that Kenyon taught a "spiritual resurrection" that denigrated Christ's physical resurrection (p.119). He actually taught, since he believed Jesus was in Hades until the resurrection, that the resurrection of Christ's spirit/soul *preceded* his bodily resurrection. "His soul was not left in Hades, neither did his body see corruption" (Acts 2:31). The turning point, so to speak, in our redemption, was when Jesus was raised from the dead by the glory of the Father (Rom. 6:4). This began when His soul, which had been an offering for sin (Isa. 53:10), was freed from its burden and justified (1 Tim. 3:16) and made alive *in spirit* (1 Pet. 3:18). Then followed the bodily resurrection.

Kenyon certainly did not deny the importance of the bodily resurrection of Christ. In emphasizing the spiritual side, Kenyon is not trying to deny the value of the physical. He just insisted that there was *more* than the physical involved.

Positive Mental Attitude

If Kenyon, or the modern Faith movement, espoused a positive mental attitude based on something men had in themselves, there might be a cause for concern (pp. 138–140). Kenyon, however, believed we could be confident in life because we were redeemed children of God. The Bible name for this concept is *hope*. W.E. Vine defines the Greek word for hope, *elpis*, as "a favorable and confident expectation, [having] to do with the future and unseen . . . the happy anticipation of good." Philippians 4:8 would seem to encourage just such a preoccupation for believers.

Elitism

McConnell seemed to understand Kenyon as creating "classes" of Christians, which fits in with McConnell's thoughts on Gnostic elitism (p. 108). Kenyon merely believed there were "carnal" Christians and "spiritual" Christians, which the apostle Paul taught (1 Cor. 3:1). This was a common teaching among the late nineteenth-century Higher Life teachers. They were calling those in the church to go deeper in their commitment and understanding of what God wanted in their lives. There was nothing exclusive about it, just a recognition that not all would enter in to the "Higher Christian Life."

Jesus Became a Demoniac in Hell

Because Kenyon taught that Jesus *became* sin with our sin (2 Cor. 5:21) and he took that literally and seriously, Kenyon has been said to believe that Jesus became a demoniac in hell (p. 127). Kenyon's language in describing Jesus' sufferings is capable of being misunderstood. Kenyon never suggests that Jesus ceased to be deity; in fact, he insisted that deity must suffer for humanity because man cannot pay for his own sins, being sinful himself. Taking *all* that Kenyon said on the subject would not paint the picture that McConnell and some others have attempted to paint.

SUMMARY

I believe D. R. McConnell sincerely wanted to help the body of Christ with his book. People have been hurt by misunderstanding teachings about faith and healing, and the results have been tragic. I empathize with McConnell's desire to keep people from error. I think, however, his approach is flawed. Thousands of people have been saved and healed through the ministry of Kenyon and those who teach the same truths.

What E. W. Kenyon wrote and taught was greatly misrepresented in McConnell's book and many have—because of the scholarly nature of the book—accepted it uncritically. This is a great injustice to E. W. Kenyon, a man who loved God and God's people.

This quick overview of some of the accusations made against Kenyon may suggest to the reader the seriousness and the flawed nature of the criticisms leveled against Kenyon. The majority of the accusations are dealt with in more detail in the text of this book.

Appendix Two

Two Witnesses?

I n building his "case" against E. W. Kenyon, D. R. McConnell in his book *A Different Gospel,* cites two witnesses who supposedly heard Kenyon freely admit to being influenced by Christian Science and making the statement that "all Christian Science needs is the blood of Jesus."

In my research into these testimonies I discovered some information that casts a different light on the reports of these two men. In this appendix I will share what I learned.

John Kennington

One witness that McConnell cites is John Kennington. Kennington knew Kenyon when he was a young man and followed Kenyon's teaching (at least what he thought was Kenyon's teaching) enthusiastically. John Kennington pastors Immanuel Temple in Portland, Oregon. William Booth-Clibborn, the pastor that preceded Kennington, was a friend of Kenyon's, and Kenyon preached there on many occasions. (Kennington succeeded Booth-Clibborn as pastor.)

McConnell quotes Kennington as saying, "I was once a blind follower of E. W. Kenyon . . . I have come to realize that E. W. Kenyon has simply 'baptized' many concepts from Christian Science. In so doing, he became a source for a form of 'Pentecostal Christian Science,' even though Kenyon himself was not a Pentecostal" (p. 15).

I contacted Kennington by phone and asked him about all this. First of all, he mentioned his disappointment that McConnell only used the *negative* things that he said about Kenyon and none of the positive. He said he had written both McConnell and his publisher to complain about it but had not heard back from either of them.

In an addendum to the paper by Kennington that McConnell quotes, Kennington stated, "In many ways Dr. Kenyon was a great man of God." In the first paper Kennington had said, "I learned much from him which I appreciate to this day . . . The 'formulas' work so much better when one is truly in touch with our heavenly Father."

In my personal conversation with him he expressed his praise for three of Kenyon's books: *The Wonderful Name of Jesus, The Two Kinds of Righteousness* and *The Two Kinds of Faith* (with some reservations). He thought Kenyon's teaching on the New Creation was excellent and much needed in the church today. He believed the healings and miracles in Kenyon's ministry were valid and of the Holy Spirit.

In the above quote and my phone conversation we see that Kennington does not share McConnell's opinion about Kenyon's teachings completely. He recognized something that I have been attempting to make clear in this book—that Kenyon rooted his teachings about principles of faith in a living fellowship with our heavenly Father.

Kennington's departure from Kenyon's teaching was the result of a brush with death. He almost died denying he was sick. He felt he was following Kenyon's teaching in denying the reality of the sickness. In the hospital he finally "gave up" and told God he didn't have faith to be healed. The next day he woke up healed!

Somehow for Kennington this seemed contrary to Kenyon's teaching. Kennington wrote, "My abandonment to God, whether for sickness or healing, to me is much more what true faith is all about." Ironically, Kenyon had a similar crisis of consecration and was also healed at his point of surrender. (See chapter six.)

Kenyon's teaching about Christ's lordship and the struggle to give up all rights to King Jesus in utter abandonment slipped past Kennington. Many people with a background in the Holiness movement assume that those listening to them already have dealt with the issue of consecration of all to the Lord. Many Bible teachers from Kenyon's generation wrongly assumed those of the younger generation were well established in the truths of consecration and surrender.

Kennington also seems to understand Kenyon's teaching to be a *denial* of symptoms rather than faith in healing. As we have pointed out in this book, Kenyon made a very clear distinction between the denial of the reality of sickness as practiced by Christian Science and believing one is healed because of Christ's finished work. (See chapter 20 on the metaphysical cults.)

I asked Kennington whether he felt it was legitimate to "reckon ourselves to be dead indeed to sin" (Rom.6:11), while still struggling with sin in our lives. He said yes, that was legitimate. I then asked him if, based on the same finished work of Christ, we could reckon ourselves "healed by His stripes?" At this point he became upset and said, "No, we cannot do that."

I pointed out to him that this was the teaching of the Faith-Cure movement and that Kenyon began his ministry around this group. He could not accept the idea that believing you have healing while symptoms still remain in the body is not the same as denying you were sick. We had reached an impasse in our conversation.

ERN BAXTER

Another significant fact about Kennington's testimony is that Kennington actually worked with Ern Baxter, McConnell's other witness. When I began to explain what I wanted to talk to Kennington about he expressed a concern that someone had challenged Kennington's assertions about hearing Kenyon's remarks about Christian Science. After I probed a little, he admitted that he was concerned that Ern Baxter didn't recall the events that Kennington reported. The alleged events took place in Baxter's presence.

In a phone conversation with another Kenyon researcher (Gier Lie of Norway), Kennington acknowledged that his source of information about Kenyon's sympathy toward Christian Science was Ern Baxter. He felt that Baxter's memory was not reliable, and he would not confirm the conversation that he said took place between himself, Kenyon, and Baxter.

In a letter from Baxter to Gier Lie, Baxter wrote:

> I was introduced to him [Kenyon] by the late William Booth-Clibborn . . . and found him to be a very pleasant, fatherly person.

From that point on I had contact with him. I invited him to come to Vancouver to speak at a service. I recall he spoke on 'The Father and His Family" with great emphasis on love. All the theological matters that have since become prominent probably due to the comparison with the faith movement, I was unaware of. He was strong on healing in the name of Jesus and spoke much of God's power. It needs to be said that no matter how it is interpreted, he stands out as a very gentle and kindly man . . .

I have pleasant memories of him. I do not recall having a discussion on the theological basis of his positions. So, you can see I am not much use to you as you are obviously looking for things of which I have no memories . . . I knew John Kennington quite well, but was not aware of his closeness to Kenyon. However, that is not to question the fact that he may have been . . . I would like to add that much of the biographical/theological/philosophical material contained in the books now published about him were new to me, so I obviously am not a major source of information. [Letter to Gier Lie, dated Sept. 28, 1992.]

Baxter and Kennington are two "firsthand" eyewitnesses upon which McConnell builds his entire case. When McConnell interviewed Baxter, he apparently remembered quite a bit about his discussions with Kenyon. It would be interesting to hear the questions McConnell asked and *all* that Baxter said in response.

It is clear that Baxter didn't agree with Kenyon's view of things from statements that Baxter had made. The question to my mind is how reliable is Baxter in regard to the things he remembers Kenyon saying? I think Ern Baxter was a great man of God, but even great men can misinterpret what others say. Or their memories can get fuzzy with age. The discussions these men are recalling had to have taken place in the 1940s. We have fifty years of consistent written testimony of Kenyon's opinion regarding the cults. It seems a bit arbitrary to take a fifty-year-old testimony that one of the witnesses did not even remember when questioned about it later, and give it more weight than all that Kenyon wrote on the subject.

What could Kenyon possibly have meant if he actually said "all Christian Science lacks is the blood of Jesus"? Christian Science teaches that God is not a person, there is no sin, disease, or Satan, and matter in non-existent. It denies the atonement of Christ and the efficacy of the blood. It denies the bodily resurrection and the reality of heaven and hell. And all it needs is the blood of Jesus?

We have fifty years of Kenyon's sermons, books, and periodicals and never does he endorse any of the errors of Christian Science listed above. Actually, he constantly refutes them from the beginning to the end of his ministry. It seems far more likely to me that Baxter misunderstood Kenyon and read into whatever he did say far more than Kenyon intended.

In the *Herald of Life* for August 1945, at age seventy-eight, Kenyon wrote an article typical of his opinion of the cults referred to throughout this book. He calls them "The New Human Religion." He wrote:

> The people who do not want the truth have exchanged the truth of God for a lie and the reality of God for the unreal.
>
> Yes, they use the phraseology of the scripture and the innocent and the ignorant of the Word are led astray.
>
> I do not know whether you thought of it or not, but if a man denies that God is a person, he is an atheist. Then these modern cults are all atheistic cults.
>
> This is religious atheism, the most dangerous thing that has ever come to our modern civilization. It can only be combatted by a real revival of real Christianity, a Christianity that unveils the miraculous, supernatural power of a living Christ.

The article was written in the same period that the alleged conversation with Baxter and Kennington took place. They would have us believe that Kenyon drew his inspiration from the cults that he considered "the most dangerous thing that has ever come to our modern civilization"?

And all it lacks is the blood of Christ?

311

NOTES

INTRODUCTION

1. The first to suggest Kenyon was teaching a form of metaphysics and gnosticism, to my knowledge, was Judith Anne Matta in her book *Born Again Jesus of the Word-Faith Teaching,* rev. ed. (Bellevue, Wash.: Spirit of Truth Ministry, 1987). Matta, building on the fact that Kenyon attended Emerson College of Oratory, where the founder was immersed in New Thought concepts, attempted to portray Kenyon as teaching a form of gnosticism. For a brief, but accurate, rebuttal of her ideas, see Richard M. Riss's article, "Kenyon, Essek William," in Stanley M. Burgess and Gary B. McGee, eds.,*The Dictionary of Pentecostal and Charismatic Movements* (Grand Rapids, Mich.: Regency Reference Library, Zondervan Publishing House, 1988), 517–8.

D. R. McConnell, possibly taking Matta's research into Kenyon's history as his starting point (he quotes her work favorably), sought to further incriminate Kenyon in his book *A Different Gospel* (Peabody, Mass.: Hendrickson Publishers, 1988). He accused Kenyon of syncretism, mixing metaphysics with Christianity. He sees Kenyon as the true father of the modern Faith movement and because he sees Kenyon as heretical, he concludes the modern Faith movement is heretical as well.

McConnell went beyond accusing Kenyon and the Faith movement of poor scholarship or weak doctrine. He actually suggested that the healings performed by Kenyon and the Faith movement aren't from the Spirit of God. On page 52 McConnell questioned . . .

> . . . whether the Jesus of the Faith Movement is the Jesus of the New Testament. The answer that will be given in this book [McConnell's] is a decisive *no.* The Jesus of the Faith movement is "another Jesus" (2 Cor.11:4) and the gospel of the Faith movement is a "different gospel"(Gal.1:6).

This incredible accusation is based on McConnell's weak case against Kenyon. He believes the modern Faith movement is healing people by a false spirit *just because they read Kenyon's books!*

Hank Hanegraaff's assault on the Faith movement, *Christianity in Crisis* (Eugene, Ore.: Harvest House, 1993), builds on the research of Matta, McConnell and a few other authors who drew similar conclusions regarding Kenyon, and assumes the accuracy of their historical research and the validity of their theological analysis.

I will show in this book that these books assume Kenyon's guilt and seek to amass circumstantial evidence for their case while casually disregarding the tremendous amount of documentable evidence readily available to the unbiased researcher.

CHAPTER 1: EARLY DAYS

1. E. W. Kenyon, *In His Presence* (Lynnwood, WA: Kenyon's Gospel Publishing Society, 1944), 130.
2. *Quincy (MA) Daily Ledger,* 29 January 1904, 1, quoted in Dale H. Simmons, *E. W. Kenyon and the Postbellum Pursuit of Peace, Power, and Plenty* (Lanham, MD: Scarecrow Press, 1997), 3.
3. E. W. Kenyon, notes from a lecture on his early years, n.d. Notes such as these throughout this book were taken from approximately thirty-five notebooks of sermon notes by Kenyon.
4. E. W. Kenyon, *The Hidden Man of the Heart* (Lynnwood, WA: Kenyon's Gospel Publishing Society, 1955), 144.
5. Ruth A. Kenyon (later Ruth Kenyon Housworth), "He Is at Rest," *Kenyon's Herald Of Life,* April 1948, 1.
6. *The Spencer (MA) Leader,* 16 February 1912, quoted in Simmons, *E. W. Kenyon,* 2.
7. E. W. Kenyon, *Sign Posts on the Road to Success* (Lynnwood, WA: Kenyon's Gospel Publishing Society, 1938), 10.
8. Margaret Goodman, "What Eternal Life Did for the Pastor," *Kenyon's Herald of Life,* April 1942, 1.
9. Ruth Kenyon Housworth to Greg Fussi, letter, 30 August 1984. Used by permission.
10. E. W. Kenyon, unpublished notes from a talk on his early life, n.d.
11. E. W. Kenyon, "Justification," *Reality,* November 1909, 133.
12. Evva Kenyon, "God's Leadings," *The Tabernacle Trumpet,* January 1901, 131. Evva, who died in 1914, was Kenyon's first wife.
13. E. W. Kenyon, "Justification," 133.
14. E. W. Kenyon, "Possessing Your Possessions" (unpublished sermon), 7 August 1927. The description "unpublished sermon" in these notes refers

to messages given by Kenyon which were taken down in shorthand by someone, then later typed and given back to Kenyon. He often made notes and adjustments on these typed versions for future reference.

15. E. W. Kenyon, Relationship and Fellowship, *Reality,* May 1909, 98.

16. Ibid.

17. E. W. Kenyon, *The Two Kinds of Life* (Lynnwood, WA: Kenyon's Gospel Publishing Society, 1943), 132.

18. E. W. Kenyon, *New Creation Realities* (Lynnwood, WA: Kenyon's Gospel Publishing Society, 1944), 68.

19. E. W. Kenyon, "Some Experiences," *Bethel Trumpet,* October 1901, 60.

20. E. W. Kenyon, "Faith" (unpublished sermon), 8 March 1916.

21. E. W. Kenyon, "Jesus as an Example," *Reality,* February 1906, 23.

22. E. W. Kenyon, "The Sufferings of Jesus" (unpublished sermon), 27 May 1928.

23. E. W. Kenyon, "The Lamb of God" (unpublished sermon), 13 May 1928.

24. E. W. Kenyon, *Father and His Family,* rev. ed. (Spencer, MA: Essek W. Kenyon, 1916; Lynnwood, WA: Kenyon's Gospel Publishing Society, 1937), 225. Two editions of this book were published, and both are cited in these notes. This revised edition is hereafter cited as *Father and His Family,* rev. ed.

25. E. W. Kenyon, "Justification," 133.

26. Ibid. Another point might be made regarding Kenyon's later understanding of sanctification and the new birth. Looking back at those days when he was out of fellowship with the Lord, Kenyon acknowledged that he was conscious of being a child of God even though he was a prodigal. But, as we will see later, his Methodist teaching in those early years would have led him to believe that he had lost his salvation when he fell into sin.

CHAPTER 2: DAYS OF DARKNESS

1. E. W. Kenyon, "Righteousness" (unpublished article), n.d., 6. The description "unpublished article" as used throughout these notes refers to an article which Kenyon dictated but apparently never published anywhere. Many of these articles appear to be chapters for books he intended to publish.

2. Kenyon, *Sign Posts,* 45.

3. Ibid., 46–47.

4. E. W. Kenyon, *The Two Kinds of Righteousness* (Lynnwood, WA:

Kenyon's Gospel Publishing Society, 1942), 5.

5. E. W. Kenyon, "Our Privileges and Responsibilities," *Reality*, May 1904, 133.

6. Kenyon, *Two Kinds of Righteousness*, 5.

7. E. W. Kenyon, "Deliverance From Fear" (unpublished article), 6 April 1934, 2.

8. E. W. Kenyon, *Jesus the Healer*, rev. ed. (Lynnwood, WA: Kenyon's Gospel Publishing Society, 1943), 6.

9. Kenyon, *In His Presence*, 177.

10. E. W. Kenyon, "Is Your Light Darkness?" (unpublished article), 11 May 1934, 1–3. When Kenyon's critics accuse him of sympathy toward the cults, they misunderstand his desire to help those deceived by them. Possibly because he himself fell into this deception for a period of time, Kenyon treats those in the cults with respect, not questioning their sincerity. But he consistently refutes and admonishes them to turn from their error back to the biblical gospel. It is also important to realize that the year he attended Emerson College concluded the three-year period he was away from the Lord, and his restoration occurred within a month of leaving Emerson.

11. Some of Kenyon's critics try to use his knowledge of the cults to prove his sympathy for metaphysical concepts. As we will discuss later, anyone in Kenyon's day who taught divine healing found it necessary to express accurately the difference between metaphysical healing and divine healing. This demanded a familiarity with the cults teachings. Kenyon does speak of the metaphysical cults, but for the most part, his statements show his awareness of their diabolical and deceptive nature, underscoring their inferiority to the gospel.

12. E. W. Kenyon, "Is Your Light Darkness?", 1.

13. E. W. Kenyon, "Resurrection Facts" (unpublished article), 9 April 1939, 9. The article is a testimony of how Kenyon overcame his doubt and "wept for joy that the Lord was raised from the dead."

14. Dr. Dale Simmons, the assistant professor of history at Bethel College in Indiana who did his Ph.D. dissertation on Kenyon, suggests that Savage may have been a relative of Kenyon's. Many of Kenyon's relatives had the last name Savage. This may explain Kenyon's attendance at Savage's services while he was out of fellowship. In those days, respectable people attended services somewhere. Dale Simmons, telephone conversation with author, 1995.

15. One of Kenyon's detractors, D. R. McConnell, in his book *A Different*

Gospel quoted the article in which Kenyon said he attended the services of Savage (p. 34). Yet McConnell failed to mention that later in the article Kenyon actually refuted what he heard Savage say. Kenyon wrote, "Some have doubtless been thinking along the lines of so called Modern New Thought, and have come to the conclusion that we are all sons of God, that all we have to do is to develop the divine element in us, and that will make us fit to dwell with God eternally. That is, they have accepted so called New Thought instead of a New Creation, and this is not a new thought at all. It is as old as the days of Cain; in him it first manifested itself. You can trace it through the entire Bible. It means, to divest it of its beautiful garments, the development of the ego or self life until it is an acceptable companion of God Almighty.

"Now, men and women, any doctrine that teaches you and me that we have an element in ourselves which can develop and grow independent of God, and make us fit to stand in the presence of God, is not true, to put it mildly. It will not stand the Book." E. W. Kenyon, "The Only Ground of Divine Justice," *Reality,* October 1904, 4–5. This article was a transcription of a sermon preached in North Abington, Massachusetts, on Sunday morning, 4 September 1904.

Kenyon attended Savage's services while he was out of fellowship with the Lord. This is obvious to the reader of the article quoted. He is refuting Savage, not commending him.

CHAPTER 3: EMERSON COLLEGE OF ORATORY

1. W. H. Daniels, ed., *Dr. Cullis and His Work,* (1885; reprint, NY: Garland Publishing, 1985), 362.
2. McConnell, *Different Gospel,* 40–43.
3. Donald E. Heady, "Charles Wesley Emerson: A Theory of Oral Interpretation" (Ph.D. diss., Wayne State University, 1972), 1, quoted in Simmons, *E. W. Kenyon,* 5.
4. E. W. Kenyon, untitled and unpublished sermon preached at the First Presbyterian Church, Hollywood, CA, 27 August 1944, 2.
5. The majority of the biographical information on Emerson is taken from John Main Coffee and Richard Lewis Wentworth, *A Century of Eloquence: The History of Emerson College, 1880–1980* (Boston, MA: Alternative Publications, 1982).
6. See Simmons, *E. W. Kenyon,* 5–10.
7. Charles Cullis, *Twenty-first Annual Report* (period ending October 1,

1885), 125, quoted in Simmons, *E. W. Kenyon,* 6.

8. Simmons, *E. W. Kenyon,* 6.
9. Coffee and Wentworth, *Century of Eloquence,* 57.
10. Daniels, *Dr. Cullis,* 362.
11. Charles Cullis, *Sixteenth Annual Report* (period ending 1880), 96–97, quoted in Simmons, *E. W. Kenyon,* 6.
12. Simmons, *E. W. Kenyon,* 6–7.
13. Ibid., 10.
14. McConnell, *Different Gospel,* 107.
15. Coffee and Wentworth, *Century of Eloquence,* 59.
16. J. Gordon Melton, ed., *Religious Leaders of America* (Detroit, MI: Gale Research, 1991), 479–80.
17. Horatio W. Dresser, *A History of the New Thought Movement* (NY: Thomas Y. Crowell, 1919), 172.
18. McConnell, *Different Gospel,* 138–9, 150–1, 156, 158.
19. Coffee and Wentworth, *Century of Eloquence,* 36–37.
20. J. D. Douglas, ed., *The New International Dictionary of the Christian Church* (Grand Rapids, MI: Zondervan Publishing House, 1978), 314.
21. This quote was found on an announcement of availability for Kenyon's evangelistic ministry. The announcement was published by Kenyon and contained endorsements from many pastors for whom he had ministered.
22. Coffee and Wentworth, *Century of Eloquence,* 30.
23. Ralph Waldo Trine, *In Tune With the Infinite* (1897; reprint, London: G. Bell and Sons, 1965), 29.
24. E. W. Kenyon, "Where Do We Live?" *Reality,* June 1906, 88.
25. E. W. Kenyon, "The Victory of the Cross," *Kenyon's Herald of Life,* April 1945, 2.
26. Jessie Penn-Lewis, *Life in the Spirit: A Glimpse Into the Heavenly Warfare* (London: Marshall Brothers, n.d.), 14. This book was created from four lectures given in 1910. Obviously, Kenyon had not read this book by 1906. Jessie Penn-Lewis's writings had been popularized through her articles in two popular British periodicals. In one, she chronicled the Welsh revival. Kenyon likely began following her writings from that time.
27. The metaphysical cults tend to use terms that have a lot of flexibility, whereas the evangelicals of the day were quite concerned with biblical accuracy.

CHAPTER 4: RESTORED

1. E. W. Kenyon, unpublished article, n.d., 4.
2. Evva Kenyon, "God's Leadings," 131.
3. Ibid.
4. Ibid.
5. E. W. Kenyon's journal. This journal is a compositions book with "E. W. Kenyon's journal" written across the top in Kenyon's elegant handwriting. Unfortunately, there are only a handful of entries in this journal; it contains many blank pages. The first page says "private meditations of a servant" and is dated "7-15-1896." The journal contains about a dozen scattered entries and a number of teaching outlines and studies. It appears he used this journal regularly for a few months and then used more generally after that. The few devotional entries are touching in the intimacy Kenyon expresses to the Lord. Kenyon really loved God.
6. Evva Kenyon, "God's Leadings," 131.
7. Ibid.
8. Much of the case presented by Kenyon's critics depends on the existence of an unproven, continuing sympathy with the cults in Kenyon's life. It also assumes he spent much time in Boston under the influence of metaphysical teachers like Emerson, Ralph Waldo Trine and Minot J. Savage. This has been guesswork on the critics' parts and here is shown to be historically inaccurate. Kenyon actually spent less than a year in Boston!
9. Evva Kenyon, "God's Leadings," 131.
10. Ibid.
11. Generally, there were only six questions (actually, five questions and a sixth step): "1. Do you, in the presence of God and this assembly, believe the whole Volume of the Scriptures, both Old and New Testaments, to be infallibly true? 2. Do you believe the Faith and Order of this church to be altogether consonant with the Holy Scriptures as far as you be acquainted with them? 3. Do you feel divinely called of God, to take upon you the office of the public ministry of the Word? 4. Are you at this time on your part, in the full fellowship of the brethren of this church? 5. Do you purpose in your heart, to earnestly contend for the faith and order of this Society and to serve the brethren as far as respects Ministerial function in the order of this Society? 6. If the answers be discreet and satisfactory, he shall receive Ordination and his credentials." William F. Davidson, *The Free Will Baptists in America, 1727–1984* (Nashville, TN: Randall House Publications, 1985), 237–8.

12. Evva Kenyon, "God's Leadings," 131. The ordination was authorized by the Chemung Quarterly Meeting of New York and Pennsylvania Yearly Meeting of Free Will Baptists. Minutes of the Twenty-Ninth General Conference of Free Baptists, 1895, 92, American Baptist Historical Society, Rochester, NY.

13. Minutes of the Twenty-Ninth General Conference of Free Baptists, 1895, 222, American Baptist Historical Society, Rochester, NY.

14. Daniel G. Reid, et al., eds., *Dictionary of Christianity in America* (Downer's Grove, IL: InterVarsity Press, 1990), s. v. "Free Will Baptists."

15. Davidson, *Free Will Baptists,* 218.

16. Ibid., 232. Footwashing became optional as an ordinance before Kenyon joined but was still practiced in some of the churches.

17. Ibid., 295.

18. Ibid., 298–9.

19. E. W. Kenyon, "The Atonement," *Reality,* May 1916, 192. This obviously took place after Kenyon's rededication but prior to his alignment with the Free Will Baptists. It also explains why the Free Will Baptists' philosophy was so agreeable to Kenyon.

20. Robert M. Anderson, *Vision of the Disinherited,* (Peabody, MA: Hendrickson Publishers, 1992), 174. Anderson is a professor of church history at Wagner College, Staten Island, NY.

21. Vinson Synan, *The Holiness-Pentecostal Movement in the United States* (Grand Rapids, MI: William B. Eerdmans, 1971), 73.

22. Ibid.

23. Ibid.

CHAPTER 5: FORMATIVE YEARS

1. Evva Kenyon, "God's Leadings," 131.

2. McConnell, *Different Gospel,* 34.

3. Both the Emerson College catalogue of 1892–1893 and Kenyon's application for admission list Kenyon as residing in Amsterdam, NY, before he attended Emerson College.

4. E. W. Kenyon, "The Seven-fold Test of the Scriptures," *Reality,* May 1916, 199.

5. McConnell, *Different Gospel,* 51.

6. E. W. Kenyon, "How to Receive the Holy Spirit," *The Tabernacle Trumpet,* October 1898, 5.

7. E. W. Kenyon, "Three Fold Call," *Reality,* March–April 1906, 44

8. McConnell, *Different Gospel*, 50.

9. Ern Baxter quoted in McConnell, *A Different Gospel*, 26. Baxter stated, "Kenyon's roots were not in propositional truth. He did not have propositional truth as the basis of his faith." Nothing could be further from the truth than this statement of Baxter's.

10. E. W. Kenyon, "Healing Not in the Dispensation" (unpublished article), 6 April 1934, 1.

11. Kenneth Mackenzie, Jr., *Divine Life for the Body* (Nyack, NY: Christian Alliance Publishing, 1900), 8–10.

12. William Arthur, *The Tongue of Fire* (London: The Epworth Press, 1856).

13. Richard Gilbertson, *The Baptism of the Holy Spirit: The Views of A. B. Simpson and His Contemporaries* (Camp Hill, PA: Christian Publications, 1993), 15–16.

14. E. W. Kenyon, *What Happened From the Cross to the Throne* (Lynnwood, WA: Kenyon's Gospel Publishing Society, 1945), 77.

15. Arthur, *Tongue of Fire*, 39.

16. McConnell, *Different Gospel*, 23.

17. I have a copy of Kenyon's application to the Assemblies of God in Kenyon's own handwriting answering the questions.

18. I have not found any mention of Gordon in McConnell's evaluation of Kenyon in *A Different Gospel*. McConnell would have us believe that Kenyon was not influenced by the "more biblically sound healing movements that arose from the Holiness-Pentecostal tradition . . . Kenyon drew from the only background in these areas he did have: metaphysics" (p. 49). McConnell makes this statement despite the fact that Gordon is quoted numerous times in Kenyon's books and that Gordon was one of the major lights in the "biblically sound healing movements that arose from the Holiness . . . tradition." I cannot imagine how Gordon's influence was overlooked.

19. Later editions of Kenyon's book *Father and His Family* contain numerous quotes from A. J. Gordon, *The Ministry of the Spirit* (1894; reprint, Minneapolis, MN: Bethany House Publishers, 1985). It was obviously a favorite of Kenyon's.

20. A. J. Gordon, *Ministry of the Spirit*, 45, 48.

21. E. W. Kenyon, *The Bible in the Light of Our Redemption [Basic Bible Course]*, (Lynnwood, WA: Kenyon's Gospel Publishing Society, 1969), 251.

22. The two earliest Bible colleges that arose out the evangelical movement were Moody's and A. B. Simpson's. Moody's was known as the Chicago

Bible *Institute,* while Simpson's was referred to as the New York Missionary Training *College.* The evidence leans towards Moody's as the likely sight of Pierson's teachings.

23. McConnell erroneously puts Kenyon in Boston under the influence of Unitarians such as Minot J. Savage " . . . from 1895 to 1899, about the time Kenyon was in Boston" (*Different Gospel,* 94). However, shortly after Kenyon's rededication he went into evangelistic work. In November 1893 Kenyon assumed a pastorate in Elmira, New York. In January 1894 Kenyon relocated to Springville, NY, where he pastored for three years. In May 1897 Kenyon accepted a call to Worcester, MA, eventually settling in Spencer, MA, where his Bible school was located. In the absence of historical information, McConnell freely speculated about Kenyon. Though many of his speculations are refuted by the facts, they unfortunately have caused considerable confusion.

24. R. A. Torrey, *What the Bible Teaches: A Thorough and Comprehensive Study of What the Bible Has to Say Concerning the Great Doctrines of Which It Treats* (NY: Fleming H. Revell, 1898–1933). See Book III, "What the Bible Teaches About the Holy Spirit," chaps. I–VI, 225–68.

25. R. A. Torrey, *The Baptism With the Holy Spirit* ([1895]; reprint, Minneapolis, MN: Bethany Fellowship, Dimension Books, 1972), 54–59.

26. This teaching of Torrey's is also very similar to the teaching of Holiness advocate Phoebe Palmer and likely reflects her direct or indirect influence. Her teaching and influence on Kenyon will be examined in chapter 6.

27. A. B. Simpson, *Part II: The New Testament* vol. 2 of *The Holy Spirit; or, Power From on High: An Unfolding of the Doctrine of the Holy Spirit in the Old and New Testaments* (Harrisburg, PA: Christian Publications, [1896?]), 23.

28. Edith Lydia Waldvogel, "The 'Overcoming Life': A Study in the Reformed Evangelical Origins of Pentecostalism," (Ph.D. diss., Harvard, 1977), 27.

CHAPTER 6: THE HOLINESS MOVEMENT

1. Kenyon, *Two Kinds of Life,* 128.

2. McConnell, *Different Gospel,* 24.

3. McConnell in *A Different Gospel* seeks to establish a "Kenyon Connection" (as he calls it) between Kenyon and the metaphysical cults. In this way he attempts to show the modern Faith movement to be heretical.

4. Charles G. Finney and Asa Mahan and the Oberlin School were also quite influential from the non-Methodist perspective. Kenyon does not seem to have been as directly influenced by these men as he was by the more Methodist-influenced wing of the Holiness movement. However, he was aware of Finney and mentioned him in his writings as a great man of God.

5. Kenyon, *Hidden Man,* 180.

6. E. W. Kenyon, "The Lordship of Christ," *Reality,* March 1910, 1.

7. Anderson, *Vision of the Disinherited,* 174.

8. E. W. Kenyon, "What This Work Stands For," *The Tabernacle Trumpet,* March 1899, 67.

9. There is not the slightest indication of any unorthodox influence in Kenyon's writings from these years. McConnell's theory of Kenyon's metaphysical influence assumes Kenyon's continued exposure to and influence by the cults. This is not historical fact but instead is clearly McConnell's strained attempt to align Kenyon with the cults.

10. Phoebe Palmer, *Faith and Its Effects* ([1848]; NY: Foster and Palmer, Jr., [1867?]), 36.

11. E. W. Kenyon, "The Lordship of Christ," 1.

12. E. W. Kenyon, "Justification," 136.

13. Kenyon wrote in 1903, "Wesleyan teaching would have us believe that when a man accepts Jesus of Nazareth as his Saviour, he simply receives remission of sins, or as they put it, the forgiveness and pardon of sins, and that the nature causing and estranging man from God is not touched in any way but remains either latent or active as the case may be in the child of God. We believe that this teaching *dishonors the finished work of Christ*" (italics added). "The Family Council," *Reality,* September 1903, 72.

14. E. W. Kenyon, "Explanation of the Incoming of the Holy Spirit" (unpublished sermon), 20 August 1927, 4. We know from Evva's testimony that Essek received the Holy Spirit in 1897.

15. See chapter 1.

16. Harold E. Raser, "Phoebe Palmer, Her Life and Thought," in *Studies in Women and Religion,* (Lewiston, NY: The Edwin Mellen Press, 1987), 22:282–3.

17. Timothy L. Smith, foreword to *The Beauty of Holiness: Phoebe Palmer as Theologian, Revivalist, Feminist and Humanitarian,* by Charles Edward White (Grand Rapids, MI: Zondervan Publishing House, Francis Asbury Press, 1986), vii.

18. White, *The Beauty of Holiness,* 12.

19. Raser, "Phoebe Palmer."

20. Palmer, *Faith and Its Effects,* 76.

21. Ibid., 113.

22. Kenyon, *Hidden Man,* 181.

23. Raser, "Phoebe Palmer," 22:185. The quotation is from Palmer, *Faith and Its Effects,* 40.

24. S. L. Brengle, *Helps to Holiness* (1896; reprint, Stoke-on-Trent, England: Harvey and Tait UK, 1990), 31.

25. E. W. Kenyon, "The Lost Testimony" (unpublished article), 6 April 1934, 1–2.

26. Daniel Steele, *Milestone Papers* (1878; reprint, Salem, OH: Schmul Publishing, n.d.), 137–40. In the section in quotes, Steele is quoting someone named Lacordaire.

27. Kenyon published the *Bethel Trumpet* from February 1901 till sometime in 1902. Many Holiness and Higher Life authors and magazines were quoted, and articles from them were printed in the *Bethel Trumpet.*

28. George D. Watson, *Love Abounding,* ([1900?]; reprint, Salem, OH: Schmul Publishing, 1988), 146–8. Notice that Watson advocates publicly confessing *unto* the blessing. He encourages his readers to confess the applicable truth of Scripture continually as a means of entering into a biblically promised experience. In other words, keep saying it until the witness comes.

29. George D. Watson, *Heavenly Life and Types of the Holy Spirit,* ([1900?]; reprint, Salem, OH: Schmul Publishing, 1994), 75–76.

30. E. W. Kenyon, "Confession," *Living Messages,* April 1930, 45.

31. George D. Watson, *White Robes* (1883; reprint, Stoke-on-Trent, England: Harvey and Tait UK, 1989), 58. The chapters of this book were first seen as articles in various Holiness magazines in the United States.

32. Hannah Whithall Smith, *The Christian's Secret of a Happy Life* (1888; reprint, NY: Fleming H. Revell, 1916), 55–56.

33. Ibid., 67–68. Notice that the idea is to say it over and over again *until* you believe it. When the faith expressed by the mouth registers on the heart, *then,* Smith says, God will enable you to walk in it.

34. Hannah Whithall Smith, *The God of All Comfort* (Chicago: Moody Press, 1956), 196–7, 201. Originally published as *Living in the Sunshine* by Fleming H. Revell in 1906. Here Smith advocates denying evidence that is contrary to the promises of God. That evidence, she says, is not a reason to doubt God's Word. She is not advocating denying the *reality* of the contrary evidence, but denying the fact that the contrary evidence can remain

unchanged in face of God's faithfulness to His promises. This is precisely Kenyon's teaching.

35. Kenyon, *Jesus the Healer,* 57.

36. E. W. Kenyon, "The Potency of Affirming What God Says," *Living Messages,* February 1930, 30.

37. *The Merck Manual,* 16th ed. (Rahway, NJ: Merck Research Laboratories, 1992), s. v. "gastrointestinal disorders."

38. E. W. Kenyon, "Why Trusting Is So Hard to So Many" (unpublished article), 6 April 1934, 1–2. For a similar example of wrestling with the lordship of Christ in this era see Norman Grubb, *Rees Howells, Intercessor* (Fort Washington, PA: Christian Literature Crusade, 1973), chap. 5.

39. E. W. Kenyon, "What The Resurrection Means To Us" (unpublished article), 6 April 1934, 8–9.

40. E. W. Kenyon, *Living Bible Studies,* 2 November 1936, vol. 8, no. 7, 8. *Living Bible Studies* were weekly studies that were mailed out to radio listeners who requested them. I might point out that this healing took place through a dedication to the lordship of Christ and the prayer of another believer. This was during the period when Kenyon was supposedly coming under the influence of the metaphysical cults and their teachers. All the evidence points decidedly away from such conclusions.

41. Ibid.

CHAPTER 7: THE FAITH-CURE

1. Asa Mahan, "Faith-Healing," *The Earnest Christian,* September 1884, 76, 78, quoted in Paul Gale Chappell, "The Divine Healing Movement in America" (Ph.D. diss., Drew University, 1983), 165.

2. Chappell, "Divine Healing Movement," 192.

3. McConnell put forth this premise about Kenyon: "His [Kenyon's] theology *does not* fit into either the Wesleyan-Holiness or the Pentecostal healing streams . . . there is a healing stream into which Kenyon's theology *does* fit. This divine healing movement is known as 'metaphysics' and encompasses such religious groups as Christian Science, New Thought, Unity School of Christianity, and Science of Mind" (*Different Gospel,* 24). This premise is lacking in any substance. As will be seen in coming chapters, Kenyon was thoroughly conversant with "second work of grace" (or Wesleyan) Holiness teaching, as well as the "Keswick" brand of Holiness teaching. These two movements, and the Faith-Cure

movement, were the seed-bed out of which Kenyon's unique perspective grew.

4. Evva Kenyon, "God's Leadings," 134. Note that Evva says the Lord "began to lead us into the knowledge of healing." There is little or no evidence that Kenyon was familiar with metaphysical healing. He did read some philosophy and metaphysics when he was away from the Lord. No evidence exists to sustain the argument that he attempted to practice metaphysical healing personally or upon others. As pointed out earlier, neither Charles Wesley Emerson, the founder of Emerson College, nor Ralph Waldo Trine, the New Thought author, were ever known to *practice* metaphysical healing. They taught the philosophy that was the foundation of much metaphysical healing but did not actually attempt to heal. Kenyon's thoughts about divine healing before he began teaching it are quoted in this chapter.

5. Ibid.

6. E. W. Kenyon, "His Name on Our Lips Brings Healing," *Kenyon's Herald of Life,* 30 August 1938, 1.

7. Evva Kenyon, "God's Leadings," 134.

8. E. W. Kenyon, "Healing in the Redemption," *The Tabernacle Trumpet,* November 1898, 15.

9. Simmons, "E. W. Kenyon" (Ph.D. diss. , Drew University, 1988), 56. A local newspaper (*The Spencer [Mass.] Leader,* 13 January 1900) reported this accusation as expressed by local pastors who were critical of Kenyon. Quoted in Dale Simmons, "The Postbellum Pursuit of Peace, Power and Plenty: As Seen in the Writings of Essek William Kenyon" (Ph.D. diss., Drew University, 1988), 56.

10 E. W. Kenyon, "The Decadence of Faith," *Bethel Trumpet,* October 1902, 133.

11. A. B. Simpson, *The Gospel of Healing,* rev. ed. 1886; (Harrisburg, PA: Christian Publications, 1915), 160.

12. A. E. Thompson, *The Life of A. B. Simpson* (New York: Christian Alliance Publishing, 1920), 73.

13. Ibid., 74.

14. A. B. Simpson, *Gospel of Healing,* 164–5.

15. Ibid., 166–7.

16. A. B. Simpson, *In Heavenly Places* (1892; reprint, Harrisburg, PA: Christian Publications, 1968), 98.

17. McConnell insists that Kenyon cannot be "historically grouped with the non-Pentecostal healers, such as John Alexander Dowie, Charles Cullis,

and a whole host of other participants in the divine healing movement who came from the Wesleyan-Holiness tradition." (*Different Gospel*, 24). He says this in spite of the fact that he later cites Cullis as one of the influences after which Kenyon patterned his Bethel Bible Institute (p. 32). In a taped interview, Ruth Kenyon Housworth (E. W. Kenyon's daughter) tells McConnell that her father actually had met Dowie in Chicago along with F. F. Bosworth (Ruth Kenyon Housworth, interview by D. R. McConnell, tape recording, 19 February 1988, Oral Roberts University Library, Tulsa, OK). As shown in this chapter, Kenyon refers to Dowie in a number of places in his writings and publications.

18. Mackenzie, *Physical Heritage in Christ,* 18–19.
19. McConnell, *Different Gospel,* cf. 24 with 32.
20. E. W. Kenyon, "The Walk of Faith," *Reality,* January 1907, 163–4.
21. R. Kelso Carter, *"Faith Healing" Reviewed After Twenty Years* (Boston, MA: Christian Witness, 1897), 109, quoted in Chappell, "Divine Healing Movement," 191.
22. Ruth Kenyon Housworth, interview by D. R. McConnell, tape recording, 19 February 1988, Oral Roberts University Library, Tulsa, Oklahoma.
23. E. W. Kenyon, "Three Realms of Faith" (unpublished sermon), n.d., 6–7.
24. Kenyon, *In His Presence,* 115.
25. E. W. Kenyon, "Faith," *Reality,* November 1908, 3.
26. For more on the status of nineteenth-century medicine, see Simmons, *E. W. Kenyon,* 199–207.
27. When I talked with a Baptist historian, James R. Lynch (director of the library, American Baptist Historical Society), he was surprised to find that the Free Will Baptists taught divine healing. He was unaware of that fact.

CHAPTER 8: MORE FAITH-CURE INFLUENCES

1. Chappell, "Divine Healing Movement," 165.
2. Palmer, *Faith and Its Effects,* 106–7.
3. Phoebe Palmer, *The Way of Holiness* (1843; reprint, Salem, OH: Schmul Publishing, 1988), 28.
4. Palmer, *Faith and Its Effects,* 77.
5. Ethan O. Allen, *Faith Healing; or, What I Have Witnessed of the Fulfilling of James V:14, 15, 16* (Philadelphia, PA: G. W. McCalla, 1881), 3–4.
6. Ibid., 4–5.
7. Fletcher claimed that he had obtained and lost his sanctification four or five times because he failed to testify to it. "I received this blessing four or

five times before; I lost it by not observing the order of God who has told us, 'with the heart man believeth unto righteousness, with the mouth confession is made unto salvation.' But the enemy offered his bait under various colors, to keep me from a public declaration of what God had wrought." John Fletcher, quoted in A. M. Hills, *Holiness And Power* (1897; reprint, Salem, OH: Schmul Publishing, 1988), 276. Palmer insisted that it was not necessary to agonize and come to a place of deep conviction in order to receive sanctification. She believed it could be claimed by faith as soon as it was desired and the condition of complete consecration was met. She called this the "shorter way." (See particularly *The Way Of Holiness.*)

8. Carrie Judd Montgomery, *The Prayer of Faith* [2nd ed.] (1880; reprint, Alameda County, CA: Office of "Triumphs of Faith," 1894), 13.

9. Probably the best history of the Faith-Cure movement is Chappell's "Divine Healing Movement." A condensed version of it appears as "Healing Movements" in Burgess and McGee, eds., *Pentecostal and Charismatic Movements*, 353-74. The article is quite good with one exception. Chappell criticizes the modern Faith movement, specifically Kenneth Hagin's role, by saying, "He [Hagin] differs from most advocates of divine healing in his use of positive confession, sensory denial (particularly as it relates to physical symptoms of illness), and implicit rejection of medical science." He indicts Hagin by tracing these supposedly "aberrant" doctrines to their root "in the metaphysical teachings of New Thought/Christian Science as presented by E. W. Kenyon" (p. 373-4).

These three ideas that Chappell suggests were introduced by Kenyon from metaphysical sources are easily documentable in the Faith-Cure movement. We see that "positive confession," a confession of faith rather than a confession of sin, is rooted in the Holiness movement and predates the metaphysical cults by many years. "Sensory denial," or claiming to be healed while symptoms of sickness remain in the body, was practiced by Ethan O. Allen, and as I will demonstrate throughout this book, was common to the divine healing movement Chappell writes about. The emphasis in evangelical divine healing, and in the writings of E. W. Kenyon, is not on *denying* the senses, as is often suggested by those who don't understand the teaching, but rather on believing you receive from God in answer to prayer *before* there is any visible change. The Bible name for this concept is *faith*. Faith *is* the evidence of thing *not seen* (Heb. 11:1). To criticize this as some strange doctrine is like suggesting that anyone who believes God has heard and answered their prayer before they see any change is denying sensory reality. No, the one praying believes God is working and bringing the answer because He promised.

"The implicit rejection of medical science," or, trusting God entirely for one's health and not relying on medical science, was, right or wrong, a common practice of many of those who taught divine healing. For many, it was *explicit*, not implicit. Many in the Holiness movement who embraced healing felt it would be unbelief not to trust God for their healing. John Alexander Dowie, who was the best-known advocate of divine healing in the country from 1894 to 1905, totally rejected the use of doctors and medicine. Charles Cullis took the opposite view, practicing homeopathic medicine and praying for the sick. All three of the teachings that Chappell suggests that Hagin got from Kenyon are clearly seen in the Faith-Cure movement, which is where Kenyon got them. Kenyon got them from the Bible, which is where the Faith-Cure movement got them as well.

10. Montgomery, *Prayer of Faith*, 14–15.
11. Ibid., 17–19.
12. Chappell, "Healing Movements," 358.
13. Kenyon had a close relationship with the Montgomerys, especially Carrie Judd's husband, George. When they developed their friendship is not clear; it was possibly not until Kenyon moved to Oakland in 1923. Mrs. Montgomery published an article from Kenyon's magazine *Reality* in her journal as early as 1914, so she was familiar with Kenyon at least that early. She also visited and taught at some of A. B. Simpson's conferences while Kenyon still lived in Massachusetts. Kenyon's respect for and familiarity with Simpson, even his preaching at Simpson's church, suggests great familiarity with Montgomery even if he had not yet met her. Kenyon did not always talk about those he knew in the divine healing ministry. He sat on the platform when Maria Woodworth-Etter ministered in New England and even testified at her trial. Interestingly, no mention of this is found in his magazine during that period of time.
14. Carrie Judd Montgomery, *The Life of Praise* (Oakland, CA: Office of "Triumphs of Faith," n.d.), 68–69. This was previously published in her journal *Triumphs of Faith*. These articles were also published by A. B. Simpson in a volume of the Alliance Colportage Library.
15. Leona Choy, *Andrew Murray: Apostle of Abiding Love* (Fort Washington, PA: Christian Literature Crusade, 1978), 139–49.
16. Andrew Murray, *Divine Healing* (Springdale, PA: Whitaker House, 1982), 35–37.

17. Kenyon, *Jesus the Healer,* 36.

18. The Willard Tract Repository grew to the place where it had offices in Boston, NY, Philadelphia, and London.

19. Chappell, "Divine Healing Movement," 106.

20. William Boardman, *The Great Physician (Jehovah Rophi)* (Boston, MA: Willard Tract Repository, 1881), 118.

21. E. W. Kenyon, "Jesus the Healer," *Kenyon's Herald of Life,* August 1940, 4.

22. Chappell, "Divine Healing Movement," 172.

23. A. J. Gordon, *The Ministry of Healing: Miracles of Cure in All Ages* (Chicago: Fleming H. Revell, 1882), 16–17.

24. Ibid., 196–7.

25. R. L. Stanton, "Gospel Parallelisms: Illustrated in the Healing of Body and Soul," *Triumphs of Faith,* April 1883, 73–74.

26. R. Kelso Carter, *The Atonement for Sin and Sickness; or, A Full Salvation for Soul and Body* (Boston, MA: Willard Tract Repository, 1884), 2–4.

27. Ibid., 5–6.

28. Kenyon, *Jesus the Healer,* 44.

CHAPTER 9: MOODY'S WARRIORS

1. E. W. Kenyon, "All Honor," *Bethel Trumpet,* September 1901, 46.

2. E. W. Kenyon, "God-Proved," *Reality,* February–March 1907, 187.

3. E. W. Kenyon, "S. D. Gordon—A Tribute" (unpublished article), n.d., 1–2.

4. E. W. Kenyon, "The Decadence of Faith," 133.

5. John Beauregard (archivist of Gordon College), letter to author, 18 December 1995.

6. Keith Bailey, foreword to *The Acts of the Holy Spirit,* by A. T. Pierson, (New York: Fleming H. Revell, 1895; Harrisburg, PA: Christian Publications, 1980), 10–11.

7. E. W. Kenyon, "Our Privileges and Responsibilities," 133.

8. E. W. Kenyon, "Preaching in the Book of Acts," *Reality,* September 1903, 75.

9. E. W. Kenyon, "The New Birth" (unpublished sermon), 17 June 1928, 2–3.

10. E. W. Kenyon, "Prayer," *Reality,* December 1903, 100.

CHAPTER 10: THE LIFE OF TRUST

1. E. W. Kenyon, "Trust—Faith—Believing" (unpublished article), April 1934, 3.
2. Evva Kenyon, "God's Leadings," 132.
3. Francis Wayland, foreword to *The Life of Trust,* by George Müller (New York: Sheldon and Company, 1878), xvii–xxvi. Wayland was a Baptist minister and one-time president of Brown University in Providence, Rhode Island.
4. Müller, *Life of Trust,* 237.
5. E. W. Kenyon, Foot Prints of Faith, *Reality,* July–October 1911, 23.
6. At the 19 October 1898 meeting of the Massachusetts Association of Free Baptists it is recorded: "A request of Rev. E. Kenyon that his name be dropped was referred to the Ministers Conference" (p. 178). The 20 October 1898 minutes record: "The Ministers Conference recommends that the name of Rev. E. W. Kenyon be dropped from our roll in accordance with his request. Report adopted" (p. 181). James R. Lynch (director of the library, American Baptist Historical Society), letter to author, 6 February 1996.
7. Evva Kenyon, "God's Leadings," 132.
8. James R. Lynch (director of the library, American Baptist Historical Society), letter to author, 6 February 1996.
9. Evva Kenyon, "God's Leadings," 133.
10. Ibid.
11. Ibid.
12. The information on Frank W. Sandford is taken from William C. Hiss, "Shiloh: Frank W. Sandford and the Kingdom, 1893–1948," (Ph.D. diss., Tufts University, 1978); Frank S. Murray, *The Sublimity of Faith: The Life and Work of Frank W. Sandford* (Amherst, NH: The Kingdom Press, 1981); Frank W. Sandford, *Seven Years With God* (1900; reprint, Mont Vernon, NH: Kingdom Press, 1957).
13. Evva Kenyon, "God's Leadings," 133–4.
14. Ibid., 135.
15. Ibid., 136.
16. Ibid.
17. E. W. Kenyon, "Some Experiences," 59–60.

CHAPTER 11: EVANGELIST, PASTOR, AND TEACHER

1. Frank W. Sabean, "Report of Annual Convention at Weymouth and New Tusket, N. S." and *Reality,* November 1903, 92–93.

2. Ibid., 95–96.

3. B. H. Lane, "Revival—Rockland, Massachusetts," *Reality,* September 1904, 191. A Methodist, Congregationalist and a Baptist church had joined together for these services.

4. "At Kingston, Massachusetts, June 5–19," *Reality,* July 1904, 175.

5. E. W. Kenyon, *Personal Evangelism Course* (Lynnwood, WA: Kenyon's Gospel Publishing Society, 1943), Lesson 1, 1–2.

6. Ibid., Lesson 2, 1.

7. Ibid., Lesson 2, 2.

8. Ibid., Lesson 3, 1.

9. Kenyon's Gospel Publishing Society, P.O. Box 973, Lynnwood, WA 98046

10. Lydia Berkey, "The Ministry of Dr. Lydia Berkey" (unpublished article), n.d., 6–7.

11. Gordon Lindsay, *The Gordon Lindsay Story* (Dallas, TX: Voice of Healing Publishing, n.d.), 5. Lindsay did express his concern that "Like all geniuses he [Kenyon] was apt to overemphasize, to get a forgotten truth across."

12. E. W. Kenyon, "God's Justice" (unpublished sermon), 20 May 1928, 2.

13. E. W. Kenyon, "Mental Characteristics of Jesus" (unpublished sermon), 15 June 1928, 8.

14. E. W. Kenyon, "The Whole Burnt Offering," *Reality,* November 1910, 81.

15. E. W. Kenyon, "The Living Word" (unpublished sermon), 18 November 1928, 1–2.

16. Ironically, this quote is from John Kennington, one of D. R. McConnell's two "witnesses." Kennington wrote two short papers on Kenyon: "E. W. Kenyon and the Metaphysics of Christian Science," 8 July 1986, and "An Addendum to My Brief Comments on E. W. Kenyon," 24 August 1994. This quote is from the "Addendum."

17. Again, ironically, this quote is from Ern Baxter, McConnell's other "witness." Ern Baxter to Gier Lie, letter, 28 September 1992. Used by permission of Lie.

18. Simmons, *E. W. Kenyon,* xv.

19. E. W. Kenyon, "A Contrast of the Four Gospels" (unpublished sermon), 12 January 1931, 7.

20. I compiled the list of materials Kenyon read by reviewing his comments in unpublished sermons and teaching notes that remained in his estate.
21. E. W. Kenyon, "Paul's Three Men" (unpublished sermon), n.d., 10.
22. E. W. Kenyon, "Mental Characteristics of Jesus," 1.
23. McConnell, *Different Gospel*, 52.
24. E. W. Kenyon, "S. D. Gordon: A Tribute" (unpublished article), n.d., 1.
25. Ibid., 2.
26. Ibid., 2–3.
27. Kenyon, *Jesus the Healer*, 104.
28. E. W. Kenyon, "Victory of the Cross," 2.

CHAPTER 12: KENYON'S BIBLE SCHOOL

1. E. W. Kenyon, Editorial Notes, *Bethel Trumpet*, July 1901, 40.
2. Another reason Kenyon gave for his falling away from the Lord was having failed to receive the Holy Spirit after he was converted. He believed he would not have fallen into sin had he invited the Holy Spirit into his life to empower him and instruct him. As a result, Kenyon always asked people to receive the Spirit after he was assured they were genuinely converted.
3. Kenyon, *New Creation Realities*, 68.
4. E. W. Kenyon, "Salvation and Discipleship," *Reality*, January 1910, 167–8.
5. E. W. Kenyon, "The Re-opening of Bethel Bible Training School, September 1904," *Reality*, June 1904, 159.
6. E. W. Kenyon, "Taking Our Rights" (unpublished sermon), preached at Rev. Norvell's church in Pasadena, California, 14 February 1926, 11–12.
7. *Spencer (MA) Leader*, 1 February 1902, quoted in Simmons, *E. W. Kenyon*, 54. Dr. Dale Simmons reported on this event that "Suicide was a surprisingly common occurrence at this time, with the local press in Worcester reporting cases on almost a daily basis. Headlines for other instances of suicide were equally tactless, and, therefore, the treatment [at Bethel] need not be viewed as a specific attack on Kenyon or Bethel" (pp. 54–55).
8. E. W. Kenyon, "Concerning the Opening of the Bible School," *Reality*, July 1904, 170.
9. E. W. Kenyon, Foot Prints of Faith, *Reality*, January 1912, 69.
10. E. W. Kenyon, "Taking Our Rights," 2.
11. Ibid.

12. E. W. Kenyon, "The Place Held by the Word of God in the Early Church" (unpublished sermon), 15 May 1928, 5.
13. E. W. Kenyon, Foot Prints of Faith, *Reality,* January 1912, 69.
14. E. W. Kenyon, "Jesus and Natural Laws" (unpublished sermon), n.d., 4.
15. E. W. Kenyon, "Trial of Faith," *Reality,* June–October, 1909, 117.
16. E. W. Kenyon, Editorial, *Reality,* May 1903, 25.
17. E. W. Kenyon, "Trial of Faith," 117.
18. Simmons, *E. W. Kenyon,* 59 n. 161.
19. *Spencer (MA) Leader,* 2 May 1942, quoted in Simmons, *E. W. Kenyon,* 69.
20. Eunice M. Perkins, *Joybringer Bosworth: His Life Story,* rev. 2nd ed. (Detroit, MI: Eunice M. Perkins, 1927), 84.
21. Smith to Ruth Kenyon Housworth, letter, 16 February 1966. Used by permission.

CHAPTER 13: PENTECOSTALISM

1. E. W. Kenyon, "The Gift of Tongues," *Reality,* May 1907, 229.
2. One such periodical, which was considered to be one of the finest of its type, was the *Missionary Review of the World* edited by A. T. Pierson. A set of this periodical is in the archives of Gordon College in Wenham, Massachusetts. Kenyon read this periodical and it is quoted in *Reality.* It was one of many such periodicals that shared any signs of revival that were emerging.

    John Beauregard, the archivist at Gordon College, told me that he received a call from one of the girls' schools at Northfield (schools originally founded by D. L. Moody in his hometown of Northfield, Massachusetts) asking him if he was interested in some old magazines that were found in the basement. He went to check and found that these old magazines were a complete set of the *Missionary Review of the World.* The school was going to throw them away! Beauregard said his car almost scraped on the pavement after he filled his trunk with all the magazines, but he (and the magazines) made it safely back to Gordon College.
3. "Evangelism in New England," *Reality,* March 1905, 66. Clearly, Kenyon was expecting and looking for signs of a worldwide revival. The school was praying for an outpouring of the Spirit. In May 1905 *Reality* published an excerpt from W. T. Stead's *Revival in Wales.* Many quotes from Evan Roberts, the young man who was being used mightily by the Lord to spread the revival, are included.
4. An article called "On the Field" in *Reality,* November 1905, reported "a

grand revival in India in the Ramabai Orphan Homes . . . The Awakening in Austria is increasing . . . the "Christian Work" [presumably a periodical] gives an account of a revival in the Island of Madagascar in the fields of the Welsh missionaries as an effect of the Welsh Revival . . . truly these are evidence of the worldwide revival for which we have been praying" (p. 176).

5. E. W. Kenyon, "Three Fold Call," 45. Kenyon exhorts his readers to personal work (evangelism), encouraging them that "The very air all over the world is full of the stirrings of the Spirit. He is working in men and women everywhere. A revival is on the world, let us arise and work."

6. E. W. Kenyon, "The Gift of Tongues," 228–9.

7. Ibid., 229.

8. Richard M. Riss, *A Survey of Twentieth Century Revival Movements* (Peabody, MA: Hendrickson Publishers, 1988), 64. It is interesting to note that Charles Parham, who was later considered by many to be the leader of the Pentecostal movement, went to John Alexander Dowie's Zion city near Chicago with the Pentecostal message in September 1906. Meeting resistance to the message, Parham found it difficult to find a place for an audience to gather. He held his first meeting in a private room at Elijah Hospice (hotel). His wife wrote that "He then began cottage meetings and many of the best homes in the city were opened for meetings. Fred F. Bosworth's home was literally converted into a meeting house" (p. 64).

9. Richard Riss, "Durham, William H." in Burgess and McGee, eds., *Pentecostal and Charismatic Movements*, 255–6.

10. Frederick Link, quoted in Edith L. Blumhofer, *The Assemblies of God*, vol. 1 (Springfield, MO: Gospel Publishing House, 1989), 61.

11. Thomas William Miller, "The Significance of A. H. Argue for Pentecostal Historiography," *Pneuma* 8 (fall 1986): 123–4.

12. William H. Durham, "The Two Great Experiences or Gifts," *Articles from Pentecostal Testimony* (n.p.: n.p.,n.d.) It is interesting to note that nowhere in this collection of articles does Durham mention the dual-nature idea. If he had been influenced by the Keswick teachers, as some have suggested, it is unlikely that the dual-nature concept would not appear. The evidence is strong in favor of Kenyon having a definite influence on Durham.

13. E. W. Kenyon, "Triumph for Truth," *Reality,* April 1912, 128.

14. Dale H. Simmons, "I Love You, but I Just Can't Marry You: E. W. Kenyon and the Pentecostal Movement" (paper presented at the annual meeting of the Society for Pentecostal Studies, Wycliffe College, Toronto, Ont.,

Canada, 9 March 1996), 10.

15. C. M. Robeck Jr., "Yoakum, Finis Ewing," in Burgess and McGee, eds., *Pentecostal and Charismatic Movements*, 907–908.

16. School Notes, *Reality*, July–October 1912, 167.

17. E. W. Kenyon, untitled and unpublished sermon, 2 January 1926, 2.

18. Carrie Judd Montgomery, *Under His Wings* (Oakland, CA: Offices of "Triumphs of Faith," 1936), 195.

19. Maria Woodworth-Etter, *Signs and Wonders* n.p.: M. E. W. Etter, 1916), 305–306.

20. "Many Testify to Faith Cures," *Boston Globe*, 28 August 1913.

21. "Defense Puts on Witnesses," *Framingham (MA) Daily Tribune*, 27 August 1913.

22. E. W. Kenyon, "The Holy Spirit," *Kenyon's Herald of Life*, May 1940, 1.

23. E. W. Kenyon, "Ye Shall Receive Power When the Holy Ghost Is Come Upon You," *Kenyon's Herald of Life*, 12 October 1937, 2.

24. Ibid.

CHAPTER 14: TRIUMPH AND TRAGEDY IN SOUTHERN CALIFORNIA

1. This quote, used later in the chapter as well, is most likely from George Hunter, a Bethel graduate who lived in the area and preached for Kenyon. This quote was in a church bulletin from Kenyon's church, Figueroa Baptist Church in Los Angeles.

2. E. W. Kenyon, *Triumphs of Faith*, October 1930, 234. This is taken from a letter Kenyon wrote to Carrie Judd Montgomery upon her husband's death. She published several letters she received from people about her husband.

3. Edith L. Blumhofer, *Aimee Semple-McPherson: Everybody's Sister* (Grand Rapids, MI: William B. Eerdmans Publishing, 1993), 390.

4. Blumhofer, *The Assemblies of God*, vol. 1 (Springfield, MO, Gospel Publishing House, 1989), 240.

5. I am grateful to Glen Gohr at the Assemblies of God archives for copies of these newspaper advertisements.

6. E. W. Kenyon, unpublished sermon, 2 January 1926, 2.

7. For this information about the Plymouth Congregational Church I am indebted to Gier Lie of Norway.

8. Robert L. Niklaus et. al., *All For Jesus* (Camp Hill, PA: Christian Publications, 1986), 262. The Dr. Farr whom Kenyon mentions is

Frederic W. Farr (1860–1930), who after graduating from Newton Theological Seminary in 1885, pastored two churches in Massachusetts. Kenyon may have made his acquaintance then. Farr was an associate pastor with A. B. Simpson for some time before pastoring the Bethlehem Baptist Church in Philadelphia for twenty years. He was also the dean of the Missionary Training College (Simpson's) for several years. In 1915, he came to Los Angeles to assume the pastorate of Calvary Baptist Church.

9. E. W. Kenyon, "Divorce" (unpublished sermon), preached at Bethel Temple, Los Angeles, 21 January 1926, 11–12.

10. E. W. Kenyon, "The Name of Jesus" (unpublished sermon), preached at Bethel Temple, Los Angeles, 24 January 1926, 7.

11. E. W. Kenyon, "Divorce" (unpublished sermon), preached at Bethel Temple, Los Angeles, 28 January 1926, 2–3.

12. I am indebted to Glen Gohr of the Assemblies of God archives in Springfield, Illinois, for sending me the copy of Kenyon's application. Thank you!

13. Clifford A. Rice, telephone conversation with author, 1995. Rice succeeded Reidt as president of the Ministerial Fellowship of the USA, now known as International Fellowship of Ministries.

14. Lake to Charles H. Parham, 24 March 1927, Assemblies of God archives, Springfield, Missouri.

15. Dale Simmons, *E. W. Kenyon,* 38.

16. "Let Me Introduce," *Living Messages,* September 1929, 18.

17. "What We Believe," *Kenyon Herald,* October 1927, 1.

18. Declaration of faith, Figueroa Baptist Church, 808 W. Ninth, Los Angeles, California, ca. 1928, 4.

19. "Our Home," *Kenyon Herald,* 23 October 1927, 2.

20. Church Notes, *Kenyon Herald,* 27 November 1927, 3.

21. Kenyon believed in the necessity of being a good public speaker. What he learned at Emerson College of Oratory about public speaking he passed on to his students both at Bethel and the churches he pastored. It is also interesting to note that he was proud of attending Emerson. He would not be quick to boast of his attendance at Emerson if it had been thought of as a place for training in New Thought which Kenyon clearly repudiated.

22. Simmons, *E. W. Kenyon,* 42.

23. E. W. Kenyon, "Is God a Person?" *Living Messages,* February 1929, 1–2.

24. E. W. Kenyon, "Another Jesus," *Living Messages,* March 1929, 1–2. Ironically, D. R. McConnell accuses Kenyon of preaching "another

Jesus." He asks, " . . . is . . . the Jesus of the Faith movement . . . the Jesus of the New Testament? The answer that will be given in this book is a decisive *no*. The Jesus of the Faith movement is 'another Jesus' (2 Cor. 11:4), and the gospel of the Faith movement is a 'different gospel' (Gal. 1:16)." *Different Gospel*, 52. He makes this claim based on his speculative premise that Kenyon was sympathetic to metaphysics!

25. E. W. Kenyon, unpublished notes, n.d.
26. McConnell, *Different Gospel*, 50.
27. Evva Kenyon died in 1914 after a prolonged sickness.
28. E. W. Kenyon, "We Are What We Think," *Living Messages*, vol. 3, no. 11, 1931, 22. Notice that this article appeared a few months after their divorce.

CHAPTER 15: THE FRUITFUL NORTHWEST YEARS

1. E. W. Kenyon, *Kenyon's Living Poems*, rev. ed. (Lynnwood, WA: Kenyon's Gospel Publishing Society, 1945), 33.
2. Gier Lie, "E. W. Kenyon: *Sekstifter eller kristen lederskikkelse?* En historisk undersøkelse av Kenyons teologi med søerlig nenblikk på deus historiske rotter og innflytelsen på samtid og ettertid." Master's thesis, Norwegian Lutheran School of Theology, October 1994. Translated to English by GierLee and William DeArteaga, n.d., 21. "E. W. Kenyon: Cult Founder or Evangelical Minister? An Historical Analysis of Kenyon's Theology With Particular Emphasis on Roots and Influences." I am grateful to Gier Lie for his research on the radio ministry of Kenyon. Thanks, Gier!
3. Norma Johnson, "Seattle Bible Institute," *Kenyon's Herald of Life*, 24 September 1935, 1.
4. M. W., "Bible School Closes May 14," *Kenyon's Herald of Life*, 12 May 1936, 2.
5. Ruth A. Kenyon (later Ruth Kenyon Housworth), "E. W. Kenyon Memorial Fund," *Kenyon's Herald of Life*, May–June 1948, 1.
6. E. W. Kenyon, "Church of the Open Door," *Kenyon's Herald of Life*, 1 October 1935, 1.
7. E. W. Kenyon, "This Past Year," *Kenyon's Herald of Life*, January 1940, 1.
8. Although Kenyon doesn't say why the book was controversial, it was likely because of his teaching on the atonement and his disagreement on sanctification with both Holiness and Keswick/Higher Life advocates.
9. G. B. McGee, "Simpson, William Wallace," in Burgess and McGee, eds.,

Pentecostal and Charismatic Movements, 787. W. W. Simpson attended A. B. Simpson's (no relation) New York Missionary Training College (later Nyack College) and headed for China the following year with other missionaries from the Christian and Missionary Alliance.

In a convention of missionaries in Taochow, China, in 1912, Simpson received the baptism of the Holy Spirit and spoke in tongues. In 1915 he returned to the States, resigned from the CMA over the issue of tongues and aligned himself with the Assemblies of God.

He eventually returned to China and evangelized in all the northern provinces, becoming one of the most respected and best-known missionaries of the Pentecostal movement.

10. W. W. Simpson, "Forty Thousand Edition of 'The Father and His Family,' printed in Chinese," *Kenyon's Herald of Life,* April 1940, 1–2. The details of Simpson's relationship with Kenyon are not very clear. Simpson had returned to the States in 1915 and became president of Bethel Bible Training School in Newark, New Jersey, in 1916. Kenyon, still overseeing Bethel Bible Institute in Massachusetts, might have become acquainted with Simpson while he was living in close proximity. This (1916) was the year Kenyon published his "controversial book" [Kenyon's description] *Father and His Family.*

At any rate, of all the books Simpson might have desired to translate into Chinese, he chose Kenyon's *Father and His Family.* Simpson translated and personally published a first edition in Chinese of only two thousand copies. Those were soon exhausted, and shortly thereafter Simpson heard from Kenyon's contact in China that Kenyon wanted to publish another ten thousand copies.

Simpson, upon learning of this, wrote to Kenyon and said, "I shall be glad to do all I can towards the second edition. Before hearing of your wish I had arranged with Brother Chang Chow Sin of the Tientsin Evangelistic Band, a self-supporting undenominational body, who had bought half of the first edition, to print another twenty thousand copies. He came to see me . . . he and I agreed to print forty thousand copies altogether" (p. 2).

11. Gerald S. Pope, "Important Message," *Kenyon's Herald of Life,* May 1947, 4.

12. See McConnell, *Different Gospel,* chapter 6, particularly 104–6.

13. Kenyon, *Jesus the Healer,* 5.

14. E. W. Kenyon, "The Character of Unbelief," *Reality,* May 1903, 20–21.

15. E. W. Kenyon, "Our New Book: 'The Two Kinds of Knowledge,'"

Kenyon's Herald of Life, 10 May 1938, 1.

16. "Evangelistic Meetings in Los Angeles, California," *Kenyon's Herald of Life,* November 1940, 1, and "Good News! Dr. Kenyon on Network," *Kenyon's Herald of Life,* December 1940, 1.

17. E. W. Kenyon, "The Meetings in California," *Kenyon's Herald of Life,* August 1943, 1.

18. Ern Baxter to Gier Lie, 28 September 1992. Used by permission of Lie.

19. E. W. Kenyon, "The Work in Los Angeles," *Kenyon's Herald of Life,* October 1945, 1.

20. Kenneth E. Hagin, *The Name of Jesus* (Tulsa, OK: Rhema Bible Church, AKA Kenneth Hagin Ministries, 1979), preface. It should be noted that in putting together *The Name of Jesus,* Hagin used material from Kenyon's *The Wonderful Name of Jesus* with Ruth Kenyon Housworth's full blessing. It is also worth mentioning that Ruth told me personally that she enjoyed a good relationship with Hagin and his ministry. Rhema Bible Training Center uses some of Kenyon's material in their classes.

21. Housworth to Mr. Roy Heather, 3 October 1991. Used by permission of Kenyon's Gospel Publishing Society.

22. E. W. Kenyon, preaching notes, 24 December 1946.

23. Housworth to Mr. Roy Heather, 6 March 1992. Used by permission of Kenyon's Gospel Publishing Society.

24. Jerry Kenyon, telephone interview with author, 8 December 1995. For personal reasons, Kenyon's son, Essek, has not been willing to discuss anything related to his father.

25. E. W. Kenyon, Strictly Business, *Kenyon's Herald of Life,* 21 June 1938, 4.

26. E. W. Kenyon, "How I Got My Healing," *Kenyon's Herald of Life,* June 1942, 4.

27. E. W. Kenyon, *Two Kind of Righteousness,* 66.

28. Ruth A. Kenyon (later Ruth Kenyon Housworth), "He Is at Rest," 1.

29. Housworth to Gier Lie, letter, 30 September 1992. Used by permission of Kenyon's Gospel Publishing Society.

30. Housworth to Bruce Barron, letter, 8 March 1985. Used by permission of Kenyon's Gospel Publishing Society.

31. E. W. Kenyon, "The Old Year," *Kenyon's Herald of Life,* February 1948, 4.

Chapter 16: The Sufferings of Christ

1. E. W. Kenyon, "The Justice of God," *Reality,* December 1907, 63.
2. For a modern, scholarly defense of this idea of Christ's drinking the cup of God's wrath, as well as a scholarly defense of the reality of Christ's dying spiritually, see Leon Morris, *The Cross in the New Testament* (Grand Rapids, MI: William B. Eerdmans Publishing, 1965), 47 (on the cup of God's wrath), 42–49 (on the separation from the Father). Morris quotes many respected scholars who believe that Christ's separation from the Father was an essential part of the atonement.
3. E. W. Kenyon, *Identification* (Lynnwood, WA: Kenyon's Gospel Publishing Society, 1941), 11–12.
4. E. W. Kenyon, "The Sufferings of the Christ in Our Redemption: Physical and Spiritual" *The Tabernacle Trumpet,* October 1900, 117.
5. Kenyon, *Two Kinds of Righteousness,* 66.
6. E. W. Kenyon, "A Heart Talk," *Reality,* January 1909, 45.
7. E. W. Kenyon, untitled sermon preached at First Presbyterian Church, Hollywood, California, 27 August 1944, 2.
8. Kenyon, *Identification,* 16. Kenyon is accurate in saying that the word *death* is plural in the Hebrew text. Scholars, however, don't necessarily draw the same conclusion Kenyon did. Hebrew scholar Franz Delitzsch calls it a plural of exaggeration "applied to a violent death, the very pain of which makes it like dying again and again." *Commentary on the Old Testament,* vol. 7 (n.d.; reprint, Grand Rapids, MI: William B. Eerdmans Publishing Company, 1982), 329. Kenyon points out, however, that "this is the only time that the word 'deaths' is used in the entire Old Testament Scriptures, except when it speaks of Satan's being cast out of Heaven, that he 'died the deaths'" [Ezek. 28:10]. *Father and His Family,* rev. ed., 126. Although this was an important Scripture for Kenyon regarding the idea of Christ's spiritual death, he used many other scriptures to justify the teaching. The fact that the use of the plural in Isaiah 53, discussing the atoning death of Christ, is one of only two times it is used in the plural in the entire Old Testament certainly must have some significance. Whether this verse (Isa. 53:9) teaches a two-fold death of Christ or not, Isaiah does teach in the aforementioned chapter both the physical death of Christ and the fact that His soul was made an offering for sin (Isa. 53:10). In the next chapter I will show many of the significant voices that taught this two-fold death of Christ in the atonement. See also next endnote.
9. I am aware that Kenyon's critics fault his interpretation of *deaths* in Isaiah

53. At this point I am showing the importance of this doctrine to Kenyon, the power he felt it had, and that he didn't teach it until he felt he had scriptural warrant for doing so. It might be pointed out, however, that A. W. Pink was in agreement with Kenyon's interpretation of Isaiah 53:9: "The margin of Isaiah 53:9 tells us that Christ was 'with the wicked in his *deaths*' for in His soul He tasted of the second death, and in His body He suffered natural death; thus He experienced both a spiritual and a natural Resurrection." *Gleanings From Paul: Studies in the Prayers of the Apostle* (Chicago: Moody Bible Press, 1967), 137.

10. Kenyon, *Identification*, 37–38.
11. Alfred Edersheim, *The Temple, Its Ministry, and Services* (n.d.; reprint, Grand Rapids, MI: William B. Eerdmans Publishing, 1986), 115.
12. E. W. Kenyon, *Blood Covenant* (Lynnwood, WA: Kenyon's Gospel Publishing Society, 1949), 36. This book was published posthumously.

CHAPTER 17: CONCURRING VOICES ON THE SUFFERINGS OF CHRIST

1. Billy Graham, *Peace with God* (New York: Simon and Schuster, Pocket Books, 1953), 97.
2. Many believed that Christ "died spiritually," that He experienced separation from God the Father as a part of the price of redemption. Quite a few believed that it was during the three hours on the cross rather than the three days and three nights after his physical death. Whether it was for three hours or for three days and nights, to believe that Christ's separation from the Father was essential to our redemption is to believe that Christ died spiritually.
3. E. W. Kenyon, "The Decadence of Faith," 1.
4. John Nelson Darby, *The Sufferings of Christ* (London: G. Morrish, 1959), 20–21. Reprinted from the periodical *Bible Treasury*, 1858–59.
5. Ibid., 23–24.
6. Ibid., 38–39.
7. H. A. Ironside, *A Historical Sketch of the Brethren Movement* (Grand Rapids, MI: Zondervan Publishing House, 1952), 77.
8. Ibid., 78–79.
9. H. A. Ironside, *Charge That to My Account* (Chicago: Moody Press, 1931), 64, 66.
10. M. J. Erickson, "Atonement, Theories of," in Reid, et al., eds., *Dictionary of Christianity*, 91.

11. John Calvin, *The Institutes of the Christian Religion*, vol. 1 (Grand Rapids, MI: William B. Eerdmans Publishing, 1949), 564.

12. The list would include Calvin, Luther, Jonathan Edwards, Spurgeon, Leon Morris, Billy Graham, J. N. Darby, P. T. Forsyth, Alexander Maclaren, James Denny, R. W. Dale, Kenneth Wuest, A. W. Pink, G. Campbell Morgan, Henry C. Mabie, R. C. Sproul, Franz Delitzsch, George Eldon Ladd, and C. E. B Cranfield, to name a few. I am not suggesting that these men would endorse everything in Kenyon's teaching about the atonement. I am saying that all of these men believed that the spiritual sufferings of Christ were as much a part of His work of atonement as His physical suffering and the shedding of His blood.

13. McConnell, *Different Gospel,* 129.

14. Hank Hanegraaff, *Christianity in Crisis* 162.

15. Charles Haddon Spurgeon, *Spurgeons's Sermons of the Cross of Christ* (Grand Rapids, MI: Kregel Publications, 1993), 40–41. Kenyon spoke frequently of Christ's work satisfying divine justice. Calvin and Spurgeon both used this concept. Kenyon has been misrepresented as holding to the ransom theory of the atonement which sees the atonement as paying *to Satan* a price for man's redemption. Kenyon never taught this theory. He believed, with Calvin and Spurgeon, that Christ's sacrifice satisfied God's divine justice.

16. Ibid., 130.

17. Ibid., 138.

18. Ibid., 30.

19. Paul Althaus, *The Theology of Martin Luther* (Philadelphia, PA: Fortress Press, 1966), 205–206.

20. R. W. Dale, *The Atonement* (The Congregational Union Lecture for 1875), 24th ed. (London: Congregational Union of England and Wales, 1905), 373.

21. Ibid., 119, 121, 123–124.

22. Ibid., 58.

23. D. R. McConnell (*Different Gospel,* chap. 7) and Hank Hanegraaff (*Christianity in Crisis,* 153) portray Kenyon (and the modern Faith movement) as teaching the ransom theory of atonement. This teaching, which a number of the early church fathers taught, suggests that Jesus was the price God paid to the devil to redeem man. William DeArteaga in the revised edition of *Quenching the Spirit,* rev. ed., (Orlando, FL: Creation House, 1996), accepts McConnell's evaluation although defending the ransom theory as a valid doctrine (pp. 240–243). Kenyon did not, how-

ever, believe that Jesus was a ransom paid to the devil. He believed, along with Calvin, Edwards, Spurgeon, Dale, and many others that Christ's sacrifice was to pay the debt of sin and satisfy God's justice. DeArteaga points out that one of the earliest to depart from the ransom theory was Anselm. Anselm stressed that the atonement was satisfaction paid by Christ to God the Father (p. 240). This is much closer to the Reformers and Kenyon's teaching. Charles Hodge in his *Systematic Theology,* vol. 2 (1873; reprint, Grand Rapids, MI: William B. Eerdmans, 1968) discusses the various views of the atonement (pp. 563–598). He begins with what he refers to as the "orthodox view:" "According to this doctrine the work of Christ is a real satisfaction, of infinite inherent merit, to the vindicatory justice of God; so that He saves his people by doing for them, and in their stead, what they were unable to do for themselves, satisfying the law in their behalf, and bearing the penalty in their stead" (p. 563). Elsewhere he writes, "It is therefore the plain doctrine of Scripture that . . . Christ saves us . . . by . . . a satisfaction to divine justice, as an expiation for sin and as a ransom from the curse and authority of the law" (p. 520). He continues, " . . . The ideas, therefore, of legal substitution, of vicarious obedience, and punishment, of the satisfaction of justice by one for all, underlie and pervade the whole scheme of redemption" (p. 521). On pages 564–566 he discusses the ransom theory held by some of the church fathers. Kenyon did not hold to the view described as the ransom theory.

24. Thomas Hywel Hughes, *The Atonement: Modern Theories of the Doctrine* (London: George Allen and Unwin, 1949), vii.
25. E. W. Kenyon, "The Sufferings of Jesus" (unpublished sermon), 27 May 1928, 3.
26. As noted above, many critics do exactly what MacLaren says we mustn't do: separate the physical sufferings of Christ from the spiritual, or think that the physical sufferings are the atonement.
27. Henry C. Mabie, *The Meaning and Message of the Cross* (New York: Fleming H. Revell, 1906), 66–67, 74, 83–84.
28. G. Campbell Morgan, *The Crises of the Christ* (New York: Fleming H. Revell, 1936), 358.
29. Charles Cuthbert Hall, *Does God Send Trouble?* (Boston, MA: Houghton, Mifflin and Co., 1895), 49–50, 54.

CHAPTER 18: THE FINISHED WORK OF CHRIST

1. Kenyon, *In His Presence,* 138.

2. E. W. Kenyon, "Divorce," *The Tabernacle Trumpet,* October 1900, 121–2.

3. Kenyon, *Father and His Family,* rev. ed., 159.

4. Kenyon, *New Creation Realities,* 71–72.

5. A. J. Gordon, *In Christ; or, The Believer's Union With His Lord* (Boston, MA: Gould and Lincoln, 1872; Grand Rapids, MI: Baker Book House, 1964), 9–10.

6. Ibid., 55.

7. Ibid., 50.

8. Arthur T. Pierson, *The Gospel: Its Heart, Heights, and Hopes* (Grand Rapids, MI: Baker Book House, 1978), 170–171. The sermons were originally preached between 1891 and 1893, and originally published as three separate books in 1892, 1893, and 1896.

9. A. J. Gordon, *Grace and Glory,* (New York: Fleming H. Revell, 1880), 32–33.

10. Ibid., 38–39.

11. A. T. Pierson, *Acts of the Holy Spirit,* 17, 24.

12. A. B. Simpson, *Part II: The New Testament* vol. 2 of *The Holy Spirit,* 14.

13. A. E. Thompson, *Life of A. B. Simpson,* 240.

14. A. J. Gordon's influence as a speaker would have been limited to 1893–94, since he died in early 1895. His books, however, would continue to influence Kenyon throughout Kenyon's life.

15. A. B. Simpson, *The Christ Life* (1888; reprint, Harrisburg, PA: Christian Publications, 1980), 20.

16. Kenyon, *Father and His Family,* rev. ed., 99–100.

17. McConnell, *Different Gospel,* 43.

18. Kenyon, *Hidden Man,* 26–27.

19. Kenyon, *Two Kinds of Life,* 82.

20. See Kenyon, *Father and His Family,* rev. ed., 146, and A. J. Gordon, *Ministry of the Spirit,* 76–77.

21. E. W. Kenyon, "Driftwood," *Bethel Trumpet,* September 1901, 50. An "anxious seat" was a place provided for seekers after peace with God so they could "pray through" to victory.

CHAPTER 19: REVELATION KNOWLEDGE

1. Kenyon, *Father and His Family,* rev. ed., 185.

2. "It is neither sky, nor grace, nor glory, nor any spatial abode, but rather the unseen world of spiritual reality." John R. W. Stott, *God's New Society* (Downers Grove, IL: InterVarsity Press, 1979), 35. He is describing the

"heavenly places" of Ephesians 1:3.

3. Kenyon, *Jesus the Healer,* 90.

4. McConnell, *Different Gospel,* 118.

5. Kenyon, *Two Kinds of Faith,* 46–48.

6. S. D. Gordon, *Quiet Talks on Prayer* ([1904]; reprint, New York: Grosset and Dunlap, Family Inspirational Library, 1972), 30.

7. G. Campbell Morgan, *Christian Principles* (New York: Fleming H. Revell, 1908), 15.

8. Kenyon, *The Wonderful Name of Jesus* (Los Angeles, CA: West Coast Publishing, 1927), 38. Kenyon's understanding on this point is strikingly similar to Morgan's. This edition is hereafter referred to as 1st ed.

9. It should be pointed out that Kenyon was not writing for theologians. He assumes a basic common ground of belief among his readers. If his language lacks theological precision, that is to be expected. In his zeal to show the glorious privileges of the believer in being called to conformity to Christ, he emphasizes, perhaps to a fault, the humanity of Jesus. In other places, however, he expresses the unique deity of Christ quite clearly.

10. Morgan, *Christian Principles,* 30.

11. Ibid., 54–55.

12. A. T. Pierson, *The Scriptures: God's Living Oracles* n.p.: Baker and Taylor, 1904; New York: Fleming H. Revell, 1913), 217–218.

13. See E. W. Kenyon's, *The Two Kinds of Knowledge* (Lynnwood, WA: Kenyon's Gospel Publishing Society, 1938) and *Father and His Family,* rev. ed., 13–17.

14. McConnell, *Different Gospel,* 105.

15. Ibid.

16. Kenyon, *Two Kinds of Knowledge,* 32–33.

17. Ibid., 35.

18. Kenyon, *In His Presence,* 82–83.

19. McConnell, *Different Gospel,* 106.

20. Kenyon, *Two Kinds of Knowledge,* 33.

21. Ibid., 39. It might be pointed out that Kenyon wrote this whole book on the subject of the two kinds of knowledge and is quite clear about the need of the mind being renewed. Kenyon felt a true submitting to the lordship of Christ to demand submitting the intellect to the authority of the written word. See pp. 47, 58, 72.

22. A. B. Simpson, *Wholly Sanctified* (1890; reprint, Harrisburg, PA: Christian Publications, 1925), 28–29.

23. Ibid., 62.

24. McConnell, *Different Gospel,* 104, 110.

25. W. H. Aldis, comp., *The Message of Keswick and Its Meaning,* rev. ed. (London: Marshall, Morgan and Scott, 1957), 59.

26. A. T. Pierson, *Lessons in the School of Prayer* (New York: H. M. Caldwell Co. Publishers, 1895), 31–32.

27. Ibid., 34–35.

28. Kenyon, *Father and His Family,* rev. ed., 185.

29. Kenyon, *Two Kinds of Life,* 68.

30. Mabie, *Meaning and Message,* 183–5.

31. G. Campbell Morgan was another voice calling the church to rise above the other two alternatives. Morgan expressed this mind-spirit conflict in another of his books. "Man was created to walk and talk with God, to think the thoughts of God after Him. All human success along the lines of science simply comes from the fact that man is struggling after that very thing. Nevertheless all the while there is a definite hiatus, a gap, between man and God. Again, according to the Biblical account, that rupture was created when man fell from the spiritual to the psychic . . . By that rebellion he lost his sense of God, and the sense of his own spiritual nature. This not to say that the psychic or the mental is essentially wrong; but it always fails when it is divorced from the spiritual. When man descended by rebellion to the level of the merely mental, he began a quest after God with the powers of his mind, and has never been able to find Him." *The Answers of Jesus to Job* (1935; reprint, Grand Rapids, MI: Baker Book House, 1973), 34–35.

In using the word *psychic,* Morgan does not mean the word as used today of occultic practices, but rather synonymously with "of the soul." (*Psyche* is the Greek word for "soul.") Morgan, in this quote, expressed the essence of Kenyon's thought regarding the effects of the Fall on man. Kenyon used the terms *revelation knowledge* and *sense knowledge* to convey the ideas (psychic or mental versus spiritual) articulated by Morgan.

CHAPTER 20: THE METAPHYSICAL CULTS

1. E. W. Kenyon, "The Limitlessness of Faith" (unpublished article), 6 April 1934.

2. Chappell, "Divine Healing Movement," 269.

3. Charles S. Braden, *Spirits in Rebellion: The Rise and Development of*

New Thought (Dallas, TX: Southern Methodist University Press, 1963), 130. Significantly, Braden points out that P. P. Quimby, recognized as the influential and pioneer teacher of metaphysical healing; Warren Felt Evans, the first articulate author of metaphysical healing concepts; and Julius A. Dresser and his wife, who were early practitioners and teachers of New Thought or mental healing; never formed any recognizable organization around metaphysical healing concepts. See Braden, chapter 5, "The Developing Movement."

4. *Times* (London), 26 May 1885, quoted in Robert Peel, *Mary Baker Eddy: The Years of Trial* (Boston, MA: Christian Science Publishing Society, 1971), 158.

5. Raymond J. Cunningham, "The Impact of Christian Science on the American Churches, 1880–1910," *The American Historical Review* 72 (April, 1967): 893.

6. E. W. Kenyon, "Jesus Christ as High Priest," *Reality*, January 1909, 33.

7. Daniels, *Dr. Cullis*, 339.

8. When E. W. Kenyon published his book on divine healing, *Jesus the Healer*, in 1940, the advertisement in *Kenyon's Herald of Life*, stated, "There has never been anything like it [Kenyon's book] since healing was first discovered by Dorothea Truedel in the Swiss Mountains. She was the first one to teach healing after the dark ages. Year by year the message has been growing clearer." August 1940, 4.

9. Paul Chappell, "Healing Movements," in Burgess and McGee, eds., *Pentecostal and Charismatic Movements*, 358–9.

10. Willa Cather and Georgine Milmine, *The Life of Mary Baker G. Eddy and the History of Christian Science* (1909; reprint, Lincoln, NE: University of Nebraska Press, 1993), 211. This was first published in serial form in *McClure's* magazine, 1907–1908.

11. Ibid., 270–1.

12. Mary Baker Eddy, *Retrospection and Introspection* (1891; reprint, Boston, MA: Trustees Under the Will of Mary Baker G. Eddy, 1920), 54.

13. S. R. Pointer, "Cook, Joseph (Flavius Josephus)," in Reid, et al., eds., *Dictionary of Christianity in America*, 318.

14. Peel, *Years of Trial*, 155.

15. A. J. Gordon, "Christian Science Not Scriptural" (Los Angeles, CA: The Bible House of Los Angeles, n.d.), 3–5,11,13.

16. A. B. Simpson, *Gospel of Healing*, 185.

17. A. B. Simpson, *The Four-Fold Gospel* (1887; reprint, Harrisburg, PA: Christian Publications, 1925), 48–49.

18. Kenyon, *Two Kinds of Life*, 93.

19. E. W. Kenyon, "The Justice of God," 61.

20. E. W. Kenyon, Notes, *Reality*, February 1910, 192.

21. E. W. Kenyon, "The Incarnation," *Reality*, December 1911, 49.

22. John Kennington, "E. W. Kenyon and the Metaphysics of Christian Science" (unpublished article), quoted in McConnell, *Different Gospel*, 15.

23. R. A. Torrey, *Divine Healing* (1924; reprint, Grand Rapids, MI: Baker Book House, 1974), 38–39.

24. Ibid., 7.

25. R. L. Marsh, *Faith Healing: A Defense; or, The Lord Thy Healer* (New York: Fleming H. Revell, 1889), 131, 142.

26. James M. Gray, *The Antidote to Christian Science* (New York: Fleming H. Revell, 1907), 69–72.

27. E. W. Kenyon, "Righteousness" (unpublished article), n.d., 6.

28. Kenyon, *Two Kinds of Faith*, 3.

29. Kenyon, *Wonderful Name of Jesus*, 1st ed., 110–112.

30. Torrey, *Divine Healing*, 33–34.

31. A. B. Simpson, *Gospel of Healing*, 89–93.

32. Montgomery, *Prayer of Faith*, 42–43, 99.

33. Maria Woodworth-Etter, *Marvels and Miracles God Wrought in the Ministry of Mrs. Maria Woodworth-Etter for Forty-Five Years* (Indianapolis, IN: M. B. W. Etter, 1922), 481–482.

34. Murray, *Divine Healing*, 42–54. Originally published in English ca. 1900.

35. F. F. Bosworth, *Christ the Healer* (River Forest, IL: F. F. Bosworth, 1924), 183. Bosworth's book in its present form (it is still in print today) includes a chapter titled "Our Confession" at the end of which he acknowledges drawing from Kenyon's writings (Old Tappan, NJ: Fleming H. Revell, 1973, chap. 10, 148). This earlier edition does not contain that material. The book, in both editions, however, is drawn from the primary voices of the Faith-Cure movement and is in many ways a statement of that earlier movement's teaching on divine healing.

36. Kenyon, *Jesus the Healer*, 22, 93.

37. Kenyon, *Hidden Man*, 109–10.

CHAPTER 21: POSITIVE CONFESSION

1. Kenyon, *In His Presence*, 44.

2. "Arlington Heights," *Reality*, November 1904, 13.

3. E. W. Kenyon, Relationship and Fellowship, *Reality,* December 1904, 38.

4. E. W. Kenyon, "Testifying or Witnessing," *Reality,* December 1904, 44–45.

5. E. W. Kenyon, "Privileges and Responsibilities," 135.

6. E. W. Kenyon, "Three Fold Call," 44.

7. E. W. Kenyon, "Can He Be Trusted?" *Reality,* November 1906, 134.

8. Pierson, *Lessons,* 97, 102–103, 106.

9. Gordon F. Atter, *The Third Force* (Peterborough, Ontario: The College Press, 1962), 63–64.

10. C. H. Pridgeon, *Faith and Prayer* (Pittsburgh, PA: The Evangelization Society of The Pittsburgh Bible Institute, 1928), 18, 21, 23, 68.

11. Jessie Penn-Lewis, Notes, *The Overcomer,* June 1910, 89.

12. C. H. Pridgeon, "Faith the Fruit of the Cross," *The Overcomer,* June 1910, 93. Pridgeon embraced and taught a form of ultimate reconciliation at some point in his ministry. He was known primarily, however, for his "prayer watch" ministry, and was a respected minister. In 1918 he began to teach the suffering of the unsaved was not eternal. Apparently, even many of his own followers did not embrace this teaching with him. Atter, *Third Force,* 64.

13. George B. Peck, *Throne-Life; or, The Highest Christian Life* (Boston, MA: Watchword Publishing, 1888), 171, 174–175, 177.

14. Montgomery, *Under His Wings,* 124.

15. A. B. Simpson, "The Faith of God," *The Herald of His Coming,* September 1995, 3–4. See also Simpson, *In Heavenly Places,* 24.

16. Carrie Judd Montgomery, "The Power of Praise and Testimony," *Triumphs of Faith,* January 1924, 3–5.

17. George Montgomery, "Standing on God's Word," *Triumphs of Faith,* January 1935, 8–9.

18. Montgomery, *Under His Wings,* 206–207.

19. Ibid., 208.

20. Hanegraaff, *Christianity in Crisis,* 89.

21. Hanegraaff, *Christianity in Crisis,* 390, n. 12.

22. A. T. Robertson, *A Grammar of the Greek New Testament in the Light of Historical Research* (Nashville, TN: Broadman Press, 1934), 500.

23. Hanegraaff, *Christianity in Crisis,* 91.

24. Albert Barnes, *Barnes Notes on the New Testament,* vol. 1, ed. Robert Frew (Grand Rapids, MI: Baker Book House, 1964), 372–373. Joseph Addison Alexander, *The Gospel According to Mark* (1858; reprint, Grand Rapids, MI: Baker Book House, 1980), 310. *Adam Clarke's Commentary*

on the Whole Bible in *The Bethany Parallel Commentary* (Minneapolis, MN: Bethany House Publishers, 1983), 312.

25. For further documentation of this kind of "defense of the faith," see James Spencer, *Heresy Hunters: Character Assassination in the Church* (Lafayette, LA: Huntington House Publishers, 1993) and James Spencer, *Bleeding Hearts and Propaganda: The Fall of Reason in the Church* (Lafayette, LA: Huntington House Publishers, 1995). See also Bob and Gretchen Passantino, *Witch Hunt* (Nashville, TN: Thomas Nelson, 1990) and DeArteaga, *Quenching the Spirit.*

26. E. W. Kenyon, "Persistence and Positiveness of Confession Needed," *Kenyon's Herald of Life,* January 1942, 2.

27. Kenyon, *Jesus the Healer,* 92.

28. Ibid., 93.

29. E. W. Kenyon, "Dare You Confess That You Are What God Says You Are?", *Kenyon's Herald of Life,* July 1941, 2.

30. Kenyon, *Hidden Man,* 109–10.

31. E. W. Kenyon, "Potency," 30.

32. E. W. Kenyon, "Confession," 45.

33. In a letter to Carrie, Kenyon mentions the fine staff at the Home of Peace. Whether Nuzum was there at the time or not is not clear. Nuzum was a missionary to Mexico for many years. She had been miraculously healed after twenty-seven years of constant pain.

34. C. Nuzum, *The Life of Faith* (Springfield, MO: Gospel Publishing House, 1956), 64.

35. Lillian B. Yeomans, *Healing From Heaven* (Springfield, MO: Gospel Publishing House, 1954), 81. Eventually moving to southern California, Yeomans taught church history and divine healing at Aimee Semple-McPherson's L.I.F.E. Bible College. She also contributed many articles on divine healing to *Triumphs of Faith,* Carrie Judd Montgomery's periodical. Her lectures at the Bible School and some of her articles were put into book form, and four resultant books on divine healing are still being published.

CHAPTER 22: THE BELIEVER'S AUTHORITY

1. Kenyon, *In His Presence,* 96.

2. Charles H. Spurgeon, *According To Promise* (London: Passmore and Alabaster, 1890; reprint, Grand Rapids, MI; Baker Book House, 1964), 43.

3. McConnell, *Different Gospel*, 56. "The heresy of the Faith movement is its denial of the sovereignty and personhood of God ... " Later McConnell wrote, "In Faith theology, a *personal* loving God does not determine what comes into the believer's life ... This is not the sovereign, personal God of the New Testament. This is the god of metaphysics" (p. 140).

4. A. J. Gordon, *Ministry of Healing*, 214–15.

5. Ibid., 157.

6. Peck, *Throne-Life*, 47–48.

7. Ibid., 47.

8. E. W. Kenyon, "Where Is the Power?," *Kenyon's Herald of Life*, August 1944, 2.

9. E. W. Kenyon, "The Miracle of the Book of John" (unpublished sermon), preached 1 June 1928, 15–16.

10. E. W. Kenyon, "A New Use for the Name," *Kenyon's Herald of Life*, September 1942, 1.

11. Ibid.

12. E. W. Kenyon, "The Power of His Name," *Bethel Trumpet*, March 1902, 93.

13. Pierson, *The Gospel*, 1891.

14. E. W. Kenyon, *The Wonderful Name of Jesus*, rev. ed., (Lynnwood, WA: Kenyon's Gospel Publishing Society, 1935), 2.

15. Ibid., 1.

16. Ibid., 17.

17. E. W. Kenyon, "Jesus' Resurrection and the Realm of Unbelief," chapter 19 in "The Deity of Christ" (unpublished manuscript), n.d., 8.

18. E. W. Kenyon, unpublished and untitled sermon preached at First Presbyterian Church, Hollywood, California, 27 August 1944, 2.

19. Kenyon, *In His Presence*, 34.

20. E. W. Kenyon, "The Deity of Christ" (unpublished sermon), preached at Bethel Temple, Los Angeles, 20 December 1925, 12.

21. Kenyon, *Wonderful Name of Jesus*, 1st ed.

CHAPTER 23: THE FATHER AND HIS FAMILY

1. Kenyon, *Father and His Family* (Spencer, MA: Essek W. Kenyon, 1916), first notes following introductions. This edition is hereafter cited to as *Father and His Family*, 1st ed.

2. E. W. Kenyon, Relationship and Fellowship, *Reality*, December 1904, 35–38.

3. Francis S. Bernauer, introduction to Kenyon, *Father and His Family,* 1st ed., 9–10.

4. Ibid.

5. Ibid., 14–15.

6. Müller, *Life of Trust,* 258–9.

7. E. W. Kenyon, "Broken Fellowship," *Reality,* December 1905, 185–6.

8. E. W. Kenyon, "Jesus as an Example," 23–24.

9. For example, see Kenyon, *In His Presence,* 11.

10. E. W. Kenyon, "Giving God His Place in Your Plans," *Kenyon's Herald of Life,* November 1940, 4.

11. Kenyon, *In His Presence,* 88–89.

12. E. W. Kenyon, "The Lordship of Christ," 1–2.

13. Kenyon, *Two Kinds of Life,* 105.

14. E. W. Kenyon, "Can I Afford It?" *Reality,* February 1912, 85–86.

15. E. W. Kenyon, "The Lordship of Christ" (unpublished sermon), preached at Bethel Temple, Los Angeles, 30 December 1926, 1.

16. James D. Jenkins, "A Letter From the Field," *Reality,* January 1906, 13.

17. Kenyon, *Father and His Family,* rev. ed., 144–5.

18. Kenyon, *Father and His Family,* 1st ed., 134, 138, 140.

19. E. W. Kenyon, "The Sufferings of the Christ," p. 122.

20. E. W. Kenyon, "Eternal Life," *Kenyon's Herald of Life,* May 1940, 1.

21. Kenyon, *Father and His Family,* rev. ed., 147.

22. For an interesting view of the Reformed influences on the Pentecostal movement, see Waldvogel, "The 'Overcoming Life'." The relevance of this thesis in this study is that the primary men she feels influenced Pentecostalism are, for the most part, the four men who influenced Kenyon as well: A. J. Gordon, A. T. Pierson, A. B. Simpson, and R. A. Torrey.

23. McConnell, *Different Gospel,* 24.

24. Kenyon, *Father and His Family,* rev. ed., 185–6, 190–1.

GLOSSARY

Affirmations. Declarations of statements of beliefs made to build confidence in the truth stated.

Annihilationism. The position held by some that after death the lost cease to exist.

Arminianism. A form of Protestant theology that arose in reaction to John Calvin's emphasis on the sovereignty of God in predestinating the elect to be saved. Arminianism emphasizes man's ability to freely choose salvation.

Brethren movement. The Plymouth Brethren were a group that began meeting in homes for the breaking of bread and Bible study. Their outstanding teacher was John Darby. They desired to return to the simplicity of apostolic days and simplicity of worship, while affirming the unity of the body of Christ. Their numerous Bible teachers (in addition to Darby) were very influential in America in the latter part of the nineteenth century.

Calvinism. A system of theology derived from the writings of John Calvin (1509–1564) which emphasized God's sovereignty in choosing the elect for salvation and man's complete helplessness to contribute anything to his salvation. Calvinism emphasizes the total depravity of man, that man's election to salvation is completely unconditional, that Christ only died for the elect, that the elect cannot resist the grace of God, and that those chosen by God will persevere in the faith and cannot apostatize (commonly known as eternal security).

Christian Science. A metaphysical healing cult founded in the nineteenth century by Mary Baker Eddy. It denies the personality of God, the reality of matter, and proclaimed itself as the true gospel of Christ. Healing was practiced by getting the patient to believe that the sickness did not exist and was an "illusion of mortal mind."

Command of faith. The practice enjoined by Jesus in Mark 11:23 to speak to "mountains" and command them to be removed. It is the primary methodology of Jesus in healing the sick.

Crisis of consecration. The nineteenth-century Holiness and Higher Life movements believed that an experience of sanctification or victory over sin could be entered into by a crisis experience where all was surrendered to God and His power for victory was received.

Dispensationalism. A system of theology associated with the Plymouth Brethren and John Darby which divided God's dealings with man into consecutive "dispensations," each having a distinctive mark in the way God dealt with man in that period. The teaching of the pre-tribulation Rapture is an integral part of the system.

Divine healing. Healing by the power of God in answer to prayer and faith.

Dual nature theory. The idea that redeemed man has two natures after conversion—a new nature and a "sin" nature, or old nature.

Entire sanctification. The term used to describe the state attained after a crisis of consecration.

Faith movement. The name given to the current movement in the church that emphasizes many of the same doctrines popularized by E. W. Kenyon—faith, divine healing, who we are in Christ, victorious living, confidence in prayer, and the authority of the believer. Kenneth Hagin, Kenneth Copeland, Charles Capps, Fred Price, and Jerry Savelle are among the primary voices of the movement, though there are many others. The Faith movement has, however, emphasized prosperity to a greater degree than did Kenyon.

Faith-Cure movement. A late nineteenth-century movement of divine healing that developed from the Holiness and Higher Life movements.

Higher Life movement. A nineteenth century -movement within the Christian church that sought a deeper experience of holiness. Rooted in the Holiness revival in the Methodist church, this movement transcended denominational borders and made Holiness teaching acceptable to many denominations.

Holiness movement. A revival of Methodist Holiness teaching that emerged in the mid-nineteenth century under the influence of Phoebe Palmer and many others. It also found expression in non-Methodist churches under the influence of Charles Finney and Asa Mahon of Oberlin college.

Incarnation. The doctrine which states that God, in the Person of Jesus Christ, was uniquely manifested miraculously in human flesh. The term was also used by many evangelical Bible teachers in a less precise way to describe the indwelling of the Holy Spirit or Christ in a believer.

Initial evidence. This is the doctrine that states that speaking in tongues is the one and only evidence that one has received the baptism of the Holy Spirit.

Metaphysical cults. General descriptive term for a number of late-nineteenth and early twentieth century pseudo-Christian groups that espoused healing and/or prosperity using Christian-sounding terminology but denying the existence of a personal God. Christian Science, New Thought, Unity, and Mind Science would be examples. All the fundamental beliefs of orthodox Christianity are denied by these cults.

New Thought. The term given to a wide variety of metaphysical teachings that affirmed the deity of man and man's ability to control his universe by right thinking and affirming. New Thought denies the existence of a personal God.

Penal substitution theory of atonement. This understanding of the atonement holds that Christ took the sinner's place as a substitute and received the punishment due the sinner on the cross.

Positive confession. A positive declaration of biblical truth as opposed to the confession of sin.

Prayer of consecration. A prayer made to God of complete surrender of the life to the will and purposes of God. This kind of prayer was enjoined by the Holiness and Higher Life movements as the point of entrance into the deeper life.

Revelation knowledge. The term used by E. W. Kenyon to describe: 1) the Bible as the source of the necessary knowledge of God that cannot be found by the senses; 2) the illumination of the Bible by the Holy Spirit to the individual that the individual might apply the truth of Scripture to life.

Sanctification. In general, the term used to describe the process (or the state) of growth in holiness. In nineteenth-century Holiness terminology it referred to a crisis experience whereby the believer entered into a victorious life of freedom from the dominion of sin.

Second work of grace. The experience of sanctification (described above) was entered into by a crisis experience known as a second work of grace to distinguish it from the first work of grace (conversion).

Sense knowledge. The term given by E. W. Kenyon to knowledge that came through the five physical senses unassisted by the Holy Spirit. This applied to understandings of the Bible which men gained without the help of the Holy Spirit as well.

Sensory denial. In the metaphysical cults this described the denial of physical matter's existence, which therefore meant that sickness was not real, only imagined.

Tongues. Speaking in an unknown (to the speaker) language by the ability of the Holy Spirit. It is one of the gifts of the Holy Spirit listed in 1 Corinthians 12.

Unity. One of the New Thought metaphysical cults. Unity denies the existence of a personal God while using much of the language of Christianity.

Unitarianism. A liberal theological perspective that invaded many of the traditional churches that denies the Trinity, deity of Christ, and the Holy Spirit.

INDEX LIST